Praise for *Boom a...*

MW00397742

"The authors of this compelling and fascinating book demonstrate clearly that U.S. monetary policy—by creating a boom and a bust—led to the financial crisis and the great recession. But they go much further. They apply their excellent analytical skills to show why policy took this unfortunate route, why alternative explanations—such as a global-saving glut—are flawed, and why monetary policymakers must return to rules-based policies in the future. *Boom and Bust Banking* is exceptionally well-written and well-reasoned. It should be read by anyone interested in improving economic policy and economic performance."

> —**John B. Taylor**, Mary and Robert Raymond Professor of Economics, Stanford University; former Member, President's Council of Economic Advisers

"Few issues remain more confused than economic upheavals like the Great Depression and Great Recession. The superb book *Boom and Bust Banking* now shows the Federal Reserve's role and provides incisive cures to end the current debacle. The real news is the emerging consensus among economists as diverse as John Taylor and Lawrence White on the monetary origins of the crisis. Everyone should read this book."

> —**Amity Shlaes**, bestselling author of *The Forgotten Man: A New History of The Great Depression*; columnist, Bloomberg News

"David Beckworth is a young intellectual leader in what has been dubbed 'market monetarism,' which focuses on monetary policy as a key factor in economic fluctuations, including in the great recession of 2008-09. Beckworth has succeeded in assembling a superb group of contributors who have written stimulating essays on this topic. *Boom and Bust Banking* is an important contribution to furthering our understanding of recent events in the U.S. and around the world."

> —**Douglas A. Irwin**, Robert E. Maxwell '23 Professor of Arts and Sciences, Dartmouth College

"**Boom and Bust Banking** is very enlightening on the banking-financial disequilibrium that began in 2002 and continues to the present, focusing on the primary culprit for the debacle—the Federal Reserve System, and how it has become a monetary-fiscal factotum for an all-encompassing government financial policy. The book explores the fundamentals of central banking existence and whether proper monetary policy must start all over again without a central bank. Now we're getting somewhere! Let's proceed along this line using this book as a starting point."

> —**Richard H. Timberlake**, Professor Emeritus of Economics,
> University of Georgia

"The preeminent economic challenge of our time finally gets the attention it deserves in the very important book from leading monetary thinkers, **Boom and Bust Banking**. Distinguished economists such as George Selgin and Lawrence White address how the boom-and-bust cycle engendered by central banks creates financial instability and dare to propose alternative monetary arrangements. Inherent throughout this volume is the fundamental question: Is the Federal Reserve capable of appropriately calibrating the money supply to the needs of the real economy? To give an informed answer—read this book."

> —**Judy Shelton**, author, *Money Meltdown: Restoring Order to the Global Currency System* and *Fixing the Dollar Now: Why U.S. Money Lost Its Integrity and How We Can Restore It*

"**Boom and Bust Banking** is a serious book for anyone who has a serious interest in learning why the financial meltdown of 2008 occurred, and what kind of reforms would be necessary to assure that we don't experience a repeat episode. The contributing scholars thoroughly document that the boom was engineered in Washington, and also that the financial hangover has been a costly and painful consequence of misguided government intrusion into our financial system. It has been labeled 'crony capitalism' for good reasons; the remedy is to get the politicians weaned off of financial sector contributions and restore the discipline inherent in true capitalism."

> —**Jerry L. Jordan**, former President,
> Federal Reserve Bank of Cleveland

"***Boom and Bust Banking*** is a valuable contribution to the burgeoning national debate about the way U.S. monetary policy and financial sector regulation is conducted. The authors join with a growing number of monetary economists and decision makers in arguing that the Federal Reserve Board's management of the fiat dollar has been shown to be prone to serious and potentially catastrophic error. The Fed's key role in creating the mid-2000s credit bubble that ended with the 2008 financial system meltdown is discussed in elaborate and informative detail. The book suggests debate-worthy fixes; such as a Fed monetary policy that targets national income instead of interest rates or financial regulation that disassembles 'full-service' banking in favor of 'limited-service' entities. Indeed, strong arguments are provided against central banking as such, particularly as it has been conducted over the last 40 years of fiat money. One compelling assertion equates modern-day central banking with the central planning that wrecked economies in the old Soviet bloc. ***Boom and Bust Banking*** will be a valuable compendium when monetary reform in the U.S. becomes imperative. That may happen sooner than we think."

   —**George Melloan**, former Deputy Editor, *The Wall Street Journal*; author, *The Great Money Binge: Spending Our Way to Socialism*

"The magnitude of the world recession that began in late 2007 merits a scholarly debate comparable to that which occurred in the 1960s and 1970s known as the monetarist/Keynesian debate. ***Boom and Bust Banking*** superbly helps launch this debate. Although the book expresses a great diversity of opinion, the contributions generally continue the monetarist tradition. The central bank should follow a rule to stabilize the growth rate of aggregate nominal demand at the economy's potential growth rate. Such a rule both allows the price system to work and prevents central banks from making the mistakes that destabilize the economy."

   —**Robert L. Hetzel**, Senior Economist and Research Advisor, Federal Reserve Bank of Richmond

BOOM AND BUST BANKING

BOOM AND BUST BANKING

The Causes and Cures of the Great Recession

EDITED BY DAVID BECKWORTH

The INDEPENDENT INSTITUTE

Oakland, California

The Independent Institute
100 Swan Way, Oakland, CA 94621-1428
Telephone: 510-632-1366
Fax: 510-568-6040
Email: info@independent.org
Website: www.independent.org

Library of Congress Cataloging-in-Publication Data

Boom and bust banking : the causes and cures of the great recession / edited by David M. Beckworth.
    p. cm.
   Includes index.
   ISBN 978-1-59813-076-8 (pbk. : alk. paper) — ISBN 978-1-59813-081-2 (hbk. : alk. paper)
   1. Monetary policy—United States—History—21st century. 2. Finance—United States—History—21st century. 3. Recessions—United States—History—21st century. 4. Financial crises—United States—History—21st century. 5. Global Financial Crisis, 2008-2009. 6. United States—Economic policy—2009- I. Beckworth, David M.
   HG540.B664 2012
   330.973'0931—dc23   2012008380

Cover Design: Keith Criss
Cover Image: Anistidesign/123rf
Interior Design and Composition by Leigh McLellan Design

"Limited-Purpose Banking," by Laurence J. Kotlikoff is excerpted from his book *Jimmy Stewart is Dead* © 2010 by Laurence J. Kotlikoff. Reproduced with permission of John Wiley & Sons, Inc.

Contents

Introduction

David Beckworth

IN 2009, the entire world economy stopped growing, the first time this had happened in well over fifty years. In the United States, the epicenter of the great recession, GDP shrank, unemployment rates skyrocketed, and budget deficits exploded. The twenty-first century had opened with optimism, as first technology and then housing boomed, but by the end of the decade confidence had been drained. Why did the boom-and-bust cycle return in such force after several decades of economic stability? Most studies answer this question by pointing to financial innovation, a global saving glut, poor governance, industry structure, housing policy, and misaligned creditor incentives.[1] Though these areas are an important part of the story, the amount of attention given to them makes it easy to ignore the errors of perhaps the single most powerful actor in the world economy today, the U.S. Federal Reserve.[2] The chapters in this book offer some much-needed perspective by shifting the focus back to the Federal Reserve. These essays conclude that the wide swings in the economic activity could not have occurred without the destabilizing policies of the Federal Reserve.

Former Federal Reserve Chairman William McChesney Martin once famously quipped that it was the central bank's job to take away the punch bowl

---

1. A notable exception is John Taylor in his 2009 book, *Getting Off Track: How Government Actions Caused, Prolonged, and Worsened the Financial Crisis* (Stanford: Hoover Institution Press, 2009).

2. For example, the Financial Crisis Inquiry Commission concluded that a host of governance, ethics, and market failures were key contributors to the financial crisis but that "excess liquidity did not need to cause a crisis." (See Financial Crisis Inquiry Commission, "Conclusion of the Financial Crisis Inquiry Commission," 2011, 12, http://c0182732 .cdn1.cloudfiles.rackspacecloud.com/fcic_final_report_conclusions.pdf.)

just as the party is getting good. The essays in this book show that rather than follow this advice, the Federal Reserve spiked the punch bowl and then kicked the hung-over economy out to the street at the worst possible time. Monetary policy was strengthening the business cycle instead of leaning against it during the 2000s.

The context for this "leaning with the wind" rather than against it by the Federal Reserve begins with the expansion that followed the 2001 recession. Though centered on housing, this expansion grew and pulled in many different parties including builders, subprime borrowers, mortgage originators, investment bankers, rating agencies, and investors from around the world. It also elevated the importance of structured finance and the shadow banking system. The pace of the expansion accelerated and soon it became the Great Boom of the 2000s. Like other big booms before, it was characterized by excessive leverage, mispricing of risk, soaring asset prices, and a pervasive "it's different this time" optimism. By 2007, however, the Great Boom had ended. It was soon followed by financial stress and the beginning of what was initially a mild recession. By late 2008, the financial stress had turned into a severe financial crisis that froze up credit markets and led to a sharp decline in the stock market. Similarly, by late 2008, the mild recession had mutated into one of the sharpest economic downturns since the Great Depression. This Great Recession was characterized by a dramatic collapse in spending and double-digit unemployment.

Chapters by Lawrence H. White, David Beckworth, Diego Espinosa, and Chris Crowe show that the leaning with the wind began when the Federal Reserve failed to tighten monetary policy sooner in the 2002–2004 period. The economic recovery was well underway by that time and yet monetary policy remained extremely accommodative throughout this period. As a result, the recovery that followed the 2001 recession got turned into the Great Boom. Chapters by Scott Sumner, Jeffrey Rogers Hummel, Bill Woolsey, and Nicholas Rowe show that when the economy began contracting in 2008, the Federal Reserve once again leaned with the wind by effectively tightening monetary policy. This response turned what was initially a mild recession into the Great Recession.

Going forward, what can be done to avoid repeating these monetary policy mistakes? Chapters by Joshua Hendrickson, William R. White, Laurence Kotlikoff, and George Selgin address this question. They acknowledge as a starting point that monetary policy should do a better job stabilizing nominal spending in a rule-based fashion. Several chapters even make the case for a nominal income-targeting rule. One implication of these chapters is that had the Federal Reserve been stabilizing nominal spending the Great Boom and the Great Recession of the 2000s may have never happened. Other chapters, however, question if stabilizing nominal spending is enough, or if it is even possible, given our current institutional arrangements for monetary policy. These essays, therefore, call for other reforms that aim to reduce the procyclical tendencies of the financial system while other chapters call for alternative monetary institutional arrangements altogether. Given the ongoing interest in reforming the Federal Reserve, these chapters provide a good starting point for considering how to do it and more generally how to maintain macroeconomic stability.

Creating the Great Boom

The chapters of the book are divided into three parts. The first explains how the Federal Reserve helped to create the Great Boom of the 2000s. Lawrence H. White begins with an overview of the U.S. monetary policy during the early-to-mid 2000s and how it contributed to the housing boom. It is well known that the Federal Reserve kept its target federal funds rate extremely low over this period. White shows that not only was it low, but that it was low relative to the Taylor Rule and a measure of the neutral federal funds rate. In other words, the Federal Reserve kept interest rates lower than what was warranted by economic fundamentals. White demonstrates that this sustained easing of monetary policy was systematically related to various measures of the housing boom. He also shows that the Fed's monetary policy influenced the types of mortgages originated during the housing boom and that the misaligned incentives in the financial system amplified the effects of monetary easing.

A natural question that follows from the first chapter is why did the Federal Reserve keep monetary conditions so easy for so long? David Beckworth explains that it was because monetary authorities failed to properly handle the productivity boom during that time. Total factor productivity (TFP) growth averaged 2.5 percent a year between 2002 and 2004, a vast increase over the average 0.9-percent growth for the preceding thirty years. He notes that such rapid gains in

TFP growth put downward pressure on the price level, expanded the capacity of the economy, and put upward pressure on the neutral federal funds rate. The Federal Reserve, however, saw the resulting disinflation and excess economic capacity as symptoms of continuing slack in aggregate demand. It feared raising the federal funds rate. As a result, the Federal Reserve loosened monetary policy and helped turn a beneficial productivity boom into a housing boom. Ironically, the Federal Reserve understood that the productivity boom was contributing to the disinflationary pressures and the growing economic capacity. The Federal Reserve, however, could not get past its fear of these developments to make the proper policy calls.

Diego Espinosa next shows that the Federal Reserve's policy not only enabled the housing boom, but it also helped bring about many of the problems in the financial system. In particular, he shows that the low-interest rate policy coupled with the expectation that it would persist signaled to investors there was a new carry-trade game in town. One could now borrow at predictably low, short-term interest rates and invest in higher-yielding long-term assets. All else equal, investors wanted to invest in relatively safe higher-yielding assets to ensure a predictable spread. The financial system responded to the increased demand for such safe assets by securitizing more mortgages, including subprime ones, through the process of structured finance. The surge in subprime lending and the growth of the shadow banking system, therefore, was tied to the Federal Reserve's accommodative monetary policy.

One critique of the view that U.S. monetary policy was a key driver of the U.S. housing boom is that the global housing market was booming too. How could the Federal Reserve be responsible for a phenomenon that was happening across the globe? Given this critique, many observers point to the saving glut hypothesis as an alternative explanation. This view holds that excess savings coming from emerging economies and oil exporters depressed interest rates globally and fueled the boom. David Beckworth and Chris Crowe respond to this critique by arguing that a more likely explanation is that the Federal Reserve is a monetary superpower with global influence. They show that the rise in global liquidity, the drop in global interest rates, and the buildup of foreign reserves during the early-to-mid 2000s can be explained by monetary policy in the United States. They also show that some of the saving glut is nothing more than U.S. monetary policy being recycled back into the U.S. economy.

Creating the Great Recession

The second part of the book examines the role the Federal Reserve had in creating the Great Recession of the 2000s. As noted above, the recession that started in December 2007 turned virulent by the end of 2008. Why did this happen? Scott Sumner explains it as a failure by most macroeconomists to see what was really happening to the economy. The standard view at this time was that the severe financial crisis in late 2008 made the recession worse, that monetary policy had been very accommodative, and that the zero interest rate bound was preventing the Federal Reserve from providing any more monetary stimulus. Sumner shows that this understanding was wrong. Monetary policy actually was tightening throughout much of 2008 and putting pressure on financial markets. This tightening was the main culprit behind the eruption of the financial crisis and worsening of the recession in late 2008. Sumner argues that had monetary authorities understood they were tightening, and that monetary policy was not limited by the zero bound, they could have prevented the Great Recession. This would have been possible if they had been paying attention to and targeting expected nominal GDP growth.

Jeffrey Rogers Hummel reaches a similar conclusion on the origins of the Great Recession in his comparison of Ben Bernanke and Milton Friedman. Hummel shows that the reason why the Federal Reserve allowed monetary policy to tighten during much of 2008 had to do with Bernanke's nonmonetary view of financial crises. For him, financial crises are an aggregate supply problem and are best dealt with by the Federal Reserve's lender of last resort role. Consequently, the Federal Reserve created numerous liquidity facilities between August 2007 and August 2008 to prop up the financial system. Milton Friedman, on the other hand, viewed financial crises as the result of monetary policy failing to respond to aggregate demand shocks. Therefore he probably would have been aghast to have seen the Federal Reserve ignore the precipitous decline in velocity in 2007 and 2008 while its attention was diverted to saving the financial system. Hummel notes that another problem with Bernanke's view is that it required the Federal Reserve to engage in the lender-of-last-resort role on a scale so large that it effectively turned the central bank into a central planner of credit.

How monetary policy caused the Great Recession is further explored by William Woolsey in his chapter on monetary disequilibrium. He shows that what happened in 2008 was the emergence of a pronounced excess money demand problem that was not attended to by the Federal Reserve. Since money lacks its own market but is traded on all other markets, any shock to the supply or demand of it will be disruptive to the entire economy. Given the severity of the excess money demand shock and that it was ignored, it is not surprising then that the economic downturn got turned into the Great Recession. Woolsey also shows that many of the problems associated with the Great Recession such as the liquidity trap, the paradox of thrift, and impaired household balance sheets are nothing more than a manifestation of the excess money demand problem. This chapter shows that to really understand what happened in the Great Recession, one must first understand monetary disequilibrium.

Excess money demand problems did not stop at the U.S. border. As Nicholas Rowe shows, the heightened demand for liquidity went global in 2008. Why it went global speaks to the very nature of what liquidity is and why it matters. Rowe explains that liquidity is the ability to turn an asset into purchasing power quickly, and the asset with the most liquidity is money. During the financial crises, the demand for liquidity and thus money increased. Not all money, however, has the same liquidity. The U.S. dollar with its reserve currency status is the most liquid currency. It is the money for all other monies. Consequently, when the global demand for liquidity spiked in late 2008 only one central bank, the Federal Reserve, was capable of responding. Eventually it did provide dollars through currency swaps to other major central banks, but not before economic conditions had already been adversely affected. Rowe notes that, although the Great Recession is over, the global demand for dollars is still strong in places like Asia. This means the Fed must continue to provide these dollars or face an excess dollar demand that could drive the U.S. economy into recession.

Creating a Better Monetary System

The last set of chapters explores what can be done to avoid the boom-bust cycle in the future. Josh Hendrickson begins this section by making the case for a more rules-based approach to monetary policy. He specially calls for a nominal income-targeting rule as a way to improve macroeconomic stability. He explains the great virtue of nominal income targeting is that it forces the

Federal Reserve to systematically respond to aggregate demand shocks while ignoring aggregate supply shocks. This focuses the Fed's attention on stabilizing total current dollar spending, while allowing it to ignore aggregate supply-driven changes in the price level. Hendrickson also compares nominal income targeting to the popular Taylor Rule. While they are very similar, a nominal income target is far easier to implement in real time. Nominal income targeting only requires one to know the current dollar value of the economy. A Taylor rule, on the other hand, requires knowledge of the appropriate inflation rate, the output gap, and the neutral federal funds rate. All of these are hard to measure with a lag, let alone in real time. Hendrickson concludes that a nominal income target would do much to reduce macroeconomic volatility going forward.

Though sympathetic to nominal income targeting, William R. White wonders whether it is sufficient to prevent credit booms from emerging. He makes the case that focusing too narrowly on aggregate demand stabilization could cause the Federal Reserve to ignore the inherent procyclicality of the financial system. Credit booms would be allowed to emerge, leading to a buildup of economic imbalances. When such economic imbalances burst, it would require the central bank to "clean up" afterwards to keep aggregate demand stable. White is concerned that such cleanups can create their own set of problems as seen in the housing boom that was fueled by the Federal Reserve's attempt to clean up after the stock market tanked in the early 2000s. He, therefore, believes that monetary authorities should not just lean against the business cycle, but against credit cycles. This could be done by adopting what he calls a "macrofinancial stability framework" for policy.

Laurence J. Kotlikoff is even more skeptical that the Federal Reserve can maintain macroeconomic stability given our current institutional arrangements. In particular, he believes that our current financial system is rigged for failure since it so easy for financial institutions to gamble with other people's money. As long as banks and other financial intermediaries have the expectation that gains will be privatized and losses socialized, they will continue to misuse creditors' funds. Kotlikoff believes the entire financial system needs to be reformed along the lines of limited-purpose banking. In this system every financial intermediary would operate strictly as a mutual fund company and live under a common set of rules. There would be two main types of mutual funds: a cash mutual fund that provides checking account services and other mutual funds that would provide investment opportunities. Under such a system, checking accounts would be 100-percent backed by highly liquid assets. This means the Federal Reserve would gain complete control over the money supply and, in principle, be able to better stabilize aggregate demand.

George Selgin closes the book by asking whether any of these reforms can truly maintain macroeconomic stability as long as there is a U.S. central bank. Selgin shows that central banks in general are inherently destabilizing by comparing them to how monetary conditions would evolve in their absence. In such a system, banks would issue banknotes that would be fractionally backed by some kind of reserve. Historically, this reserve was specie, but in the modern context it could be the U.S. monetary base. Banknotes would circulate much like checks do today and be cleared by banks returning rivals' banknotes directly to them or through a central clearinghouse. Any net dues owed by one bank to another would be settled by transferring reserves. This interbank clearing of banknotes and the resulting transfer of reserves would prevent private banks from issuing too many banknotes given the existing level of money demand. If money demand suddenly changed, then banks would know from the level of interbank clearings whether to increase or decrease the amount of banknotes. In the aggregate, this would result in a stable level of total current dollar spending. Central banks are fundamentally destabilizing, explains Selgin, because they are not subject to the discipline and knowledge created by such interbank clearings. Without this information, then, the Federal Reserve will never know enough to truly stabilize aggregate demand.

The Federal Reserve was more than just a bit player over the past decade. The essays in this book make a strong case that U.S. monetary policy took what would have been an ordinary business cycle and turned it into the Great Boom and the Great Recession. The other contributing factors to the business cycle at this time—including financial innovation, a global saving glut, poor governance, industry structure, housing policy, and misaligned creditor incentives—were of lesser importance. Yes, these developments all came together to form a perfect global financial storm. But a global financial storm needs a global economic force strong enough to catalyze it. This book points to that force being the Federal Reserve.

References

Financial Crisis Inquiry Commission. 2011. Conclusion of the Financial Crisis Inquiry Commission. http://co182732.cdn1.cloudfiles.rackspacecloud.com/fcic_final_report_conclusions.pdf

Taylor, John. 2009. *Getting Off Track: How Government Actions Caused, Prolonged, and Worsened the Financial Crisis.* Stanford: Hoover Institution Press.

PART I

Creating the Great Boom

1

Monetary Policy and the Financial Crisis

Lawrence H. White

An Overview

THE U.S. HOUSING BOOM of 2001–06 and the subsequent bust were not the results of laissez-faire or deregulation in the monetary and financial system.[1] The boom and bust were the results of the interaction of an unanchored government fiat monetary system with a perversely regulated financial system. Overly expansionary monetary policy fueled imprudent lending that was incentivized by "too-big-to-fail" and other regulatory distortions.

President George W. Bush famously explained the boom and bust by analogy (off the record, but someone in the room made a cell phone recording): "Wall Street got drunk! It got drunk and now it's got a hangover."[2] To extend the metaphor, it was the Federal Reserve's cheap credit policy that spiked the punchbowl. The housing boom-and-bust cycle of 2001–07 was driven by Federal Reserve credit expansion.

To use a much-repeated phrase, the Fed in 2001–06 kept interest rates "too low for too long" by injecting too much credit. From 2002 to 2005, the

---

1. Joseph Stiglitz, for one, has attributed the crisis to deregulation. (*See* Joseph Stiglitz, *Freefall: America, Free Markets, and the Sinking of the World Economy* (New York: Norton, 2010).) But the only major (partial) deregulatory measure in recent memory was the Gramm-Leach-Bliley Act of 1999 (GLB), while important new regulations (e.g., HUD affordable-housing mandates to Fannie Mae and Freddie Mac) were added between 1999 and 2007. Stiglitz does not explain how the GLB could have caused the crisis.
2. Leonard Doyle, "Bush: 'Wall Street got drunk and now it's got a hangover'," *The Independent*, 24 July 2008, http://www.independent.co.uk/news/world/americas/bush-wallstreet-got-drunk-and-now-its-got-a-hangover-875780.html.

overnight federal funds (interbank lending) rate was below 2 percent. In 2004, it was 1 percent. In an environment of increasing federal subsidies and mandates for widening home ownership through relaxed creditworthiness standards, the credit flowed disproportionately into housing. Real estate lending grew by 10–15 percent per year for several years, an unsustainable path. Low interest rates and easy terms meant that house buyers could afford larger mortgages and therefore pricier houses, driving house prices up dramatically. Federal Reserve Chairman Alan Greenspan in 2004 and his successor Ben Bernanke in 2005 assured observers that there was no national bubble in housing prices.

Rising prices and extended low interest rates made "creative" lending seem to pay off: for a time, default rates were low, even on "nonprime" mortgages that by contrast with traditional standards had low down payments, high loan-to-income ratios, poorly documented income, and monthly payments that would rise once market interest rates rose. The temporary success of creative mortgages encouraged further expansion of real estate lending to non-creditworthy borrowers. Lenders offered "nonprime" mortgages secured not by 20 percent *down,* but essentially by the hope that the trend in prices would give the borrower 20 percent equity *soon.* With rising interest rates beginning in 2005 and the reversal in real estate prices beginning in 2006, the bubble burst. Mortgage defaults rose, first on nonprime mortgages and eventually even on conventional mortgages.

The bursting of the housing bubble brought down a surprisingly large array of financial institutions. Fannie Mae and Freddie Mac, the nation's two largest mortgage financiers, became insolvent. They remain in federal "conservatorship" with losses ever mounting by the hundreds of billions. Investment house Bear Stearns failed and was sold to JPMorgan Chase only after the Federal Reserve Bank of New York injected capital by overpaying for the worst assets. Lehman Brothers failed and was resolved. The insurance giant AIG failed and was placed on federal life support. Wachovia Bank, Washington Mutual, and Merrill Lynch had to be absorbed by other institutions. Goldman Sachs, Morgan Stanley, Bank of America, Citibank, and other large institutions lined up for federal capital injections under the Troubled Asset Relief Program, and (we later learned) received quiet capital injections from the Federal Reserve in the form of loans at below-market interest rates.

Causes of the Housing Boom and Bust[3]

In the recession of 2001, the Federal Reserve System, under Chairman Alan Greenspan, began aggressively easing U.S. monetary policy. There is more than one method for judging whether monetary policy is too tight or too easy, but all indicators point toward excessive ease beginning in 2001. Year-over-year growth in the M2 monetary aggregate rose briefly above 10 percent and remained above 8 percent entering the second half of 2003. The Fed repeatedly lowered its target for the federal funds interest rate until it reached a record low. The rate began 2001 at 6.25 percent and ended the year at 1.75 percent. It was reduced further in 2002 and 2003; in mid-2003, it reached a then-record low of 1 percent, where it stayed for one year. The *real* Fed funds rate was negative—meaning that nominal rates were lower than the contemporary rate of inflation—for more than three years. In purchasing power terms, during that period a borrower was not paying, but rather gaining, in proportion to what he borrowed.

The "Taylor Rule"—a formula devised by economist John Taylor of Stanford University—provides a now-standard method of estimating what level of the current nominal federal funds rate (the overnight interbank borrowing rate that the Federal Reserve uses as its operating instrument) would be consistent, conditional on current inflation and the "output gap" between the economy's estimated potential real output and current real output, while keeping the inflation rate to a chosen target rate. Figure 1.1 contrasts the federal funds rate target path indicated by the Taylor Rule, assuming a 2-percent inflation target, with the actual federal funds rate path. The figure shows that the Fed pushed the actual federal funds rate below the Taylor Rule–estimated target rate starting in the late 1990s, and that this gap had become especially large—200 basis points or more—between mid-2003 and mid-2005.[4]

The real federal funds rate (adjusted for contemporaneous inflation) shows a similar pattern. Figure 1.2 indicates that the ex post real federal funds rate (measured by the federal funds rate minus the CPI inflation rate) was persistently

---

3. This section draws heavily on Lawrence H. White, "How Did We Get Into This Financial Mess?" (Cato Institute Briefing Paper no. 110, November 18, 2008), http://www.cato.org/pub_display.php?pub_id=9788
4. Figure courtesy of David Beckworth.

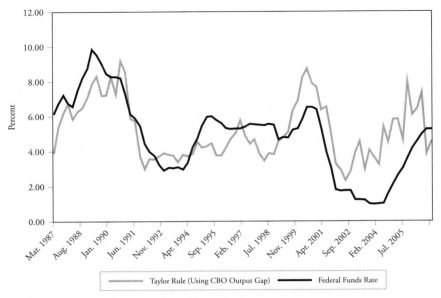

Figure 1.1. The Federal Funds Rate and the Taylor Rule

Source: FRED Database, Author's Calculations

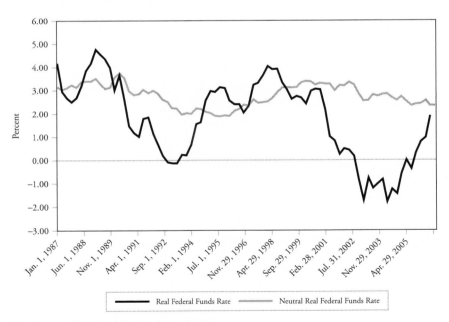

Figure 1.2. The Real Federal Funds Rate

Source: FRED Database, Laubauch and Williams (2003)

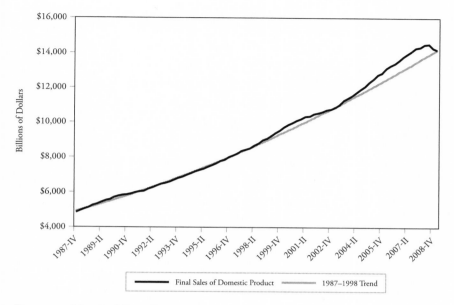

Figure 1.3. Nominal Spending
Source: FRED Database, Author's Calculations

negative for more than three years between 2002 and 2005, getting as low as −1.77 percent. This figure also shows that during this time the real federal funds rate was more than 300 basis points below the "neutral" real federal funds rate level as estimated by Thomas Laubach and John C. Williams.[5] By either measure, then, monetary policy was overly loose.

By pursuing a monetary policy so expansionary as to hold the real federal funds rate too low, the Fed drove nominal spending above its established path. Figure 1.3 shows that the final sales of domestic product grew at a fairly stable rate between 1987 and 1998.[6] In mid-1998, however, the Fed deviated and lowered the federal funds rates even though the economy was experiencing robust economic growth. The demand bubble it created set the stage for the recession of 2001. The Fed acted similarly from mid-2002 to mid-2004 by lowering the federal funds rate even after the recovery was underway. The second period of

---

5. Thomas Laubach and John C. Williams, "Measuring the Natural Rate of Interest," *Review of Economics and Statistics* 85 (2003): 1063–70. Figure courtesy of David Beckworth.
6. Figure courtesy of David Beckworth.

easy money set the stage for the recession of 2007–09. The Fed's policy, in the words of economist Steve Hanke, "set off the mother of all liquidity cycles and yet another massive demand bubble."[7]

This new demand bubble went heavily into real estate. From mid-2003 to mid-2007, while the dollar volume of final sales of goods and services was growing at 5 percent to 7.5 percent annually, real estate loans at commercial banks were growing at 10–17 percent. Figure 1.4 shows how mortgage lending grew from $541 billion in January 2001 to a peak of $1,647 billion in April 2006.[8] The rapidly growing volume of mortgage lending pushed up the inflation-adjusted sales prices of existing houses and encouraged the construction of new housing on undeveloped land, in both cases absorbing the increased dollar volume of mortgages. Because real estate is an especially long-lived asset, its market value is especially boosted by low interest rates. The Federal Housing Finance Agency (FHFA) housing price index exhibited annual nominal growth rates of 7–12 percent and annual real growth rates of 5–7 percent over the 2001–2006 period.

Can the rapid appreciation in house prices be explained simply by the economic fundamentals that normally drive home prices? No, it cannot. Figure 1.5 shows that the FHFA housing price index grew 73 percent more than personal income per capita over the 2001–2006 period.[9] The figure also shows that housing prices grew about 30 percent more than owners' equivalent rent over that same time. Housing prices, therefore, were growing faster than warranted by the growth in the ordinary fundamentals. Monetary policy helps to explain the housing bubble.

Figure 1.6 provides further evidence that the Fed's low interest rate policy was an important contributor to the housing boom.[10] The figure shows that over the Greenspan Fed period (1987–2006) a large amount of the non-fundamentals-driven movement in house prices, measured alternatively as the ratio of house prices to rents and as the ratio of house prices to personal income per capita, can be explained by prior deviations of the federal funds rate from the Taylor Rule federal fund rate target. Much of the extraordinary rise of house prices during the

---

7. Steve Hanke, "Greenspan's Bubbles," *Finance Asia* (June 2008), http://www.cato.org/pub_display.php?pub_id=9448
8. Figure courtesy of David Beckworth.
9. Figure courtesy of David Beckworth.
10. Figure courtesy of David Beckworth.

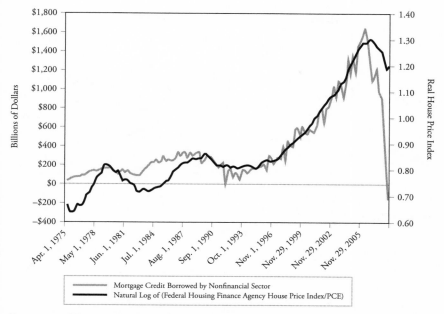

Figure 1.4. Housing Boom and Credit Growth
Source: FRED Database, Flow of Fund Data

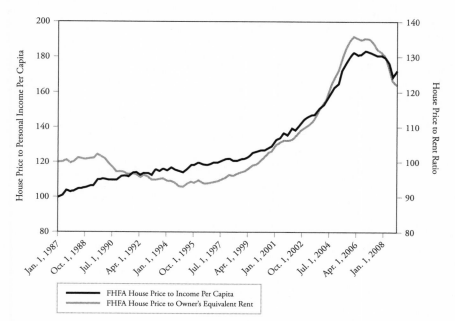

Figure 1.5. Housing Boom and Economic Fundamentals
Source: FRED Database, BLS

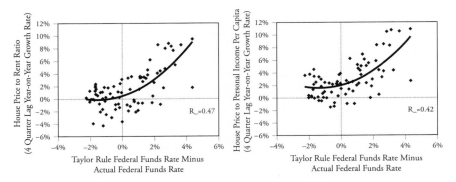

Figure 1.6. Taylor Rule Deviations vs. Housing Boom Indicators

Source: FRED Database, Author's Calculations

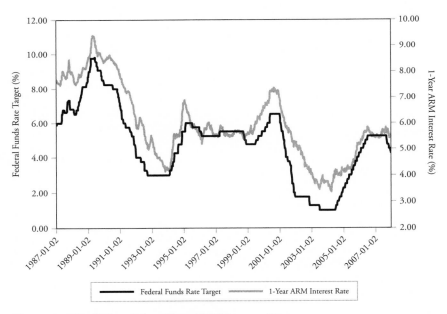

Figure 1.7. The Fed and the 1-Year ARM Interest Rate

Source: FRED Database

boom thus traces to the period of too-low path movement of the federal funds rate in 2002–2005. Other evidence similarly links much of the housing boom to the Federal Reserve's too-low federal funds rate targets.[11]

The Fed's policy of lowering short-term interest rates not only fueled growth in the dollar volume of mortgage lending, but also had unintended consequences for the *type* of mortgages written. By pushing the federal funds rate down so dramatically between 2001 and 2004, the Fed lowered all short-term interest rates relative to longer-term rates. Adjustable-rate mortgages (ARMs), typically based on a one-year interest rate, became increasingly cheap relative to thirty-year fixed-rate mortgages. Figure 1.7 shows the Fed's influence on ARM interest rates by charting the federal funds rate target together with and the average one-year ARM interest rate.[12] Back in 2001, the one-year ARM interest rate on average was about 0.90 percent lower than the average thirty-year fixed mortgage interest rate (7.05 percent versus 7.97 percent). By 2004, as a result of the low federal funds rate target, the average gap had more than doubled, growing to 2.08 percent (3.72 percent vs. 5.80 percent). The Fed not only created the gap, but also created the expectation that it would persist by explicitly committing itself in 2003 to keep the federal funds rate low for a "considerable period."

Not surprisingly, increasing numbers of new mortgage borrowers were drawn away from mortgages with thirty-year rates into ARMs. Studies have shown that households deciding whether to take out an ARM mortgage or a fixed-rate mortgage consider the expected path of interest rates.[13] By creating the expectation that the gap between the ARM interest rate and the thirty-year

---

11. Marek Jarocinski and Frank R. Smets, "House Prices and the Stance of Monetary Policy," Federal Reserve Bank of St. Louis *Review* (July/August 2008): 339–65; John B. Taylor, Getting Off Track: How Government Actions and Intervention Caused, Prolonged, and Worsened the Financial Crisis (Stanford: Hoover Institution Press, 2009); Rudiger Ahrend, "Monetary Ease: A Factor Behind the Financial Crisis? Some Evidence from OECD Countries," *Economics: The Open Access, Open Assessment Journal* 4 (2010): 12; George A. Kahn, "Taylor Rule Deviations and Financial Imbalances," *Federal Reserve Bank of Kansas City Review* (2nd quarter 2010): 63–99.

12. Figure courtesy of David Beckworth.

13. Emanuel Moench, James Vickery, and Diego Aragon, "Why is the Market Share of Adjustable Rate Mortgages So Low?" *Current Issues in Economics and Finance* 16, no. 8 (December 2010): 1–11.

Figure 1.8. The Fed and ARM Market Share

Source: FRED Database, FHFA Monthly Interest Rate Survey

fixed-rate mortgage interest rates would persist for a "considerable period," the Fed made ARMs more attractive to borrowers. Figure 1.8 shows the percent of all mortgages that were ARMs, along with a measure of the mortgage interest rate gap. The gap measure shows the difference between current rates on thirty-year fixed-rate mortgages and the expected one-year ARM rate, as measured by the average one-year ARM rate over the past three years.[14] The greater the gap, the more attractive the ARM will be. Figure 1.8 indicates changes in this gap are an important contributor to changes in the ARM share of mortgage originations.[15]

Figure 1.8 shows that during the housing boom period the market share of ARMs went from around 11 percent (in the first half of 2001) to a high of 40

14. Figure courtesy of David Beckworth. Construction of the expected mortgage interest rate gap follows Moench et. al (2010). The justification for using the lagged three-year average on the one-year ARM is the hypothesis that households use this average to forecast future ARM interest rates.

15. The R^2 between the two series is 56.39 percent for the 1990:1–2005:12.

percent (in mid-2004). Unsurprisingly, the surge in ARM originations coincided with the Fed-induced rise in the mortgage interest rate gap. The Fed's monetary policy was thus the key reason for the sharp rise in ARMs. The rise in ARMs is an important part of the story of how mortgage defaults became such a problem. An adjustable-rate mortgage shifts the risk of refinancing at higher rates from the lender to the borrower. Many borrowers who took out ARMs implicitly (and imprudently) counted on the Fed to keep short-term rates low indefinitely. These borrowers faced severe problems as their monthly payments adjusted upward. Default rates have been much higher on ARMs than on fixed-rate mortgages. The shift toward ARMs thus compounded the mortgage-quality problems arising from regulatory mandates and subsidies.

The riskiness of loans to less creditworthy borrowers was hidden for several years by the upward trend in housing prices. When the bubble burst, borrowers could no longer make mortgage payments by cash-out refinancing or home-equity borrowing.

The Financial System Amplifies the Monetary Stimulus

The Fed's monetary ease set off a housing boom in a financial system distorted by housing mandates and moral hazard problems. Creditors to Fannie Mae and Freddie Mac, Citibank, Bank of America, and the large investment banks believed that they were protected by government backing, whether guarantees were explicitly stated or not.

The U.S. banking system has received ever-increasing protection through its history, amplifying—rather than mitigating—the problems of weak banks and unsound banking. Each attempt to patch the system, to make it less prone to crisis, has unintentionally sown the seeds of a later crisis. In the early republic, restrictions against branch banking, intended to secure local monopoly privileges, left banks under-diversified and undercapitalized. Partly to fix the resulting problem of insecure and heterogeneous banknotes, the National Currency Acts passed during the Civil War required banks to hold federal bonds as collateral against notes (which also served to compel them to buy federal war bonds). The unintended result was a currency so "inelastic" that peak seasonal demands for currency set off financial panics like the Panic of 1907. To address the problem of panics, Congress, in 1913, created the Federal Reserve System, rather than undoing legal restrictions to move toward a system more like the panic-free Canadian banking system.[16]

The Federal Reserve System was supposed to remedy panics by providing an elastic currency and by acting as a lender of last resort. In the 1920s, the Fed experimented with its new powers by engaging in expansionary monetary policy, unintentionally inflating an asset price boom that went bust in 1929. The Fed failed to alleviate the multiple banking panics of 1930–33 and failed to offset the resulting sharp contraction in the money stock. A new patch was added in 1933 with the creation of federal deposit guarantees administered by the FDIC. As is now widely recognized, deposit guarantees have unintentionally bred moral hazard. In adapting to deposit insurance, U.S. banks have lowered their capital ratios and learned to take on greater portfolio risk.

To patch the problem of the incentive to hold inadequate capital, the Basel agreements among central bankers have imposed required capital ratios that are arbitrarily risk-weighted. The unintended result has been that banks have hidden high-risk assets off the balance sheet in "structured investment vehicles," and in other ways have made their risk-taking more opaque. Reported balance-sheet capital ratios have become almost completely uninformative, remaining at the mandated level even for banks whose market-valued capital (share price times number of shares)—which reflects informed estimates of the actual market values of the bank's assets and liabilities—has declined toward zero.

In the recent crisis, it became clear that moral hazard problems have been amplified greatly by implicit guarantees to all creditors and counterparties of even non-bank institutions considered "too big to fail" (TBTF). Moral hazard grows under TBTF because even creditors and counterparties not officially covered by the FDIC consider their claims guaranteed. They therefore have little reason to put a price on risk-taking by requiring a riskier bank to pay higher interest rates before they will lend to it. Money-center banks have adapted to the bigness requirement for this implicit coverage by growing large not for efficiency reasons, but to maximize the credit subsidy.

---

16. George A. Selgin and Lawrence H. White, "Monetary Reform and the Redemption of National Bank Notes, 1863–1913," *Business History Review* 68 (Summer 1994): 205–43; Vera Smith, *The Rationale of Central Banking* (Indianapolis: Liberty Funds, 1990).

The Fed's monetary easing made for a volatile mix with this pronounced moral hazard. With short-term interest rates held low, TBTF financial institutions could very cheaply finance bets on higher-yielding assets like subprime mortgages and collateralized debt obligations. The increased demand for higher-yielding assets was met by Fannie, Freddie, and TBTF banks securitizing more mortgages, including subprime mortgages. The process sustained itself as long as housing prices continued to soar and interest rates remained low.

The Housing Boom Comes to an End

The Federal Reserve, in June 2004, began slowly raising the federal funds rate in 0.25-percent increments. The national house price trend reversed after the spring of 2006, and mortgage defaults consequently began to rise. Delinquency rates on one-year-old securitized subprime mortgages made in 2003 and 2004 were roughly 3 percent and 4 percent, respectively. Delinquency rates were roughly *four times* higher on similar mortgages made in 2006 and 2007 (12 percent in 2006, 16 percent in 2007). Fannie Mae, Freddie Mac, and investment banks were caught holding highly leveraged portfolios overweighted with mortgage-backed securities, or exotic derivatives based on such securities. AIG was caught with a highly leveraged portfolio of default swaps it had sold on collateralized debt obligations backed by subprime loans. "Highly leveraged" means that AIG kept too little capital to absorb losses on its portfolios.

The Fed-induced housing boom was over. What we have learned about regulatory policy, and should already have known, is that the moral hazard of "too big to fail" powerfully corrodes financial prudence, especially in combination with policies that encourage originators to shred traditional standards of creditworthiness when making mortgage loans. What we have learned about monetary policy, and should already have known, is that the Federal Reserve should not promote asset-price bubbles by over-expanding credit. We should now consider alternative monetary institutions in which the Fed no longer has the arbitrary power to expand credit, or even in which the Fed no longer exists. The failures of the Fed should reinvigorate research on alternative monetary institutions.

References

Ahrend, Rudiger, "Monetary Ease: A Factor Behind the Financial Crisis? Some Evidence from OECD Countries," *Economics: The Open Access, Open Assessment Journal* 4, 2010–12.

Jarocinski, Marek and Frank R. Smets, "House Prices and the Stance of Monetary Policy," *Federal Reserve Bank of St. Louis Review*, July/August 2008, 339–65.

Kahn, George A., "Taylor Rule Deviations and Financial Imbalances," *Federal Reserve Bank of Kansas City Review* (Second Quarter, 2010) 63–99.

Laubach, Thomas, and John C. Williams, "Measuring the Natural Rate of Interest," *Review of Economics and Statistics* 85, 1063–1070.

Moench, Emanuel, James Vickery, and Diego Aragon, "Why is the Market Share of Adjustable Rate Mortgages So Low?" *Current Issues in Economics and Finance* 16(8), December 2010, 1–11.

Neely, Christopher J., and David E. Rapach, "Real Interest Rate Persistence: Evidence and Implications," *Federal Reserve Bank of St. Louis Review* 90 (November–December 2008).

Selgin, George A., and Lawrence H. White, "Monetary Reform and the Redemption of National Bank Notes, 1863–1913," *Business History Review* 68 (Summer 1994): 205–43.

Smith, Vera, *The Rationale of Central Banking*. Indianapolis: Liberty Funds, 1990.

Stiglitz, Joseph, *Freefall: America, Free Markets, and the Sinking of the World Economy*. New York: Norton, 2010.

Taylor, John B., *Getting Off Track: How Government Actions and Intervention Caused, Prolonged, and Worsened the Financial Crisis*. Stanford: Hoover Institution Press, 2009.

White, Lawrence H., "How Did We Get Into This Financial Mess?" Cato Institute Briefing Paper no. 110 (18 November 2008). http://www.cato.org/pub_display .php?pub_id=9788

2

Bungling Booms

How the Fed's Mishandling of the Productivity Boom Helped Pave the Way for the Housing Boom

David Beckworth

Introduction

MANY CLAIM THAT the Fed contributed to the housing boom of 2002–2006 by setting the federal funds rate target at levels that proved, in retrospect, to be too low for too long. According to this view, both the extent of the housing boom and the severity of the consequent bust would have been less severe had the Fed pursued a less accommodative monetary policy.[1]

Such claims raise an important question. Why did the Fed behave as it did? The answer laid out in this chapter is that the Fed's actions were the consequence of its inability to properly handle the U.S. productivity boom at the time. Between 2002 and 2004, total factor productivity grew at an average rate of about 2.5 percent a year. This was a vast increase over the average growth of just under 0.9-percent growth over the previous thirty years.[2] This productivity surge reduced upward pressures on the price level by expanding the capacity of the economy. These changes in turn meant that the federal funds rate needed to be higher to prevent monetary policy from becoming too expansionary. The Fed had a hard time seeing these developments this way. The Fed assumed that the disinflation was the result of harmful deflationary pressures and that the excess capacity was a symptom of slack demand. Raising the federal funds rate, therefore, would be contractionary. In short, the Fed approached these developments as though they were the result of a decline in aggregate demand rather

---

1. See, e.g., John Taylor, *Getting Off Track* (Stanford, CA: Hoover Institution Press, 2009).
2. These averages are measured using the Fernald total factor productivity series. See John Fernald, "A Quarterly, Utilization-Adjusted Series on Total Factor Productivity" (unpublished manuscript, Federal Reserve Bank of San Francisco, August 16, 2009).

than an increase in aggregate supply. Consequently, the Fed kept monetary policy excessively accommodative for an extended period of time.

Ironically, at the time, the Fed recognized that the productivity gains were contributing to the deflationary pressures and the growing economic capacity. Yet it could not get past its fear of these developments to see the implications of this understanding: further monetary easing was not necessary for most of the 2002–2004 period. Constrained by fear, the Fed simply could not respond in an appropriate manner to the productivity boom. The U.S. economy, therefore, was subjected to rapid gains in both aggregate demand and aggregate supply for a prolonged period in the early-to-mid 2000s. As a result, the Fed helped turn a beneficial productivity boom into an ultimately destructive housing boom.

In this paper, I chronicle this bungling of booms by the Fed. First, I document the Fed's fear of deflation at this time, its influence on policy, and how this fear was ultimately misplaced, given the pickup in the productivity growth rate. Second, I show that the Fed was also concerned about the excess capacity in the economy or the "negative output gap," why it too was a misplaced concern given the productivity gains, and why the Fed's response to it and the deflationary pressures was distortionary. Third, I show that contrary to the Fed's lowering of the federal funds rate during this time, the rapid productivity growth implied that the Fed should have raised its policy interest rate much sooner in the 2002–2004 period. Finally, I conclude with some implications for monetary policy.

The Fed and Deflation

The Deflation Scare of 2002–2004

Throughout the 2002–2004 period, Fed officials were concerned about deflationary pressures that were pushing down the inflation rate. By 2002, the CPI inflation rate had fallen below 2 percent and would remain there for most of the year. Despite a brief pickup in inflation in late 2002, it fell again throughout most of 2003 and early 2004, landing below 2 percent. While some Fed officials saw this decline as beneficial—it would allow them to maintain monetary ease without fear of inflation pressures building—the sustained nature of the decline also became increasingly worrisome for the Fed. These concerns became evident by the first FOMC (Federal Open Market Committee) meeting of 2002, which opened with several presentations on what monetary policy could do at the "zero bound," the point at which the federal funds rate bottoms out at zero percent and can no longer provide conventional monetary stimulus.

The zero bound is only a problem when inflation is low, and thus the discussion of the zero bound at the January 2002 FOMC meeting was motivated by concerns about the decline in inflation. In subsequent FOMC meetings that year, Fed officials continued to discuss the low inflation and the possibility of further disinflation should there be additional weakening of aggregate demand. These discussions were important in shaping the FOMC's decision to maintain ongoing monetary easing during 2002. For example, the June 2002 FOMC minutes record the following: "In the current situation, retention of the currently accommodative policy stance was desirable. . . . Inflation was still edging down, inflation expectations appeared to be low and stable, and going forward the member's forecasts . . . implied that unit costs and prices would remain subdued for some time." For most of the year, then, the Fed kept the federal funds rate unchanged at 1.75 percent.

The Fed's concerns about deflationary pressures appear to have increased in late 2002. During the November meeting, FOMC members, having gone so far as to consider the possibility of outright deflation, voted to lower the federal funds rate to 1.25 percent.[3] Later that month, Governor Ben Bernanke gave a speech entitled "Deflation: Making Sure 'It' Doesn't Happen Here."[4] According to many observers, this speech provided the intellectual justification for the Fed's low-interest rate policies over the next year and a half.[5] That speech was followed in December by one from Alan Greenspan entitled "Issues for Monetary Policy," in which Greenspan discussed the dangers of deflation and, in particular, argued that deflation is inherently more damaging to an economy than is inflation.[6]

---

3. Another related concern was the slack in the economy or the negative output gap. I discuss this concern in the next section.

4. Ben S. Bernanke, "Deflation: Making Sure 'It' Doesn't Happen Here" (speech to National Economists Club, 2002), 2.

5. David Wessel's *In Fed We Trust: Ben Bernanke's War on the Great Panic*, Crown Business, 2009.

6. Alan Greenspan, "Issues for Monetary Policy" (speech to Economics Club of New York, 2002).

The concerns expressed by Bernanke and Greenspan were echoed in FOMC meetings throughout 2003. The minutes for the January 2003 meeting state that "the members anticipated that consumer price inflation probably would edge down over the next several quarters from an already low level." The minutes for the May 2003 FOMC meeting note that "the probability of further disinflation was higher than that of a pickup in inflation." FOMC concerns appear to have escalated still further by the June 2003 FOMC meeting, at which the threat of deflation became the dominant theme. This meeting began with presentations by the Fed staff on the use of unconventional monetary policy, should the Fed face the zero bound problem. Though similar to the presentations on unconventional monetary policy in the January 2002 FOMC meeting, the presentations at the June 2003 FOMC meeting were far longer and more detailed. They included discussions on using the Fed's balance sheet and the managing of expectations as a tool that "would allow monetary policy to combat economic weakness and forestall any unexpected tendency for a pernicious deflation to develop," according to the minutes of the June 2003 meeting. At that meeting, the Fed staff also provided supplemental material on liquidity traps and produced a forecast that suggested the probability of deflation in 2004 and 2005 was as high as 40 percent. The minutes summarized the mood at this meeting by noting how members were "cognizant of the risk of substantial further disinflation, which could have potentially adverse economic effects." Given this growing apprehension about deflationary pressures, the FOMC decided at this meeting to cut the federal funds rate to 1 percent.

The Fed remained concerned about deflationary pressure through most of 2003. Press releases for the August, September, and October FOMC meetings all noted "an unwelcome fall in inflation exceeds that of a rise in inflation from its already low level" and stated, "The Committee judges that, on balance, the risk of inflation becoming undesirably low remains the predominant concern for the foreseeable future." By December 2003, the Fed stated in its FOMC press release that though inflation was still "quite low" the "probability of an unwelcomed fall in inflation has diminished. . . ." Nonetheless, there was still some concern at the Fed about further disinflation through the early part of 2004. Minutes from the March 2004 FOMC meeting record that members believed that "the cost to the economy associated with a further decline in inflation likely outweighed those associated with a comparable increase." Gradually, these concerns receded, and by the June 2004 FOMC meeting, members believed the threat had passed and that it was safe to begin tightening monetary policy.

Was the Fed's Deflation Scare Warranted?

Over most of the 2002–2004 period, the Fed viewed the disinflation as being driven by harmful deflationary pressures, so it responded by maintaining a highly accommodative monetary policy. Were these concerns warranted? Was the disinflation during this time truly posing a threat to the economy?

To answer this question, one must first determine what was driving the deflationary pressures during the 2002–2004 period. The standard aggregate demand–aggregate supply model indicates deflationary pressures can occur for two reasons: a decrease in aggregate demand, or an increase in aggregate supply.[7] The first type of deflationary pressure is a consequence of a collapse in spending that, in the presence of nominal rigidities like inflexible wages, drives actual economic activity below its potential and creates economic slack. This harmful form is what most observers invoke, sometimes implicitly, in their discussions of deflation. For example, Ben Bernanke, in his 2002 deflation speech, says that the "sources of deflation are not a mystery. Deflation is in almost all cases a side effect of a collapse in aggregate demand—a drop in spending so severe that producers must cut prices on an ongoing basis in order to find buyers."[8] This type of deflation occurred during the Great Depression in the 1930s and was associated not only with a weakened economy, but also with decreased financial intermediation as asset prices (i.e., collateral values) fell, real debt burdens increased, and thousands of banks became insolvent.

The second type of deflationary pressure, on the other hand, is the result of positive aggregate supply shocks. Such aggregate supply shocks are the result

---

7. See Chapter 9 in this volume: Joshua R. Hendrickson, "Nominal Income Targeting and Monetary Stability," for a more thorough discussion of the differences between these two forms of deflation.
8. Ben S. Bernanke, "Deflation: Making Sure 'It' Doesn't Happen Here" (speech to National Economists Club, 2002), 2, http://www.federalreserve.gov/boarddocs/speeches/2002/20021121/default.htm

of surges in productivity or factor input growth that lower per-unit costs of production and, in conjunction with competitive market forces, create downward pressure on output prices. Unlike a collapse in aggregate demand, positive aggregate supply shocks generate benign deflationary pressures that are entirely consistent with robust economic activity. Consider, for example, the case of a sustained increase in the productivity growth rate. In this case, not only are the deflationary pressures associated with strong economic growth, but also financial intermediation is not being harmed as asset prices are increasing and any unexpected increases in real debt burdens are being offset by unexpected increases in real income.[9] Bernanke acknowledges this type of deflationary pressure in his 2002 deflation speech: "Deflation could also be caused by a sudden, large expansion in aggregate supply, arising, for example, from rapid gains in productivity and broadly declining costs. . . . Note that a supply-side deflation would be associated with an economic boom rather than a recession."[10] Although rare today, deflationary pressures like this did occur in the United States during the Postbellum period of 1866–97, as can be seen in the first graph of Figure 2.1. During this time, real GNP growth averaged about 4 percent a year, while the price level declined on average about 2 percent a year. The second graph in this figure shows that financial intermediation trended up during this time, as measured by the deposit-to-currency ratio and the loans-to-GNP ratio.[11] Both of these measures grew on average about 5 percent a year. Deflationary pressures, therefore, are not necessarily associated with economic weakness and a breakdown in financial intermediation. It all depends on the source of the downward price pressures.

So what was driving the disinflation during the 2002–2004 period? Was it harmful deflationary pressures caused by faltering aggregate demand? Or, was

---

9. Asset prices are increasing, since the productivity gains are raising current and expected future earnings from the assets. Likewise, the productivity gains are creating higher income that can be used to pay for the increased real debt burden.

10. Ben S. Bernanke, "Deflation: Making Sure 'It' Doesn't Happen Here" (speech to National Economists Club, 2002).

11. For more on this deflation experience see David Beckworth (2007), "The Postbellum Deflation and its Lessons for Today," *North American Journal of Finance and Economcis*, 18(2), 195–214.

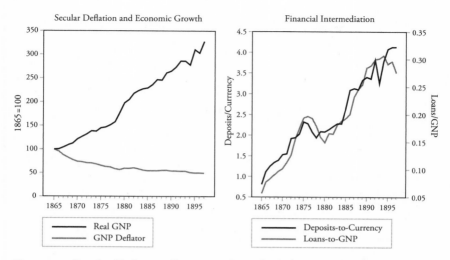

Figure 2.1. Secular Deflation, Economic Growth, and Financial Intermediation

Source: U.S. Bureau of the Census (1949), Friedman and Schwartz (1963), Balke and Gordon (1989), Johnston and Williams (2003), Mitchell (2003), Author's Calculation

it the benign deflationary pressures caused by surging aggregate supply? Figure 2.2 provides the answer. The first graph in this figure shows that aggregate demand, as measured by final sales of domestic product, bottomed out by the end of 2002:Q1 and started a sustained recovery in 2002:Q3. Domestic demand, as measured by final sales to domestic purchasers, shows an even earlier recovery that began in 2002:Q1. Aggregate spending, therefore, stabilized and began to recover in 2002, well before the Fed dropped the federal funds rate to the then-historically-low level of 1 percent. Weakening demand could not have been the source of the deflationary pressures at this time. The second graph in Figure 2.2 reveals the real driving force: robust productivity growth. There were two big surges in the productivity growth rate, as measured by total factor productivity, during this time, and these surges coincided with the two sustained drops in the inflation rate. Surging aggregate supply, then, is a far better explanation than faltering aggregate demand for the deflationary pressures during 2002–2004. Consequently, the Fed's concerns at this time were misplaced: the disinflation was simply the benign byproduct of the surge in productivity. This disinflation should not have been feared by the Fed.

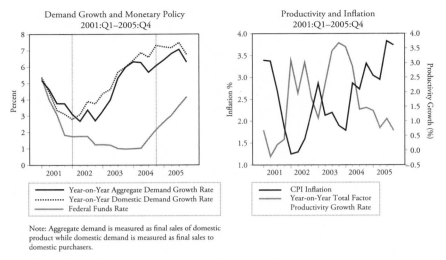

Figure 2.2. Monetary Policy, Demand Growth, Productivity, and Inflation
Source: Fernald (2009), FRED Database, Author's Calculation

Ironically, FOMC members during this time understood that the productivity gains were probably contributing to the low inflation. For example, the March 2002 FOMC minutes state that the members believed that "the prospects of relatively robust growth in productivity in a highly flexible and competitive economy likely would moderate the extent of any potential buildup in inflationary pressures in the future." The FOMC also understood that the productivity gains were most likely shoring up economic growth as noted in its June 2003 press statement: "The Committee continues to believe that an accommodative stance of monetary policy, coupled with still robust growth in productivity, is providing important ongoing support to economic activity." The productivity surge, in fact, became a common point of discussion in FOMC meetings over the 2002–2004 period. Richard G. Anderson and Kevin L. Kleisen show that though the FOMC was slow to appreciate the full extent of what was happening, it ultimately understood there was a productivity boom.[12]

___

12. Richard G. Anderson and Kevin L. Kleisen, "FOMC Learning and Productivity Growth (1985–2003): A Reading of the Record," *Federal Reserve Bank of St. Louis Review* (March/April 2010): 129–53.

Despite this understanding, FOMC members responded to the productivity-driven disinflation as if it indicated a weakening of aggregate demand. There were conversations justifying the highly accommodative stance of monetary policy, as indicated in the minutes for the May 2003 FOMC meeting: "Members commented that substantial additional disinflation would be unwelcome because of the likely negative effects on economic activity and the functioning of financial institutions and markets, and the increased difficulty of conducting an effective monetary policy. . . ." Some of the FOMC's confusion was motivated by concerns about excess economic capacity pushing down inflation rates. But, as shown in the next section, these concerns were misguided since the growing economic capacity was the result of the productivity surge, not faltering aggregate demand. Apparently, the FOMC members were so constrained by their fear of deflation that they were unable to differentiate between the harmful implications of aggregate demand-induced deflationary pressures and the benign implications of aggregate supply-induced deflationary pressures.[13] As a result, the FOMC treated all deflationary pressures as if they were driven solely by a weakening in aggregate demand. This was one of the biggest policy mistakes of this period.

The Fed and the Output Gap

Concerns over the Negative Output Gap

Another concern of the Fed officials during this time was the persistence of excess economic capacity. Throughout much of the 2002–2004 period, actual output was less than potential output, and this negative output gap was perceived by the FOMC to be problematic. Specifically, there was a belief that insufficient aggregate demand had generated economic slack that, in addition to the productivity gains, was pushing down the inflation rate to an uncomfortably

---

13. One exception to this was Minneapolis Fed President Gary Stern. He expressed reservations about the deflation fears in meetings and speeches in 2003. See, e.g., Gary Stern, "Top of the Ninth: Should We Accept the Conventional Wisdom about Deflation?" *Minneapolis Federal Reserve Bank The Region* (September, 2–6, 2003), http://www.minneapolis fed.org/publications_papers/pub_display.cfm?id=3352

low level. For example, the June 2003 FOMC minutes report that with "the economy thought likely to operate below its potential for an extended period and productivity growth expected to remain robust, the members believed that the current low-inflation environment would persist over the next several quarters and indeed that some further disinflation could be in store. In this regard, there was concern that inflation could be approaching a level that would begin to complicate the implementation of monetary policy. . . ." Even as late as May 2004, FOMC minutes record that with "inflation low and resource use slack, the Committee saw a continuation of its existing policy stance as providing a degree of support to the economic expansion that was still appropriate." One manifestation of the negative output gap that particularly bothered FOMC members was the weak recovery in the labor markets. Meaningful job creation, as seen by sustained growth in non-farm business payroll jobs, did not begin to materialize until the second half of 2003. This negative output gap, then, was another reason Fed officials were concerned about the deflationary pressures. But were their concerns warranted? Did the negative output gap truly indicate that aggregate demand was faltering and posing a threat to the economy?

We have already shown in Figure 2.2 that a sustained recovery in aggregate demand was underway by late 2002. A weakening of aggregate demand, then, could not have been the cause of the negative output gap at this time. To better understand what was behind the excess economic capacity, let us return to the aggregate demand–aggregate supply (AD-AS) model.

Earlier, we showed with this model that deflationary pressures can arise for two reasons: a decrease in aggregate demand, or an increase in aggregate supply. For these same two reasons, a negative output gap can emerge and is illustrated in Figure 2.3. This graphical representation of the AD-AS model is shown with output, Y, on the horizontal axis, and the inflation rate, π, on the vertical axis. In this model, the long-run aggregate supply (LRAS) represents the potential or natural rate level of output. The short-run aggregate supply (SRAS) curve shows the positive relationship that exists between the inflation rate and output in the short run, given the existence of nominal rigidities (i.e., sticky prices). The aggregate demand (AD) curve shows total current dollar or nominal spending for a given inflation rate and real output.

In the first graph of Figure 2.3 we see the type of negative output gap presumed by the FOMC: a fall in AD from AD^1 to AD^2 that temporarily pushes

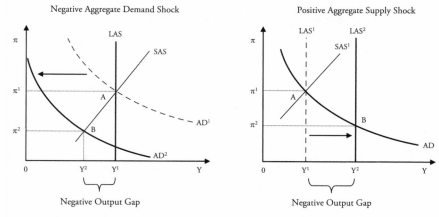

Figure 2.3. Two Types of Negative Output Gaps
Source: Drawn by David Beckworth

output from its potential, Y¹, to a lower level, Y². This drop in AD is also accompanied by a decline in the inflation rate. In this case it makes sense to talk about monetary policy "closing the gap" since output has contracted and the harmful type of deflationary pressures are present. As noted above, however, this scenario does not fit the data for the 2002–2004 period. What does fit the data for this time period is found in the second graph of Figure 2.3. Here, the LAS has shifted, due to the positive productivity shock. The SAS curve, however, has yet to shift out because of sticky prices and, and as a result, output is still at Y¹ instead of Y². In short, the economy has yet to grow into its new added capacity. In this scenario, there is a negative output gap, but there has been no contraction; the outlook is for strong economic growth, and the disinflation is benign. Thus, it makes less sense here to talk about monetary policy needing to "close the gap," which will happen automatically as the SAS shifts to the new equilibrium output, Y². Not all negative output gaps, then, are the same.

With this understanding, it is worth considering what the output gap during the 2002–2004 period would have looked like had there been no productivity surge. To do this, we estimated a structural vector autoregression for the period 1970:Q1–2006:Q4 that includes the output gap, total factor productivity, and final sales of domestic product as variables. I identify productivity shocks and conduct what is called a historical decomposition to determine how important these

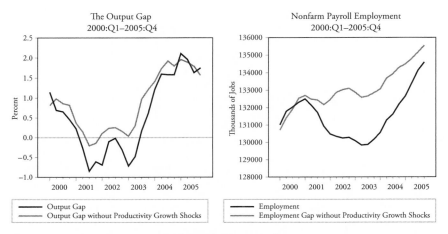

Figure 2.4. The Output Gap and Employment with
and without Productivity Shocks

Source: Fernald (2009), Laubach and Williams (2003), FRED Database, Author's Calculation

shocks were to the output gap.[14] Doing so allows us to see what the output gap
would have been had there been no productivity shocks. The first graph in
Figure 2.4 shows the actual output gap, and an output gap constructed without the estimated productivity shocks. This graph shows that after accounting
for the productivity surge, the output gap only turned negative in 2001, the
year the NBER (National Bureau of Economic Research) dates the recession.
The adjusted output gap remains close to zero, but positive through mid-2003,
and then rapidly grows through 2004. This evidence indicates the observed
negative output gap of 2002–2004 seems largely to have been the result of the
rapid productivity gains during this time.

These findings are consistent with those from research that has examined the
effect of productivity shocks on employment.[15] Starting with Gali (1999),[16] there
have been a number of studies that show positive productivity shocks lead to a

14. The specifics of the VAR are in the data and methods appendix.
15. Technically, these shocks are called "technology" shocks in the literature.
16. Gali (1999), "Technology, Employment, and the Business Cycle."

temporary decline in hours worked.[17] The interpretation given to these findings is that given sticky prices, firms initially respond to productivity gains by using less labor. Only as prices become more flexible (i.e., the SRAS curve shifts right) do firms employ more labor and push the economy to its full economic potential. Thus, these studies imply that a productivity boom of the kind experienced during 2002–2004 should initially lead to some slack in resource utilization.

To further examine this implication, we estimated another VAR identical to one above except now nonfarm business employment replaced the output gap in the model.[18] We again use the historical decomposition technique to construct an alternative nonfarm employment series that has the effect of productivity shocks removed from it. This adjusted employment series and the original one is plotted in the second graph of Figure 2.4. This graph shows that after accounting for the productivity surge, employment has only a mild decline during this period and recovers much sooner than the actual employment series. This evidence, therefore, also points to the productivity boom being the main reason for the excess economic capacity and slack in resource utilization during this time.

Both theory and evidence, then, indicates that not all negative output gaps are created equal. Some are truly harmful while others are benign. The negative output gap during the 2002–2004 period was largely of the benign form. The FOMC, however, viewed all negative output gaps the same, as if they were the result of a weakening in aggregate demand. As we show next, this failure to treat negative output gaps differently was another big mistake made by the FOMC.

---

17. There have been some studies that show hours worked increase immediately after a positive productivity shock (e.g., Lawrence J. Christiano, Martin Eichenbaum, and Robert Vigfusson, "What Happens After a Technology Shock?" NBER Working Paper 9819 (2003)). Serious questions, however, have been raised about the methodological assumptions used in these studies. Recent work suggests the findings that show a temporary decline in hours worked to a positive productivity shock is a more robust finding (e.g. Susanto Basu & John G. Fernald & Miles S. Kimball, "Are Technology Improvements Contractionary?" *American Economic Review*, 96 no 5 (2006):1418–48; Karl Whalen, "Technology Shocks and Hours Worked: Checking for Robust Conclusions," *Journal of Macroeconomics* 31 (2009): 231–39).
18. See the data and methods appendix for details of the VAR.

What is Wrong with "Closing the Gap"?

One objection to the above analysis is that despite the fact the negative output gap during this time was largely benign, the FOMC was helping restore macroeconomic equilibrium by expediting the "closing of the gap." What harm could possibly come from the Fed increasing aggregate demand so as to shorten the time it takes for the economy to reach its full potential? After all, if it makes sense to close the gap for an aggregate demand-induced negative output gap, then why not do the same for aggregate supply-induced negative output gap?

To answer these questions, let us once again look to the AD-AS model and consider two ways in which this benign negative output gap could close. The first graph in Figure 2.5 shows the first way is to simply let the SRAS curve shift out on its own and close the gap between Y^1 and Y^2. This approach maintains a fairly stable level of aggregate demand (AD) as the SRAS shifts from point A to B. This shift can be seen by noting that changes in the inflation rate are offset by changes in output so that AD remains relatively stable. This stabilization of nominal spending is an important feature of this approach. It means there will not be any sudden changes in total current dollar spending that would, in the presence of nominal rigidities like sticky prices, push the economy away from its new equilibrium level, Y^2.

The second way in which the gap could close is for the Fed to loosen monetary policy so as to increase AD. This approach is portrayed in the second

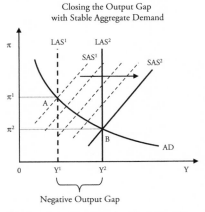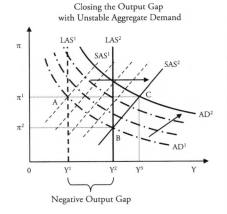

Figure 2.5. Closing the Output Gap

graph of Figure 2.5. Note that with this approach, the increase in AD is being accompanied by the shift out in the SRAS. Now, if the FOMC in its decision to increase AD is also aiming for inflation stability—so as to avoid deflationary pressures—a likely outcome is point C. At this point the AD shift has maintained the original inflation rate and the SRAS has reached its final destination. This outcome is not sustainable since output has been pushed to Y^3, a point beyond its sustainable output level of Y^2. Thus, the negative output gap was replaced by a positive one.[19] So much for expediting the "closing of the gap." This unsustainable boom was created because the Fed failed to stabilize nominal spending. In other words, the economy was simultaneously buffeted by positive AD and AS shocks, a double stimulus that was too much. Interestingly, the unsustainable pickup in actual output occurs without any alarming increases in inflation. Thus observers, like the FOMC, who view stable inflation as sign of macroeconomic stability could be lulled into complacency.

This second way of closing the output gap and its associated problems is what transpired in the 2002–2004 period. Though aware of the productivity boom, the FOMC responded to the deflationary pressures and the negative output gap as if they were symptoms of faltering aggregate demand. They did so by keeping monetary policy highly accommodative during this time. As a result, nominal spending surged along with productivity. This helped set off a housing boom. Instead of closing the output gap, then, this response by the Fed simply created a new one as seen in first graph of Figure 2.4. The FOMC did this by keeping the federal funds rate below the neutral federal funds rate for an extended period of time. We explain next what this means, and why it too was not warranted.

The Fed and the Neutral Rate of Interest

The FOMC and the Neutral Federal Funds Rate

The FOMC's mishandling of deflationary pressures and the negative output gap during the productivity boom meant that it was also mishandling the

---

19. Lawrence Christiano, Roberto Motto, and Massimo Rostagno show a similar result more formally in "Two Reasons Why Money and Credit May be Useful in Monetary Policy," NBER Working Paper 13502 (2007).

federal funds rate, the rate with which the FOMC sets monetary policy. To understand how the FOMC botched its handling of the federal funds rate, some background on how the Fed conducts monetary policy is in order.

Monetary policy in the United States has long been based on interest-rate targeting, that is, on selecting a target value for a particular interest rate, and adjusting the growth rate of the monetary base in a manner calculated to make the actual rate hit the target. The federal funds rate, the interest targeted by the FOMC, is the one for overnight interbank reserve borrowings or "federal funds." When the federal funds rate rises above its targeted value, the Fed's open-market desk responds by increasing its net purchases of government securities, thereby adding to the supply of bank reserves; when the rate falls below target, it reduces its net purchases, and may even engage in net sales. Because the cost of acquiring federal funds to cover temporary reserve shortages is an important determinant of banks' own willingness to lend, raising the federal funds rate target tends to check overall credit expansion, other things being equal, while lowering the federal funds rate target tends to encourage credit expansion.

The FOMC's challenge can be understood as that of achieving a "neutral" monetary policy stance, meaning one that strives to close the output gap and thus avoid contributing either to booms or busts.[20] The federal funds rate consistent with such a monetary policy stance is sometimes referred to as the neutral (and sometimes as the "natural") rate of interest. Were the neutral rate directly observable, implementing a neutral monetary policy would be a simple matter. In fact, the rate is both unobservable and impossible to estimate precisely. The fundamental and cyclical determinants of that rate are nevertheless well understood.[21] The fundamental determinants are generally understood to be the growth rate of the population, long-term saving preferences of households, and the growth rate of total factor productivity (TFP). Of these, the TFP growth rate is seen as responsible for most variations in the neutral interest rate in the U.S. economy.[22] An increase in the total factor productivity growth rate leads,

---

20. Tom Bernhardsen and Karsten Gerdrup, "The Neutral Real Interest Rate," Norges Bank *Economic Bulletin* 78, no. 2 (2007): 52–64.
21. For a more thorough but accessible discussion of the neutral interest rate, *see* Bernhardsen and Gerdrup, "The Neutral Real Interest Rate."
22. Between 1970 and 2006, the total factor productivity (TFP) growth rate ranged from

all else equal, to an increase in the real (i.e., inflation-adjusted) neutral interest rate. This is because productivity gains increase both investment demand and consumer demand by raising the expected return on capital and the expected household income. The cyclical determinants are spending shocks that create either positive or negative output gaps. In this situation, a positive (negative) spending shock will lead to a higher (lower) neutral interest rate so as to close the output gap.

Though the real neutral federal funds rate cannot be measured precisely, there have been many attempts to estimate it.[23] Here, a simple estimate of it is provided, one that accounts for the importance of productivity innovations and cyclical influences on the real neutral interest rate. The approach is to treat the real neutral interest rate as simply being equal to the long-run average real neutral interest rate, which is generally assumed to be about 2 percent, plus the difference between the currently forecasted (TFP) growth rate and the mean rate of TFP growth.[24] More formally,

$$r_t^n = r^n + (g_t^e - g),$$

where r_t^n is the real neutral interest rate for period t, r^n is the long-run neutral real interest rate, g_t^e is the expected year-on-year TFP growth rate for period t, and g is the mean year-on-year TFP growth rate for the sample. This approach stresses the importance of expected TFP growth rate deviations from trend—the higher the productivity is expected to be above its trend the higher will be the real neutral interest rate and vice versa. It also allows for cyclical influences since

---

as high as 4 percent to as low as –3 percent, with many relatively sharp swings, the most recent of which has been the so-called productivity "surge" that began in the mid-1990s, which was interrupted by the dot.com crash, and then resumed with still greater vigor until 2004. The U.S. population growth rate, in contrast, has been relatively stable during this time, hovering around 1 percent. The contribution of changes to the rate of time preference to the neutral rate is, on the other hand, very uncertain, as there are no reliable and consistent estimates of it (see Shane Frederick, George Loewenstein, and Ted O'Donoghue, "Time Discounting and Time Preference: A Critical Review" *Journal of Economic Literature* 40, no. 2 (2002): 351–401).

23. *See*, e.g., Thomas Laubach and John C. Williams, "Measuring the Natural Rate of Interest" *Review of Economics and Statistics*, 85 (2003): 1063–70.

24. The data appendix explains how we estimate these series.

our TFP measure is a non-cyclically adjusted one (i.e. it is affected by technology shocks as well as changes in unobserved input utilization).[25]

Figure 2.6 shows this measure of the real neutral interest rate along with the actual real federal funds rate for the period 1970:Q1–2006:Q4. This figure indicates that the real federal funds rate has often deviated significantly from the real neutral interest rate. These deviations can be viewed as departures from optimal monetary policy. Consequently, they provide a measure of the stance of monetary policy. Unsurprisingly, these deviations are closely tied to subsequent swings in the output gap, as seen in Figure 2.7. This figure shows that the spread between our real neutral interest rate measure and the real federal funds rate, plotted against the output gap, lagged 5 quarters. The relationship has a R^2 of almost 60 percent. This indicates that non-neutral moves in U.S. monetary policy explain a significant portion of subsequent swings in the business cycle. Because in this simple framework the real neutral rate changes only owing to changes in the growth rate of productivity, this spread can be referred to as the "Productivity Gap." The Productivity Gap can be formally stated as follows:

$$P_t = r_t^n - r_t,$$

where r_t^n is the real neutral interest rate calculated above and r_t is the actual real federal funds rate. Thus, the larger the Productivity Gap the greater the monetary easing and vice versa.

The Productivity Gap and the Stance of Monetary Policy During the Housing Boom[26]

The Productivity Gap is plotted in Figure 2.8, along with two other measures of the stance of monetary policy. The first one is the "Taylor Gap," the

---

25. The cyclical influences act upon TFP in a manner that serves as a proxy for spending shocks. For example, if there is a positive spending shock that leads to increased unobserved input utilization, it will cause TFP to be overstated. The higher TFP, in turn, will imply a higher neutral interest rate. This result is consistent with that implied by a positive spending shock that creates pressure for a positive output gap to emerge (i.e., a higher neutral interest rate is needed to keep the output gap closed).

26. This section draws heavily on David Beckworth, George Selgin, and Berrak Bahadir "The Productivity Gap: Productivity Surges as a Source of Monetary Excesses," (2011), University of Georgia working paper.

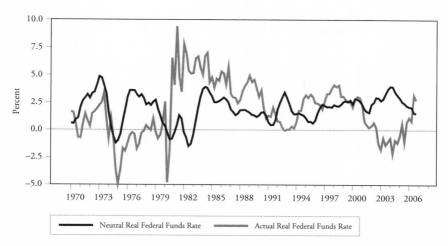

Figure 2.6. The Neutral and Actual Real Federal Funds Rate, 1970:Q1–2006:Q4
Source: Fernald (2009), FRED Database, Author's Calculation

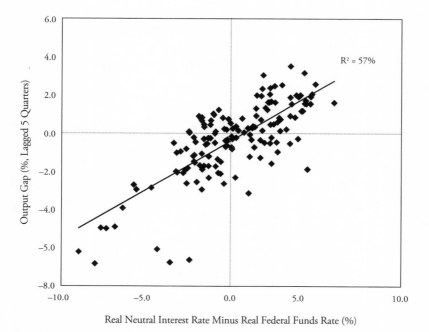

Figure 2.7. Monetary Policy and the Output Gap, 1970:Q1–2006:Q4
Source: Fernald (2009), Laubach and Williams (2003), FRED Database, Author's Calculation

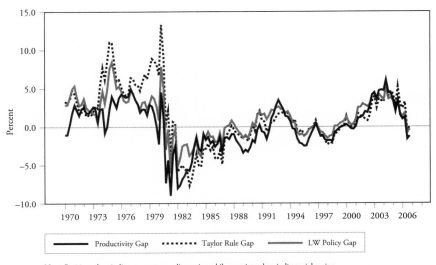

Note: Positive values indicate monetary policy easing while negative values indicate tightening.

Figure 2.8. Monetary Policy Gaps, 1970:Q1–2006:Q4
Source: Fernald (2009), Laubach and Williams, FRED Database, Author's Calculation

difference between the federal fund funds rate target suggested by the Taylor Rule and the actual federal funds rate. The widely-known Taylor Rule determines the optimal federal funds rate target based on three factors: (1) a baseline estimate of the neutral federal funds rate, (2) deviations between economic and potential output, and (3) deviations between the actual and target inflation rate.[27] The second measure is "LW Policy Gap" and is the difference between the natural interest rate estimate from Laubach and Williams[28] and the actual real federal funds rate. This LW Policy Gap measure represents one of the more sophisticated attempts to estimate the natural or real neutral interest rate and its implications for monetary policy. Together, the Taylor Rule Gap and the LW Policy Gap provide a robustness check against our simple Productivity Gap measure. Figure 2.7 shows that all three gaps are highly correlated and thus show similar periods of monetary easing and tightening. It follows that the Fed's departures of the federal funds rate from the Taylor Rule and the real

---

27. See Chapter 9 in this volume: Joshua R. Hendrickson, "Nominal Income Targeting and Monetary Stability," for a thorough discussion of the Taylor Rule.
28. Laubach and Williams, "Measuring the Natural Rate of Interest."

federal funds rate from the natural interest rate may be understood as being frequently due to its failure to adjust the federal funds target appropriately to changes in the economy's productivity growth rate.

The direction and magnitude of monetary policy errors implied by the Productivity Gap are roughly consistent with conventional wisdom. Fed policy was, according to this measure, excessively easy throughout the 1970s, although less so in the immediate wake of the initial OPEC-induced oil supply shock than at other times, while it was excessively tight during the Volcker anti-inflation campaign. During the 1990s policy was at first easy and then somewhat (though not dramatically) tight. During the period immediately surrounding the tech bubble crash, monetary policy appears to have been neutral. Finally, beginning around 2002, monetary policy became increasingly easy as the Fed drove the real federal funds rate into negative territory despite strong productivity growth. The Productivity Gap during this time reached its largest value in the sample period. Figure 2.8 indicates, then, that the FOMC's failure to respond appropriately to the productivity boom when setting the federal funds rate target caused it to create one of the greatest monetary easing periods in recent history.

This great monetary expansion has been shown by numerous studies to have been an important contributor to the 2002–2006 housing boom.[29] Figure 2.9 provides further evidence on the link. It shows that swings in the productivity gap are typically followed by similar swings in the housing market as measured by housing starts. Once again, we see that the Fed's bungling of the productivity boom helped pave the way for the housing boom.

Policy Implications

This paper has shown that the Fed's inability to handle the implications of the 2002–2004 productivity boom for the inflation rate, the output gap, and the federal funds rate help put into motion the housing boom. Though the Fed's

---

29. Marek Jarocinski and Frank R. Smets, "House Prices and the Stance of Monetary Policy," *Federal Reserve Bank of St. Louis Review* (July/August 2008): 339–65; John Taylor, *Getting Off Track*; George A. Kahn, "Taylor Rule Deviations and Financial Imbalances," *Federal Reserve Bank of Kansas City Review* (2nd quarter 2010): 63–99; Rudiger Ahrend, "Monetary Ease: A Factor Behind the Financial Crisis? Some Evidence from OECD Countries," *Economics: The Open Access, Open Assessment Journal* 4 (2010), 12.

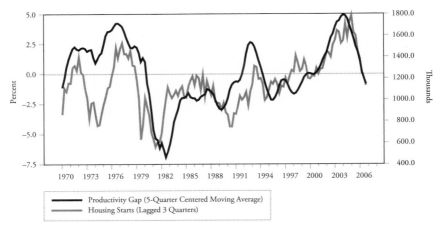

Figure 2.9. The Productivity Gap and Housing, 1970:Q1–2006:Q4

Source: Fernald (2009), FRED Database, Author's Calculation

response during this time was one of the greatest failures of monetary policy, it was not unique. Rather, it reflected the Fed's tendency to ease monetary policy when responding to productivity surges. This tendency can be seen in Figure 2.10, which shows the average responses of total factor productivity (TFP), the federal funds rate, the inflation rate, the unemployment rate, and the output gap to a typical (i.e., one standard deviation) positive shock to the TFP growth rate for the period 1970:Q1–2006:Q4.[30] This figure reports the cumulative responses, which means it shows the effect of the TFP growth rate shock on the level of these variables. The dashed lines in the figure are simulated standard error bands.

Figure 2.10 shows that, ceteris paribus, a positive TFP shock during this time increased the level of TFP which, in turn, put downward pressure on the inflation rate. Consistent with our discussion in the section above, the TFP shock also typically increased unemployment for a short time, indicating that firms temporarily used fewer workers, given the productivity gains. The figure further indicates that the Fed typically responded to such developments by dropping the federal funds rate as a means to push the inflation and unemployment rates back to their pre-shock levels. Doing so, however, means the federal funds rate

---

30. The specifics of the VAR are in the data and methods appendix.

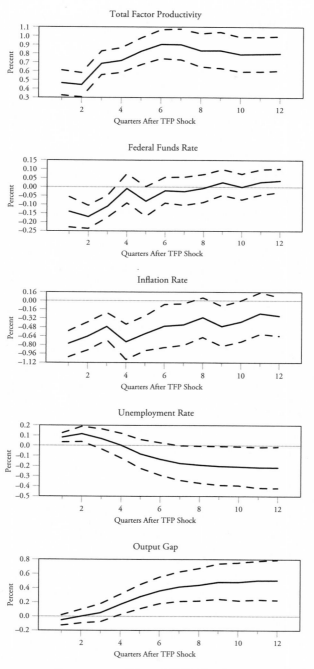

Figure 2.10. Response to a Typical TFP Shock, 1970:Q1–2006:Q4

Source: FRED Database and Author's Calculations

is not allowed to reflect the changes in productivity—it is held below its neutral rate level. As a result, this response has usually pushed the economy beyond its sustainable output level as seen in the increase in the output gap.

Historically, then, the Fed's fear of deflationary pressures has caused it to systematically respond in an inappropriate manner to productivity surges. Thus, what the Fed did in 2002–2004 was nothing new. What was unique about this experience was the magnitude of the productivity gains. During the 2002–2004 period, total factor productivity averaged 2.5-percent growth, compared to the 0.9-percent average growth rate over the previous thirty years. In other words, the Fed finally met a productivity surge that did it in.

What is needed, then, is a systematic approach to monetary policy that allows the Fed to respond appropriately to productivity surges, but at the same time keeps aggregate demand stable. Such an approach would allow productivity booms to translate into lower inflation and vice versa and keep the interest rates nearer the neutral rate level. It would also need to keep total current dollar spending growing at a stable rate. The way to do this is for the Fed to adopt some kind of nominal income targeting rule such as a nominal GDP target. This approach to monetary policy is covered in this book in Chapter 5, "How Nominal GDP Targeting Could Have Prevented the Crash of 2008," by Scott Sumner; and Chapter 9, "Nominal Income Targeting and Monetary Stability," by Josh Hendrickson.

Data and Methods Appendix

Data Sources

Total factor productivity comes from John Fernald,[31] while the output gap measure comes from Laubach and Williams.[32] The rest of the variables—the federal funds rate, the CPI, the unemployment rate, and housing starts—all come from the FRED Database at the St. Louis Federal Reserve Bank.

---

31. John Fernald, "A Quarterly, Utilization-Adjusted Series."
32. Laubach and Williams, "Measuring the Natural Rate of Interest."

Vector Autoregression Methods (VAR)

The first VAR is estimated for the period 1970:Q1–2006:Q4, uses 5 lags to eliminate serial correlation, and the data identifies the productivity shock using long-restrictions (i.e., final sales of domestic product cannot permanently affect productivity, but productivity can permanently affect itself and final sales; also, productivity cannot permanently affect the output gap). The use of long-run restrictions to identify productivity shocks is a common approach that goes back to Jordi Gali, "Technology, Employment, and the Business Cycle: Do Technology Shocks Explain Aggregate Fluctuations?" *American Economic Review* 83 (1999): 402–415; with recent examples being William Lastrapes, "Inflation and the Distribution of Relative Prices: The Role of Productivity and Money Supply Shocks," *Journal of Money, Credit, and Banking* 38, no. 8 (2006): 2159–98; and Karl Whalen, "Technology Shocks and Hours Worked: Checking for Robust Conclusions," *Journal of Macroeconomics* 31 (2009): 231–39. The variables are ordered in the VAR as follows: output gap, total factor productivity, and final sales of domestic output. Except for the output gap, which is already in rate form, the variables are logged and first differenced. See the data appendix for data sources. For more on the historical decomposition technique, see James Fackler and Randall Parker, "Accounting for the Great Depression: A Historical Decomposition," *Journal of Macroeconomics* 16, no. 2 (1994): 193–220.

In the second VAR, the variables are ordered as follows: total factor productivity, nonfarm business employment, and final sales of domestic output. The identifying restrictions, lags, and sample period in the previous VAR are used here. All variables are logged and first differenced. The estimated first difference data from the historical decomposition, which approximates a growth rate, was applied to the 1999:Q4 non-farm business employment data point in level form to construct the alternative level series.

The third VAR uses 5 lags to eliminate serial correlation and identifies the TFP shock using long-run restrictions (i.e., only shocks to the TFP series can permanently affect itself). The TFP series is logged and first differenced while the other series—which are already in rate form—are just first differenced to induce stationarity.

Neutral Rate and Productivity Gap Construction

The neutral real federal funds rate is based on the equation, $r_t^n = r^n + (g_t^e - g)$, where r_t^n is the current period neutral real interest rate, r^n is the long-run, steady neutral real interest rate, g_t^e is the current expected year-on-year TFP growth rate, and g is the mean year-on-year TFP growth rate for the sample. I assume $r^n = 2$ percent and estimate g_t^e using an exponential weighted moving average process of past year-on-year TFP growth rates with the current period weight receiving a value of 0.70. As noted in the text, the Productivity Gap, P_t, is calculated as follows: $P_t = r_t^n - r_t$, where r_t is the actual real federal funds rate. The real federal funds rate is calculated as the federal funds rate minus the year-on-year inflation rate.

References

Anderson, Richard G., and Kevin L. Kleisen. 2010. "FOMC Learning and productivity Growth (1985–2003): A Reading of the Record." *Federal Reserve Bank of St. Louis Review* (March/April): 129–53.

Basu, San, John Fernald, and Miles Kimball. 2006. "Are Technology Improvements Contractionary?" *American Economic Review*, American Economic Association, vol. 96(5), pages 1418–48, December.

Bernhardsen, Tom, and Karsten Gerdrup. 2007. "The Neutral Real Interest Rate." *Norges Bank Economic Bulletin* 78 (2): 52–64.

Fackler, James and Randall Parker. 1994. "Accounting for the Great Depression: A Historical Decompostion." *Journal of Macroeconomics*, 16(2), 193–220.

Federal Reserve System, Board of Governors. Federal Open Market Committee Transcripts. At http://www.federalreserve.gov/monetarypolicy/fomc_historical.htm

Ferguson, Roger. 2004. Chairman Ferguson, October 29. "Equilibrium Real Interest Rate: Theory and Application." Remarks delivered at the University of Connecticut School of Business, October 29, http://www.federalreserve.gov/boarddocs/speeches/2004/20041029/default.htm

Fernald, John. 2009. "A Quarterly, Utilization-Adjusted Series on Total Factor Productivity." Unpublished manuscript, Federal Reserve Bank of San Francisco, August 16.

Frederick, Shane, George Loewenstein, and Ted O'Donoghue. 2002. "Time Discounting and Time Preference: A Critical Review." *Journal of Economic Literature*, 40(2), 351–401.

Gali, Jordi. 1999. "Technology, Employment, and the Business Cycle: Do Technology Shocks Explain Aggregate Fluctuations?" *American Economic Review* 83, 402–15.

Gordon, Robert. 2010. "Revisiting U.S. Productivity Growth over the Past Century with a View of the Future." *NBER Working Paper* 15834.

Lastrapes, William. 2006. "Inflation and the Distribution of Relative Prices: The Role of Productivity and Money Supply Shocks" *Journal of Money, Credit, and Banking* 38(8), 2159–98.

Laubach, Thomas, and John C. Williams. 2003. "Measuring the Natural Rate of Interest" *Review of Economics and Statistics*, 85, 1063–70.

Lombardi, Marco, and Silvia Sgherri. 2007. "(Un)Naturally Low? Sequential Monte Carlo Tracking of the US Natural Interest Rate." *ECB Working Paper* 794.

Oliner, Stephen, Daniel Sichel, and Kevin Stiroh. 2007. "Explaining a Productive Decade." *Brookings Papers on Economic Activity*, 1:2007, 81–137.

Selgin, George. 1997. *Less Than Zero: The Case for a Falling Price Level in a Growing Economy*. London: Institute of Economic Affairs.

Stern, Gary. 2003. *Top of the Ninth: Should We Accept the Conventional Wisdom about Deflation?* Minneapolis Federal Reserve Bank, *The Region*, September, 2–6.

Sutherland, Donald. 2009. "Monetary Policy and Real Estate Bubbles." Working paper, Institute for SocioEconomic Studies, February 11.

Tambalotti, Andrea. 2003. "Optimal Monetary Policy and Productivity Growth." Unpublished manuscript, Princeton University, February 11.

Taylor, John. 2009. *Getting Off Track*. Stanford, CA: Hoover Institution Press.

Weidener, Justin, and John C. Williams. 2009. "How Big is the Output Gap?" San Francisco Federal Reserve, *Economic Letters*, 2009–10, 1–3.

Williams, John C. 2003. "The Natural Rate of Interest." *Federal Reserve Bank of San Francisco Economic Letter* 32 (October 31).

Whalen, Karl. 2009. "Technology Shocks and Hours Worked: Checking for Robust Conclusions." *Journal of Macroeconomics*, 31, 231–39.

3

Chain Reaction

*How the Fed's Asymmetric Policy
in 2003 Led to a Panic in 2008*

Diego Espinosa

My daughter came home from school one day and said, "Daddy,
what's a financial crisis?" And without trying to be funny, I said,
"It's the type of thing that happens every five, ten, seven, years."
And she said: "Why is everybody so surprised?" So we shouldn't
be surprised . . .   —JPMorgan CEO Jamie Dimon

THE U.S. ECONOMY has been subject to many financial crises
over the past thirty years. In the 1980s, there was the Latin debt crisis, the savings & loan crisis, and a major stock market crash. In the 1990s, there was a
credit crunch and a bond market crisis, followed a few years later by the stock
market crash of the early 2000s. All of these events are evidence that JPMorgan
Chase & Co. CEO Jamie Dimon could point to in support of his view that
financial crises are not uncommon in the United States.[1] Yet in an important
way, Dimon was wrong. What happened in 2008 was more than just a financial crisis; it was a banking panic. Banking panics are systemic events that
adversely affect an entire economy. They are often associated with deflation
and debt restructuring that can take years to resolve. None of the "crises"
discussed above, however, led to a systemic panic. In fact, such panics have
been absent from the U.S. economy since the early 1930s. This relative financial stability, however, came to a screeching halt in 2008. Why this sudden

---

1. Video, Testimony of Jamie Dimon before the Financial Crisis Inquiry Commission,
January 13, 2010.

change? What caused the end of the seventy-plus–year run of no systemic banking panics in the United States?

In this paper, I argue that the root cause of the 2008 banking panic was a change in the character of the U.S. Federal Reserve ("the Fed") monetary policy in 2002–2003, the years when the Fed extended the goals of policy to a guarantee that deflation would not occur. In support of that goal, and for the first time, the Fed signaled it would do the following: always provide liquidity to protect the financial system from a precipitous fall in asset prices; keep interest rates low for a long time; and afterwards, only raise rates at a predictable pace. These promises created new incentives that changed the workings of the U.S. financial system in three important ways.

First, investors within the shadow banking system responded by crafting an optimal investment portfolio: not one with risky assets, but one with low-risk, collateralized assets. For the Fed had just told them that they could make a predictable spread on safe investments and depend on the liquidity of the collateral to mitigate risk. Consequently, these "banks" went to the financial system and said, "Please send us more low-risk assets to invest in." The financial system—in particular, large banks and investment houses—responded by taking loans and converting them into largely AAA-rated securities through the production process of structured finance, i.e., tranching and pooling.

Second, at the other end of the financial system, where credit originated, the signal was clear: "Send us more loan 'raw material' to convert to AAA." The suppliers of subprime, Alt-A, home equity and commercial mortgages responded by ramping up origination volumes. They could only do so, however, by lowering underwriting standards. Falling standards and low-payment loans effectively minted new buyers, creating higher demand, higher prices, lower defaults, and justification for even lower standards.

Finally, the result was the ballooning of portfolios invested in processed AAA-rated securities. The missing element in the optimal portfolio was leverage, for leverage transformed meager returns into attractive ones. To lever the portfolios, the shadow banking system used repo (and other short-term) funding in a form of "carry trade." Essentially, they accessed overnight repo "deposits" that were collateralized with the same processed AAA-rated securities. It was concern over the safety of this repo collateral—concern sparked by rising delinquencies—that set off the modern-day version of a run on bank deposits, which in turn led to the banking panic (Gorton 2010).[2]

It is important to note that these changes had underpinnings that were not new. The originate-and-securitize model for asset-backed securities existed since the mid-eighties without causing much instability. Wall Street greed has always been with us. Low-income-housing incentives had been in place for decades. The repo market dates back to the eighties. Arguably, the competence of banking system regulators did not change, nor did their lack of immunity to "regulatory capture." The credit cycle existed during the entire post-FDIC era without producing a banking panic. Finally, the government-sponsored enterprises ("GSEs")—Fannie Mae and Freddie Mac—that were important purchasers of subprime securities, had been around for decades. Though these factors were necessary conditions for the boom-bust cycle in the financial system to occur, they did not combine to form a reaction until a catalyst appeared. That catalyst was a change in Fed policy.

In the sections that follow, I explain how the Fed's actions led to the build-up of financial system fragility that eventually paved the way for the banking panic. The focus is on tracing the ripple effects of Fed policy through the system, from the creation of shadow bank investment portfolios to the formulation of lending standards and, ultimately, to the run on the liabilities of the shadow banking system.

The Fed's New Role: Carry Trade Enabler

One of the difficult parts of any Fed official's job is to weather perennial second-guessing over the Fed's policy stance. The experience of the last decade is no exception, as some blame the Fed for causing the housing bubble by holding rates down below optimal "rules-based" levels when emerging from the 2001 recession, while others argue that the Fed tightened too much after 2005 and precipitated the crisis. This type of criticism—too easy/too tight—is something that could be leveled at any Fed at any time during its existence.

---

2. Gary Gorton, *Slapped by the Invisible Hand: The Panic of 2007* (New York: Oxford University Press: 2010).

It therefore misses the fact that, early in the decade, the Fed was engaging in something new, a change in the character of policy that also gave birth to a different set of risks for the financial system. This "new thing" was the Fed's attempt to fight deflation by making a set of commitments about future policy actions to the financial markets.

The genesis for the Fed's policy change was the fall in U.S. core inflation that occurred after the 2001 recession, coupled with the consensus perception that the Bank of Japan, by allowing deflation, was responsible for Japan's painful "lost decade." As it had following previous episodes, U.S. core CPI steadily declined in the months following the 2001 recession. The difference was that core inflation started from a lower base, so that by April of 2003, the economy experienced three consecutive months of zero or near-zero core CPI. The fall in inflation was ominous in the wider context of Japan. Regarding the threat of deflation in the United States, the Fed Chairman Ben Bernanke wrote in a 2002 speech: "That this concern is not purely hypothetical is brought home to us whenever we read newspaper reports about Japan, where what seems to be a relatively moderate deflation—a decline in consumer prices of about 1 percent per year—has been associated with years of painfully slow growth. . . . While it is difficult to sort out cause from effect, the consensus view is that deflation has been an important negative factor in the Japanese slump."[3]

Given this "consensus view" and the deflationary threats of Long-Term Capital Management ("LTCM") in 1998, the 2000 Nasdaq crash, the 2001 recession, and the 9/11 attacks, it is no surprise that the Fed adopted an explicit policy of fighting not only deflation, but deflation risk. The result was twofold:

First, monetary policy became asymmetric in support of asset prices. The Fed promised to make deflation fighting its priority, and to keep it that way as long as the deflationary environment persisted. Steep asset market corrections signal heightened deflationary risk. So, logically, markets should expect the Fed to ease aggressively in reaction to asset market sell-offs. In Bernanke's words: "As suggested by a number of studies, when inflation is already low and the fundamentals of the economy suddenly deteriorate, the central bank should act more preemptively and more aggressively than usual

---

3. Ben S. Bernanke, "Deflation: Making Sure 'It' Doesn't Happen Here," (speech, National Economists Club, Washington, D.C., 2002).

in cutting rates. . . . By moving decisively and early, the Fed may be able to prevent the economy from slipping into deflation, with the special problems that entails."[4] Admittedly, the market's idea of a commitment by the Fed to ease in response to falling asset prices dates back to former Fed Chairman Alan Greenspan's rapid intervention following the stock market crash of 1987, followed by similar actions taken during the 1998 LTCM crisis. This "Greenspan Put," however, now had a more identifiable policy rationale for defending asset prices—avoiding deflation risk. Moreover, the Fed itself admitted that inflation-fighting did not require capping asset prices. In the market's mind, this asymmetry led to the natural expectation that the Fed would support asset prices but not "pop" bubbles. Further, as long as deflation risk prevailed, even slow growth was a reason to hold rates down.

Second, the Fed became much more explicit in defining the path of policy. In an effort to shape expectations, the Fed began to tell markets what it planned to do under a reasonable range of forecasts. This was new. Prior to 1999, the Fed gave very little information about the future path of policy beyond an intermeeting bias toward easing or firming. Following the LTCM crisis, the Fed moved to an indication of whether the balance of risks in the economy was weighted toward inflation or a slowdown. In May 2003, the Fed highlighted the risk of an "unwelcome substantial fall in inflation," and moved toward longer-term guidance on its deflation-fighting plans. Despite a relatively benign view on economic growth prospects, the Committee stated that because of the potential for deflation, the balance of risks was "weighted towards weakness over the foreseeable future." By August, the Committee had explicitly committed to interest rates staying low for a "considerable period."[5] In a July speech, Bernanke thought the change in communications tactics important enough to highlight:

> A crucial element of the statement was an implicit commitment about future monetary policy; namely, a strong indication that . . . monetary policy will maintain an easy stance. Particularly at very low inflation rates, a central bank's ability to make *clear and credible commitments*

4. Bernanke, "Deflation."
5. FOMC meeting statement (August 12, 2003), http://www.federalreserve.gov/board docs/press/monetary/2003/20030812/default.htm

about future policy actions . . . is crucial for influencing longer-term interest rates and other asset prices, which are themselves key transmission
channels of monetary policy.

   . . . [with] short-term nominal interest rates are at historical lows, the
success of monetary policy depends more on how well the central bank
communicates its plans and objectives *than on any other single factor.*[6]
[Emphasis added]

Bernanke, above, specifically cites long-term interest rates and asset prices
as the target of the Fed's new approach. How exactly would a "clear and credible commitment" affect those targets? He doesn't say, but it is reasonable to
assume that a mechanism for translating the commitment into both lower
long-term rates and higher asset prices is what traders call the "carry trade."

A carry trade is simply when a speculator borrows overnight in a low-
yielding currency to invest in an asset with a higher return. There are essentially two types of carry trades involving low-risk assets. The first involves
exploiting "maturity transformation," or the spread between very short duration funding and a longer-term investment—in essence, the yield curve. A
hedge fund might borrow overnight from a prime broker at just over 1 percent
and invest in five-year Treasuries at over 3 percent—an unlevered spread of
around two percentage points, one that could produce returns of 20 percent
with leverage of ten times. The risk for this trade was the possibility that the
Fed would raise short-term rates faster than anticipated, or so-called "duration
risk." The second takes advantage of "liquidity transformation," or using overnight funding to invest in a longer-maturity floating-rate asset. For example,
the off-balance sheet vehicle (a conduit or "SIV") of a commercial bank might
use commercial paper paying LIBOR+.25 percent to fund AAA-rated CDOs
(along with a fixed-to-floating interest rate swap) paying LIBOR+.75 percent.
The small spread of .50 percent in that admittedly simplified example could
produce returns of 15 percent with leverage of thirty times. In this case the
risk to the trade was "liquidity risk," or the inability to roll over short-term
funding, which would force the trader to liquidate the longer-term maturity
asset at a discount.

---

6. Ben S. Bernanke (remarks made before the Economics Roundtable, University of
California, San Diego, La Jolla, California, 2003).

How did the Fed's policy commitments affect these carry trades? To a banker, a central bank's commitment to hold down rates is an attractive inducement to make a marginal loan. To a speculator, the effect of the commitment is an order of magnitude greater. It provides the fundamental rationale for entering into a trade. Getting direction and timing right equals profit, and the Fed was almost guaranteeing the timing of the trade. Using the maturity transformation carry trade example above, a promise by the Fed not to raise rates quickly effectively removed much of the key risk (duration risk) during the period covered by the Fed's promise. In the liquidity transformation example, the Fed's promise to ease—thus providing liquidity for sales of longer maturity assets—also seemingly erased much of that trade's risk (liquidity risk) for that time. Moreover, by seeming to want to support asset prices, the Fed was also virtually eliminating the already-low risk that AAA-rated collateral might suffer a ratings downgrade in the period. The result of each of these factors was that carry traders could employ more and more leverage as they gained faith in the Fed's commitments.

In the Fed's own view, the May 2003 change in communications strategy was successful in setting market expectations. Vince Reinhart, a Fed economist, offered the FOMC an update on the behavior of Fed funds futures—the market's predictions about future Fed rate actions—during the September 2003 meeting.[7] In it, he describes how the volatility of expected Fed funds rates has fallen, and how it tends to be stable even in the face of positive economic data. The markets now expect the Fed to keep rates steady for about one year. He concludes: "Taken together, this suggests that the Committee has been able to anchor expectations about the very near term course of policy—in effect making them less volatile and less sensitive to revisions to the expected path of the economy."

In other words, asymmetric policy was having a direct impact on market expectations; because that was the case, it follows that traders would act on these same expectations. The carry trade was "on."

Various Fed officials have countered the charge that they fueled speculation by pointing out that much of the "froth" occurred when the Fed was

---

7. Transcript, FOMC Meeting, September 16, 2003, 75."

already raising rates. However, this ignores the character of carry trades that we outlined above. As long as markets could predict when and how the Fed would raise rates, the timing was still a known variable and duration risk was manageable. In fact, this was the effect of the Fed's "measured pace" language in describing future rate hikes. Interestingly, the FOMC debated the beneficial impact of the words "measured pace" on financial markets for twenty-five pages of the roughly one hundred pages of the May 5, 2004, FOMC meeting transcripts. Changing the behavior of financial markets was not a by-product of Fed policy; rather, it was the intended effect. Douglas Diamond and Raghuram Rajan reach a similar conclusion: [8]

> Our model suggests that the crisis of 2007–2009 may not be unrelated to the actions of the Federal Reserve earlier in the decade, not only in convincing the market that interest rates would remain low for a sustained period following the dot-com bust because of its fears of deflation, but also in promising to intervene to pick up the pieces in case of an asset price collapse—the so-called Greenspan put. The behavior of the central bank may have contributed to bank investment in illiquid assets (the now infamous mortgage-backed securities as well as vehicles such as SIVs and conduits) as well as bank leverage. . . .

Think of the Fed's actions in the context of insurance. Traders make decisions based on simplified concepts about expected future events—narratives of likely cause and effect, or heuristics. Without these narratives, the sheer complexity of future scenarios, and "unknown unknowns," would swamp traders' abilities to make decisions.[9] This doesn't mean that traders totally ignore tail risk (the risk that an asset or portfolio of assets will move more than three standard deviations away from its current price); instead, they hedge against it with some form of insurance. Excess liquidity on an investment-bank balance

---

8. Douglas W. Diamond and Raghuram Rajan, "Illiquidity and interest rate policy" (NBER Working Paper 15197, 2009), 33, http://www.nber.org/papers/w15197
9. "Knightian Uncertainty and the Resilience-Stability Trade-off," *Macroeconomic Resilience Blog*, January 30, 2010, http://www.macroresilience.com/2010/01/30/knightian-uncertainty-and-the-resilience-stability-trade-off/

sheet, for instance, is insurance against unknown future systemic risk, as is the decision by a hedge fund to maintain sub-optimal leverage or days-to-liquidate.

In a deflationary environment, the problem is that hedging activity can create an adverse feedback loop, one in which traders hedge against uncertainty by reducing leverage, which begets asset sales and lower prices, which create margin calls and further reduces leverage, all leading to lower velocity and ever higher deflation risk. So it is logical to believe that the Fed's communication strategy targeted, directly, the appetite of carry traders for insurance in order to reduce deflation risk. In doing so, it rendered the system less liquid, more levered, and more susceptible to tail risk.

The above discussion is somewhat academic, but my personal experience during the time of the crisis is that the Greenspan Put (later the "Fed Put") heuristic was dominant during the decade. "Negative skew" bets were the norm from 2003–2007; that is, traders sought out low-volatility assets and levered them up to the hilt, and in return accepted the tail risk of being wiped out—after all, the Fed stood ready to prevent that tail "event" from occurring. To an investor in shadow banking institutions, negative skew bets seemed like "safe" forms of arbitrage; products of the genius of the carry traders. These investors shunned vehicles with volatile returns and poured more funds into carry trade vehicles, which in turn helped "squeeze out" more and more (downside) volatility. In this environment, shorting credit or stocks was the truly "risky" trade.

Now that the carry trade and the Fed's potential effect on it have been outlined, the question remains: who were the carry traders? In 2003, "carry trade" could be used to describe the activity of the so called shadow banking system: hedge funds, off-balance sheet special investment vehicles ("SIVs") and conduits, investment bank prime brokerage and prop desks, and non-bank mortgage originators. All of these shadow bank components were created explicitly to employ leverage to profit from the potential spread between short-term funding and long-term assets.

The point is that while the business of the banking system is banking, the business of the shadow banking system is speculation through carry trades. It was this horsepower that the Fed harnessed in pursuit of its deflation-fighting goals. What was the impact on the shadow banking system itself?

Impact on the Shadow Banking System: A Marked Acceleration in Asset Growth

The thesis that Fed policy fueled the carry trade implies there should have been a rather distinct kink—an acceleration in growth—in the charts depicting shadow banking system assets around 2002, when the Fed first made deflation fighting its priority. We will now look at the asset growth of three shadow banking system components: investment banks, mortgage originators, and hedge funds.

Investment Banks

The locus of the financial panic was investment bank balance sheets, including the investment banking portion of large commercial banks. Lehman Brothers and Bear Stearns obviously failed, but concerns also surfaced over the viability of Merrill Lynch, Morgan Stanley, and Citigroup during the fall of 2008, not to mention non-U.S. institutions such as UBS.

Investment banks were a critical part of the shadow banking system. They were, in fact, the "factory" that produced carry trade securities. As a by-product of securitization, investment bank balance sheets held securities that were in the process of being sold. Given the short holding period needed to securitize a pool of assets, we can assume that this activity was not the major contributor to investment bank balance sheet growth. Instead, two other activities were mostly responsible: carry trade assets that were held either short term (classified as "trading" or "held for sale") or long term (classified as "held for investment"). Diamond and Rajan, when examining bank holdings of mortgage securities, came to a similar conclusion: "The amounts of MBS held seemed too high to be purely inventory. Some holdings could have been portions of the package they could not sell, but then this would not explain why banks held on to AAA-rated securities, which seemed to be the most highly demanded of mortgage-backed securities. The real answer seems to be that bankers thought these securities were worthwhile investments, despite their risk."[10]

---

10. Douglas W. Diamond and Raghuram Rajan, "The Credit Crisis: Conjectures about Causes and Remedies" (NBER Working Paper 14739, 2009), 4. http://www.nber.org/papers/w14739.

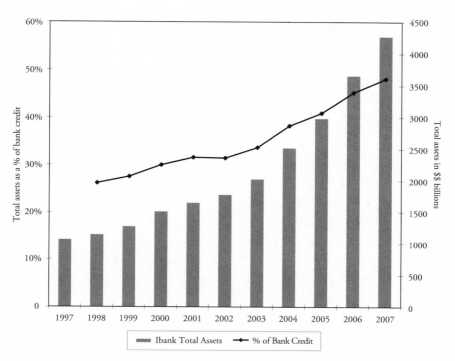

Figure 3.1. Total Assets of Major Stand-alone Investment Banks
Source: Company SEC filings, Federal Reserve H.8 Report

As stated earlier, we use as evidence of the Fed's impact the timing of any acceleration in the expansion of bank balance sheets. Figure 3.1 shows that total assets for the largest stand-alone investment banks (Lehman Brothers, Morgan Stanley, Goldman Sachs, Merrill Lynch, and Bear Stearns) did, in fact, reach an inflection point as the Fed adopted asymmetric policy.

Assets grew by about 60 percent from 1997 to 2002, and in the next five years they climbed 140 percent. The percentage growth, however, does not tell the whole story. By the end of the second period, assets were 45 percent of bank credit compared with 17 percent in 2002. The post-asymmetric-policy asset growth was—relative to the traditional banking system—much stronger.

Some would argue that a 2004 rule change relaxing leverage requirements drove investment bank growth. While important, this rule change did not happen in a vacuum: It was requested by the securities firms themselves (arguing leverage ceilings put them at a disadvantage versus European Union competitors), and it came on the back of strong asset growth, rather than preceding it. The impact of the rule change was significant in some cases and negligible in others. Bear Stearns, for instance, maintained gross leverage of around 28× throughout the period (until it jumped in 2007 due to write-offs). Goldman Sachs, on the other hand, saw its leverage climb from 17× in 2002 to 26× in 2007.

We also note that Figure 3.1 counters the commonly heard argument that the "originate and securitize" model provided an incentive for securitizers to reduce lending standards. As was the case with the mortgage originators (see "Mortgage Originators" section below), securities firms were retaining significant exposure to securitized assets through carry trades. Merrill Lynch, for instance, had approximately $27 billion of (mostly AAA-rated) subprime collateralized debt obligations (CDO) and ABS exposure in the months leading up to its sale to Bank of America. Clearly, it had an incentive to construct quality CDO portfolios.

Hedge Funds

Hedge funds are the most unfettered of the classes of carry traders we examine. They are somewhat constrained by the broad mandate they use to attract funds—macro, fixed income, long-short equity, etc. Beyond that, they are free to invest in whatever the manager chooses. Hedge funds are also components of the shadow banking system in that they lever themselves with short-term collateralized funding (from investment banks) and supply funds for longer-dated securities.

Not all hedge funds employ pure carry-trade strategies, but even the ones that do not employ them saw their activities lubricated by the carry trade. For example, corporations drew on low-cost, bridge financing from investment banks to complete mergers; "event" hedge funds, in turn, profited from engaging in a related "merger arbitrage" equity trade. Perhaps more important, all hedge funds were able to borrow more cheaply and readily from investment bank prime brokerage arms, which in turn funded themselves using overnight repos. As evidence of the importance of hedge funds to their lenders, we note that Fitch Ratings (2005) estimated that hedge funds drove up to 25 percent of the earnings of the larger investment banks.

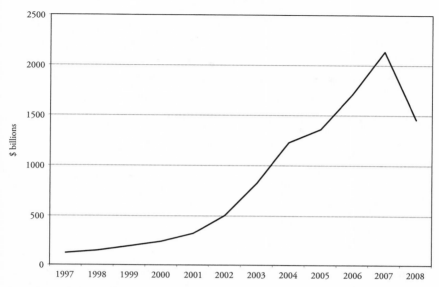

Figure 3.2. Hedge Fund Assets Under Management
Source: BarclayHedge

Figure 3.2 shows the rapid growth of hedge fund assets under management following the Fed's adoption of asymmetric policy. Again, we would note that growth in the 1997–2002 time frame, while strong, was coming off a much lower base. Relative to the size of bank credit, hedge funds became a much more important part of the shadow banking system after 2002.

Ironically, Fitch Ratings published a report in 2005 on hedge fund structured-finance carry trades that highlighted their contribution to systemic risk:[11]

> In the past few years, hedge funds have emerged as a dominant force in the capital markets, benefiting from a relatively benign environment of low interest rates and easy credit.
>
> Hedge funds remain reliant on short-term financing to pursue leveraged investment strategies, and the impact on the credit markets could be fairly broad-based if several credit-oriented hedge funds were forced to deleverage. A far-reaching liquidity squeeze and price dislocation across

---

11. "Hedge Funds, an Emerging Force in the Global Credit Markets" (Fitch Ratings, 2005).

multiple, interlocking credit markets could ensue simply due to hedge funds' presence in most, if not all, of the major segments of the credit markets. The effects of such an event would be felt first and foremost in the form of price declines and credit spread widening across multiple sectors of the credit markets. In turn, this could present challenges to some market value structures with mark-to-market and deleveraging triggers. Beyond potential trading losses, including among some prime brokerage banks, cost-effective financing for all forms of credit could be adversely affected.

Mortgage Originators

Another shadow-bank carry trade was the balance sheets of mortgage originators such as Countrywide, New Century, and Indymac. Prior to 2002, the strategy of these companies was originate-and-sell. Their profits resulted from the spread between their cost of acquiring mortgages and what they earned when selling them to third parties. This changed in 2002, when, like the securities firms, the mortgage originators began to retain portions of their own securitizations (these securitizations were structured as financing vehicles rather than outright whole loan sales). These were funded by short-term credit lines from investment banks or by the securitization vehicles themselves. The securities of the latter, in turn, were often purchased by carry traders relying on repo financing.

Figure 3.3 shows that the assets of three large subprime/Alt-A mortgage originators jumped around 2002. The chart provides further evidence that the carry trade became an attractive vehicle for a number of originators that had previously securitized most of their product. We note that many large subprime originators failed during the LTCM (Long-Term Capital Management) crisis, when lenders pulled their funding, and until 2002, originators were famously reluctant to put subprime mortgages on their own books. Here we see the nexus of Fed policy and the behavior of shadow-banking-system components. The Fed targeted the monetary transmission mechanism, and as a result, minds were changed; institutions that shunned balance sheet risk for valid historical reasons reversed course and began to engage in the carry trade, borrowing short term

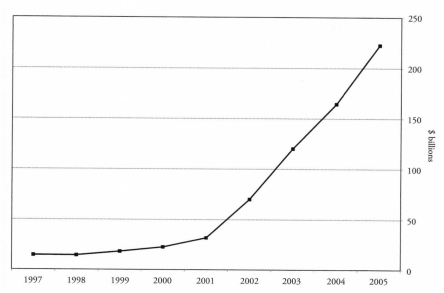

Figure 3.3. Total Assets of Countrywide, New Century, Indymac
Source: Company SEC filings

to invest in their own securitizations. In short, leaving aside considerations of whether the quality of the securitizations themselves was suspect, this was a case in which the Fed achieved its stated aim.

GSE-Retained Portfolios—An Exception

Was there a group of large shadow-banking components that did not respond to the change in Fed policy? At first glance, the GSEs (government-sponsored enterprises)—Fannie Mae and Freddie Mac—seem to fit that bill. Figure 3.4 shows that GSE total assets remained stable after 2002. This would seem to challenge our thesis that asymmetric policy had an impact on all carry traders. However, a closer look tells us that the GSEs were the exception that proves the rule. Before we get to that, it is useful to understand that GSEs were made up of two distinct businesses, one traditional and one relatively new.

The traditional part of the GSEs was the guarantee business—purchasing and pooling mortgages that met their standards, and then securitizing

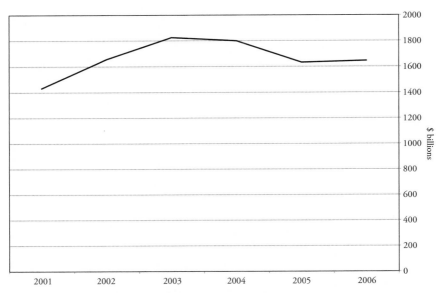

Figure 3.4. Fannie Mae and Freddie Mac Total Assets
Source: Company SEC filings

and selling them off with a guarantee attached. The guarantee business itself changed little during most of this period. Underwriting standards for purchased mortgages were relatively stable (33 percent debt-to-income ratios, mortgage insurance required on loan-to-value ratios over 80), and the GSEs, as a result, lost significant market share to subprime, jumbo, and Alt-A securitizers.

The non-traditional business was the retained portfolio, where the GSEs purchased mortgage securitizations (their own and others') for their own balance sheet. To give a sense of the order of magnitude of this business, the GSEs' portfolio of guaranteed-but-not-owned residential mortgage-backed securities ("RMBS") totaled approximately $3.2 trillion, whereas the combined retained portfolios totaled approximately $1.6 trillion.

The GSE-retained portfolios were not strictly carry trades, but ratings-arbitrage vehicles. GSE debt carried an implicit guarantee from the U.S. Treasury, and therefore GSEs could exploit the spread between their low funding cost and the returns on balance sheet assets. Driven by this arbitrage, the portfolios grew rapidly from around $500 billion in 1997 to more than $1.5 trillion by

2003. In that year, the GSEs voluntarily curtailed the growth of the portfolios in reaction to a series of accounting scandals. Finally, after the scandals were resolved, Congress decided to formally cap the size of the portfolios in early 2006. The result of these two factors was a stagnation of total GSE assets after 2003.

Why then was the GSE the exception that proved the rule? First, the Fed-engineered reduction in liquidity risk gave the GSEs an incentive to invest in slightly-higher yielding, less-liquid AAA-rated assets while still remaining within the cap on assets; and second, the effect of Fed policy was arguably to reduce the profit from ratings arbitrage on plain-vanilla mortgages (the agency funding cost advantage over, say, investment banks, shrank as credit spreads fell). The GSEs reacted by purchasing AAA-rated non-agency mortgage securitizations. According to company filings, close to 100 percent of Fannie Mae's retained portfolio subprime and Alt-A holdings were rated AAA. They were able to find these low-risk securities because, as I argue below, Fed-induced demand for low-risk investments is what led to the growth of subprime and Alt-A mortgage issuance. Finally, note that this view runs counter to arguments that low-income housing mandates forced Fannie and Freddie to buy or securitize non-prime mortgages (Wallison 2009). Occam's Razor applies here: The simplest explanation is that the profit motive drove the GSEs' actions, and that the Fed, plus the implicit guarantee and wildly excessive leverage, made the "trade" an attractive one.

In this section, the case was made that several classes of shadow banks stepped up their carry-trade activities in response to the Fed's intended policy of stimulating the financial system. In the case of Fannie and Freddie, we begin to see how much of this carry trade was targeted at low-risk assets. I now turn to the question of why and how these low-risk assets were produced, and, more important, how this production affected mortgage underwriting standards.

At the Heart of the Carry Trade: A Search for AAA-Rated Securities

Carry trades drove shadow-banking-system asset growth following the introduction of asymmetric monetary policy. Equally important is how these carry trades were executed. A common conception, even among those that ascribe a share of blame to asymmetric policy, is that the "Greenspan Put" led to increased risk-taking on the part of the shadow banking system. This is somewhat correct: The all-important carry trade involved taking on additional duration and liquidity risk for incremental yield. However, what this concept misses is that, at the core of the shadow banking system, actors sought to take on *very little* incremental credit risk. In fact, they invested in the safest securities they could find beyond sovereign (or sovereign-guaranteed) debt. These were AAA-rated securities produced through structured finance.

A credit crisis caused by firms seeking only a marginal increase in credit risk is counterintuitive. However, it is less so when viewed through the lens of the carry trade. The Fed provided incremental information about the future path of interest rates. Given this information, the purest form of arbitrage involved borrowing as short-term as possible and investing in longer-duration securities with non-volatile returns. Adding more return volatility—in the form of credit risk—would have diluted the value of that marginal piece of information. The greatest potential arbitrage was "funding short," "lending long and safe," and using leverage to raise expected returns.

I am not arguing that the Fed did not encourage risk-taking. My own experience is that the "Greenspan Put" was a part of the conventional wisdom cited by traders as a rationale for entering into riskier trades ("Don't fight the Fed" was another trader nostrum). Instead, I argue that the sequence of events matters. First, Fed policy encouraged a pure arbitrage of the expected path of future policy rates; then the demand for low-risk securities climbed; then the price of assets financed by those securities boomed and the appetite for risk-taking—an aspect of any credit cycle—boomed. In the end, investors were flocking to payment-in-kind (PIK), highly leveraged, covenant-light, buyout loans that allowed leveraged buyout firms to defer interest payments during a recession. This extreme of risk-taking was achieved in 2007, during the peak of market exuberance, and not in 2003. In hindsight, the years leading up to the financial crisis seem compressed and simultaneous; at the time, to traders with daily P&Ls, they stretched ahead like eras. As a result, some of the causality leading up to a crisis tends to get washed out as the distance increases between the observer and the event.

Below, we look at the state of the market for AAA-rated securities before and after the Fed's change in policy.

AAA-Rated Securities Prior to Asymmetric Policy

What information does an AAA rating confer? Ironically, the ratings agencies make few outright representations. The rating is relative and generally means that the issuer or security has the top rating among a group of peers. Further, the ratings agencies provide some guidance of what the range of ratings have meant historically. According to Moody's Investors Service, "The average default rate from 1970–2000 for AAA-rated securities over a ten-year period was only 0.67 percent. . . . However, as one descends the rating scale into the speculative-grade section, the default rate increases dramatically. For B-rated securities, the ten-year probability of default is 44.57 percent."[12]

For a trader with a short horizon, the probability of suffering a collateral loss on an AAA-rated security was close to zero, making it an attractive vehicle for carry trades. Prior to 2002, however, the supply of AAA-rated securities was relatively fixed. The bulk of securities sharing that rating in the United States were either direct U.S. government obligations (Treasuries, Ginnie Maes) or those holding a quasi-government guarantee (agencies and GSE-guaranteed mortgages). The percentage of non-government AAA-rated securities was negligible, and according to Fitch, included only about 1 percent of corporate bonds outstanding.

From 1996 to 2001, the stock of AAA-rated Treasuries, agencies, and GSE RMBS grew from $7.1 trillion to about $9.5 trillion—or 6 percent per annum—with most of that growth supplied by the need to finance the expansion of the GSE retained portfolios.

AAA-Rated Securities Outstanding Surge
Following Adoption of Asymmetric Policy

Following asymmetric easing, the stock of governmental non-mortgage AAA-rated debt grew as a function of the U.S. fiscal deficit. Together, Treasury and agency debt outstanding grew from about $5.3 trillion in 2001 to about $7.5 trillion in 2006. Of this $2.2 trillion increase, a substantial por-

12. Moody's Investor Service, "Moody's Ratings Definitions" (2010), http://www.moodys korea.com/english/definition.asp#7

tion satisfied demand for AAA-rated securities from reserve-accumulating countries: China alone accumulated about $700 billion by the end of 2006.[13]

Thus, the shadow banking system was presented with a problem starting in 2002. The Fed had begun to encourage the carry trade through its low-interest-rate policy. However, not only was the stock of government-issued AAA-rated securities relatively fixed, but the private markets faced competition for those securities from Japan, China, and other reserve accumulators. These foreign exchange reserves, in turn, were growing partly as a function of the need for fixed-exchange-rate countries to recycle their balance of payment surpluses (it is not a stretch to tie those same surpluses back to Fed policy, but that argument lies outside the scope of this chapter).

The shadow banking system responded to the demand for safe investments by manufacturing them. Enter structured finance, in which the cash flow from a pool of underlying securities is securitized into different tranches, each with a different loss position. The first loss, or mezzanine tranche, is hit for any initial shortfalls in cash flow due to credit losses; once the mezzanine tranche is depleted, the BBB-rated tranche absorbs any losses, and so on, until, finally, losses may accrue to the AAA-rated tranche. This "waterfall" loss exposure means that the AAA tranche is protected by the subordination of all lower-rated tranches. In structured finance, virtually any pool of securities, no matter how risky the underlying loans, may be securitized to produce a sizeable AAA-rated tranche. It was just a matter of making the subordinated tranches large enough to reduce the probability of a loss accruing to the AAA-rated tranche.

The surprising outcome of this manufacturing process was that around 80 percent of the value of a typical subprime ABS securitization was rated AAA by the ratings agencies.[14] This means that for every dollar of risky loans originators supplied to securities firms, they produced eighty cents of lowest-risk securities. Clearly, from the investor's perspective, without foreknowledge, the purpose of subprime loan origination was to supply the market with safe investments. In their thorough study of structured finance credit ratings and subsequent downgrades, Efraim Benmelech and Jennifer Dlugosz concur: "If

---

13. Brad W. Setser and Arpana Pandey, "China's $1.5 Trillion Bet: Understanding China's External Portfolio" (Council on Foreign Relations Working Paper, 2009), 16.
14. Adam B. Ashcraft and Til Schuermann, "Understanding the Securitization of Subprime Mortgage Credit" (Staff Report 318, Federal Reserve Bank of New York, 2008).

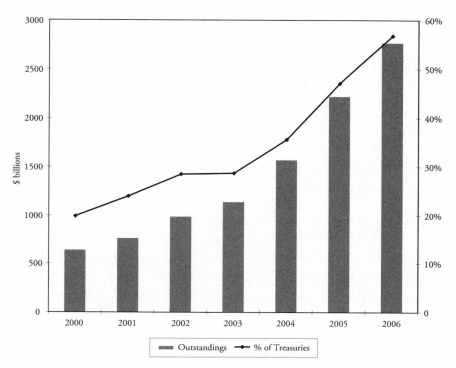

Figure 3.5. AAA-Rated Asset-Backed Securities Outstanding
Source: Fitch, Sifma

investors use heuristics to classify assets . . . and only AAA-rated securities are perceived to be riskless, then issuers would cater to investor demand by carving out large portions of their deals as AAA. [We] argue that the uniformity of CDO structures suggest that investor demand in general is an important determinant of deal structures."[15]

Figure 3.5 shows the growth of non-agency, mortgage-related securitizations (comprising mostly subprime, Alt-A, commercial real estate, jumbo loans, and home equity lines) estimated to have been rated AAA. From about $1 trillion in 2002, the amount grew to over $2.7 trillion by 2006. Approximately $800 billion of this increase came from the growth in subprime loans outstanding,

15. Efraim Benmelech and Jennifer Dlugosz, "The Credit Rating Crisis" (Working Paper 15045, 2009), http://www.nber.org/papers/w15045

with more coming from subprime CDOs (not including double-counting, as the purpose of CDOs was to use pooling and diversification to achieve yet more AAA-rated tranching). For purposes of comparison, $2.7 trillion amounted to 57 percent of Treasuries outstanding in 2006. By that measure, the shadow banking system's expansion of available AAA-rated investments was a ringing success.

The Originators' Response: "To Make More AAA, We Need More Bodies"

In 2006, as a hedge fund manager, I attended a "beauty contest"—a series of hedge fund "pitches" to an audience of wealthy clients and institutional investors. The sponsoring securities firm also brought in one of its structured finance specialists to discuss, with a panel of fixed income hedge funds, the prospects for subprime securitizations. This managing director, in her introductory speech, made a comment that seemed important enough to note down: "We expect that the pipeline of subprime originations will continue to be strong, mostly because we see such a big appetite from *technical* buyers."[16]

The other panelists concurred and went on to discuss the bright prospects for their subprime investments. This concept of technical demand was, at the time, a bit of a mystery to me. What did it mean? Later, it became clear that "technical" meant "arising from CDO issuance." The speaker was saying that the surging demand for CDOs (collateral debt obligations) was creating demand for more originations, and not the other way around.

A second anecdote: Later I went to visit the management of a San Diego–based subprime originator. I asked one of the executives, "How do you set production targets for any given month?" The response was, "It depends on the demand for our paper—our capital markets group is always in touch with securities firms to gauge the appetite." Again, the same message: It was investor demand for subprime securitizations (which in turn, according to that investment bank managing director, came from demand for CDOs) that drove their origination volumes.

---

16. Presentation, Bank of America Prime Brokerage Conference, San Francisco, March, 2006.

How did an originator with already significant market share "turn the dial" on near-term production volumes? Paying out more commissions to mortgage brokers was one possibility, although it also reduced origination margins. The more profitable alternative was to reduce underwriting standards and/or allow for more exceptions to those "guidelines." According to the New Century Bankruptcy Examiner (who interviewed most of the principals), this is exactly what happened.

The Examiner cites among the factors behind the bankruptcy, "New Century's increasing origination, from 2004 onward, of increasingly risky products, such as stated income loans . . . . 80/20 loans, with such higher-risk features often combined through a so-called layering of risks."[17]

In 2004, the year the Examiner cites, industry subprime outstandings *jumped by 40 percent*. The report contains charts noting the progression of no-doc loans, 80/20 loans, and interest-only payment loans, all increasing over this period. The clear implication is that, as demand for subprime securitizations from investors seeking safe investments rose, the originators responded by reducing standards to bring in more applicants. The Examiner, after studying a litany of weak credit processes and internal audit capabilities, concluded: "New Century measured loan quality primarily in terms of whether it was successful in selling loans to investors. So long as investors continued to purchase New Century loans, New Century did not believe it needed to significantly improve loan quality . . ."[18]

Was New Century different from other originators? Its securitizations did suffer from above-average credit losses; however, the company was not far ahead of the curve in terms of setting loan underwriting standards. The industry as a whole moved toward setting guidelines that eliminated the principal barriers that restricted the applicant pool:

- Not enough money for a down payment (solved by 80/20, no-money-down loans).
- Not enough verifiable income to qualify (solved by stated-income loans).

---

17. Michael J. Missal, "Examiner's Report: Final Report of Michael J. Missal, Bankruptcy Court Examiner" (United States Bankruptcy Court for the District Delaware, In re: New Century TRS Holdings, Inc., a Delaware corporation, et al., 2008).
18. Missal, "Examiner's Report."

- Not enough actual income to make monthly payments (solved by interest-only payments).

By 2006, the three classes of volume "solutions" accounted for the following percent of subprime dollar issuance: 80/20, 25 percent; stated income, 45 percent; interest only, 33 percent. Of course, the three were not mutually exclusive, but layered together to bring in the most marginal borrower. Meanwhile, the solutions penetrated upward into the prime space: Alt-A mortgages with those attributes were used to increase the pool of high-FICO buyers who could purchase ever-more expensive homes.

To summarize: The Fed aimed to activate the monetary transmission mechanism with asymmetric policy; carry traders responded by demanding AAA-rated assets; demand for AAA-rated securities led to structured finance demand for subprime and Alt-A loans; and surging demand for those loans caused originators to reduce standards in order to boost the applicant pool.

We will look at one more link in the chain reaction before returning to the banking panic itself. It is the impact of declining standards on house prices.

Standards: "If You Lower Them, They Will Buy"

The effect of reducing standards to bring in more applicants was to shift out the demand curve for houses. At any given house price, more buyers were available to make a purchase than before. The analysis of the California housing market below, which I undertook in 2005, underscores just how powerful this effect was on the state's house prices.

The question is: how many more *potential* buyers did the lower standards in California create? First, using a no-money-down product, we include all buyers regardless of available savings for a down payment. Second, by allowing for stated income, we bring in all buyers regardless of ability to qualify based on income. The only remaining filter is actual ability to pay, which is where the lower-payment products come in. By the first quarter of 2005, according to Corelogic, a firm that tracks mortgage lending for the industry, roughly two-thirds of California ARM [adjustable rate mortgages] purchase mortgages were interest only, up from 10 percent in 2002. More surprising—even in hindsight—was that over a quarter of these had a negative amortization fea-

Table 3.1. Annual Income Required to Purchase a Median Home

	Monthly Payment	Annual Income Required
30-yr Fixed	$3,300	$125,000
5/1 ARM	$3,100	$110,000
5/1 Interest-Only	$2,600	$95,000
1% Neg-Am	$1,300	$55,000

Source: Author's 2005 analysis based on published mortgage rates

ture (option ARMs) in which the borrower made a low-cash interest payment (1 percent–2 percent) and deferred the remaining interest, which was then added to the principal balance. Overall, interest only mortgages comprised 44 percent of total California (ARM and fixed rate) purchase mortgages for the full year in 2005.

The median house price in California in 2005 was around $570,000. Let us first see how much annual income was required to make the payment on this mortgage (based on a mortgage, taxes and insurance payment of 33 percent of gross income) under the different payment products (each with a successively lower payment due to the interest reset feature).

Table 3.1 shows that to purchase a median home, a borrower needed an annual gross income of only $55,000 with an option ARM mortgage. This is roughly half the income needed for a conventional thirty-year mortgage. The next question is: how many more California borrowers did the option ARM mortgage bring in? In other words, at the same price—$570,000—how far did the demand curve shift to the right as a result of the lowest-payment product? The calculations below were based on California household income distribution data:

Table 3.2 shows that 50 percent of California households had incomes over $55,000 and could afford the payment on the option ARM mortgage, whereas only 16 percent of households could make the payment on the conventional thirty-year mortgage. In other words, the effect of option ARM loans was to *triple* the number of households that could potentially buy a home in California. This is why the California home-price-to-income ratio was more than three standard deviations higher than the historical mean in 2005.

Table 3.2. Percentage of CA Households That Could Afford a Median Home

	Required Income	**% of CA Households**
30-yr Fixed	$125,000	16%
5/1 ARM	$110,000	19%
5/1 Interest-Only	$95,000	22%
1% Neg-Am	$55,000	50%

Source: Author's 2005 analysis, CA Comptroller's Office

What occurred in California could be seen to a degree in other "bubble" states (Florida, Arizona, Nevada, New York, and New Jersey) and, to a much lesser extent, elsewhere. Together, the "bubble" states accounted for about 60 percent of subprime and Alt-A mortgage issuance. What is important to note here is (1) the incidence of low defaults on subprime and Alt-A mortgages was caused by high home-price appreciation that allowed delinquent borrowers to cure late payments with cash-out refinancings; and (2) this low-delinquency experience fed into models that *risk-seeking* investors—those taking on the lower tranches of securitizations, for instance—used to justify asset purchases at lower and lower returns, which, in turn, they compensated for with higher and higher leverage. As I stated above, what started out as a search for safe yield created the conditions under which investors ultimately increased their appetite for risky assets and leverage. In our opinion, the same dynamic occurred in other asset markets, such as commercial real estate, leveraged buyouts, and high-yield debt.

I have now examined the important connections to the banking panic, from the Fed's adoption of asymmetric policy all the way to higher asset prices and peak leverage across the financial system. Some of the evidence, while substantial, is unavoidably circumstantial. However, the question is: what is a logical expectation to have about the impact of Fed actions? In other words, the Fed set out to fight deflationary expectations by influencing long-term rates and asset prices. It would seem that a reasonable next step from that policy might be to activate some portion of the financial system, inducing it to borrow and lend. Further, that portion might loosen standards, on the margin, to increase lending volumes. The resulting increase in asset prices and demand would, in turn, result in more leverage and yet further lending, creating additional demand and finally allaying deflation fears. In other words, much of what happened from 2002 to 2007 happened *as intended for the risk-taking channel* in the first place. In fact, Fed officials did not much protest developments as they unfolded; instead, they frequently took pains to downplay the buildup of risk in the financial system (Greenspan's famous "housing froth" quote), and in the early years of the housing recovery they correctly identified that a strong housing sector was leading the way into a more robust recovery (FOMC transcripts 2003). It was not until early 2006, months after California house prices had peaked, that the Fed finally eliminated the word "measured" from its meeting-statement release.

Full Circle: AAA-Rated Mortgage Collateral + Flat Home Prices = Banking Panic

I open this section with a final anecdote from my own experience. The question for any investor—particularly one using leverage—is not how events will unfold, but when. Timing is critical, and markets are littered with the bodies of speculators who attempted to time the bursting of various investment bubbles and failed. Knowing this, I needed a reliable indicator of when housing equities might reverse. It came out of the analysis of Southern California lending standards.

The option ARM was the ultimate mortgage product in terms of bringing in marginal buyers. Where could the industry go next? A zero-payment mortgage was not that different from a 1-percent option ARM, so the number of buyers that change could attract was small, even if it were practical (investors did have some standards). Cash-out refinancings at 120 percent were tentatively tried out, but only by fringe lenders and not for securitization. The answer to the above question is, "nowhere": a 1 percent stated-income, no-down-payment, negatively amortizing (option-Arm) mortgage was the final innovation possible. Therefore, once the penetration of option ARM mortgages into the California market leveled off, the industry would have finished expanding the demand curve for housing, and house prices would, at the very least, stabilize. Armed with this view, I used a major option ARM originator—Countrywide Financial—as a proxy. Whenever Countrywide's percentage of option ARM originations (released monthly by the company) flattened, it was a signal that the turn in housing was near. This did, in fact, occur in the summer of 2005, which coincided with the peak in California home prices.

Once house prices stabilized, I expected that subprime borrowers could no longer "cure" delinquencies with cash-out refinancings. Data from New Century showed that California subprime delinquencies were below 2 percent at the time, compared with the mid-teens in Midwestern states without high home-price appreciation. Therefore, it was reasonable to expect that California (and other bubble state) delinquencies would spike once prices leveled. Once those delinquencies spiked, it was not difficult to envision a chain of events—falling demand for securitizations, tighter loan standards, lower housing demand, falling house prices, more credit losses, levered, illiquid shadow bank failures—that would ultimately threaten the financial system.

I recount this experience because it helps to directly establish causality. As I detail later in the chapter, a run on shadow banking system liabilities, caused by concerns over AAA-rated collateral, directly resulted in the banking panic.[19] The question is, did a Fed policy error (excessively tight monetary policy) result in deflationary fears that then drove the concerns over collateral; or did concerns over collateral cause a panic, which then resulted in a crash of inflation expectations in late 2008? If the former is true, the Fed caused the panic by being too tight in the months before Lehman Brothers failed. If the latter is true, the Fed erred by, years earlier, creating a system vulnerable to even a slight shock.

The impact of level house-price appreciation and rising delinquencies was a string of ratings downgrades. These appeared first in the lower subprime tranches (BBB) and progressed up the capital structure until finally hitting the highest tranche *before* the Lehman Brothers failure. A total of 11,327 downgrades of AAA-rated securities occurred in the first three quarters of 2008. As of October of that year, the downgrades of predominantly AAA CDO exposure at AIG, Citigroup and Merrill alone totaled close to $90 billion.[20]

If a collapse in growth expectations was sufficient to cause the downgrade of AAA collateral, then one would expect those downgrades to also have af-

---

19. Gorton, *Slapped by the Invisible Hand.*
20. Benmelech and Dlugosz, "The Credit Rating Crisis."

fected AAA-rated securities in other sectors of the economy. In fact, very few, if any, AAA-rated corporate bonds were downgraded in 2008.[21]

A similar phenomenon occurred in collateral backing a short-term funding "cousin" of the repo market, the asset-backed commercial paper (ABCP) market, where outstandings had fallen by 33 percent in the twelve months prior to August 2008 (due to collateral concerns), while non-ABCP remained stable. In fact, in that August, a year after BNP Paribas suspended withdrawals from three money market funds due to ABCP issues, the spread of non-ABCP over Fed funds remained close to zero.[22]

This is not to say that markets were not under some stress. As I noted above, some indicators of expectations (the S&P 500, the VIX, oil and other commodities prices) had started to deteriorate. However, these signals were not inconsistent with the mild recession already underway. For instance, in September 2008, the S&P level of 1300 was just 5 percent below its 200-day moving average, and only 16 percent from the prior year's peak. Moreover, all of these quiescent indicators of deflation expectations occurred at a time when markets expected the Fed to maintain its policy stance. The Fed held the rate at 2.00 percent in the summer of 2008, when commodities prices spiked. By mid-August of that year, markets assigned a 70 percent probability to the Federal Open Market Committee ("FOMC") leaving the Fed funds rate at 2 percent at their September meeting (Figure 3.6). In other words, the Fed's actions in September (leaving rates unchanged) were in line with market expectations and would have been already incorporated into asset prices. If the markets feared a deflationary crash, then it stands to reason asset prices would have reflected much more concern given the markets' expectations for Fed inaction.

Overall, I find it difficult to isolate a set of indicators that were at levels consistent with a crash in expectations that could lead to doubts over AAA-rated collateral. In contrast, into the summer of 2008, there were strong indications that the Fed's efforts to stabilize housing and shadow banks might lead to higher

21. Benmelech and Dlugosz, "The Credit Rating Crisis."
22. Marcin Kacperczyk and Philipp Schnabl, "When Safe Proved Risky: Commercial Paper During the Financial Crisis of 2007–2009" (NBER Working Paper 15538, 2009).

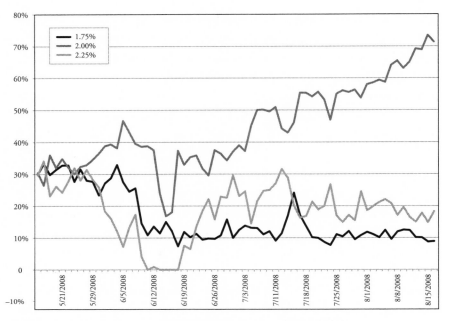

Figure 3.6. September 2008 FOMC Meeting Outcome Probabilities

Source: Federal Reserve Bank of Cleveland

inflation. The 60 percent move in the CRB commodities index that occurred from late 2006 to the summer of 2008 was the steepest rise since 1973, the dollar was relatively weak, and many emerging markets stock markets—hardly deflation beneficiaries—were hitting new highs.

Stepping back, we can see that 2008 was quite different from 1933, or even December 1930, the month that the Bank of the United States became the first large bank casualty of the Great Depression. In 2008, a panic of national importance arose—one that threatened virtually all the major banks—within months of a peak in the inflation rate, money growth and commodity prices; and during a normal stock market correction. By the fall of 1930, in contrast, the price level, commodities prices, monetary aggregates, and output had contracted significantly, and the stock market was down 37 percent from its peak.

In short, it appears that the system was exposed to an event as benign as a year or so of level house-price appreciation, and that this development resulted in a panic not seen for seventy years. What I have attempted in this chapter is to trace the cause of this fragility back to the Fed's attempts to target the expectations of carry traders and their shadow banking institutions—the new elements of the monetary transmission channel. Our final step is to tie the shadow banking system's response to Fed policy directly to the mechanism of the banking panic itself: the run on the repo and other short-term funding for the system.

The Mechanics of the Panic: A Run On Repos

The previous section dealt mostly with the performance of AAA-rated assets on the asset side of the shadow banking system balance sheet. For purposes of actually identifying the proximate cause of the 2008 banking panic, the liability side is what is important. The common feature of any systemic banking panic is a "run" on that system's liabilities. A run results from individual depositors doubting the safety of collateral backing their deposits, which in turn leads them to demand their funds back from an individual bank before that bank's access to liquid funds is exhausted by other depositors demanding the same. The rush by individuals to withdraw funds leads, in aggregate, to the system running short of funds to pay depositors, which in turn leads banks to engage in fire sales of assets, which lowers the prices of collateral and creates further doubts over their safety.

Prior to the establishment of the FDIC, banking rested on the "information insensitivity" of deposits.[23] The depositor did not need to know about the quality of a bank's loan book, or its overall health, before deciding to make a deposit. During the onset of a recession, deposits would lose this information insensitivity as banks' loan portfolios became suspect. In the absence of more information about which loans, and which banks, were most affected, depositors would withdraw funds from the banking system, hoarding currency and precipitating a panic. FDIC insurance provided, of course, a means of maintaining the information insensitivity of deposits even during a deep recession. The success of the insurance mechanism governing the deposits of the traditional banking system explains the prolonged absence of banking panics.

By 2008, the insurance mechanism described above was no longer effective in guaranteeing the immunity of the financial system to panics. This

---

23. Gorton, *Slapped by the Invisible Hand.*

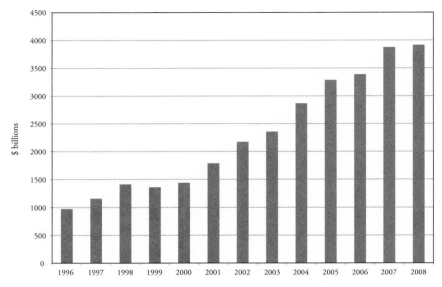

Figure 3.7. Total Primary Dealer Repos Outstanding
Source: Federal Reserve Bank of New York

was simply because, as percentage of total short-term system liabilities, the non-insured portion grew to a critical mass. The most important instrument in that non-insured portion was the short-term repo, the primary funding mechanism for the shadow banking system. Short-term repos were essentially collateralized loans, with the AAA-rated assets described earlier serving as collateral. Not surprisingly, the growth in overnight repos mirrored the same "kink," or acceleration, exhibited by shadow banking system assets following the Fed's 2003 policy shift. While banks used repos for years prior to 2002, what clearly stands out in this cycle is how repo financing exploded beginning in that year (Figure 3.7). At its peak, repo funding was roughly twice the deposits of the banking system).[24] Further, investment banks increasingly relied on overnight funding, with the use of overnight repos doubling between 2000 and 2007.[25]

---

24. Joseph S. Tracy, "What the Fed Did and Why" (remarks at the Westchester County Bankers Association, New York, 2010).
25. Markus K. Brunnermeier, "Deciphering the Liquidity and Credit Crunch 2007–2008," *Journal of Economic Perspectives* 23 (Winter 2009): 80.

If the repo was the critical funding vehicle for the shadow banking system, then the impact of structured finance was to manufacture more "information insensitive" collateral for repos. Repo depositors did not discriminate between classes of AAA collateral pre-crisis.[26] In fact, the Federal Reserve Bank of New York ("NY Fed") estimated that "illiquid collateral" (a substantial portion of which was structured finance) backed 55 percent of all primary dealer repos by 2006.[27] Thus, the web of repo transactions that connected shadow banking institutions with each other would have been suffused with structured finance product.

To come full circle, I have described above how the Fed's policy shift encouraged carry trades, how this led to rapid growth in shadow banking system AAA-rated assets, and how this growth in turn reduced the quality of AAA-rated collateral. The result of all of those asset-side reactions was an increase in the use of repo and other non-insured financing for the financial system, to the point that the system was no longer protected from runs by the deposit insurance mechanism. This brings us to 2007, when concerns over AAA-rated subprime mortgages first began to impact banking system funding.

The presence of small-scale "runs" on financial institution liabilities began in August 2007. In that month, rising subprime defaults and ratings culminated in BNP Paribas's suspension of investor withdrawals from three subprime-related funds. The significance of the announcement was that BNP argued it could not ascertain the value of the (mostly AAA-rated and AA-rated) subprime securities in its fund portfolios. In essence, BNP was announcing to the markets that AAA-rated subprime collateral was now "information sensitive." As a result, interbank lending spreads spiked and the Asset Backed Commercial Paper and repo markets experienced collateral calls.

Stepping back, the question is why a more generalized run on financial system liabilities did not begin in August 2007, but only happened once Lehman failed a year later? One can think of the chain of events as a continuous process, one in which concern over AAA-rated repo and ABCP collateral caused

---

26. Gorton, *Slapped by the Invisible Hand*, 35.
27. Tobias Adrian, Christopher R. Burke, and James J. McAndrews, "The Federal Reserve's Primary Dealer Credit Facility," *Currency Issues in Economics and Finance* 15, no. 4 (2009).

brief, localized "runs" on successive shadow banking institutions: starting with the off-balance-sheet carry trade vehicles of banks (conduits, SIV's) through the fall of 2007, and then moving to the balance sheets of investment banks (Bear Stearns) in the spring of 2008, to the GSEs (summer), and finally, to Lehman, Merrill, and Morgan Stanley (September), then broadening out to money market funds, GSE debt, derivatives books, AIG; and then culminating in the threat of a wide-scale, generalized run on the non-insured liabilities of the financial system in October, 2008. At each step of the way, the Fed tried to contain the runs by acting to reduce the information sensitivity of shadow bank collateral through "backstopping."[28] This started with a coordinated (with the ECB (European Central Bank) and BOJ (Bank of Japan)), public liquidity injection in August, 2007, and then was followed by rate cuts; the establishment of short-term lending vehicles (TALF (Term Asset-Backed Securities Loan Facility), PDCF (Primary Dealer Credit Facility) to replace lost repo and other short-term financing; the bailout of Bear Stearns and GSE creditors; and finally, the commitment to purchase repo collateral directly and in size (through the Fed's $1.25 trillion in mortgage purchases).

In the end, the Fed and the Treasury won the battle and stemmed the run on the system, preventing a full-blown panic. The panic that did occur, however, cost the financial system and the economy dearly. The shadow banking system has contracted in size, from $20 trillion in credit outstanding to $16 trillion (NY Fed 2010, 65); and it became virtually absent from performing some of its earlier functions (i.e., providing mortgage lending). Despite the Fed-engineered growth in bank reserves, traditional bank credit continued to contract well into 2010. Perhaps most important, borrowers, especially households, remain saddled with debt contracts that were entered into at higher asset prices, inducing them to de-lever. This de-levering, in turn, depresses the recovery in nominal spending. All of these factors continue to weigh on the fragile recovery from the 2008 recession, such that the overall cost to the economy of the banking panic still remains to be tallied.

---

28. Adrian et al., Shadow Banking, Staff Report No. 458, Federal Reserve Bank of New York, July, 2010, pp. 58–64.

Counterfactual: No Panic Without Asymmetric Policy

I turn to the question of what the Fed should have done differently before the crisis. Given our thesis, to eliminate the possibility of a bank panic in the fall of 2008, the Fed had a few obvious choices. Any scheme that did not rescue structured finance AAA-rated securities would not fix the repo (and ABCP) collateral problem. It was unlikely that deeper cuts to the Fed funds rate in the spring of 2008 would have prevented expectations for additional ratings downgrades. The same applies to any pre-panic attempt to formally raise inflation expectations that did not also commit the Fed to raising home prices and/or rents (after all, shelter is approximately 40 percent of core CPI), or if not, then reigniting the spike in commodities prices and headline CPI. Both of those tactics would have risked the "bag of chips" effect, where pulling harder on both sides of the bag to open it results in nothing until finally, by exerting enough force, the bag bursts open, raining chips into the air (the "chips" in this case being inflation).

Compare the above pre-panic prescriptions to the following counterfactual: What would have happened if instead of opting for asymmetry, the Fed made no commitments regarding the path of policy in 2003? It is possible that deflationary expectations might have taken hold; and yet, just a few years later, the risk of those expectations was to come back with a vengeance anyway. Arguably, the financial system was in much better shape to take on deflationary risk without outsized intervention in 2003 than in 2008. Household balance sheets were in better shape, and, as I have shown, the shadow banking system was much smaller. Asset prices—particularly those of Nasdaq stocks and high-yield communications sector bonds—were in the process of clearing without creating systemic risk in the shadow banking system.

The interaction between policy and the soup of other variables is too murky for counterfactuals to be anything more than indicative. Perhaps the cost of not withdrawing uncertainty under the deflationary threat was higher than I perceive. Regardless, the more important point, the one I set out to prove, is that without asymmetric policy, the shadow banking system, and its uninsured liabilities, would not have grown in such a way as to ultimately produce a banking panic.

Conclusion: To Improve Policy, Recognize Its Limitations

I leave specific policy recommendations to other chapters of this book. The implication of this chapter, however, is that any proposed policy regime should take into account the limits of Fed power. I have argued that Fed policy can cause chain reactions in markets that can lead to systemic risk and financial panics. Below, I look briefly at two other limitations: (1) the inherent conflict between the Fed's deflation-fighting goals and risk management; and (2) the Fed's own organizational shortcomings.

Today, the Fed remains in deflation-fighting mode. It may be too easy or too tight, but one thing is certain: By holding rates at zero and engaging in Quantitative Easing, the Fed is implicitly trying to convince carry traders to once again reduce insurance (against deflation and illiquidity) and take on leverage. To be successful, this policy has to allow carry traders to profit from the trade for as long as it takes to tame deflation risk. The problem is that, if the Fed is successful in avoiding deflation, it may again create system fragility in the medium term. How can the Fed communicate to markets so as to reduce insurance taking, while at the same time controlling the risks associated with too-low insurance? It is not clear that the Fed can be both weatherman (issuing sunny forecasts) and flood control manager (in charge of the building of levies). Any policy regime that targets market expectations to manufacture stability should take this conflict into account.

The second limitation on policy involves organizational culture. Is the Fed capable of gauging and managing the tail risk? On its face, the evidence from the past twelve years or so is not encouraging: The Fed repeatedly failed to anticipate the crisis-inducing failures of over-levered shadow banking institutions (LTCM (Long-Term Capital Management), Bear Stearns, Lehman Brothers). Yet the issue goes deeper than the Fed's ability to "see around" any single corner. The Fed seems unable to recognize the limits of its own understanding. If known unknowns are questions for which they do not have an answer; then unknown unknowns are questions they are unable to formulate (Morris 2010).[29] The Fed shows signs of a chronic inability to ask the right questions.

---

29. Errol Morris, "The Anosognosic's Dilemma: Something's Wrong But You'll Never Know What It Is (Part 1)," *New York Times*, June 20, 2010.

Fed Vice-Chairman Kohn, for instance, has defended the Fed by argu-ing that bubbles are hard to identify before they crash (Kohn 2008).[30] This is beside the point. The question is not whether we can identify bubbles, but whether we can measure and control shadow-banking-system fragility (high leverage, reliance on overnight funding, and rising carry trader demand for correlated, leveraged bets are all reliable indicators). Unfortunately, there is little evidence that the Fed is engaged in a thorough examination of this ques-tion. A San Francisco Fed economist recently published a paper dismissing the notion that low rates might produce imbalances[31] by saying that the link between the two is "quite erratic and poorly understood." To us, it sounds like the Fed official is saying, "If we do not understand something, we can afford to ignore it." Further, there is a body of research that does establish the link for emerging economies.[32]

Bernanke himself believes that the financial crisis was mostly a failure of regulation.[33] This is inarguable. Less numbers of stated-income loans would have been a good thing. However, in 2005, prohibiting California stated-income loans would have caused house prices there to fall, and fall hard. No regulator wanted to be blamed, at the time, for harming homeowners. So the question is: can we count on regulators to make the right trade-offs when we give them discretion? Again, there is little sign that the question is being asked.

I noted that in the 1980s, a wave of social science research culminated in the idea that government bureaucrats were incapable of forecasting the follow-on effects of their policies on individuals and society. Somehow, the post-1970s Fed was exempted from that view. Perhaps it is time to remove that exemption.

30. Donald L. Kohn, "Monetary Policy and Asset Prices Revisited" (presentation at the Cato Institute's 26th Annual Monetary Policy Conference, Washington, D.C., 2008).

31. Glenn D. Rudebusch, "The Fed's Exit Strategy for Monetary Policy," *FRBSF Eco-nomic Letter* (2010): 18.

32. Moritz Schularick and Alan M. Taylor, "Credit Booms Gone Bust: Monetary Policy, Leverage Cycles and Financial Crises, 1870–2008" (NBER Working Paper 15512, 2009), http://www.nber.org/papers/w15512

33. Ben S. Bernanke, "Monetary Policy and the Housing Bubble" (speech given at the Annual Meeting of the American Economic Association, Atlanta, Georgia, 2010), http://www.federalreserve.gov/newsevents/speech/bernanke20100103a.htm

I have looked at three limits on policy: (1) chain reactions; (2) conflicts between policy goals and risk-taking; and (3) organizational limitations. To us, the three limits argue that the Fed should use extreme caution when expanding the commitments—such as no more deep recessions—that it makes to markets and society at large. Without this caution, we risk creating a repeat of the shadow banking panic of 2008.

References

Adrian, Tobias, Christopher R. Burke, and James J. McAndrews. 2009. The Federal Reserve's primary dealer credit facility. *Current Issues in Economics and Finance*. 15 (4).

Adrian, Tobias and Hyun Song Shin. 2008. Liquidity, monetary policy, and financial cycles. Current Issues in Economics and Finance. 14 (1).

Ashcraft, Adam B. and Til Schuermann. 2008. Understanding the Securitization of Subprime Mortgage Credit. Staff Report 318. Federal Reserve Bank of New York. New York.

Benmelech, Efraim and Jennifer Dlugosz. 2009a. The credit rating crisis. Working Paper 15045. http://www.nber.org/papers/w15045

———. 2009b. The alchemy of CDO credit ratings. NBER Working Paper 14878. http://www.nber.org/papers/w14878

Bernanke, Ben S. 2002. Deflation: Making Sure "It" Doesn't Happen Here. Speech given at the National Economists Club, Washington, D.C.

———. 2003. Remarks made before the Economics Roundtable, University of California, San Diego, La Jolla, California

———. 2010. Monetary Policy and the Housing Bubble. Speech given at the Annual Meeting of the American Economic Association, Atlanta, Georgia. http://www.federalreserve.gov/newsevents/speech/bernanke20100103a.htm

Brunnermeier, Markus, K. Deciphering the liquidity and credit crunch 2007–2008. 2009. *Journal of Economic Perspectives*. 23 (Winter): 77–100.

Diamond, Douglas W. and Raghuram Rajan. Illiquidity and interest rate policy. 2009. NBER Working Paper 15197. http://www.nber.org/papers/w15197

————. 2009. The credit crisis: conjectures about causes and remedies. NBER Working Paper 14739. http://www.nber.org/papers/w14739.

Examiner's Report. 2008. Final Report of Michael J. Missal, Bankruptcy Court Examiner. United States Bankruptcy Court for the District Delaware. In re: New Century TRS Holdings, Inc., a Delaware corporation, et al.

Fitch Ratings. 2005. Hedge Funds, an Emerging Force in the Global Credit Markets.

FOMC meeting statement. May 6, 2003. http://www.federalreserve.gov/boarddocs/press/monetary/2003/20030506/default.htm

————. May 6, 2003. http://www.federalreserve.gov/monetarypolicy/files/FOMC 20030506meeting.pdf

————. August 12, 2003. http://www.federalreserve.gov/boarddocs/press/monetary/2003/20030812/default.htm

————. May 4, 2004. http://www.federalreserve.gov/monetarypolicy/files/FOMC 20040504meeting.pdf

Gorton, Gary B. 2010. *Slapped by the Invisible Hand: The Panic of 2007.* New York: Oxford University Press.

Kacperczyk, Marcin and Philipp Schnabl. 2009. When Safe Proved Risky: Commercial Paper During the Financial Crisis of 2007–2009. NBER Working Paper 15538.

Kohn, Donald L. 2008. Monetary Policy and Asset Prices Revisited. Presented at the Cato Institute's 26th Annual Monetary Policy Conference. Washington, D.C.

Macroeconomic Resilience blog. Knightian uncertainty and the resilience-stability trade-off. http://www.macroresilience.com/2010/01/30/knightian-uncertainty-and-the-resilience-stability-trade-off/

Moody's Ratings Definitions. 2010. Moody's Investor Service. http://www.moodys korea.com/english/definition.asp#7

Morris, Errol. The Anosognosic's Dilemma: Something's Wrong But You'll Never Know What It Is (part 1). *New York Times*, June 20, 2010.

Pozsar, Zoltan, Tobias Adrian, Adam Ashcraft, and Hayley Boesky. 2010. Shadow Banking. Federal Reserve Bank of New York Staff Reports, no. 458 July 2010.

Rudebusch, Glenn D. 2010. The Fed's Exit Strategy for Monetary Policy. FRBSF Economic Letter. 2010–18.

Schularick, Moritz and Alan M. Taylor. 2009. Credit Booms Gone Bust: Monetary Policy, Leverage Cycles and Financial Crises, 1870–2008. NBER Working Paper 15512. http://www.nber.org/papers/w15512

Setser, Brad W. and Arpana Pandey. 2009. China's $1.5 Trillion Bet: Understanding China's External Portfolio. Council on Foreign Relations Working Paper.

Tracy, Joseph S. 2010. What the Fed Did and Why. Remarks at the Westchester County Bankers Association. New York.

Wallison, Peter J. The Price for Fannie and Freddie Keeps Going Up. *Wall Street Journal*, December 29, 2009.

4

The Great Liquidity Boom and the Monetary Superpower Hypothesis

David Beckworth and Christopher Crowe

Introduction

THE ECONOMIC BOOM of the early-to-mid 2000s was not just a U.S. phenomenon. It was a global one. Beginning in the early 2000s, the world economy began an expansion that had the fastest sustained economic growth in thirty years. At its peak during this boom, the global economy was growing at about a 5.0-percent annual average growth rate[1] compared to about a 3.5-percent average for the 1970–2001 period. This global economic boom has been attributed to the opening up of Asia, technological gains, and the ongoing liberalization of the real economy throughout the world. It has also been attributed, however, to a rapid expansion of global liquidity.[2]

This surge in global liquidity can be seen in Figure 4.1. This figure shows that both narrow and broad measures of the money supply in the G-5 countries (France, Germany, Japan, the United Kingdom, and the United States) start growing faster than the underlying economies around 2002.[3] Global foreign

---

1. This average is for the 2004–2007 period. "Global Prospects and Policies," *World Economic Outlook*, October 2008, 3–48.
2. Bank for International Settlements, "Rescue, Recovery, and Reform" (Annual Report for the Bank for International Settlements, 2009: 3–14); Ansgur Belke and Daniel Gros, "Global Liquidity, World Saving Glut and Global Policy Coordination" (Discussion Paper 473, DIW Berlin, 2010).
3. Narrow money is seasonally adjusted M1, except for the United Kingdom where M0 is used. Broad money is seasonally adjusted M3, except for the United Kingdom where M4 is used. Quarterly world nominal GDP is an interpolated version of the IMF's (International Monetary Fund's) annual world nominal GDP. It is interpolated using the Chow and Lin method where an indicator series, here the OECD quarterly nominal GDP, is used to aid the interpolation (*see* Gregory Chow and AnLoh Lin, "Best Linear Unbiased

exchange reserves also take off, going from about $2 trillion in 2002 to over $5 trillion by the end of 2006. They, too, grow faster than the underlying global economy. Given this rapid growth of the global money stock, the global real short-term interest rate turns negative and deviates significantly from the global real GDP growth rate during this time.[4] If one views the global real GDP growth rate as an indicator of the return to investing in the global economy and the global real interest rate as the cost of financing that investment, then the large gap that emerges between them means there was a strong incentive to leverage up and invest in the global economy. The next few graphs in the figure indicate that this is exactly what happened. They show that the amount of debt securities in the global economy sharply increased at this time.[5] Finally, Figure 4.1 reveals that the surge in global liquidity coincided with a global housing boom, a finding consistent with other studies that show global asset prices in general were supported by the rise in global liquidity.[6] The global economic boom of the early-to-mid 2000s, then, was closely tied to a global liquidity boom during this time.

What explains this global liquidity boom? One view, associated in particular with Federal Reserve Board Chairman Ben Bernanke, posits that a global "saving glut" was behind the global liquidity boom. This view holds that in a number of countries, most notably China and a number of oil exporters, desired savings exceeded desired investment. This global excess savings was manifested in higher current account surpluses for these countries and meant that other economies, mainly the United States and some other Anglo-Saxon countries, had

---

Interpolation, Distribution, and Extrapolation of Time Series by Related Series," *Review of Economics and Statistics* 53 (1971): 372–75). All the data in Figure 4.1 come from the IMF's International Financial Statistics database, the IMF's World Economic Outlook database, and the OECD (Organisation for Economic Co-ordination and Development) online database.

4. The G5 real interest rate is used as the measure of global real interest rates. It is a GDP-weighted average of the individual G5 ex-post real interest rate. The global real GDP measured is constructed the same way as global nominal GDP using the real counterparts.

5. The debt securities are the sum of the Bank for International Settlements' domestic and international debt securities series.

6. Sebastian Becker, "Global Liquidity 'Glut' and Asset Price Inflation: Fact or Fiction?" (Deutsche Bank Research Note, May 29, 2007); Jacopo Carmassi, Daniel Gros, and Stefano Micossi, "The Global Financial Crisis: Causes and Cures," *Journal of Common Market Studies* 47 (2009): 977–96.

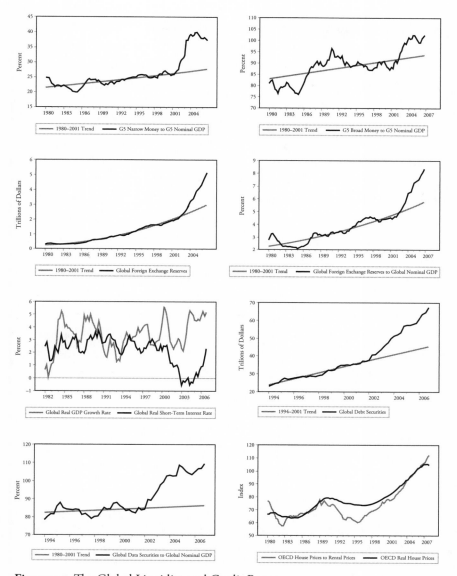

Figure 4.1. The Global Liquidity and Credit Boom

Source: IMF IFS Database, BIS Database, FRED Databases, and Authors' Calculations

to use the excess savings by running current account deficits.[7] The global liquidity boom, therefore, was nothing more than the surge in excess saving finding its way around the world to these advanced economies. Along the way, it depressed real long-term interest rates, which in turn discouraged domestic saving and increased asset values (particularly in housing) in these recipient economies. The excess savings also encouraged the U.S. financial sector to create new "safe" and liquid financial assets (e.g., asset-backed securities linked to housing loans) to satisfy this foreign thirst for financial claims on the United States.[8]

Others, however, have disputed this view, arguing that there is little evidence for a saving glut as a cause rather than a consequence of the global liquidity boom. They see the highly accommodative stance of U.S. monetary policy in the early-to-mid 2000s in conjunction with the decision of other countries to peg their currency to the dollar being behind the buildup of global imbalances. According to this view, U.S. monetary policy got recycled back to the advanced economies via the dollar-pegged economies acquisition of foreign exchange reserves. These economies had to buy up dollars to maintain their dollar pegs as U.S. monetary policy loosened. In turn, these dollars were used to purchase securities from the advanced economies, mainly the United States. What appeared, then, as a saving glut finding its way to the advanced economies was instead a recycling of U.S. monetary policy.[9]

---

7. Ben Bernanke. "The Global Saving Glut and the U.S. Current Account Deficit" (speech delivered to the Virginia Association of Economists, 2005); B. Bernanke, "Global Imbalances: Recent Developments and Prospects" (speech delivered to Bundesbank in Germany, 2007).

8. Ricardo Caballero and Arvind Krishnamurthy, "Global Imbalances and Financial Fragility," *American Economic Review: Papers and Proceedings* 99 (2009): 584–88; Ben Bernanke, "Global Imbalances: Links to Economic and Financial Stability" (speech delivered to Banqe de France Financial Stability Review in France, 2011).

9. Daniel Gros, Thomas Mayer, and Angel Ubide, "A World Out of Balance?" (Special Report of the CEPS Macroeconomic Policy Group, 2006); Thierry Bracke and Michael Fidora, "Global Liquidity Glut or Global Savings Glut? A Structural VAR Approach" (European Central Bank Working Paper 911, 2008); J. Carmassi et al., "The Global Financial Crisis"; Maurice Obstfeld and Kenneth Rogoff, "Global Imbalances and the Financial Crisis: Products of Common Causes," *Asia Economic Policy Conference Volume* (Federal Reserve Bank of San Francisco, October 19–20, 2009): 131–72; M. Vermeiren, "The Global Imbalances and the Contradictions of U.S. Monetary Hegemony," *Journal of International Relations and Development* 13 (2010): 105–35.

This perspective also holds that because U.S. monetary policy was being exported to much of the world through the dollar-pegged countries, the Bank of Japan and the European Central Bank also had to follow to some extent the stance of U.S. monetary policy lest their currencies become overvalued. The Federal Reserve, therefore, was effectively a monetary superpower that created a global liquidity boom.[10] Finally, the low global interest rates caused by the global liquidity boom created a "search for yield" by fixed-income investors while encouraging other investors like hedge funds to take on more leverage. These developments, along with the purchase of U.S. securities by the dollar-pegged economies, are what encouraged the U.S. financial sector to convert risky assets into "safe" assets.

Assessing which explanation for the global liquidity boom is the most plausible is not easy. The global economy, already highly complex, became even more so over the course of the past decade, as globalization of trade and investment flows and financial innovation continued at a bewildering pace. It is hard to condense such a complex system to a simple analytical model with a clear path from cause to effect. As a result, many different explanations are consistent with much of the data. In order to bring some clarity to this debate, we first provide a brief narrative account of the global economy over the period, focusing on the principal facts that any theoretical account of global liquidity boom has to account for.

The Global Economy, 2000–2010

The decade commenced as the long boom of the 1990s, a period of high economic growth and low volatility in the U.S. economy, was giving way to renewed uncertainty. During the 1990s, the United States had provided a relatively safe investment environment. Stock returns were high as a result of the "tech boom"—productivity-enhancing innovations in the information technology sector that were gradually diffusing through the economy. Meanwhile, low inflation and fiscal consolidation reduced perceptions of macroeconomic risk.

---

10. David Beckworth, "Aggregate Supply-Driven Deflation and Its Implications for Macroeconomic Stability," *Cato Journal* 28 (2008): 363–84.

The U.S. performance looked particularly impressive in the context of greater global volatility in emerging markets—exemplified by the trauma of the crises in East Asia, Russia, and Brazil—and a relatively sluggish performance in Europe and Japan. However, as the tech boom looked increasingly unsustainable and the Fed raised rates in 1999 and 2000, the U.S. economy slowed, creating widespread fears that the U.S. could follow Japan into a destabilizing period of deflation. Uncertainty increased further in the wake of the 9/11 attacks. In response, the Fed lowered policy rates to historically low levels, and rates remained extremely low for several years. Concurrently, fiscal policy was loosened significantly via tax cuts and increased expenditure.

As a result, the U.S. economy avoided deflation, although jobs growth remained sluggish even as the economy recovered. An unwinding equity price boom was soon replaced with a new and even more pronounced surge in house prices and housing investment. Consumption grew more strongly than incomes, driven in part by increased nominal housing wealth made available through housing equity withdrawal, and the domestic savings rate fell to historic lows. Both house prices and home ownership trended upwards. Although income and job growth remained fairly stagnant, financial innovation, in the shape of lower lending standards and widespread securitization of home lending, made home ownership more affordable—at least as long as house prices were expected to continue their upwards trajectory. Increased affordability was also supported by historically low long-term interest rates.

In the second half of the 1990s, the counterpart of high levels of corporate investment had been savings from the fiscal and external sectors, in the shape of a fiscal surplus and external current account deficit, respectively. By contrast, the counterpart of high levels of residential housing investment and declining household savings in the years after 2000 was an even wider current account deficit, not least as the fiscal position had moved sharply from surplus to deficit. Foreign buyers were particularly active in markets for paper issued by the federal government (Treasury securities) and asset-backed securities, notably collateralized debt obligations created by securitizing prime and (increasingly) subprime mortgages.

Foreign central banks and sovereign wealth funds, in fast-growing Asian economies and commodity exporting countries, were increasingly providing the flow of foreign savings. For commodity exporters (particularly oil exporters), the rationale was obvious: high commodity prices reflected a temporary increase in wealth which called for a significant portion of the windfall to be saved; in addition, accumulating foreign exchange reserves via sterilized intervention would help to minimize real exchange rate appreciation and prevent the erosion of export competitiveness through so-called "Dutch disease" effects.

Asian countries—particularly China—faced a different dilemma. For many emerging markets, particularly in Asia, the lesson of the Asian financial crisis had been the critical importance of building up sufficient reserves to protect the currency in the event of a speculative attack. Policy-makers noted that speculative capital inflows during good times could easily reverse direction once panic took hold—particularly since domestic capital would likely join the exodus. A sharp currency devaluation could be devastating for the domestic economy—as events in Indonesia in particular testified—since corporations tended to become highly indebted as they sought to grow their businesses in the high growth phase, and currency mismatch was almost inevitable if investment was funded through capital inflows.

Countries in the Asian region—notably China—hoped to avoid this fate via large-scale reserves accumulation. This could limit the risks of an Indonesian-style implosion via three channels. First, reserves accumulated through sterilized foreign exchange market intervention would help prevent real exchange rate appreciation and thus the gradual erosion of competitiveness that had helped to trigger the Asian crisis. Second, if the currency did come under pressure, the accumulated reserves could be used to counter any speculative attack or at least ease the adjustment to a new equilibrium exchange rate. Third, the hard currency could be used to recapitalize any domestic financial institutions caught up in such a crisis, without resorting to fire-sales to foreign banks or excessively weakening the central bank or government balance sheets.

Imbalances were thus emerging simultaneously across sectors and regions of the world economy. Countries in Asia, particularly China, were recording increasing current account surpluses driven by exports of labor-intensive manufactured goods. As capital was also flowing into the region to support increasing levels of investment, the counterpart of these flows was significant reserves accumulation, mostly of U.S. Treasuries. The high level of global growth was simultaneously driving up demand for raw materials. As a result, commodity prices (including oil prices) were driven up to record levels, creating additional surpluses in commodity exporting countries, which were again offset by reserves accumulation. Meanwhile, low levels of inflation in the U.S., caused in part by imported price deflation from low-cost Asian imports, led the Fed to maintain interest rates at record lows until 2004. At the same time, low interest rates supported a new asset price boom in the housing sector—not just in the U.S., but also across a surprisingly broad range of countries.[11]

Understanding the ultimate driving force behind these developments and their relationship to the global liquidity boom has taxed policymakers and academic economists, and the issue has become the center of a key debate in international macroeconomics. Assessing causality is particularly hard in this case because key decision-makers made policy choices conditional on choices made—or expected to be made—by other "players." Assessing causality then comes down to deciding between the plausibility of different counterfactuals: given the choices of others, could a particular player have behaved differently?

According to the "saving glut" hypothesis, the key exogenous factor behind the global liquidity boom was the imbalance of savings over investment in oil producing countries and Asian economies, which drove down global interest rates and created deflationary pressures in the world economy. In this view, agents in the United States—home buyers and central bankers alike—were simply responding to the incentives created by these flows. The counterfactual under this hypothesis is that if these countries had increased their domestic demand (through fiscal or monetary stimulus or by letting their currencies appreciate, increasing effective income levels and promoting imports), then the saving glut would have evaporated, long-term interest rates would have increased to their equilibrium levels, and the house price boom would have been largely ameliorated.

An alternative hypothesis for the global liquidity boom is that the main exogenous factor was the behavior of the Federal Reserve, in lowering interest rates so precipitously in 2000–2001 and keeping them at such low levels through 2004. Low interest rates discouraged saving in the United States and created the conditions for rapid house price growth driven by a surge in household borrowing. Low interest rates also meant the dollar-pegged economies

<hr>

11. For more on the growth of global capital flows during this time, see Martin Wolf, *Fixing Global Finance* (Baltimore: The Johns Hopkins University Press, 2010).

had to buy up dollar assets to maintain their peg, channeling additional credit to the U.S. economy. Collectively, these developments elevated U.S. demand and thus widened the deficit on the external current account.

In loosening policy, the Fed was responding in part to deflationary pressures arising from the impact of low-cost Asian imports as well as technological change. Essentially, the global economy faced a series of positive supply shocks, which allowed U.S. output to increase strongly on the back of loose monetary policy even while inflation remained low and stable. Exacerbating the problem was the fact that central banks globally were becoming increasingly focused on inflation as the sole arbiter of imbalances in the economy, at precisely the moment that global disinflationary shocks made headline inflation a poor measure of domestic overheating. In fact, positive supply shocks called for an increase in long-run interest rates, but policymakers responded by pushing down short-term rates, leading to increased imbalances in the economy.

The impact of these monetary policy actions was all the greater because they occurred concurrently with a loosening of fiscal policy as well as widespread financial innovation that helped to drive up house prices and strengthened the financial accelerator effect on demand. In this account, the counterfactual has the Fed loosening more conservatively in 2000–2001, and raising rates earlier in the recovery. Because U.S. monetary policy gets exported to the dollar-pegged economies and, to some extent, to other advanced economies, the Federal Reserve's monetary loosening had a multiplier effect on global demand, driving up asset prices (particularly prices of commodities and housing) worldwide. With a tighter monetary stance, the commodity and house price surge would have been much less pronounced, and the global liquidity boom and related imbalances that emerged during the course of the decade would have been substantially eliminated.

We would stress that—in a world of increasingly complex linkages between economies and sectors—no policymaker has complete freedom of action. The fact that other central banks pegged their currencies to the dollar limited the Fed's ability to set U.S. monetary policy independently. Similarly, deflationary price pressures and the weak job growth caused by intensified competition from low-cost manufacturers in Asia created a bias towards monetary easing, given the Fed's mandate to maintain a stable price level consistent with full employment. At the same time, however, central banks in Asia were given every incentive to maintain the exchange rate peg and restrain domestic demand, given that they were able to import dollar price stability from the U.S., and that the relatively loose monetary stance emanating from the U.S. was already creating concerns of overheating in sectors of the domestic economy, such as housing. The key question is which player in this policy game had the greater ability to act autonomously. Our view—which we outline in more detail in the "Policy Implications" section below—is that the Fed alone had the power to act more or less independently and was ultimately the source of the global liquidity boom. Thus, the only credible counterfactual is one in which U.S. monetary policy took a less expansionary path from 2000–2001 onwards. But before we progress to this discussion, we discuss in more detail the case for and against the saving glut hypothesis.

The Saving Glut Hypothesis

The saving glut hypothesis is most closely associated with two speeches by Fed Chairman Ben Bernanke[12] on global imbalances and the U.S. current account deficit. Bernanke points to increased current account surpluses on the part of emerging market economies as the main counterpart of the increased current account deficit in the U.S., with these surpluses in turn driven by changes in savings and investment behavior in the countries involved. A key underlying factor was these countries' response to the financial crises of the late 1990s, which led them to accumulate "war chests" of foreign exchange reserves "as a buffer against potential capital outflows." [13] Mercantilist motivations may also have been at work, since reserves were also accumulated "in the context of foreign exchange interventions intended to promote export-led growth by preventing exchange-rate appreciation."[14] Governments acted as financial intermediaries, issuing debt to domestic savers and using the proceeds to buy up foreign assets, primarily U.S. Treasury Bills. In turn, this glut of emerging market savings (demand for assets in advanced economies,

---

12. Bernanke, "The Global Saving Glut"; Bernanke, "Global Imbalances: Recent Developments and Prospects."
13. Bernanke, "The Global Saving Glut."
14. Bernanke, "The Global Saving Glut."

particularly that of the United States) drove up the price for these assets. Prior to 2000, much of the asset demand flowed into the stock market, driving up stock prices. Following the end of the tech boom, demand instead flowed into the bond market, leading to higher prices (lower yields). This in turn reduced the incentive for consumers in the affected advanced economies to save.

Bernanke goes on to ask "why the current-account effects of the increase in desired global saving were felt disproportionately in the United States relative to other industrial countries." His first answer is that the United States was (or at least appeared) a more attractive investment destination than many other advanced countries—because of the high growth enjoyed during the tech boom, as well as the uniquely liquid nature of U.S. asset markets, as demonstrated, for instance, by the kind of financial innovations that allowed U.S. households to sell housing equity created by the house price boom. Thus, Bernanke argues that "external imbalances are to a significant extent a market phenomenon and, in the case of the U.S. deficit, reflect the attractiveness of both the U.S. economy overall and the depth, liquidity, and legal safeguards associated with its capital markets."[15] Caballero and Krishnamurthy make a similar point, arguing that there was a surge in the global demand for safe debt instruments which created incentives for the innovative U.S. financial sector to create new "safe" assets from the pooling and tranching—via securitization—of relatively risky underlying assets.[16]

Bernanke's second answer to his rhetorical question is that in fact the trends identified in the United States, of widening current account deficits, surging housing markets and declining domestic savings, were common to many advanced economies. Germany and Japan were the sole significant exceptions to this trend.[17]

---

15. Bernanke, "The Global Saving Glut"; Bernanke, "Global Imbalances: Links to Economic and Financial Stability" (speech delivered to Banqe de France Financial Stability Review in France, 2011).
16. Caballero and Krishnamurthy, "Global Imbalances and Financial Fragility."
17. Other analysts have come to a broadly similar view to Bernanke. Thus, the IMF (see IMF, "Global Imbalances: A Saving and Investment Perspective," *World Economic Outlook*, September 2005, 91–124) argues that the main cause of global current account imbalances was global savings and investment trends. Specifically, the key trends were the decline in public saving (increase in the budget deficit) in the United States, demographic changes in Japan and Europe, and a decline in investment in Asia (excluding

However, the saving glut hypothesis has been disputed by other analysts. Obstfeld and Rogoff argue that a global saving glut could not have caused the decline in real interest rates in the United States and elsewhere in the early 2000s, because the real interest rate started to decline in 2000, whereas desired savings only increased significantly later on.[18] Obstfeld and Rogoff argue that a decline in expected productivity growth following the bursting of the tech bubble, combined with the aggressive monetary easing that followed, are a more convincing explanation for the decline in real interest rates in 2000–2001. Specifically, they argue that "coupled with low long-term interest rates, the accommodative stance of monetary policy, particularly U.S. monetary policy, played a key role in the expansion of both housing-market excesses and the global imbalances starting in 2004." The Bank for International Settlements came to a similar conclusion in 2009, arguing that U.S. monetary policy easing probably had an impact on global credit conditions that was more than proportionate to the U.S. economy's size.[19]

Obstfeld and Rogoff argue that a saving glut becomes a plausible explanation *after* 2004 (i.e., after the period identified by Bernanke), when several trends converged: (1) global savings rates increased markedly, (2) current account deficits in the United States and other advanced economies widened significantly, and (3) long-run real interest rates remained low despite global monetary policy entering a tightening phase. However, Obstfeld and Rogoff attribute this saving glut in part to the earlier monetary easing—which raised global growth rates, driving up commodity prices—as well as exchange rate intervention by emerging market surplus countries.

Laibson and Mollerstrom (2010)[20] make a similar point, arguing that global savings rates did not show a robust upward trend during the 1996–2006 period

China) following the Asian financial crisis. Like Bernanke, these authors argue that the global imbalance of desired savings over investment drove down real long-term interest rates; however, they argue that a low level of investment (relative to the economic cycle), driven by corporate sector behavior, rather than a high level of savings, was the key factor.

18. Obstfeld and Rogoff, "Global Imbalances and the Financial Crisis."

19. Bank for International Settlements, *Annual Report 2009,* 3–14.

20. David Laibson and Johanna Mollerstrom, "Capital Flows, Consumption Booms and Asset Bubbles: A Behavioral Alternative to the Savings Glut Hypothesis," NBER Working Paper 15759, 2010.

identified by Bernanke. Moreover, their model-based analysis suggests that countries receiving a significant capital inflow during the period should have experienced an investment boom; whereas investment in the United States did not increase significantly during the period. By contrast, consumption rose significantly, in concert with increased household wealth driven by a surge in house prices. While the saving glut hypothesis argues that increasing house prices are an effect of capital inflows, Laibson and Mollerstrom argue that house price bubbles in fact played a causal role in driving global imbalances. Their explanation does not provide an account of why house price bubbles occurred—as they acknowledge. More significantly, their explanation does not explain why bubbles should arise in so many countries at the same time.

To shed some light on this discussion, Figure 4.2 and Figure 4.3 show the evolution of key data series over the 1990–2010 period: the global savings rate, the U.S. current account balance, the federal funds rate, and longer-term interest rates on U.S. Treasury securities.[21] The key argument behind the saving glut hypothesis is that long-term U.S. interest rates were low from the early 2000s onwards, thanks to a rapid increase in global savings, the source of the global liquidity boom. It is certainly true that global savings rates increased sharply between 2002 and 2007, from a trough of around 20.5 percent of global GDP to a peak of more than 24 percent. At the same time, long-term U.S. interest rates remained fairly low—the ten-year Treasury interest rate tops out at about 5 percent—despite a ramp-up in the policy rate to 5.25 percent (from a low of 1 percent) between mid-2004 and mid-2006. Could high global savings rates have been a factor preventing the long-term rate from responding more elastically to the policy tightening?

Looking at Figures 4.2 and 4.3, we see that the evidence is mixed. On one hand, the response of long-term interest rates seems consistent with a forward-looking bond market simply pricing in anticipated policy rate changes. Long-term interest rates are generally considered to be equal to the average of expected short-term interest rates over the same horizon plus a term premium, the additional compensation an investor gets for the risk of holding longer-term securities

---

21. The global savings rate comes from the IMF *World Economic Outlook*. It is calculated by the world savings divided by world GDP, all in USD. The U.S. current account and all the interest rates come from the St. Louis Federal Reserve Bank's FRED Database.

Figure 4.2. The Global Savings rate and the U.S. Current Account Balance
Source: IMF IFS Database, FRED Database, Authors' Calculations

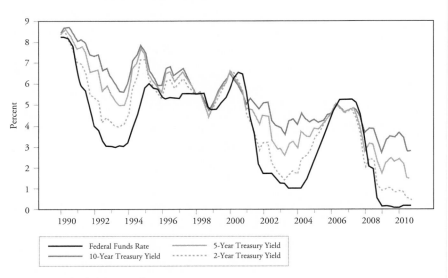

Figure 4.3. U.S. Interest Rates
Source: FRED Database

Thus, bond yields across the term structure increased by about 100 basis points between mid-2003 and mid-2004, *before* the Fed started its tightening cycle, as the bond markets anticipated a move away from the extraordinarily loose policy stance that was maintained through mid-2004. In addition, the trough-to-peak increase in longer-term interest rates was not insignificant: the ten-year yield increased by 145 basis points, the five-year yield by 242 basis points, and one-year yield by 357 basis points. Compared to the 425-basis-point increase in the target federal funds rate, these changes seem reasonable given the linkages across the term structure of interest rates.

Still, Figure 4.3 indicates that long-term interest rates in 2005 and 2006 did not increase proportionally as much as they had in previous monetary policy tightening cycles. One explanation for this so called "interest rate conundrum" is that the bond market was once again pricing in expected policy rate changes. This time, however, it was pricing in policy rate cuts in anticipation of weakening in the U.S. economy. According to this view, the U.S. housing boom was headed for a bust, and the relatively low long-term interest rates were simply part of an inverting yield curve that signaled a recession was imminent.[22]

An alternative interpretation for the "interest rate conundrum" is that the rise in global savings kept long-term interest relatively low during this time, especially in 2005 and 2006. For example, Bernanke argued that, among other things, the rise in global savings kept the demand for long-term U.S. Treasuries elevated and thus drove down the term premium.[23] Some studies that have estimated this effect have found that long-term interest rates were anywhere from 50 to 100 basis points lower than they otherwise would have been.[24] Figure 4.2 and Figure 4.3 do lend some support to these findings. They show that the rise in global savings does coincide with an increase in the U.S. current account deficit and a drop in U.S. long-term interest rates.

There are, however, problems with this story. First, though long-term interest rates do fall with the growth of global savings and the U.S. current

---

22. Mark Trumball, "Why That Cheap Home Loan May Signal Trouble Ahead," *The Christian Science Monitor*, October 14, 2005; Paul Krugman, "Economic Storm Signals," *New York Times*, December 1, 2006.

23. Ben Bernanke, "Reflections on the Yield Curve and Monetary Policy" (speech delivered to the Economic Club of New York, March, 2006).

24. Harm Bandholz, Jorg Clostermann, and Franz Seitz, "Explaining U.S. Bond Yield Conundrum," *Applied Financial Economics* 19 (2009): 539–50; Rorger Craine and Vance L. Martin, "Interest Rate Conundrum," *B.E. Journal of Macroeconomics* 9 (2009): 1–27; Francis Warnock and Veronica Warnock, "International Capital Flows and U.S. Interest Rates," *Journal of International Money and Finance* 38 (2009): 903–19.

account deficit, they do so only through mid-2003. Thereafter, long-term interest rates *rise* even though the global savings and the U.S. current account deficits continue to grow. The only way to reconcile these facts with the saving glut hypothesis is to argue that after mid-2003 the rise in global saving caused long-term U.S. interest rates to rise to less than they otherwise would. Second, even if true, it does not rule out the possibility that the rise in global savings itself was the result of dollar-pegged economies acquiring vast sums of foreign exchange reserves to counteract the Federal Reserve's loose monetary policy. To maintain their dollar pegs at this time, these countries had to buy up dollars and sell their currencies. This kept their currencies undervalued, raised the price of domestic consumption, and ultimately led to a higher savings rate. The saving glut, then, may have been a by-product of loose U.S. monetary policy working through dollar-pegged exchange rate regimes.

To the extent the saving glut did matter, we believe the recycling of U.S. monetary policy interpretation to be the best explanation for it. More generally, we believe the global liquidity boom and the coordinated appearance of housing booms across a wide range of economies can be traced back to U.S. monetary policy shocks being transmitted to other economies. In addition to the recycling of U.S monetary policy, the channels of transmission include direct market effects, as lower U.S. interest rates drove down yields in other markets, as well as policy transmission, as other central banks followed the Fed in loosening policy. Our view is that the Federal Reserve, alone among central banks, has the ability to determine global monetary conditions. This is not to deny that other central banks have some limited room for independent policy action. For instance, central banks can choose to intervene in foreign exchange markets in order to fix the value of the domestic currency, and in some cases this likely exacerbated the pattern of global imbalances.[25] However, as we argue in the next section, the Federal Reserve exerts a disproportionate influence over global monetary conditions. Thus, the Fed policy decisions can explain the simultaneous appearance of a global liquidity boom and house price booms across a wide range of economies. Moreover, the Fed's status as

---

25. Although in this case, the central bank in question also surrenders whatever autonomy it might have to set monetary policy independently (unless it also maintains effective capital controls, as in the case of China, but probably few other emerging markets).

a monetary "superpower" makes the saving glut hypothesis—in which the U.S. monetary authorities act as passive bystanders overwhelmed by global forces beyond their control—an implausible explanation of global imbalances.

The Monetary Superpower Hypothesis

We believe the most convincing explanation for the global liquidity boom is what we call the "monetary superpower hypothesis." This understanding holds that the Federal Reserve is a monetary superpower capable of shaping global liquidity conditions. Given this power, the Federal Reserve's unusually accommodative monetary policy during the early-to-mid 2000s created a global liquidity boom and the related buildup of economic imbalances. The idea that the Federal Reserve can influence global liquidity is not new. Many studies have shown that U.S. monetary policy can affect monetary conditions and interest rates across the world.[26] Federal Reserve officials have acknowledged as much. Federal Reserve Vice Chair Janet Yellen, for example, in 2010 reports the following from a 2009 fact-finding trip to Asia:

> For all practical purposes, Hong Kong delegated the determination of its monetary policy to the Federal Reserve through its unilateral decision in 1983 to peg the Hong Kong dollar to the U.S. dollar. . . . As in Hong Kong, Chinese officials are concerned about unwanted stimulus from excessively expansionary policies of the Fed. . . . Overall, we encountered concerns about U.S. monetary policy, and considerable interest in understanding the Federal Reserve's exit strategy for removing monetary stimulus. Because both the Chinese and Hong Kong economies are further along in their recovery phases than the U.S. economy, current U.S. monetary policy is likely to be excessively stimulatory for them.[27]

---

26. *See*, for example, Soyoung Kim, "International Transmission of U.S. Monetary Policy Shocks: Evidence from VAR's," *Journal of Monetary Economics 48* (2001): 339–72; Ansgar Belke and Walter Orth, "Global Excess Liquidity and House Prices: A VAR Analysis for OECD Countries" (Ruhr Economic Paper No. 37, 2007); Carmassi, et al., "The Global Financial Crisis."

27. Janet Yellen was president of the San Francisco Federal Reserve Bank at this time. As president, though, she was still an influential Federal Reserve official.

Federal Reserve Chairman Ben Bernanke similarly acknowledged the global influence of U.S. monetary policy in a 2011 speech.[28] While there is this recognition of the Federal Reserve's power, no study or U.S. monetary official has documented the extent of it or followed it through to its logical conclusion. Here we do that by explaining why the Federal Reserve is a monetary superpower, by showing how extensive its global influence is, and by connecting it to the global liquidity boom.

The Federal Reserve's superpower status comes from the fact that it manages the main reserve currency of the world to which many countries either explicitly or implicitly peg their currency. By pegging to the dollar, these countries give up their monetary policy autonomy and allow their domestic monetary conditions to be set by U.S. monetary authorities. Because of its influence on these dollar-pegged countries, the Federal Reserve also will influence to some extent monetary policy in Japan and the Eurozone. Too see this, consider what would happen if the Federal Reserve were to lower interest rates. This easing of U.S. monetary policy would be transmitted to the dollar-peggers, causing their currencies, along with the U.S. dollar, to depreciate relative to the yen and the euro. As we show below, the dollar-bloc countries are a large portion of the global economy. Therefore, the Bank of Japan and the European Central Bank (ECB) could not afford to ignore such a development. At some point, they too would ease monetary policy to prevent their currencies from getting too expensive against the dollar-bloc currencies. Thus, they would effectively adopt U.S. monetary policy too.

That is the story, but does the evidence support it? Figure 4.4 shows just how big the dollar-bloc countries are as a percent of world GDP. Using PPP-adjusted values, this figure shows that those countries that use or are linked to the U.S. dollar make up about 40 percent of world GDP. By comparison, the European Central Bank (ECB) makes up about 18 percent, and the Bank of Japan approximately 7 percent. The only real contender, then, with the

---

28. His recognition is more implicit in that he responds to critics who say U.S. monetary policy is exported to emerging markets not by disagreeing but by arguing that the emerging markets should adjust their exchange rate regimes and macroeconomic policies to prevent this from becoming a problem. In other words, Bernanke is saying "Yes, our monetary policy is affecting you, but that is your problem to fix."

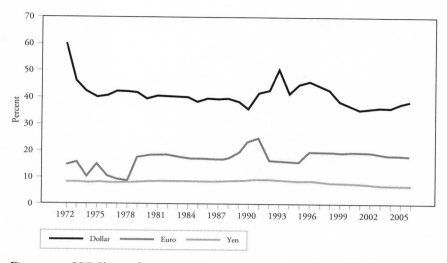

Figure 4.4. PPP Share of World GDP

Source: IFS Database, Authors' Calculations

Federal Reserve in terms of influence is the ECB. However, because the dollar-bloc share of world GDP is so relatively large, the ECB is also influenced by U.S. monetary policy. As we demonstrate shortly, there is strong evidence that Fed policy influences the monetary environment in the Eurozone, with no evidence of any influence in the opposite direction. Thus, these numbers understate the true influence that the Federal Reserve has on global monetary conditions.

Figures 4.5 and 4.6 and Table 4.1 indicate just how much influence the Federal Reserve has on the ECB. Figure 4.5 shows the target policy interest rate for both central banks.[29] It shows that since its inception in 1999, the ECB has consistently followed policy interest rate changes by the Federal Reserve with a lag (the ECB decided to start hiking rates in April 2011, while the Fed maintained its easing stance, being a recent exception). Figure 4.6 shows that not only were target policy interest rates alike, but also the extent of excessive easing or tightening by ECB was also very similar to the Federal Reserve during

---

29. The policy interest rates are the federal funds rate for the Federal Reserve and the deposit facility rate for the ECB.

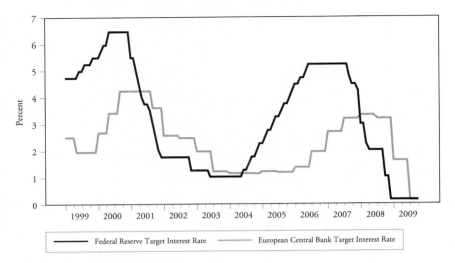

Figure 4.5. Follow the Leader

Source: FRED Database, Eurostat Database, Authors' Calculations

this time.[30] This figure shows how much each central bank's target interest rate deviated from that prescribed by a standard Taylor Rule—the Taylor Rule Gap.[31] The Taylor Rule prescribes what the policy interest rate should be given the state of economy. Any deviation from the Taylor Rule can be

---

30. John B. Taylor notices this relationship too. Like us, he makes the case that the Federal Reserve's policies probably influenced the ECB. See John B. Taylor, *Getting Off Track: How Government Actions and Interventions Caused, Prolonged, and Worsened the Financial Crisis* (Stanford, CA: Hoover Institution Press, 2009).

31. The Taylor Rule is defined as follows: $i_t^* = i_t^n = 0.5(y_t - y_t^p) + 0.5(\pi_t + \pi^*)$, where i_t^* is the target nominal federal funds target, i_t^n is the neutral federal funds rate and consist of the real neutral federal funds rate, r_t^n, and the inflation target, π_t. In both cases, the neutral real interest rate is set to 2 percent and the target inflation rate is 2 percent. This is standard for the U.S. Taylor Rule. According to Garnier and Wilhelmsen, it is also a reasonable approximation for the ECB. (See Julien Garnier and Bjorn-Roger Wilhelmsen, "The Natural Real Interest Rate and the Output Gap in the Euro Area: A Joint Estimation" (European Central Bank Working Paper 546, 2005). For the output gap we use the percent deviation of industrial production from its trend for the ECB, while for the Federal Reserve we use the Laubach and Williams output gap estimate. (See Thomas Laubach and John Williams, "Measuring the Natural Rate of Interest" *Review of Economic and Statistics* 85 (2003): 1063–70. Finally, for the ECB we use the harmonized CPI index from the OECD, while for the Federal Reserve we use the CPI.

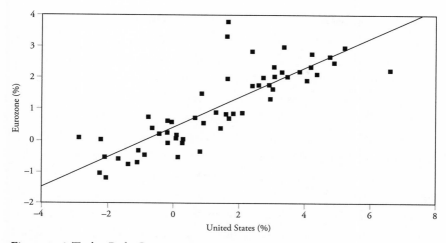

Figure 4.6. Taylor Rule Gaps 1997:Q1–2010:Q4

Source: FRED Database, Eurostat Database, Authors' Calculations

Table 4.1

Lags	The Federal Reserve U.S. Monetary Policy Shocks Do Not Granger Cause 1-Month Euribor Rate P-Value	The European Bank European Monetary Policy Shocks Do Not Granger Cause the Federal Funds Rate P-Value
1	0.283	0.989
2	0.015	0.833
3	0.031	0.121
4	0.003	0.335
5	0.013	0.430
6	0.025	0.457
7	0.040	0.467
8	0.136	0.599
9	0.260	0.673
10	0.208	0.747
11	0.139	0.475
12	0.202	0.523
13	0.025	0.613
14	0.060	0.231
15	0.007	0.315
16	0.015	0.369
17	0.008	0.422
18	0.002	0.470

viewed as monetary policy easing or tightening not warranted by economic conditions. Remarkably, the deviations are very similar.

It could be that these similarities are due to the Federal Reserve and the ECB responding to developments that affect them both, rather than the Federal Reserve independently driving changes in the ECB. To check this possibility, we use the Barakchian and Crowe monetary policy shock measures[32] to determine whether truly exogenous changes in U.S. monetary policy—changes that cannot be explained by other developments—affected short-term market interest rates in the Eurozone during this time. Likewise, we check whether such exogenous changes in ECB monetary policy influenced short-term market interest rates in the United States.[33] To do this, we run Granger causality tests that assess whether the monetary policy shocks can improve upon forecasts of the short-term market interest rates that rely only on lagged values of the short-term interest rates. Table 4.1 reports the results of this exercise using monthly data for the period 1992:2–2010:2. Various lag lengths are used to be robust.[34] Here, the null hypothesis is that the monetary policy shocks do not "Granger" cause changes in the other region's short-term interest rates. A rejection of this null—a p value of less than 0.10—indicates that the monetary policy shocks may be causing changes in the other regions' short-term interest rates.

Consistent with the monetary superpower hypothesis, Table 4.1 reveals that U.S. monetary policy shocks do influence Eurozone short-term interest rates, while Eurozone monetary policy shocks do not influence U.S. short-term interest rates.[35] U.S. monetary policy, then, truly was influencing monetary policy in the Eurozone. Figure 4.7 shows its influence was significant: for the Eurozone, up to 56 percent of the short-term interest rate forecast error and up

---

32. Syed Barakchian and Christopher Crowe, (IMF Working Papers 10/230, 2010).

33. The Barakchian and Crowe shock measures are constructed using futures contracts on short-term interest rates targeted by the central banks. (For details, see Barakchian and Crowe, "Monetary Policy Matters.")

34. Following Barakchian and Crowe, the shock series is accumulated into levels and the interest rate data is not first differenced to account for the possibility of cointegration. A vector autoregression is used to estimate the relationship. See Barakchian and Crowe, "Monetary Policy Matters."

35. Similar results are found in Ansgur Belke and Daniel Gros, "Asymmetries in Transatlantic Monetary Policy-making: Does the ECB Follow the Fed?" *Journal of Common Market Studies* 43 (2005): 921–46.

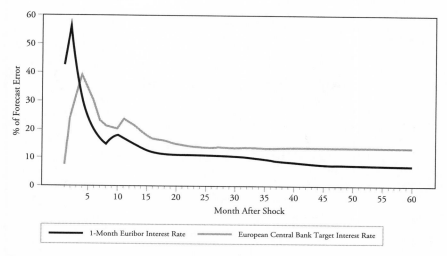

Figure 4.7. Forecast Error Explained by U.S. Monetary Policy Shocks
Source: Eurostat Database, Authors' Calculations

to about 40 percent of the policy interest rate forecast error can be explained by U.S. monetary policy shocks. This figure indicates that the Federal Reserve accounts for a sizable share of the non-predicted movement in short-term interest rates in the Eurozone.[36]

Since the Federal Reserve controls monetary policy for the dollar-bloc region and heavily influences monetary policy in the Eurozone, as shown above, its influence must be felt across the global economy. Figure 4.8 shows that, in fact, this is the case. This figure reveals that for the 1999–2009 period, the Federal Reserve's target policy interest rate helped shape short-term interest rates throughout the world.[37] Generally, the target federal funds rate led these other short-term interest rates. The only notable exception is China before

---

36. The forecast errors come from a vector autoregression of 13 lags that includes the interest rates and the U.S. monetary policy shocks.
37. The oil-exporting countries are Saudi Arabia, Kuwait, Bahrain, Qatar, Oman, and Norway. The emerging market asia countries are Singapore, South Korea, Hong Kong, Thailand, Philippines, Malaysia, and Taiwan. A GDP-weighted average of each country's short-term interest rate was used to contruct the regional short-term interest rate. For each country the shortest interest rate available was used. The data sources include the IMF's International Financial Statistics database, the OECD's online database, and in some cases central bank websites.

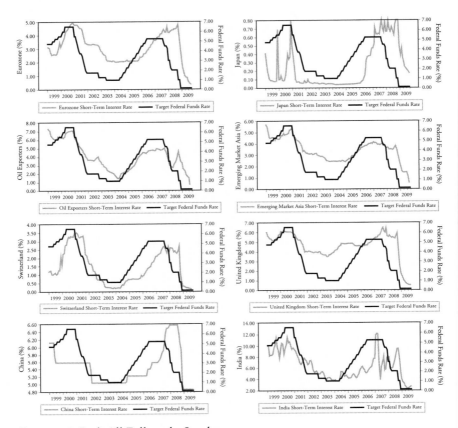

Figure 4.8. Let's All Follow the Leader

Source: OECD database, Eurostat Database, FRED Database,
   IMF IFS Database, Authors' Calculations

2002. This exception, however, reflects the fact that China did not enter the WTO (World Trade Organization) until 2001. After its entry, the Chinese short-term interest rate does follow the target federal funds rate with a lag. The Federal Reserve is indeed a monetary superpower.

The monetary superpower hypothesis claims not only that the Federal Reserve is a monetary superpower, but also that because of its unusually accommodative monetary policy in the early-to-mid 2000s, it created a global liquidity boom and the related economic imbalances. A key part of this story is that the dollar-pegging countries had to acquire vast sums of foreign exchange reserves to counteract the loosening of U.S. monetary policy. This buildup of foreign exchange reserves, in turn, got recycled back to the United States as these countries bought up U.S. securities. This increased the demand for safe U.S. assets and put downward pressure on long-term interest rates. For this story to hold, then, it must be established that the loose U.S. monetary policy was closely tied to buildup of foreign exchange reserves during this time.

Figure 4.9 shows that there is, in fact, a close relationship between the stance of U.S. monetary policy and the growth of foreign exchange reserves. This figure plots the Taylor Rule gap used in Figure 4.6 against the year-on-year growth rate of foreign exchange reserves. The R^2 between these two series is just under 50 percent for the entire period. For the period up through the end of the housing boom in 2006, the R^2 is 63 percent. A positive value for the Taylor Gap means monetary policy is excessively loose. Thus, the 2002–2004 easing by the Fed was excessive and matched by a sharp increase in the growth of foreign exchange reserves.

Figure 4.10 completes the story by showing that the Taylor Gap was also systematically related to the related buildup of economic imbalances associated with the global liquidity boom. Here we see that the U.S. current account deficit, the amount of global debt securities, the growth of the OECD real housing price index, and global nominal spending are all closely related to the Federal Reserve's easy monetary policy at this time.[38] Given the Federal Reserve's monetary superpower status, the easiest interpretation for these scatter plots is that the Federal Reserve's monetary policy created a global liquidity boom that led to the growth of these imbalances. Other studies have come to similar conclusions.[39]

---

38. The global nominal spending shock is calculated as the difference between the year-on-year growth rate of global nominal GDP and a rolling ten-year average of the year-on-year global nominal GDP growth rate. The idea here is that the ten-year rolling average provides a forecast for the current global nominal GDP growth rate. Any deviation from that forecast is a shock.

39. Gros et al., "A World Out of Balance?"; Bracke and Fidora, "Global Liquidity Glut or Global Savings Glut?"; Carmassi et al., "The Global Financial Crisis"; Obstfeld and Rogoff, "Global Imbalances and the Financial Crisis"; Vermeiren, "The Global Imbalances and the Contradictions of U.S. Monetary Hegemony."

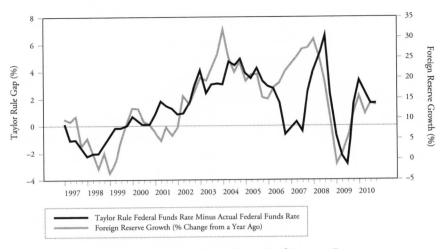

Figure 4.9. U.S. Monetary Policy and the Growth of Foreign Reserves

Source: IMF IFS Database, FRED Database, Authors' Calculations

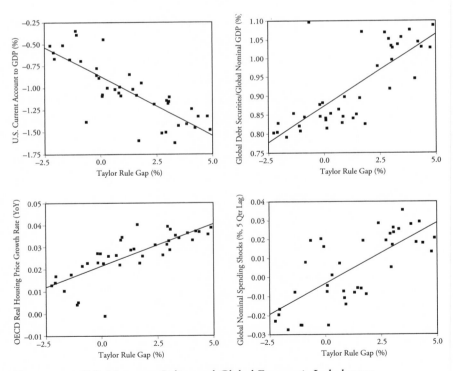

Figure 4.10. U.S. Monetary Policy and Global Economic Imbalances

1997:Q1–2006:Q4

Source: IMF IFS Database, FRED Database, BIS database, Authors' Calculations

An important implication of these findings is that the transformation of risky assets into supposedly safe AAA-rated securities during this time was, in part, a byproduct of recycled loose U.S. monetary policy. Bernanke et al. in a 2011 paper show that because the dollar-pegged countries were acquiring most of the traditional safe assets, U.S. Treasury and GSE securities, the remaining demand for safe U.S. securities was met by structured finance creating safe assets out of risky ones.[40] Had U.S. monetary policy been less accommodative, there would have been less demand for safe assets by these countries and thus, less need for structured finance to work its magic. Tighter monetary policy would have reduced the demand for safe assets in other ways too. First, many fixed-income investors such as pension funds and insurance companies have fixed nominal return targets. The Federal Reserve's low interest rate policy at this time made it difficult for them to meet their targeted nominal return. Consequently, there was a "search for yield" by these investors that led them to look for other safe, but higher-yielding assets. Second, the lower interest rates also created the incentive for other investors like hedge funds and broker-dealers to borrow at low funding rates and then invest in safe, higher-yielding assets. Both types of investors increased the demand for safe assets and that was met by transforming risky assets into safe ones.[41] The Federal Reserve, thus, increased the demand for safe assets from foreign and domestic investors alike.

The evidence presented above strongly suggests that the Federal Reserve through its influence on global monetary conditions created a global liquidity boom in the early-to-mid 2000s that fueled the rise of global economic imbalances. What appeared to be a global saving glut to some was actually the global recycling of loose monetary policy from the world's monetary superpower. The policy implications of the Federal Reserve's monetary superpower status are considered next.

40. Ben Bernanke, Carol Bertaut, Laurie Pounder Demarco, and Steven Kamin, "International Capital Flows and the Returns to Safe Assets in the United States, 2003–2007" (Federal Reserve Board of Governors, International Finance Discussion Paper, 2011), 1014.
41. Tobias Adrian and Hyun Song Shin, "Liquidity, Monetary Policy, and Financial Cycles," Federal Reserve Bank of New York, *Current Issues in Economics and Finance* 14, no. 1 (2008); L. Gambacorta, "Monetary Policy and the Risk-Taking Channel," *BIS Quarterly Review*, December, 2009, 43–53; Diego Espinosa, "Chain Reaction: How the Fed's Assymetric Policy in 2003 Led to a Panic in 2008," Chapter 3 in this volume, *Boom and Bust Banking* (Oakland, CA: The Independent Institute, 2012).

Policy Implications

The main policy implication of the monetary superpower hypothesis is that the Federal Reserve needs to be more cognizant of its global economic influence. In particular, when making monetary policy decisions, the Federal Reserve needs to take into account that its actions get amplified into broader global liquidity conditions. Thus, in the early-to-mid 2000s, the Federal Reserve's sustained easing of monetary policy created a global liquidity boom that put the global economy on an unsustainable path. Likewise, in mid-to-late 2008, as global financial conditions were worsening, the demand for the main reserve currency of the world spiked. The Federal Reserve, however, was slow to respond to this dollar demand shock. This allowed global output to contract more than it probably otherwise would have. Being more cognizant of its global influence is not easy for the Federal Reserve, given its domestic mandate. Still, the understanding that U.S. monetary policy can influence global liquidity conditions, which can in turn affect the U.S. economy, should give the Fed pause. It is in the Federal Reserve's self-interest to pay closer attention to the international dimension of its role as a monetary superpower.

What makes the Federal Reserve a monetary superpower is the fact that numerous countries peg their currency to the one that the Federal Reserve controls. These countries do so because the dollar is the currency of the largest economy in the world with the deepest financial system. The Federal Reserve cannot control this decision by these dollar-pegging countries. It can, however, respond more forcefully to domestic economic conditions and, by doing so, better manage its influence on global monetary conditions. For example, had the Federal Reserve tightened faster during the U.S. housing boom, it would have also reined in global liquidity conditions. Similarly, had the Federal Reserve responded more quickly to the weakening U.S. economy where the financial crisis started, then the global financial crisis would have been less severe and the global dollar demand shock would have been muted.

This is not to say that monetary policy that is best for the U.S. economy will always be best for the global economy, as many emerging economies learned in 2010. During this time, the U.S. economy languished while the emerging economies were experiencing rapid growth. The Federal Reserve, as a consequence, began a large monetary stimulus program called QE2. Though arguably appropriate for the U.S. economy, it was way too accommodative for the dollar-pegged emerging economies. Not wanting to let their currencies rapidly appreciate against the dollar, and not being able to sterilize all of the related capital inflows, these economies found QE2 to be too stimulative and inflationary for them. Still, they chose to maintain their link to the dollar.

Barry Eichengreen predicts that eventually the dollar will lose its reserve currency status and become one of three important global currencies.[42] When that happens, the Federal Reserve's monetary superpower status will diminish too. Though that time appears far off, there are some signs that could be viewed as moving the global economy in that direction. First, because of QE2, the dollar-pegged economies are losing their export competitiveness. As noted above, these countries are getting higher-than-desired inflation with QE2. This is making their exports more expensive and defeating the very purpose of linking cheaply to the dollar. If U.S. monetary policy continues to be too easy for them, over time it might make them less eager to peg to the dollar. Second, the ECB in early 2011 chose to begin raising its target interest rate. If it follows through, then the ECB may be finally moving out of the Federal Reserve's orbit of influence. Though interesting, these developments may prove inconsequential for the Federal Reserve monetary superpower status. For the emerging economies still need the U.S. economy to buy their goods, and it is an open question as to whether the ECB can really allow the Euro to strengthen too much against the dollar.

What is sure is that for now, the Federal Reserve is a monetary superpower. It will continue to influence global monetary conditions and influence economies far beyond its domestic mandate. Therefore, it is time for Federal Reserve officials to acknowledge this monetary superpower status and act accordingly.

References

Adrian, T. and Shin, H. 2008. "Liquidity, Monetary Policy, and Financial Cycles." Federal Reserve Bank of New York, *Current Issues in Economics and Finance*, 141.

---

42. Barry Eichengreen, *Exorbitant Privilege: The Rise and Fall of the Dollar and the Future of the International Monetary System* (New York: Oxford University Press USA, 2011).

Bandholz, H., Clostermann, J. and Seitz, F. 2009. "Explaining U.S. Bond Yield Conundrum." *Applied Financial Economics*, 19, 539–50.

Barakchian, S. M. and Crowe, C. 2010. "Monetary Policy Matters: New Evidence Based on a New Shock Measure." IMF Working Papers 10/230.

Becker, Sebastian. 2007. "Global Liquidity 'Glut' and Asset Price Inflation, Fact or Fiction?" Deutsche Bank Research Note, May 29.

Beckworth, D. 2008. "Aggregate Supply-Driven Deflation and Its Implications for Macroeconomic Stability." *Cato Journal*, 28, 363–84.

Belke, A. and Orth, W. 2007. "Global Excess Liquidity and House Prices: A VAR Analysis for OECD Countries." Ruhr Economic Paper No. 37.

———. 2005. "Asymmetries in Transatlantic Monetary Policy-making: Does the ECB Follow the Fed?" *Journal of Common Market Studies*, 43, 921–46.

———. 2010. "Global Liquidity, World Saving Glut and Global Policy Coordination." Discussion Paper 473, DIW Berlin.

Bernanke, B. 2005. "The Global Saving Glut and the U.S. Current Account Deficit." Speech delivered to the Virginia Association of Economists.

———. "Reflections on the Yield Curve and Monetary Policy. Speech delivered to the Economic Club of New York, March, 2006.

———. 2007. "Global Imbalances: Recent Developments and Prospects." Speech delivered to Bundesbank in Germany.

———. 2011. "Global Imbalances: Links to Economic and Financial Stability." Speech delivered to Banqe de France Financial Stability Review in France.

Bernanke, B., Bertaut, C., Demarco, L., Kamin, S. 2011. "International Capital Flows and the Returns to Safe Assets in the United States, 2003–2007." Federal Reserve Board of Governors, International Finance Discussion Paper 1014.

BIS. 2009. "Rescue, Recovery, and Reform" in the Annual Report for the Bank of International Settlements, 3–14.

Bracke, T. and Fidora, M. 2008. "Global Liquidity Glut or Global Savings Glut? A Structural VAR Approach." European Central Bank Working Paper 911.

Caballero, R. and Krishnamurthy, A. 2009. "Global Imbalances and Financial Fragility." *American Economic Review: Papers and Proceedings*, 99, 584–88.

Carmassi, J., Gros, D., and Micossi, S. 2009. "The Global Financial Crisis: Causes and Cures." *Journal of Common Market Studies*, 47, 977–96.

Chow, G. and Lin, A.1971. "Best Linear Unbiased Interpolation, Distribution, and Extrapolation of Time Series by Related Series." *Review of Economics and Statistics*, 53, 372–75.

Craine, R. and Martin, V. 2009. "Interest Rate Conundrum." *B.E. Journal of Macroeconomics*, 9, 1–27.

Eichengreen, B. 2011. *Exorbitant Privilege: The Rise and Fall of the Dollar and the Future of the International Monetary System*. Oxford University Press.

Espinosa, Diego. 2011. "Chain Reaction: How the Fed's Assymetric Policy in 2003 Led to a Panic in 2008." Chapter in this volume.

Gambacorta, L. 2009. "Monetary Policy and the Risk-Taking Channel." *BIS Quarterly Review*, December, 2009, 43–53.

Garnier, J. and Wilhelmsen B. 2005. "The Natural Real Interest Rate and the Output Gap in the Euro Area: A Joint Estimation." European Central Bank Working Paper 546.

Gros, D., Mayer, T. and Ubide, A. 2006. "A World Out of Balance?" Special Report of the CEPS Macroeconomic Policy Group.

IMF 2008. "Global Prospects and Policies." *World Economic Outlook*, October, 3–48.

Kim, S. 2001. "International Transmission of U.S. Monetary Policy Shocks: Evidence from VAR's." *Journal of Monetary Economics*, 48, 339–72.

Krugman, P. 2006. Economic Storm Signals. *New York Times*, December 1, 2006.

Laubach, T. and Williams, J. 2003 "Measuring the Natural Rate of Interest." *Review of Economic and Statistics,* 85, 1063–70.

Obstfeld, M. and Rogoff, K. "Global Imbalances and the Financial Crisis: Products of Common Causes," in Asia Economic Policy Conference Volume, Federal Reserve Bank of San Francisco, October 19–20, 131–72.

Taylor, J. 2009. *Getting Off Track: How Government Actions and Interventions Caused, Prolonged, and Worsened the Financial Crisis*. Hoover Institution Press. Stanford, California.

Trumball, M. 2005. "Why That Cheap Home Loan May Signal Trouble Ahead." *The Christian Science Monitor*, October 14, 2005.

Vermeiren, M. 2010. "The Global Imbalances and the Contradictions of U.S. Monetary Hegemony." *Journal of International Relations and Development*, 13, 105–35.

Warnock, F. and Warnock, V. 2009. "International Capital Flows and U.S. Interest Rates." *Journal of International Money and Finance*, 38, 903–19.

Wolf, Martin 2010. *Fixing Global Finance*. The Johns Hopkins University Press, Baltimore, Maryland.

Yellen, J. 2010. "Hong Kong and China and the Global Recession." Federal Reserve Bank of San Francisco Economic Letter, February 8, 2010.

PART II

Creating the Great Recession

5

How Nominal GDP Targeting Could Have Prevented the Crash of 2008

Scott Sumner

IN THIS PAPER, I will show how a NGDP (national gross domestic product) futures targeting regime would have prevented a severe financial and economic crash in the fall of 2008. In the section below entitled "Why Did Macroeconomists Misdiagnose the Crisis?" I discuss how and why the crash of 2008 has been widely misdiagnosed by economists. Most economists seem to have assumed that extreme financial distress in late 2008 triggered a severe recession, that the major central banks adopted a policy of monetary ease during this period, and that the zero interest rate bound (aka "liquidity trap") prevented monetary policymakers from arresting the sharp decline in aggregate demand. I will show that all three of those assumptions are incorrect, and then argue that this misdiagnosis is the root cause of the recession of 2008–09. Put simply, macroeconomists, not bankers and bank regulators, are to blame for the current economic crisis.[1]

In the section below entitled "Why NGDP Is Important," I discuss how monetary policy affects the economy, particularly in an environment where nominal interest rates are close to zero. We will see that expected NGDP growth is the best indicator of the stance of monetary policy, far superior to interest rates or the money supply. I then show why nominal GDP growth is a more useful

---

1. Robert Hetzel, Earl Thompson, and Tim Congdon were among the few who correctly saw that excessively tight money worsened the recession in the second half of 2008. *See* Robert L. Hetzel, "Monetary Policy in the 2008–2009 Recession," *Federal Reserve Bank of Richmond Economic Quarterly* (Spring 2009): 201–33; Earl A. Thompson, "Free Banking under a Labor Standard—The Perfect Monetary System" (manuscript, UCLA, 1982); Tim Congdon, "The Unnecessary Recession," *Standpoint* (June 2009): 40–45, http://www.imr-td.com/graphics/recentresearch/article6.pdf.

macroeconomic variable than inflation. In most situations in which economists use inflation, NGDP growth better reflects the economic concept that is appropriate to the model. I then show why stable nominal GDP growth, with "level targeting," is superior to inflation targeting (flexible or otherwise).

In the section below entitled "How an NGDP Futures Market Can Assist Policymakers," I argue that we need a forward-looking monetary policy that targets expected NGDP. Macroeconomics is currently hamstrung by a number of superstitions, including the view that good economists are those who successfully predict the business cycle, or asset market crashes. We need to move beyond models that rely on policymakers being smarter than markets, and restructure macro around market expectations. A successful policy is not one that stabilizes actual NGDP; rather, it is one that stabilizes expected NGDP. Macroeconomic instability comes from sudden changes in the *expected future path* of NGDP; changes expected to persist over a period of several years. If we can stabilize NGDP expectations, then key asset markets and labor markets will also be relatively stable, as both asset prices and wages are set using forecasts of future NGDP.

Why Did Macroeconomists Misdiagnose the Crisis?

Sophisticated modern economies are not governed by suicidal policymakers. Public officials have little to gain from producing the sort of severe economic crisis we have recently experienced, or the Great Depression of the 1930s. The losses from these slumps vastly outweigh the gains. Millions of workers lost jobs. Investors in stocks, corporate bonds, and commodities suffered severe losses. Many banks failed or saw severe declines in market value. The few gainers (Treasury bondholders) were not influential enough to cause consecutive Republican and Democratic administrations to pursue disinflationary policies. Instead, Federal Reserve policy has essentially reflected the consensus view of well-meaning economists, and failed to achieve its objective.

It may seem counterintuitive that this sort of economic crisis could result from a flawed worldview among a few thousand macroeconomists. In order to make that argument, I am going to first discuss the Great Depression; a qualitatively similar but much more severe crisis. As I do so keep in mind that *at the time* the standard view of the Great Depression was quite similar to the standard view of the current crisis. And also keep in mind that the *current view* of the Great Depression is quite similar to my (quite heterodox) explanation for our current crisis.

During the 1930s, the excesses of the Roaring Twenties were seen as a root cause of the Great Depression. The high stock prices of the late 1920s were viewed as a sort of "bubble." The market crash of October 1929 was seen as triggering the initial contraction. The empty skyscrapers completed in 1930 and 1931 were symbols of "malinvestment." The persistent bank panics that began in late 1930 were believed to have worsened the downturn, and the international debt and exchange rates crises of 1931 were seen as the last straw, the shock that turned a severe slump into a Great Depression.

Monetary policy was seen as being very accommodative during the 1930s. Interest rates were cut repeatedly between 1929 and 1933, bringing them to very low levels. The monetary base increased sharply. This led to a perception that monetary policy is ineffective during depressions, as there are few willing borrowers when demand is weak.

Today the consensus view of the Great Depression is almost completely reversed from the standard view of the 1930s. The main problem was a huge drop in aggregate demand, which caused nominal spending to fall by more than 50 percent between late 1929 and early 1933. There is some dispute about the specific factors that caused this decline, but most macroeconomists now think that monetary policy, broadly defined, was the key problem. Friedman and Schwartz pointed to the sharp plunge in the broader monetary aggregates in the U.S. Others blame the gold standard, which constrained monetary policy-makers and spread deflationary shocks to all countries that maintained a stable gold price peg. It is still not clear how much the Fed could have done under the constraints of the gold standard, but almost everyone agrees that if the United States had abandoned the gold standard and targeted inflation, it would have been possible to prevent a severe decline in nominal spending.

Most of the factors that were once regarded as causing the Depression now look more like symptoms of falling demand. The stock crash of 1987 was almost identical to the crash of 1929, and yet it did not have any discernable impact on aggregate demand. Even allowing for differences in the ratio of stocks to GDP between 1929 and 1987, it is hard to account for the complete absence of economic weakness in late 1987 and early 1988. More likely, the stock market crashed in late 1929 because investors saw (correctly) that the United States was entering a severe recession. The empty office buildings of the 1930s do not indicate malinvestment; in any major depression there will be projects completed right before the downturn that look foolish in retrospect. And the first banking crisis, which didn't occur until November–December 1930, was almost certainly a consequence of the Depression, not a cause. Given the severity of the initial slump (which by late 1930 was already more severe than the recent recession in the United States), it is surprising that the banking system did not experience any major distress for fifteen months. And when banking distress did begin in November 1930, the initial "panic" was quite mild. That's not to say that the banking distress had no impact on the economy. But its impact on aggregate demand could have been offset with monetary expansion. Any 50 percent decline in NGDP is primarily a failure of monetary policy.

Why did almost everyone get it so wrong at the time? The fundamental problem is that some of the side effects of deflationary monetary policy look very much like factors that could cause economic weakness, while other side effects make it difficult to interpret the stance of monetary policy. Consider the effects of severe deflation:

1. Debtors have more trouble repaying loans. Bank failures increase.
2. If wages are sticky, output falls and unemployment rises.
3. Falling prices and output depress the demand for credit. As a result, nominal interest rates fall to low levels.
4. Near-zero nominal interest rates and banking distress lead to high demand for liquidity. The monetary base increases sharply in real terms (and perhaps nominal terms as well).

All of these things occurred during the early 1930s. Now let's think about how people might have perceived these events, using a sort of "common-sense" framework. During normal times, the Fed conducts "easy money" policies via open market purchases, which increase the monetary base and reduce interest rates. In many peoples' minds, the term "easy money" is almost synonymous with low interest rates. Because interest rates were low throughout most of the 1930s, very few people blamed the Depression on "tight money."

If Fed policy wasn't seen as being contractionary, then how did economists explain the Depression? During the 1930s, the most obvious culprit was the financial system. The financial distress experienced in late 1929 and throughout the early 1930s was exactly what you'd expect to occur when NGDP falls very sharply. But at the time, those financial shocks seemed either inexplicable (the stock market crash) or reflective of poor decision-making (the bank failures). Even if the bank panics were caused by the steep decline in nominal income, which made it far more difficult to repay debts, it is only natural that the first banks to go under would be those who made the most foolish decisions. So it was easy to point fingers and engage in "blaming the victims."

In the current crisis, the situation was slightly different, and even easier to misdiagnose. This time the "victims" really did deserve to be blamed. Banks had made extensive mortgage loans that could only be repaid under the assumption that housing prices would keep increasing. Some of these loans were securitized and sold off, but many of the mortgage-backed bonds were repurchased by banks. After the housing market peaked in mid-2006, construction of new homes declined steadily for several years. By 2007, prices were falling in many of the so-called "subprime markets" (California, Nevada, Arizona, and Florida). This put increasing stress on the U.S. banking system. By April 2008, the IMF (International Monetary Fund) estimated total losses at $945 billion, and a major investment bank (Bear Stearns) was bailed out by the federal government.

The severe and prolonged housing slump from mid-2006 to mid-2008 did not produce a major recession. Although the business cycle peak was officially dated as December 2007, by mid-2008, unemployment had risen only modestly, and most forecasters continued to predict economic growth ahead. In the second quarter of 2008, real GDP continued to grow. This is how market economies are supposed to work. When there has been overinvestment in one sector (housing), resources should migrate into those sectors that are still booming (services and exports). And that is precisely what did occur for a period of about two years, as the housing sector declined in a very orderly fashion. Then, beginning in August 2008, the downturn in housing spread all across the economy. (See Figure 5.1.) By October 2008, both the U.S. and world economies were in near free-fall. Indices of exports and industrial output in many countries were falling at rates not seen since the Great Depression.

In retrospect, it is not surprising that most observers saw the severe slump that began in August 2008 as simply more of the same. The sharp fall in industrial production during August was not announced until late September,

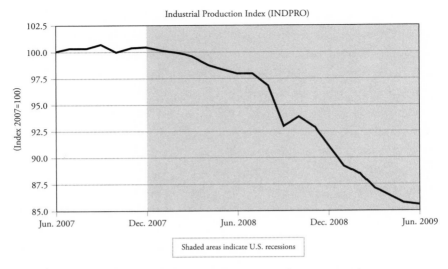

Figure 5.1. U.S. Monthly Industrial Production; Mid-2007 to Mid-2009
Source: Board of Governors of the Federal Reserve System

by which time the news was dominated by a worsening of the financial crisis, especially the failure of a major investment bank (Lehman Brothers). In fact, the nature of the crisis changed dramatically between July and October 2008. What had been a period of sluggish growth and the reallocation of resources out of housing, turned into generalized decline in aggregate demand, which depressed output and prices in many sectors unrelated to housing. It was as if a common cold had quietly turned into pneumonia, but was still being treated as a cold virus. By October 2008, the only "antibiotic" capable of arresting the decline was monetary stimulus, but the Fed was focused on rescuing the financial system, and it let monetary policy drift.

In my view, the crisis of September–October 2008 was quite similar to the crisis of September–October 1929 (or September–October 1937, for that matter). There was a sudden loss of confidence in monetary policy, which led to a sharp decline in NGDP growth expectation going several years out into the future. Unfortunately, we do not have a liquid NGDP futures market, but there is strong circumstantial evidence for this expectations shift in the behavior of asset prices and non-housing output. The following changes occurred in late 2008:

1. Real interest rates rose sharply. Between mid-July and late November 2008, the real yield on five-year Treasury Inflation Protected Securities (TIPS) rose from 0.57 percent to over 4.2 percent.
2. Inflation expectations plunged sharply. The spread between conventional and indexed bonds briefly inverted, indicating deflationary expectations.
3. Commodity prices plunged. The IMF index fell from 218 in July 2008 to only 98 in December 2008.
4. The price of foreign exchange fell as the dollar appreciated. The euro fell from about $1.57 in early July to roughly $1.25 in mid-November 2008.
5. Stock prices plunged. The S&P 500 fell from 1285 in early July to a low of 752 on November 20, 2008.
7. The decline in housing prices spread from the subprime markets to formerly stable areas such as Texas.
8. The commercial property market, which had held up well during the initial housing downturn, also became severely depressed.

None of these indicators, considered in isolation, provides conclusive proof that monetary policy became tighter in the second half of 2008. But together they provide a wealth of circumstantial evidence that policy tightened. Why then did most economists seem to assume that Fed policy was "easy" or "accommodative" during this period? And if monetary policy did tighten during late 2008, precisely what did or didn't the Fed do that caused this change in the stance of monetary policy? And how can we measure the stance of monetary policy?

For a variety of reasons, most people (both economists and non-economists) think of monetary policy in terms of interest rates. There are a variety of reasons for framing policy in this way. First, interest rates are the easiest way to visualize the transmission mechanism of monetary policy. Later I will argue this is not an important transmission mechanism, but we can all visualize how an individual or small business might be more likely to borrow and invest in a new house or factory if interest rates were to decline. In addition, because prices are sticky in the short run, changes in the money supply often move short-term interest rates in the opposite direction. This "liquidity effect" is actually surprisingly hard to identify, but nonetheless is what most people have in mind by "monetary policy." Easy money is equated with low interest rates, whether achieved by monetary injections or decreases in the demand for credit.

More sophisticated economists might point to real interest rates as being the more appropriate indicator of monetary policy. However, when interacting with economists, I find little evidence that they pay much attention to real rates. When I point out that money was quite tight during late 2008, many are rather shocked and ask why I consider it to have been tight, despite very low interest rates. I respond that interest rates are a very poor indicator of the stance of monetary policy; after all, rates are high during hyperinflation, and almost no one considers money to have been tight. Often the economist will then suggest that real interest rates are the appropriate indicator. But I soon discover that very few are even aware that real interest rates (TIPS yields) soared between July and November 2008, right when the economy turned sharply lower. (See Figure 5.2.) Although economists pay lip service to the importance of real rates, it seems few even bother to examine the level of this supposedly important variable.

In fact, as a monetary policy indicator, real interest rates are only slightly better than nominal rates. Robert King showed that in a forward-looking model with rational expectations, a tight money policy can depress both nominal and real interest rates, by depressing the expected growth rate in real GDP.[2] Something like that may have happened in December 2007, when a more contractionary than expected Fed policy statement depressed Treasury yields from three months to thirty years, and also caused a roughly 2 percent drop in the S&P 500 right after the 2:15 p.m. announcement.

The problems with using interest rates as monetary policy indicators is (or should be) well known. In the number one money and banking textbook, Frederic Mishkin emphasizes the following three ideas:[3]

1. It is dangerous always to associate the easing or the tightening of monetary policy with a fall or a rise in short-term nominal interest rates.

2. Other asset prices besides those on short-term debt instruments contain important information about the stance of monetary policy because

---

2. Robert G. King, "Will the New Keynesian Macroeconomics Resurrect the IS-LM Model?" *Journal of Economic Perspectives* 7, no. 1 (1993): 67–82.
3. Frederic Mishkin, *The Economics of Money, Banking and Financial Markets* (Boston: Pearson Education Inc., 8th ed. 2008), 606–07.

Figure 5.2 Real Interest Rates on Treasury Bonds with a
Roughly 5-year Maturity; July to November 2008
Source: Dow Jones & Company, Haver Analytics

they are important elements in various monetary policy transmission
mechanisms.

3. Monetary policy can be highly effective in reviving a weak economy even
if short-term rates are already near zero.

It is difficult to look at that list without thinking of the current crisis. Have
economists actually absorbed these basic ideas? In commenting on the situation
in Japan, Milton Friedman expressed some doubts about how much progress
we have made in identifying the stance of monetary policy:[4]

Low interest rates are generally a sign that money has been tight, as in
Japan; high interest rates, that money has been easy. . . . After the U.S.
experience during the Great Depression, and after inflation and rising
interest rates in the 1970s and disinflation and falling interest rates in
the 1980s, I thought the fallacy of identifying tight money with high

4. Milton Friedman, "Reviving Japan," *Hoover Digest*, 1998, no. 2.

interest rates and easy money with low interest rates was dead. Apparently, old fallacies never die.

If it were merely a question of interest rates, I doubt that most economists would have overlooked the contractionary nature of Fed policy during late 2008; the identification problem in monetary policy is hardly a secret. But there was a second factor that made it even more difficult to identify the stance of policy. Between September and November 2008, the monetary base roughly doubled. Almost all of the monetary injections ended up in excess reserves. Unfortunately, the monetary base is nearly as unreliable a policy indicator as interest rates. During the early 1930s, the monetary base increased sharply, and yet today most economists (including Ben Bernanke) argue that policy was far too contractionary during that period.

One way the current crisis differed from the Great Depression was that the broader aggregates actually increased during 2008, whereas the aggregates fell sharply in the early 1930s. But during the 1980s, most economists came to the conclusion that the monetary aggregates are also not reliable monetary policy indicators. Demand for M1 and M2 tends to rise when interest rates are falling, as during 1982 and 2008.

At this point, it may seem as if there are no reliable indicators of policy. Lars Svensson argued that central banks should not focus on intermediate targets, but rather should directly try to target the forecast of the goal variable.[5] Thus if the central bank has a goal of 2 percent inflation, then the monetary instrument should be adjusted until the forecast equals the goal, that is, until 2 percent inflation is expected. If the policy goal was 2 percent inflation, but 3 percent inflation was expected, then policy could be said to be too expansionary, and vice versa. Under this sort of "targeting the forecast" approach, the stance of monetary policy is always defined relative to the policy goal. This approach recognizes that there is no objective standard by which to call a monetary policy "expansionary"; rather, all we can say is that the policy is "expansionary relative to the policy goals."

---

5. Lars E.O. Svensson, "What is Wrong with Taylor Rules? Using Judgment in Monetary Policy Through Targeting Rules," *Journal of Economic Literature* 41 (2003): 426–77.

Next we need to determine the Fed's actual policy goal. Here we seem to run into a problem, as the Fed does not have an explicit policy goal, rather it has a dual mandate; stable prices and high employment. It is widely believed that the Fed does have an *implicit* inflation target, that it defines "price stability" as roughly 2 percent inflation. But there is also evidence that it doesn't strictly target inflation, but rather has some sort of "flexible inflation target," which takes into account both inflation and deviations in output from potential. The most famous example of a flexible inflation target is the Taylor Rule, in which the short-term policy rate is adjusted to keep inflation close to 2 percent and output close to potential. For our purposes, the exact form of the Taylor Rule is not important. No one believes that the Fed follows any particular rigid formula; rather, what matters is that it aims for roughly 2 percent inflation in the long run, and it attempts to "lean against the wind" when output is above or below potential.

There are obvious similarities between NGDP rules and the Taylor Rule. Both aim to maintain low and stable inflation in the long run, but both allow for some fluctuation in inflation during supply shocks. Thus, higher than 2 percent inflation might be appropriate during periods in which output is depressed, and vice versa. Nor is this sort of dual mandate particularly novel. Liaquat Ahamed argued that as far back as the 1920s, New York Fed President Benjamin Strong was basing monetary policy decisions on "the trend in prices and the level of business activity."[6]

If the Fed's monetary policy goal was something closely akin to NGDP targeting, then how can I claim that NGDP targeting would have prevented the crash of 2008? There are three answers to this question. First, Fed policy tends to be somewhat backward-looking, like someone steering a ship while looking backward, not in the direction that one hopes to travel. In contrast, the Svenssonian approach would have the Fed set its steering in such a way that, taking wind and currents into account, the captain *expected* to end up precisely where he *wished* to end up.

A perfect illustration of the distinction between forward and backward-looking monetary policies occurred on September 16, 2008. The Fed met to

---

6. Liaquat Ahamed, *Lords of Finance: The Bankers Who Broke the World* (New York: Penguin Press, 2009), 294.

discuss monetary policy just a couple days after the markets had been unnerved by the failure of Lehman. After the meeting the Fed issued a statement that pointed to roughly balanced risks of inflation and recession, then decided to keep the short-term target rate unchanged at 2 percent. It is easy to understand why the Fed would have cited a risk of recession in September 2008, after all, the U.S. economy had actually been in a mild recession since December 2007, and conditions had worsened in recent weeks. More troubling is the Fed's concern about inflation. Although the Fed did not explicitly say so, it was clear that the "risks" it referred to were risks of *excessively high* inflation, not low inflation. And it is not hard to understand why: we had just been through a period of high oil prices, which had pushed headline inflation to worrisome levels.

Nevertheless, a forward-looking Svenssonian approach would have reached exactly the opposite conclusion. The implied five-year inflation forecast in the TIPS markets showed the expected inflation rate falling from over 2 percent in mid-2008, to only 1.23 percent on the eve of the meeting. After the Fed decided not to cut rates, it fell again to 1.03 percent on the following day. In fact, at the time of the Fed meeting the risks were of recession and *excessively low* inflation, far below the Fed's implicit target. Under those circumstances, the Fed clearly would have eased if it had been following a forward-looking Svenssonian approach. We now know that the TIPS markets were much closer to the truth than the Fed, as inflation since September 2008 has fallen to very low levels.

The second problem with Fed policy is that it relies too heavily on nominal interest rates as the instrument of policy. It has long been known that a policy of simply pegging nominal interest rates at a fixed level will leave the price level indeterminate. During normal times, the Fed is able to use nominal interest rates as a policy instrument, as long as it moves them aggressively enough to keep the price level anchored. The Taylor Principle suggests that the policy rate must rise and fall more than one-for-one with changes in the expected inflation rate, in order to move real interest rates in the appropriate direction.

Although interest rate targeting worked pretty well during the "Great Moderation," there is a problem with using interest rates as a policy lever; nominal rates cannot fall below zero. To return to the analogy of steering a boat, the steering mechanism becomes locked in one direction once the rate hits zero. Again, the Fed is well aware of this problem, and Bernanke has emphasized the importance of avoiding this sort of "liquidity trap" at all costs. The Fed's eagerness to avoid this situation (especially after observing the hapless Bank of Japan) probably explains why the Fed lowered the fed funds target down to 1 percent in 2003, when there were fears of deflation. Later this policy was blamed for inflating the housing bubble. I'm not convinced that Fed policy was decisive in the housing bubble (low rates don't imply easy money), but this perception probably goes a long way toward explaining why the Fed was reluctant to immediately lower rates below 2 percent when the crisis intensified in September 2008.

Later we will see that the so-called "liquidity trap" is not a trap at all. Nonetheless, the zero bound on interest rates can become a problem if the central bank does not know how to use unconventional monetary tools, or is too conservative to do so. In that case markets may rationally expect monetary policy to fail, and the economy to undershoot the Fed's inflation and output goals. And if the markets expect policy to fail, then the Fed has a much more difficult time steering the economy. As we will see in the section below entitled "Why NGDP Is Important," markets react much more strongly to future expected policy than they do to the current stance of policy.

For simplicity, I will henceforth refer to the Fed's dual mandate as a single goal, roughly 5 percent NGDP growth. Why pick 5 percent? First, this is roughly the average growth rate in NGDP between 1992 and 2008. And second, the long-term U.S. growth rate of real GDP is roughly 3 percent, and hence the Fed's implicit inflation target of about 2 percent suggests that they are aiming for approximately 5 percent NGDP growth. None of the following assertions hinge on that specific number being exactly right, rather it provides a simple way to visualize the dual mandate, and should at least allow us to identify periods where policy had gone far off course.

By early October 2008, the markets were rapidly losing confidence in the Fed's ability to maintain roughly 5 percent NGDP growth going forward. It was obvious to almost everyone that the world was slipping into a severe slump. The Fed eventually did move on October 8, cutting the feds funds target from 2.0 percent to 1.5 percent, but this was far too little, too late. Rates on T-bills were already much lower, and the United States was widely seen as having entered a liquidity trap, even with the Fed still holding 150 basis points of "unused ammunition." There was increasing discussion of the need for fiscal stimulus.

Even worse, the Fed introduced a new and highly contractionary policy in early October 2008: interest on reserves. The Fed decided to implement this policy on Friday, October 3, and it announced the decision on Monday, October 6. The policy had the effect of increasing the demand for excess reserves, and effectively sterilized the massive reserve injections that were occurring at this time. It was essentially the same mistake the Fed made in 1936–37, when it doubled reserve requirements out of fear that the huge overhang of excess reserves would eventually lead to inflation. And the effects were similar to 1937; in 2009, the United States saw the largest decrease in NGDP since 1938. During the first ten days of October, stock investors probably realized that the Fed would not or could not prevent a severe drop in nominal spending. The stock market crashed, with the S&P 500 falling by 23 percent in just the first ten days of the month.

The final mistake in Fed policy was the most costly; it engaged in targeting inflation rates, rather than price levels. The Fed has a "memory-less" approach, which means it doesn't try to correct for previous undershoots or overshoots of its target variables. The alternative policy of "level targeting" doesn't mean that one must keep the price level or NGDP fixed. Rather, it requires the Fed to set a target trajectory for the goal variable and commit to return to that target path should that variable temporarily fall short or overshoot. In late 2008, it became clear that NGDP growth would fall far short of the Fed's implicit target over the next few months, and, even worse, that the Fed had no plan to catch up. All the focus was on rescuing banking; monetary policy had been effectively placed on a back burner.

Unfortunately, the weakening economy was rapidly eroding bank balance sheets. The Fed was bailing water out of a leaky boat without first taking the time to plug the hole through which water was pouring in. The "hole" was sharply falling NGDP expectations one, two, three years out, which fed back and reduced current assets prices. As asset prices fell, bank balance sheets worsened dramatically. By April 2009, IMF estimates of U.S. banking system losses had tripled from a year earlier, when the subprime crisis was already well understood. Later in this paper, we will see just how costly the Fed's mistake was.

Even when presented with all this information, some economists have trouble grasping the idea that monetary policy became much tighter in late 2008. What exactly caused this to occur? And why did it occur at that particular time? Unfortunately, because interest rates are poor indicators of monetary policy, we can only speculate. Part of the problem was clearly the Fed's tardiness in cutting rates. The fed funds target remained at 2 percent from late April to early October 2008, even as the economy was weakening rapidly. Some economists visualize policy in terms of Wicksell's natural rate of interest, i.e., the rate which leads to macroeconomic stability (stable prices, in Wicksell's example). Using this approach, it is likely that the worsening financial environment and weakening housing sector reduced the natural rate of interest. As the natural rate fell further and further below the unchanging policy rate, monetary policy became effectively much tighter.

If one examines policy from the perspective of supply and demand for money, the mistake occurred when the Fed failed to supply enough liquidity during the initial stages of the crisis, and then later locked up a liquidity injection with the interest rate on reserves program after October 6, 2008. But I think the best way of visualizing the policy failure is in terms of the Fed's failure to credibly communicate a strategy. Ben Bernanke is well aware of the advantages offered by level targeting. Level targeting tends to stabilize expectations if prices begin to fall, as the expected rate of inflation would then automatically tend to increase. In 2003, Bernanke recommended that the BOJ (Bank of Japan) adopt just such a policy.[7] But when the United States entered a period of falling prices and near-zero interest rates in late 2008, the Fed proved just as timid as the BOJ, unwilling to experiment with the sort of price level targeting that Bernanke had recommended (correctly in my view) as a solution to the Japanese zero rate bound problem.

Why NGDP Is Important

In this section, I discuss how monetary policy affects NGDP, and why it is preferable to inflation as both a policy indicator and a policy target. I'd like to begin by suggesting why the traditional Keynesian and monetarist transmission mechanisms are inadequate.

In the cutting edge of macroeconomic theory, there is increasing emphasis on the role of policy expectations. For instance, Michael Woodford argues that changes in the expected future path of policy are much more important than

---

7. Ben Bernanke, "Some Thoughts on Monetary Policy in Japan" (speech given to the Japan Society of Monetary Economics, May, 31, 2003).

changes in the current stance of policy.[8] In an earlier paper (1993),[9] I stumbled on this idea with the following thought experiment: Suppose the Fed suddenly doubles the money supply, and also commits to pull the money out of circulation a year later. What will be the impact on the price level, and NGDP? The simplest version of the Quantity Theory of Money would predict that prices and NGDP should immediately double, and then fall back to the original level a year later. But even a moment's thought makes clear that this cannot be the equilibrium path if the policy is anticipated. Why would someone pay $400,000 for a house expected to be worth only $200,000 a year later (after the money is withdrawn from circulation)? Instead, nominal interest rates would fall close to zero, and the extra money would be mostly hoarded. Prices might rise slightly, but only enough so that the deflation that was expected to return prices to their original level offered cash holders a real return equal to the real rate of interest. The key point is that the current price level and current NGDP are far more affected by the future expected money supply than they are by the current money supply. Woodford showed that the same principle applied to interest rates.

In 1993, I had no idea that within twenty years both the Bank of Japan (BOJ) and the Fed would attempt an experiment quite similar to what I just discussed. Both central banks dramatically increased their monetary bases, and in both cases they promised that the monetary injections were temporary, so as to reduce fears of runaway inflation. Indeed, the BOJ later withdrew much of its currency injections from 2002–03.

In 1933, we saw a very different kind of experiment. This time the government actually wanted to raise prices higher and therefore enacted a policy that would credibly lead to higher future money supplies and higher future price levels. Interestingly, there were no monetary injections and no significant cut in interest rates. Instead, FDR sharply devalued the dollar. Because the public understood that in the long run the dollar would be re-attached to gold at a lower value, and that a higher price of gold meant inflation in the long run, inflation expectations increased as the dollar depreciated. The efficient markets hypothesis tells us that an increase in future expected prices will immediately

---

8. Michael Woodford, *Interest and Prices* (Princeton: University of Princeton Press, 2001).

9. Scott Sumner, "Colonial Currency and the Quantity Theory of Money: A Critique of Smith's Interpretation." *Journal of Economic History* 53, no. 1 (1993): 139–45.

increase the current price of assets traded in auction-style markets. As a result, the prices of commodities and equities rose rapidly as the dollar depreciated.

The strong rally in asset prices during 1933 was actually due to two distinct factors. First, the devaluation of the dollar increased the future expected price level. That would tend to increase the current prices of flexible price goods and assets. Second, because the economy was severely depressed in 1933, higher expected prices and nominal GDP also increased the expected rate of real GDP growth. Industrial production shot up by 57 percent between March and July 1933. Expectations of recovery also increased the real prices of cyclical assets such as stocks, commodities and commercial real estate. If this sounds familiar, it is exactly the reverse of what occurred in late 2008, when asset prices plunged in response to falling NGDP expectations.

Robert A. Mundell called the 1933–34 dollar devaluation the pivotal event in twentieth century monetary policy.[10] I would argue that it was the most powerful monetary shock in American history—creating inflation of over 20 percent at the wholesale level, despite record unemployment rates. (See Figure 5.3.) This experiment shows that monetary policy works exactly as Woodford suggested; changes in expected future monetary policy and aggregate demand drives current changes in aggregate demand. Our trade balance actually worsened, so the terms of trade effects were minor. The devaluation powerfully influenced asset prices, despite almost no change in current levels of interest rates and the monetary base. Real interest rates may have fallen, but, as Robert King showed,[11] even that result isn't necessary for a monetary shock to have a stimulative effect. All that is required is that the policy change be credible, i.e., that the policy is expected to change the path of prices and NGDP over time.

The same transmission mechanism occurs during normal times, but it is much harder to identify because the changes are smaller and monetary policy is usually merely trying to prevent random shocks from moving the economy off target. Under those conditions, interest rates *seem* to be important, but are actually a sort of epiphenomenon, disguising the real transmission mechanism. Central banks send signals about future policy intentions through a variety

---

10. Robert A. Mundell, "A Reconsideration of the Twentieth Century," *American Economic Review* 90, no. 3 (2000): 327–40.

11. King, "Will the New Keynesian Macroeconomics Resurrect the IS-LM Model?"

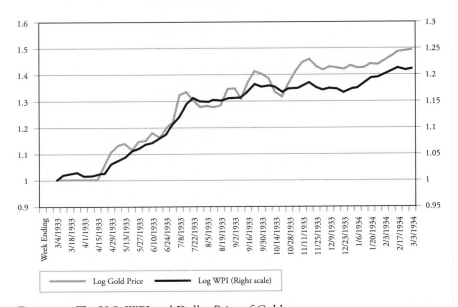

Figure 5.3. The U.S. WPI and Dollar Price of Gold

Sources: The gold prices are from various issues of the *New York Times* from 1933.
The wholesale price index is from various issues of the *Federal Reserve Bulletin* from 1933.

of channels, including interest rate targets. A change in the interest rate target affects the expected future money supply. Because the quantity theory holds in the long run, expectations of future excess cash balances tends to increase future expected NGDP. This immediately impacts the current prices of stocks, commodities and real estate. And finally, the changes in both future expected NGDP and current asset prices impact current aggregate demand.

But why focus on NGDP growth rather than inflation? There are a number of reasons. Let's start with the concept of the "liquidity trap" or zero rate bound. Most economists see this problem as something that occurs when an economy is mired in deflation. Japan, Hong Kong, and China all experienced deflation in the late 1990s, yet only Japan ran up against the zero rate bound. The reason is not hard to understand. Although all three countries experienced mild deflation, Hong Kong and China had much more rapid trend rates of real GDP growth than Japan, and hence much higher rates of nominal GDP growth. A liquidity trap is not so much associated with low inflation as it is with low

NGDP growth. This is because the two components of interest rates—the real rate and the expected inflation rate—are closely linked to the two components of expected NGDP growth: expected real growth and expected inflation. The expected inflation components are identical, and the real interest rate is positively correlated with the expected real GDP growth rate.

Another example occurred in Australia, which for many years has had significantly higher nominal interest rates than most other developed economies. There were two primary reasons for Australia's relatively high nominal interest rates. First, its trend rate of inflation was a bit higher than that of most other developed countries. But more importantly, its trend real GDP growth rate was significantly higher than that of most other developed economies. This was partly a reflection of respectable growth in per capita real GDP, and partly a reflection of a much higher-than-typical population growth rate (driven by high rates of immigration). Interestingly, Australia avoided a liquidity trap in 2008–09, and it was also the only developed country to avoid outright recession. I don't want to make too much of these examples. Other factors undoubtedly played a role, but when we think about the risks of liquidity traps, we need to pay more attention to NGDP growth and less attention to inflation. Japan has had about 1 percent per year deflation (using the GDP deflator) since 1994. The United States got by with mild deflation at times during the nineteenth century; but Japan has slow growth and a falling population, making it perhaps the worst place in the world to be conducting deflationary monetary policies.

The second great advantage of NGDP targeting is that (compared to inflation targeting) it would reduce the severity of recessions when the economy is buffeted by a supply shock. Both NGDP and inflation targeting try to fully offset a change in velocity. It is during supply shocks such as an oil embargo that NGDP targeting is superior. If the price of imported oil were to rise sharply, then under an inflation target, the Fed would be forced to deflate all non-oil prices. If we assume that nominal wages are somewhat sticky, then the deflation of non-oil prices would raise unemployment. With NGDP targeting, the Fed allows the overall inflation rate to rise a bit above normal when an adverse supply shock depresses real output, and vice versa when there is strong growth in the economy's supply side, as during the late 1990s. It doesn't prevent real shocks from having an effect on real GDP, but when those shocks occur it reduces the scale of job losses resulting from disequilibrium in the labor market.

Table 5.1. IMF Forecasts of Key Macro Variables and
Total U.S. Financial System Losses

Date of Forecast	2009	2010	2009+2010	Est. Financial Losses
April '08 RGDP	+0.6%	+3.0%*	+3.6%	($945b.)
April '08 CPI	+2.0%	+2.0%*	+4.0%	
Oct. '08 RGDP	+0.1%	+3.0%*	+3.1%	($1405b.)
Oct. '08 CPI	+1.8%	+2.0%*	+3.8%	
Jan. '09 RGDP	−1.6%	+1.6%	0.0%	($2216b.)
April '09 RGDP	−2.8%	0.0%	−2.8%	
April '09 CPI	−0.9%	−0.1%	−1.0%	($2712b.)
July '09 RGDP	−2.6%	0.8%	−1.8%	($1868b.)
Oct. '09 RGDP	−2.7%	+1.5%	−1.2%	($1025b.)
Oct. '09 CPI	−0.4%	+1.7%	+1.3%	
Jan. '10 RGDP	−2.4%	+2.0%	−0.4%	
April '10 RGDP	−2.4%	+3.0%	+0.6%	($885b.)
April '10 CPI	−0.3%	+2.1%	+1.8%	

*No 2010 forecasts were available in 2008. The 3% RGDP growth and 2% inflation figures
represent long-run trend. Forecasts for the "out years" are typically close to trend, hence
these estimates should be accurate enough to show the sharp change in expectations.

Most U.S. recessions since World War II have not been accompanied by
extreme financial distress. Nevertheless, the events of the past several years show
that it would be better if the monetary policy target reduced the likelihood of
a major financial panic. I do not wish to claim that NGDP targeting would
eliminate the risk of financial crisis. Some have argued that a 5 percent NGDP
target during 2004–06 would have led to a tighter monetary policy, and thus
restrained the housing bubble. I think this is partly true, but I am not certain
how significant the difference would have been. On the other hand, I am very
confident that NGDP targeting would have reduced the severity of the subsequent housing bust and financial crisis.

In the following table, I have provided IMF forecasts of U.S. RGDP growth,
inflation, and estimates of the eventual size of losses to the U.S. financial system
since the crisis began in 2007. In generally, macro forecasts more than one year
into the future are quite difficult. I have assumed that the IMF forecasts during
2010 would have been roughly equal to the long-run trend rates of real growth
and inflation in the United States. (Those forecasts are shown with a asterisk.)

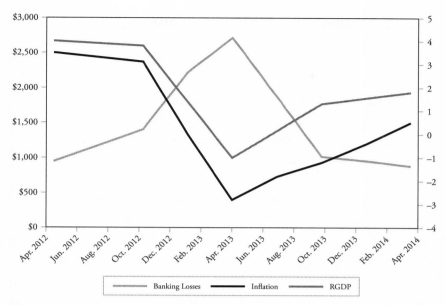

Figure 5.4. IMF Estimates of U.S. Banking Losses (in Billions), as Well as Inflation and RGDP Growth Rates for 2009 and 2010 (Combined)

Source: IMF's *Global Financial Stability Report,* various issues.

Slight adjustments in that assumption would not have significantly changed the qualitative results in this table. I have also constructed an (admittedly crude) estimate of the IMF's implied NGDP forecasts, by adding RGDP growth and CPI inflation forecasts (Table 5.1).

No 2010 forecasts were available in 2008. The 3-percent RGDP growth and 2-percent inflation figures represent long-run trend. Forecasts for the "out years" are typically close to trend; hence these estimates should be accurate enough to show the sharp change in expectations.

A few observations:

1. All three series show a similar pattern. RGDP growth and inflation forecasts deteriorated steadily until about April 2009, and then rebounded. Estimated eventual U.S. financial system losses from the beginning of the crisis in 2007 showed the same pattern. Estimated losses peaked when the economic forecasts were weakest and then fell sharply. (See Figure 5.4.)

2. The dates in Figure 5.4 refer to the IMF reports and may lag actual economic changes by about a month. This suggests the economy's actual low point may have been March 2009, which is also when U.S. equity markets hit their lows.

3. The most dramatic deterioration in growth forecasts occurred between October and April 2009, which was when the financial crisis got much worse. This suggests that if the Fed had maintained 5 percent NGDP growth in 2009 and 2010, the financial crisis would have been far milder. It is possible that the financial crisis would have intensified even if the Fed had maintained faster NGDP growth; however, in that case, the subsequent improvement in RGDP and inflation forecasts should not have dramatically reduced estimated financial system losses.

Some might argue that if the Fed had stimulated faster NGDP growth, it would have merely bailed out "irresponsible" borrowers. Exactly the reverse is true. Loans made between 2000 and 2007 presumably reflected an expectation of roughly 5 percent NGDP growth, as that had been the historical norm. It was the Fed's decision to allow much lower NGDP growth that distorted the credit markets. The Fed's passivity meant that borrowers faced an unfair burden, which could not rationally have been forecast when the loans were made. This is not to say that there weren't many irresponsible loans. Note that as early as April 2008, even before NGDP began falling, there were already massive expected loan losses, many as a result of foolish subprime lending. The Fed's mistake was to make a pre-existing problem much worse.

Some might ask why I focus on how NGDP growth affected the financial crisis. More often one hears discussions of how lenders and borrowers are impacted by inflation, not NGDP growth. But NGDP is indeed the right variable. Most loans are nominal debt, and thus nominal income is the best indicator of a borrower's ability to repay a loan. If prices fall 10 percent in a period of stable output, it is much harder for borrowers to repay debts. But this is equally true if real output falls 10 percent in a period of stable prices. It is NGDP growth, not inflation, which best measures the impact of macroeconomic conditions on credit markets.

Another advantage of NGDP is that it more accurately measures the size of nominal shocks hitting the U.S. economy. Existing price indices are highly flawed, especially when the economy is buffeted by a demand shock. Consider the closely watched core CPI. The BLS (Bureau of Labor Statistics) reported in July 2009 that the core CPI had risen 1.7 percent over the past twelve months. During the same period, the housing component of the core CPI was reported to have increased by 2.1 percent. That's right, during the greatest housing price collapse in American history, the BLS reported that housing costs were increasing, even in real terms! And because housing is 39 percent of the core CPI, this had a major impact on the reported rate of inflation. If the housing component had fallen 2.1 percent, instead of risen by that amount, then reported inflation would have be approximately zero. This might have led the Fed to be much more aggressive in its program of "quantitative easing."

The BLS data does not take into account the rapidly falling prices of new houses, but instead relies on the "rental equivalent." But even rents are not measured accurately. The BLS surveys both new and existing rental agreements, even though the latter are not true "prices."[12] And it ignores the widespread practice of offering one to two months rent free on new leases, which was much more common in the depths of the recession. In simple terms, the way the BLS measures the cost of living has only a weak correlation with the economic concept of "price" that is relevant in macro models of the economy. In contrast, NGDP data did show a severe nominal shock between mid-2008 and mid-2009, with nominal NGDP falling about 4.0 percent, or more than 9 percent below trend.

In my view, one of the strongest arguments for NGDP targeting is political. One important lesson coming out of this crisis is the acute need for more policy transparency. As of mid-2008, markets expected the Fed to allow for substantial growth in NGDP over the next year. Both wage and debt contracts were negotiated on that assumption. Yet once the crisis hit, the Fed allowed NGDP growth expectations to fall far below the historical norm. In late 2008, it wasn't clear where nominal aggregates were headed, nor what the Fed planned to do about it. By late 2009, many Fed officials were discussing the need to tighten monetary policy, despite that fact that every single major aggregate had risen far slower than the assumed Fed target and was expected to continue undershooting for

---

12. Calling the rent payment on an existing rental contract a "price" is conceptually equivalent to calling a monthly payment on a twenty-year old mortgage a price.

the foreseeable future. These Fed officials warned of the danger of higher inflation (even though TIPS markets were expressing exactly the opposite fear, as
well as fears that low interest rates could trigger more asset bubbles). Was the
Fed targeting asset prices, macro aggregates, or some combination? No one
seemed to know, and the Fed wasn't saying (Fed committee members probably
didn't agree among themselves).

Under those circumstances, a clear nominal target, almost any target, would
be better than the current confusion. But which target? In my view, NGDP is
the only possible monetary policy target that might achieve a strong enough
political consensus to be implemented. At first this might appear surprising, as
inflation targets are increasingly common throughout the world. But there was
strong Congressional opposition to a simple inflation target even before the current crisis, and the Fed's inept performance since 2008 can hardly have softened
that opposition. Inflation targets are increasing seen as a shield that conservatives
hide behind when they are opposed to additional monetary stimulus. Many on
the left assume that proponents of inflation targeting care only about the bond
market, not unemployed workers. I don't think those charges are entirely fair,
but I just don't see any prospect of getting a political consensus behind a simple
inflation target, regardless of the rate.

In contrast, NGDP targeting has advantages that appeal to people on both
the left and the right. For those on the left, it offers a policy target that puts
equal weight on prices and output. Because employment is strongly correlated
with output at cyclical frequencies, it implicitly addresses the Fed's dual mandate: prices and employment. During the current recession, a NGDP target
would have forced the Fed to become much more aggressive. It was possible
for inflation hawks at the Fed to hide behind the 1.7 percent twelve-month core
inflation in mid-2009, insisting that inflation was close to target. In contrast,
NGDP growth had fallen more than 9 percent below trend. Given the current
conservative bias at most central banks, liberals might welcome an explicit
target that weakens the position of the inflation hawks.

For those on the right, NGDP targeting offers other equally important
advantages. First, it provides a nominal anchor that would effectively control
inflation in the long run. For instance, a 4- percent NGDP target would probably result in roughly 1 percent to 2 percent inflation in the long run, given

current projections of future RGDP growth. In addition, it is a statistic that is not easily manipulated by government bureaucrats for political reasons. If politicians were to pressure the BLS to stop doing quality adjustments so that Social Security recipients could get higher benefits, that action will have no effect on monetary policy under NGDP targeting. A third advantage is that it preserves a single policy target. Conservative economists tend to emphasize the fact that the Fed can only control one variable, and worry that if employment becomes a policy target then the Fed might lose control of inflation. Others worry that the dual mandate gives the Fed too much discretion. An explicit NGDP target would severely restrict the Fed's strategic discretion; they would no longer be able to pick and choose which aspect of their dual mandate to focus on at a particular point of time.

George Selgin found that nominal income rules were very popular in the interwar period, with well-known proponents such as Friedrich Hayek.[13] Selgin himself is sympathetic to the idea, although he prefers a slightly different version that would stabilize aggregate factor prices.[14] Nominal GDP targeting can appeal to monetarists because it is easy to explain using the Equation of Exchange; the money supply adjusts to offset changes in velocity. Ironically, this should also appeal to Keynesians, as their traditional complaint about strict money supply targets is that they don't account for instability in velocity. Because it places equal weight on price level and output stabilization, NGDP targeting resembles some versions of the highly popular Taylor Rule.

Finally, there is the advantage of simplicity, which makes NGDP a sort of focal point in an area where there is enormous disagreement. Given that there are almost as many proposed policy rules as there are macroeconomists, it's unlikely that a consensus could be reached on minimizing some loss function of price and output deviations that was expressed in a complex equation, even if it was slightly better that an NGDP target, which implicitly puts equal weight on the two components.

---

13. George Selgin, "The 'Productivity Norm' vs. Zero Inflation in the History of Economic Thought," *History of Political Economy* 27 (1995): 705–35.
14. George Selgin, "Less Than Zero: The Case for a Falling Price Level in a Growing Economy" (London: Institute of Economic Affairs Occasional Paper, 1997).

How an NGDP Futures Market Can Assist Policymakers

Suppose the Fed decides to target NGDP growth at some number like 4 percent or 5 percent. How does it actually implement the policy? Here we need to return to Lars Svensson's "target the forecast" maxim. The most important thing for the Fed to do is stabilize NGDP expectations, not actual NGDP.

Why are expectations so important? I believe their importance lies in the fact that labor contracts are negotiated based on NGDP growth expectations. As they do with debt contracts, many analysts are used to thinking in terms of how inflation affects wage negotiations, but in fact it is NGDP growth that really matters. Consider the following examples. Suppose there is an economy where NGDP per capita grows at 8 percent, and inflation is 2 percent. In most cases you'd expect fairly rapid wage growth, reflecting the fact that nominal national income was rising rapidly. Now assume that NGDP growth falls to 4 percent, but inflation remains at 2 percent. If inflation determined wage growth, you'd expect no change in the rate of nominal wage increases. But in fact, wage growth would almost certainly slow dramatically. This example shows roughly what happened between the high-growth 1960s and slow-growth 1990s in countries like Italy. Or, consider what happened to wage growth in the United States during 2006–08. Inflation rose rapidly (due to high oil prices) but NGDP growth actually slowed slightly. If inflation determined wage growth, one might have expected wages to be rising much faster in mid-2008 than in 2006.

If nominal wage negotiations mostly reflect NGDP expectations, then the best way of stabilizing employment is to have NGDP expectations rise at a stable rate. This will ensure that each new round of wage contract negotiations will be based on roughly the same set of expectations, which means that workers employed under older contracts will not have wage rates that have drifted far from the equilibrium level for newly negotiated contracts. If one pursued the logical implications of this line of reasoning, then a nominal wage rate target would be superior to even an NGDP target. Earl Thompson proposed this idea back in 1982.[15] But having the Fed target nominal wage rates would be a difficult sell politically, and there are also serious measurement issues involved in estimating the average nominal hourly wage rate for the entire economy.

---

15. Earl A. Thompson, "Free Banking under a Labor Standard—The Perfect Monetary System" (UCLA, manuscript, 1982).

The first step toward stabilizing NGDP growth expectations would be the creation of a NGDP future market, in order to derive market forecasts of future NGDP growth. Currently no such market exists; as we will see, this is actually an advantage for policymakers. Suppose the federal government set up a NGDP futures market and subsidized trading to ensure adequate liquidity. In that case, policymakers would be able to make real-time comparisons between their policy target and market NGDP forecasts. One method of subsidizing trading would be to pay a slightly above average rate of return on margin account balances.

There may be a difference between expected future NGDP and the price of a NGDP futures contract, particularly if investors are risk-averse. However, most studies suggest that the risk premium in commodity futures markets is relatively small, and, because no NGDP futures market currently exists, we can infer that the demand for hedging NGDP shocks is rather low. So there is no reason to expect a wide divergence between the NGDP futures price and the rational expectation of future NGDP. Furthermore, a risk premium would not be of much macroeconomic importance unless it was time-varying.

The existence of an NGDP futures market would almost certainly assist monetary policymakers and also make policy decisions more transparent. As we will see, however, this sort of market can do much more than assist policy-makers; it can entirely remove discretion from the policy process.

An NGDP Futures Targeting Regime

Suppose we decide to have the Fed target NGDP expectations. The next questions are: whose expectations, and how do we target them? Lars Svensson suggested that the Fed should target its own inflation forecast, which would be made by an internal economic research group.[16] Why didn't he recommend targeting a market forecast of inflation, such as the TIPS spreads? Svensson was worried about the "circularity problem" discussed in papers by Bernanke and Woodford,[17] and also by Garrison and White.[18]

---

16. Svensson, "What is Wrong with Taylor Rules?"
17. Ben Bernanke and Michael Woodford, "Inflation Forecasts and Monetary Policy," *Journal of Money, Credit and Banking* 29 (1997): 653–84.
18. Roger W. Garrison and Lawrence H. White, "Can Monetary Stabilization Policy be Improved by CPI Futures Targeting?" *Journal of Money, Credit and Banking* 29 (November 1997): 535–41.

The problem is as follows: Suppose the Fed targeted inflation at 2 percent. If inflation expectations ever rose above 2 percent in the TIPS markets, then the Fed would tighten policy until inflation expectations returned to 2 percent. But if the market knew this, and if the policy was credible, then inflation expectations would never rise in the first place. In that case, there would be no signal given for the Fed to tighten monetary policy. It is called a "circularity problem" because the Fed is watching the markets, and the markets are watching the Fed. Even today there is a bit of this circularity problem, but because the Fed doesn't react one-for-one with market forecasts, it hasn't led to an indeterminacy problem.

The circularity problem would be just as much a potential problem for NGDP futures targeting as for inflation targeting. Fortunately, there is another way of using NGDP futures markets that sidesteps the circularity problem. Bernanke and Woodford argued that what was really needed wasn't so much market forecasts of the goal variable (inflation or NGDP), but rather market forecasts of the monetary instrument setting that would achieve the policy goal.[19] Unfortunately, they overlooked the fact that my 1989 NGDP futures targeting proposal (as well as Kevin Dowd's 1994 inflation futures targeting proposal) had done just that.[20]

Because this is such an unconventional policy concept, it will be useful to approach it in a roundabout fashion.[21] Let's suppose that the Federal Open Market Committee (FOMC) is instructed to set the monetary base at a level expected to produce 5-percent NGDP growth over the following twelve months. How do we motivate the FOMC members? The prediction market literature suggests that when money is at stake, you are more likely to get truthful revelation of beliefs.[22] One option would be to have the committee vote on an instrument setting for the base, and then reward committee members, ex post, on the basis of the accuracy of their vote. The actual policy setting would be

---

19. Bernanke and Woodford, "Inflation Forecasts and Monetary Policy," 653–84.

20. Kevin Dowd, "A Proposal to End Inflation," *Economic Journal* 104 (1994): 828–40.

21. The following is based on an argument made in Scott Sumner, "Let a Thousand Models Bloom: The Advantages of Making the FOMC a Truly 'Open Market'," *Berkeley Electronic Journals, Contributions to Macroeconomics* 6, no. 1, art. 8 (2006).

22. See J. Wolfers and Eric Zitzewitz, "Prediction Markets," *Journal of Economic Perspectives* 18, no. 2 (2004): 107–26.

the median vote. For instance, suppose the medium vote was for a base of $923 billion. Also suppose that a year later NGDP came in above target, say at 6.3 percent growth. In that case, each member who favored a monetary base setting below $923 billion would be deemed correct and would get a monetary reward. The more dovish voters who favored an even larger monetary base would be viewed as having erred, and would pay a monetary penalty.

By itself, the preceding thought experiment might not seem that radical. Most FOMC members are probably pretty idealistic, and presumably do the best they can even without monetary incentives. But once you start looking at policy this way, it is easy to see how the size and scope of the regime could be radically enlarged. For instance, why limit the FOMC to twelve members? Why not allow all 6.8 billion humans to vote? And why one-man-one-vote? In financial markets we typically assume that one-dollar-one-vote produces the most efficient outcome.

If we are serious about setting monetary policy in such a way as to stabilize market NGDP expectations, then logically we'd want the "market" and the FOMC to be identical. The Fed would create and subsidize trading in NGDP futures contracts, with twelve-month or perhaps twenty-four-month maturities. They would establish a highly liquid market by offering to buy or sell unlimited amounts of these contracts at a price equal to the policy target. For instance, suppose that for twelve-month contracts, the payoff value was equal to [(future NGDP/current NGDP)*$1000.] In that case, the Fed would agree to buy or sell unlimited twelve-month NGDP futures at a price of $1,050. Traders might be required to put 10 percent into a margin account, which would earn a competitive rate of interest. The most important aspect of this particular futures market is that each trade would trigger a parallel open market operation in Treasury securities. For example, investors who expected less than 5 percent NGDP growth would sell NGDP futures to the Fed, and each sale would trigger an open market purchase of bonds. Trades would continue until the monetary base was at a level where the market expected on-target NGDP growth.

If the government was serious about using NGDP futures markets, it should probably generate monthly estimates of NGDP (which shouldn't be hard because most of the components are derived from monthly data). It could then estimate daily NGDP by simply taking the weighted average of two consecutive monthly estimates. This would allow a new NGDP contract to be traded each day, which would reduce the problem of traders waiting until the last minute to observe how other traders were impacting the monetary base. Alternatively, there could be auctions of NGDP futures that are contingent on various hypothetical instrument settings. In that case, the only contracts that would be implemented are those at the instrument setting that roughly equated the net long and short positions of traders.

Under this sort of policy regime, NGDP expectations would always remain on target. It would not prevent all fluctuations in real GDP. Real shocks could still occur, but it would reduce the severity of business cycles. It would not completely eliminate financial distress (a subprime crisis could occur even with stable NGDP growth), but it would at least prevent instability in NGDP expectations from needlessly intensifying a financial panic.

Is the preceding policy regime actually feasible? When I presented this idea at the New York Fed in 1989, the general view seemed to be: "interesting idea, but we have a good research staff and can forecast just as well as the markets." While I'm tempted to say "I told you so," in all honesty I don't believe the Fed's problem in 2008 was a lack of forecasting ability, but rather a flawed policymaking apparatus. When Ben Bernanke called for fiscal stimulus in 2008, he surely knew that nominal spending was likely to come in lower than the Fed would have liked. Why else would he have called for fiscal stimulus? Instead, it seems clear that even as the Fed saw demand falling far below its implicit target, it was reluctant to take additional steps due to some sort of fear of the unknown, or perhaps worry that it might spook the markets and overshoot toward high inflation. Whatever the problem, it almost certainly was not the Fed's lack of awareness that NGDP growth for 2009 would come in far below 5 percent.

During the "Great Moderation," I had come to the conclusion that the Fed could do a pretty good job of stabilizing NGDP growth even with the assistance of futures markets. After seeing the recent debacle, I began to favor NGDP futures targeting not because I think the markets can forecast better than the Fed, but rather because NGDP futures targeting would basically force the Fed to do something it should be doing anyway, but isn't. It would force the Fed to implement Svensson's idea of targeting the forecast. In late 2008, the Fed's forecast for NGDP growth was well below any plausible implicit target. It failed to target the forecast.

The good news is that if I am right about the Fed being able to forecast nearly as well as the markets, then we may be able to begin targeting NGDP expectations even without the future market apparatus described above, which is admittedly a long shot. Even better, the Bernanke/Woodford "circularity" critique of targeting market forecasts only applies to policy regimes that try to rigidly peg market forecasts. If the Fed uses forecasts as one tool among many, forecasts can still be quite useful.[23]

The most effective way for the Fed to improve its targeting accuracy is to adopt level targeting. Under level targeting, if NGDP rose 3 percent while the target was 5 percent, then in the following year the Fed would aim for 7 percent NGDP growth, to return nominal income back to the original target trajectory. This approach has one very important advantage over memory-less growth rate targeting. During late 2008, when NGDP started falling, market expectations of future NGDP growth would have automatically risen. And higher nominal growth expectations tend to raise velocity. Under a level targeting regime with a 5 percent NGDP growth trajectory, it is very unlikely that policy would ever run aground on a liquidity trap. In contrast, under the current memory-less regime, the fall in AD during late 2008 did not lead to increases in expected future NGDP growth; forecasts of future NGDP growth were also scaled back at all horizons for which we have data. The market saw the U.S. economy falling below the Fed's implicit target, and expected it to fall further below in the future.

The stabilizing properties of level targeting are very similar to an exchange rate band under a fixed exchange rate regime. As long as the policy is credible, speculators will tend to buy a currency when it has fallen near the bottom of the target band, and vice versa. Under level targeting, if NGDP or prices fall below target, then investors will expect above normal inflation and NGDP growth, which will lower real interest rates and increase investment.

Concluding Remarks

In macroeconomics, things are rarely as they seem. The symptoms of demand-side recessions (falling asset prices, falling consumer confidence, a

---

23. The trade-off here is that the more the Fed relies on market forecasts, the more the "signal-to-noise ratio" deteriorates.

weakening financial system, etc.) can look like causes of the recession. Money doesn't look tight during recessions because low demand for credit reduces nominal interest rates. As a result, during almost every recession that I can recall, economists will say, "Most recessions are due to tight money, but this time it's different."[24] A few decades later, they look back and see falling inflation and falling NGDP growth, and categorize it as a garden-variety demand shock. If I am right that we have misdiagnosed the current crisis, then a similar re-evaluation should occur at some point in the future. The Great Recession that began in 2008 will be seen as resulting from inadequate NGDP growth, just as the Great Depression is now viewed that way.

Monetary remedies for demand shortfalls can look foolhardy to those who see events as a sort of morality play—speculative excess followed by the inevitable hangover the morning after. A suggestion that we "print more money" can sound like we are merely papering over some real weaknesses in the economy. In fact, much of what are viewed as structural problems are actually symptoms of monetary policy that has been excessively contractionary. The real problem is nominal—insufficient nominal expenditure. But the transmission mechanism for monetary policy (changes in future expected NGDP, as the excess cash balance mechanism eventually makes monetary injections neutral) is extremely hard to visualize. Most people have trouble understanding how swapping cash for T-bills could have any sort of significant impact on the economy, especially when T-bill yields are close to zero. But monetary injections do have a long-run inflationary impact, and expectations of those long-run effects can have a powerful impact on current conditions, as long as the policy is credible.

In my view, we need to rebuild macroeconomics from the ground up. Current models revolve around the concept of policy lags, which adds a bit of mysticism to the entire enterprise. Monetary injections work through "long and variable lags." After engaging in fiscal and/or monetary stimulus, we are told

---

24. The exception might be 1981–92. That was the one case in which the Fed intentionally engineered a sharp slowdown in NGDP growth. Because the Fed usually reflects the consensus view of economists, private sector economists are only likely to attribute recessions to the Fed when the outcome is viewed as desirable. In 1981, inflation had become such a problem that a recession was viewed as necessary.

that we need to "wait and see" how the policies are working. I envision a macro-economics built around futures markets in key nominal aggregates. In that world there are no more "long and variable lags," no more "wait and see." Monetary and fiscal policies affect the actual economy with a lag, but they effect NGDP growth expectations immediately. As soon as we start thinking in terms of NGDP expectations, then there is no longer a need for policymakers to rely on macro models of the economy. Keep NGDP expectations growing at a stable rate, and any actual deviations of NGDP from trend will be short-lived and will not significantly impact wage growth.

There is an interesting connection between this approach and the nineteenth century international gold standard. A regime of NGDP futures targeting combines the real-time precision of the gold standard with the stabilizing properties of steady growth in NGDP expectations. The problem with the gold standard wasn't that the Treasury or the Fed couldn't stabilize the price of gold, but rather that a stable gold price was not necessarily consistent with a stable overall price level, or NGDP growth rate. This led some economists to suggest that the Fed might want to stabilize an index of commodity prices. But as we saw in 2008, commodity prices can deviate quite far from the CPI or NGDP.

So why not try a commodity standard that includes all components of the CPI? There are two problems with this idea: (1) many prices are sticky, and (2) the CPI is not available in real time. Thus the Fed cannot peg the CPI. The obvious solution is to peg a CPI futures contract. But once we take that step and move toward targeting the expected future price level, then there is no reason not to target the future level of the nominal aggregate that is most consistent with macroeconomic stability—i.e., NGDP. An NGDP futures targeting regime would in many ways be like a gold standard. The central bank would peg the price of a NGDP contract, much as the nineteenth century central banks pegged the price of gold. The advantage of NGDP futures targeting is that a stable expected NGDP growth path is much more conducive to macroeconomic stability than a stable price of gold. The Great Contraction in the United States occurred during a period in which the price of gold was fixed at $20.67/oz., while NGDP fell in half. Admittedly the gold standard could have been managed much more effectively. But if we need effective government monetary policies to make the gold standard work, then it loses its one alleged advantage over fiat money regimes: the ability to prevent irresponsible governments from destabilizing the price level.

If NGDP futures targeting had been in effect in mid-2008, then the subsequent financial crisis would have been far smaller. This is not to suggest that there aren't real problems with our financial system, such as the privatization of gains and the socialization of losses, but those problems would be easier to address through regulatory changes if NGDP expectations grew at a steady rate. Positive NGDP growth in 2008–09 would have also greatly reduced the rise in unemployment during 2009. Again, this doesn't mean that there aren't real problems with our labor market; sharply higher minimum wage rates and greatly extended unemployment insurance benefits have made the U.S. job market less flexible and contributed to the rise in unemployment. But falling NGDP growth effectively raised the real minimum wage rate, and the sharp fall in NGDP raised unemployment, which almost certainly pushed Congress to pass the 99-week unemployment benefits extension.

Free market economists sometimes lose sight of the fact that NGDP instability is the free market's worst enemy. Because the effects of tight money are not transparent, the political class will almost always blame the "free market" when deflationary monetary policies cause a severe recession. This can lead to a backlash against laissez-faire and the implementation of statist policies. It happened in the United States during the 1930s. It happened in Argentina in 2002. And it is happening in America today. A stable NGDP growth path can help make the world safe for capitalism.

References

Ahamed, Liaquat. 2009. *Lords of Finance: The Bankers Who Broke the World*. Penguin Press.

Bernanke, Ben. 2003. "Some Thoughts on Monetary Policy in Japan." Speech given to the Japan Society of Monetary Economics, May, 31, 2003. http://www.federalreserve.gov/boarddocs/speeches/2003/20030531/default.htm

Bernanke, Ben, and Michael Woodford. 1997. "Inflation Forecasts and Monetary Policy," *Journal of Money, Credit and Banking*, 29, pp. 653–84.

Congdon, Tim. 2009. "The Unnecessary Recession." *Standpoint.* June, pp. 40–45. http://www.imr-ltd.com/graphics/recentresearch/article6.pdf

Dowd, Kevin. 1994. "A Proposal to End Inflation." *Economic Journal,* 104, pp. 828–40.

Friedman, Milton. 1998. "Reviving Japan." *Hoover Digest,* No. 2.

Garrison, Roger W. and Lawrence H. White. 1997. "Can Monetary Stabilization Policy be Improved by CPI Futures Targeting?" *Journal of Money, Credit and Banking.* 29 (November): 535–41.

Hetzel, Robert L. 2009. "Monetary Policy in the 2008–2009 Recession." *Federal Reserve Bank of Richmond, Economic Quarterly.* (Spring) pp. 201–33.

International Monetary Fund. 2008–2010. *Global Financial Stability Report.* Various issues.

King, Robert G. 1993. "Will the New Keynesian Macroeconomics Resurrect the IS-LM Model?" *Journal of Economic Perspectives.* 7, 1, pp. 67–82.

Mishkin, Frederic. 2008. *The Economics of Money, Banking and Financial Markets.* 8th Edition. Boston: Pearson Education Inc.

Mundell, Robert A. 2000. "A Reconsideration of the Twentieth Century." *American Economic Review* 90, 3, pp. 327–40.

Selgin, George. 1995. "The 'Productivity Norm' vs. Zero Inflation in the History of Economic Thought." *History of Political Economy* 27: 705–35.

———. 1997. "Less Than Zero: The Case for a Falling Price Level in a Growing Economy." London: Institute of Economic Affairs Occasional Paper.

Sumner, Scott. 1989. "Using Futures Instrument Prices to Target Nominal Income," *Bulletin of Economic Research* 41, pp. 157–62.

———. 1993. "Colonial Currency and the Quantity Theory of Money: A Critique of Smith's Interpretation." *Journal of Economic History* 53, 1, pp. 139–45.

———. 2006. "Let a Thousand Models Bloom: The Advantages of Making the FOMC a Truly 'Open Market'." *Berkeley Electronic Journals, Contributions to Macroeconomics* 6, 1, Article 8.

Svensson, Lars E. O. 2003. "What is Wrong with Taylor Rules? Using Judgment in Monetary Policy Through Targeting Rules." *Journal of Economic Literature* 41, pp. 426–77.

Thompson, Earl A. 1982. "Free Banking under a Labor Standard—The Perfect Monetary System." UCLA, manuscript.

_____. 2009. "What President Obama Should Know about Recessions." *American Thinker*. March 22, 2009.

Wolfers, J. and Zitzewitz, Eric. 2004. "Prediction Markets." *Journal of Economic Perspectives* 18 (2): 107–26.

Woodford, Michael. 2003. *Interest and Prices*. Princeton: University of Princeton Press.

Yglesias, Matthew. 2010. "Yellen Touts 'Maximum Employment'." Post in Yglesias blog, April 29, 2010, 3:58 pm. http://yglesias.thinkprogress.org/2010/04/yellen-touts-maximum-employment/

6

Ben Bernanke Versus Milton Friedman

The Federal Reserve's Emergence
as the U.S. Economy's Central Planner

Jeffrey Rogers Hummel[1]

BEN S. BERNANKE and Milton Friedman are both economists who studied the Great Depression closely. Indeed, Bernanke admits that his intense interest in that event was inspired by reading Milton Friedman and Anna Jacobson Schwartz's *Monetary History of the United States, 1867–1960*. Bernanke agrees with Friedman that what made the Great Depression truly great, rather than just a garden-variety depression, was the series of banking panics that began nearly a year after the stock market crash of October 1929. And both agree that the Federal Reserve was the primary culprit by failing to offset, if not by initiating, that economic cataclysm within the United States. As Bernanke, while still only a member of the Fed's Board of Governors, put it in an address at a ninetieth-birthday celebration for Friedman: "I would like to say to Milton and Anna: Regarding the Great Depression. You're right, we did it. We're very sorry. But thanks to you, we won't do it again."[2]

This seeming similarity, however, disguises significant differences in Friedman's and Bernanke's approaches to financial crises, differences that have played an enormous yet rarely noticed role in the recent financial crisis. Not only have

1. I would like to thank David Beckworth, Warren Gibson, David R. Henderson, Daniel Klein, Arnold Kling, Kurt Schuler, George Selgin, Scott Sumner, Robert Wenzel, and Bill Woolsey for their helpful comments and edits. Any remaining errors are entirely my own.
2. Ben S. Benanke (remarks at the Conference to Honor Milton Friedman, University of Chicago, Chicago, November 8, 2002), http://www.federalreserve.gov/boarddocs/speeches/2002/20021108/default.htm; Greg Ip, "Long Study of Great Depression Has Shaped Bernanke's Views," *Wall Street Journal*, December 7, 2005, A1; Milton Friedman and Anna Jacobson Schwartz, *A Monetary History of the United States, 1867–1960* (Princeton, NJ: Princeton University Press, 1963).

those differences resulted in another Fed failure—not quite as serious as during the Great Depression, to be sure, yet serious enough—but they have also resulted in a dramatic transformation of the Fed's role in the economy. Bernanke has so expanded the Fed's discretionary actions beyond merely controlling the money stock that it has become a gigantic financial central planner. In short, despite Bernanke's promise, the Fed *did* do it again.

Conflicting Lessons of the Great Depression

The banking panics associated with the Great Depression were not only the worst in the history of the United States; they were also the largest in the history of the world. The differences between Bernanke and Friedman center on why those panics generated economic catastrophe. For Friedman and Schwartz, the causal mechanism was the resulting changes in the money stock and therefore in the equilibrium price level. The panics brought about a collapse of the broader measures of the money stock over the four years from 1929 to 1933: a one-third fall in M2 and a one-fourth fall in M1. This collapse induced, in their view, a further fall in money's velocity (or increase in the portfolio demand for money, which is the same thing), requiring an enormous contraction in nominal income. Without full and immediate flexibility of all prices and wages, a one-third contraction in the economy's real output was the consequence. In other words, Friedman conceives of the bank panics as an enormous shock to *aggregate demand*.

This analysis leaves unanswered the prior questions of what triggered the banking panics in the first place and why the U.S. banking system was so uniquely vulnerable after so much government intervention to prevent such a crisis. Friedman and Schwartz attribute the panics to inept Fed policy, along with legal restrictions on the issue of money substitutes by private clearinghouses, but other economists have come up with myriad alternative explanations, ranging from the Smoot-Hawley tariff, through misplaced adherence to the gold standard, to an attack of Keynesian animal spirits. Despite disagreement about what initiated the panics, however, there is a fair consensus that the collapse of the banking system, once underway, made the Depression far more severe than it otherwise would have been.

Yet in contrast to Friedman's analysis, Bernanke's major article on the Great Depression, originally published in the *American Economic Review* in 1983, is openly entitled "*Nonmonetary* Effects of the Financial Crisis in the Propagation of the Great Depression [emphasis mine]." Banks were the economy's premier financial intermediaries, channeling savings from households to firms, which used the savings to maintain and accumulate capital, and to other households engaged in consumption. The failure of more than nine thousand banks caused a massive interruption of this credit flow, and in Bernanke's view, that was the primary reason for the contraction in output and its long duration. Even in his tribute to Friedman, Bernanke reiterated his belief that during the Great Depression "banking panics contributed to the collapse of output and prices through nonmonetary mechanisms" by "creating impediments to the normal intermediation of credit."[3]

At first glance, Bernanke appears to be arguing that the bank panics constituted an enormous shock to *aggregate supply*. Despite finding "this possibility . . . intriguing," he actually develops (especially in subsequent articles) a convoluted explanation of why a banking collapse would instead depress aggregate demand, even without any impact on the money stock. He speculates that such a disruption of what he calls "the credit channel" in effect will induce households and firms to hold more money rather than spend it on consumption and investment. True to his New Keynesian inclinations, what Bernanke is thus saying is that the failure of banks brings about a prolonged, negative velocity shock, although he never expresses this idea in such straightforward terms. Although the supply-side effects of bank failures would seem to make Bernanke's emphasis on the credit channel more compelling, either avenue clearly posits a mechanism for severe economic dislocations distinct from Friedman and Schwartz's explanation.[4]

---

3. Ben S. Bernanke, "Nonmonetary Effects of the Financial Crisis in the Propagation of the Great Depression," *American Economic Review* 73 (June 1983): 257–76; reprinted in Bernanke, *Essays on the Great Depression* (Princeton, NJ: Princeton University Press, 2000).

4. Bernanke, *Essays on the Great Depression*, 56; Bernanke, "Monetary Policy Transmission: Through Money or Credit?" Federal Reserve Bank of Philadelphia *Business Review* (September–October 1988): 3–11; and Bernanke and Mark Gertler, "Inside the Black Box: The Credit Channel of Monetary Policy Transmission," *Journal of Economic Perspectives* 9 (Fall 1995): 27–95. Joseph E. Stiglitz and Bruce Greenwald, *Towards a New Paradigm in Monetary Economics* (Cambridge: Cambridge University Press, 2003), offer a highly technical argument that bank failures do indeed cause significant supply shocks.

These two explanations for the Great Depression's severity are admittedly not mutually exclusive, as Bernanke himself has pointed out. Financial panics clearly constitute a hit both to the money stock and to financial intermediation. But very different policies are implied depending on which is the primary effect. If the danger from bank panics is a collapse of the money supply, then the proper response is a *general* injection of liquidity into the financial system, in order to prevent a drastic fall in aggregate demand and the price level. The survival of particular financial institutions is *at most* of secondary significance, and indeed those that are already insolvent because of taking on excessive risk, corrupt management, or other reasons can safely be permitted to go under if money and prices remain stabilized. So long as very few banks fail because of a pure liquidity squeeze that forces the selling off of assets at fire-sale prices, the damage should be contained.[5]

On the other hand, if the danger from bank panics is a choking off of credit that reduces either aggregate supply or aggregate demand, then targeted bailouts may be the proper response. A general stabilization of the money stock in order to hold up prices will be utterly inadequate if major financial institutions are insolvent. The economy will still suffer from a throttling of financial intermediation, making these institutions too big to fail. Even should contagion effects have no significant impact on money, they might in and of themselves bring about a serious economic contraction. Notice that this view bestows upon the financial sector a privileged status that no other economic sector enjoys. Threats to the financial sector's solvency are uniquely dangerous to the economy.[6]

Bernanke did not make these policy implications explicit in his scholarly writings, nor do they *necessarily* follow from his focus on the credit channel. As George Selgin points out, "So long as some banks are pre-run solvent, a sufficient dose of base money should suffice to keep those banks afloat, and in the presence of an efficient interbank market would do so even if the dose were administered via the open market"—through the Fed's purchase of Treasury

5. Anna J. Schwartz makes the point in "Real and Pseudo-financial Crises," in *Financial Crises and the World Banking System*, Forrest Capie and Geoffrey E. Wood. eds. (New York: St. Martin's Press, 1986).
6. For an appreciation of this distinction, see Robert L. Hetzel, "Monetary Policy in the 2008–2009 Recession," *Federal Reserve Bank of Richmond Economic Quarterly* 95 (Spring 2009): 201–33.

securities or federal-agency issues on the market. "Friedman and Schwartz took for granted that the same base creation that would have sufficed to maintain M2 would also suffice to maintain the flow of credit, though not without allowing some perhaps substantial change in banks' credit market shares. The mere change in credit-market shares itself needn't entail any credit-channel effects" and therefore no "fall in aggregate intermediation."[7]

It was left for the British monetary theorist Charles Goodhart to extend Bernanke's analysis into a rationale for targeted bailouts. He concludes that it is necessary to keep specific banks afloat, mainly because rebuilding relationships between borrowers and lenders takes time, so that financial intermediation can be impaired even if the central bank preserves aggregate liquidity. Nonetheless, we can see more than a glimmer of Goodhart's argument in Bernanke's initial article. Both believe that what distinguishes banks from other financial intermediaries is not merely that deposits are used as money but also that banks, in Bernanke's words, "specialize in making loans to small, idiosyncratic borrowers whose liabilities are too few in number to be publicly traded." Because bank loans are especially unmarketable, a bank collapse interrupts the flow of funds more than the insolvency of other financial institutions does. Bernanke concedes that "some of the slack" might be "taken up by the growing importance of alternative channels of credit," but "in a world of transaction costs and the need to discriminate among borrowers, these shifts in the loci of credit intermediation must have at least temporarily reduced the efficiency of the credit allocation process." It is no giant leap from Bernanke's claim that commercial banks in general are uniquely vital to financial intermediation to Goodhart's suggestion that some banks in particular are vital, especially if they are very big.[8]

Moreover, Bernanke clearly reveals in his original *American Economic Review* article that he considers *direct* government aid essential for the survival of

7. George Selgin, email to author (September 9, 2010).
8. C[harles] A. E. Goodhart, "Why Do Banks Need a Central Bank?" *Oxford Economic Papers*, new ser. 39 (March 1987): 84–89; Goodhart, "Price Stability and Financial Fragility," in *Financial Stability in a Changing Environment*, Kuniho Sawamoto, Zenta Nakajima, and Hiroo Taguchi, eds. (New York: St. Martin's Press, 1995), both articles reprinted in Goodhart, *The Central Bank and the Financial System* (Cambridge, MA: MIT Press, 1995); Goodhart, *Money, Information and Uncertainty*, 2nd ed. (Cambridge, MA: MIT Press, 1989), 188–93, 202–04; Bernanke, *Essays on the Great Depression*, 50–53.

certain forms of lending. "To the extent that the home mortgage market did function in the years immediately following 1933," he writes, "it was largely due to the direct involvement of the federal government. Besides establishing some important new institutions (such as the FSLIC [Federal Savings and Loan Insurance Corporation] and the system of federally chartered savings and loans), the government 'readjusted' existing debts, made investments in the shares of thrift institutions, and substituted for recalcitrant private institutions in the provision of direct credit." He goes on to state that "[s]imilar conditions obtained for farm credit and in other markets." Thus, "it seems safe to say . . . that the financial recovery would have been more difficult without extensive government intervention and assistance."[9]

The dividing line between Bernanke and Friedman's differing policies can sometimes be hazy. The failure of a single large bank can in theory set off a panic that causes a monetary contraction. Thus, Friedman and Schwartz did imply that the Fed might have done more to shore up the Bank of United States, to whose failure in December 1930 they attach special importance in spreading the Great Depression panic. Scholars still debate the extent to which banks succumbed to insolvency rather than liquidity problems during that episode, and Friedman does endorse deposit insurance as a cure for bank panics. But Friedman and Schwartz's central complaint about Fed operations during the Great Depression is that its expansion of the monetary base with open market operations was too little and too late. Indeed, Friedman contends in his *Program for Monetary Stability* that central banks can dispense altogether with making loans to individual banks through discounts and rely exclusively on open market operations. Among other benefits, he believes this reform would prevent the widespread "confusion between the 'monetary' effects of monetary policy—the effects on the stock of money—and the 'credit' effects—the effects on recorded rates of interest and other conditions in the credit market."[10]

One objection to Friedman's remedy for financial crises comes from Keynesian economists. With their focus on fluctuations in money demand (in other

9. Bernanke, *Essays on the Great Depression*, 64–65.

10. Friedman and Schwartz, *Monetary History*, 309–12, 357–58; Charles W. Calomiris, "Banking Crises," in *The New Palgrave Dictionary of Economics*, Steven Durlauf and Lawrence Blume, eds., 2nd ed. (New York: Palgrave Macmillan, 2008), 1:348–52; Milton Friedman, *A Program for Monetary Stability* (New York: Fordham University, 1960), 43.

words, velocity shocks) as the main source of business cycles, they have argued that the demand for money can become so elastic that no increase in the money stock, no matter how large, can offset the fall in output and employment. This is the infamous Keynesian liquidity trap, possibly prevailing during the Great Depression or even currently, in which firms and households end up just hoarding any new money. Friedman himself believes that severe changes in velocity are caused by volatile monetary policy, and that so long as money growth remains constant, velocity will change at a fairly predictable and stable rate. But it is Bernanke, with unintentional irony (as we shall see), who offers the definitive refutation of the liquidity trap. He points out that, through what has somewhat misleadingly come to be called "quantitative easing," a central bank can ultimately buy up everything in the entire economy—except that sometime before it has done so people will certainly start spending. This is the argument that earned him the sobriquet "Helicopter Ben."[11]

What is crucial for our purpose, however, is that a bank panic that causes a drastic *decrease* in such measures of money as M2 or M1 stems from an *increased* demand for currency and reserves, the two forms of base money. In this case, a fall in the broader money stock and a fall in the velocity of the monetary base are exactly the same thing, and they become alternative ways of describing what happened during the Great Depression. Indeed, once banking panics were well under way, the Fed did start expanding the supply of base money but not enough to counteract either the fall in the broader monetary supply or the fall in base velocity, however we choose to describe what was going on. Thus, whether we label a particular decline in aggregate demand a monetary shock or a velocity shock can depend on how broadly or narrowly we define the money stock. Although Friedman's primary worry is monetary shocks, the internal

---

11. Ben S. Bernanke, "Japanese Monetary Policy: A Case of Self-Induced Paralysis" (paper presented at the Allied Social Science Associations meeting, December 1999), 14–15; and reprinted in Ryoichi Mikitani and Adam S. Posen, eds., *Japan's Financial Crisis and Its Parallels to U.S. Experience* (Washington: Institute for International Economics, 2000); Bernanke, "Deflation: Making Sure 'It' Doesn't Happen Here," (remarks before the National Economists Club, Washington, D.C., November 21, 2002), http://www .federalreserve.gov/boarddocs/speeches/2002/20021121/default.htm. Bernanke's argument was anticipated in an unpublished paper by George Selgin, "Japan: The Way Out" (September 1999).

logic of his position requires a central bank response to velocity shocks as well. He even implicitly accepts this equivalence when, in a 2003 *Wall Street Journal* op-ed, he applauds Alan Greenspan's deft offsetting of the M2 velocity bubble of the mid to late 1990s.[12]

Offsetting negative shocks to money or velocity (that is, stabilizing the growth rate of *M* times *V* in the equation of exchange) with untargeted, general injections of liquidity, as consistent with Friedman's analysis, has the added advantage of helping to clarify which banks are simply illiquid and which are also insolvent, whereas direct bailouts, as implied by Bernanke's analysis, obscures the distinction. The United States has experienced at least two episodes of extensive bank insolvencies unaccompanied by any major macroeconomic downturns. These episodes would seem to confirm Friedman's emphasis on monetary shocks rather than Bernanke's emphasis on intermediation shocks. Throughout the decade of the 1920s, inordinate numbers of rural banks were failing because of agricultural distress, but these years were boom times for the U.S. economy generally, and no one as far as I know has assigned those failures any major causal role in the Great Depression.

More recently, as a result of the savings and loan (S&L) crisis of the 1980s, more than two thousand financial institutions failed. This more recent episode is obviously not as clear-cut, because there was a bailout that cost taxpayers $130 billion. Among the many regrettable features of federal deposit insurance—aside from moral-hazard-induced, excessive risk-taking, which brought on the crisis in the first place—is that some government agency must decide when a depository is thrown into bankruptcy rather than leaving the decision to private parties on

---

12. Milton Friedman, "The Fed's Thermostat," *Wall Street Journal*, 19 August 2003, A8. As far as I know, James C. W. Ahiakpor, in "On the Definition of Money: Classical vs Modern," a paper reprinted in his *Classical Macroeconomics: Some Modern Variations and Distortions* (London: Routledge, 2003), 55–56, is the only economist to have noticed the equivalence of monetary and velocity shocks in describing the Great Depression. Even some Austrian-school economists have acknowledged the desirability of a system that prevents both types of shocks, starting with Friedrich A. Hayek, *Prices and Production*, 2nd ed. (London: Routledge, 1935), 27, 113–34, and including such advocates of free banking as George A. Selgin, *The Theory of Free Banking: Money Supply under Competitive Note Issue* (Totowa, NJ: Rowman and Littlefield, 1988); Lawrence H. White, *The Theory of Monetary Institutions* (Malden, MA: Blackwell, 1999); and Stephen Horwitz, *Microfoundations and Macroeconomics: An Austrian Perspective* (London: Routledge, 2000).

the market, as would be the case with most firms. But the bailout mainly went to cover depositor losses, not to keep insolvent institutions in business. The major exception, the nationalization of Continental Illinois National Bank and Trust Company in 1984, did involve temporary discount loans of as much as $7 billion. The Fed also extended credit to certain Ohio thrifts insured by a state fund that was in trouble in 1985 and in 1989 eased collateral requirements for a few thrifts as the final details of the federal resolution were debated in Congress. However, the scope of and sums involved in these Fed interventions were small relative to the overall cost of shutting down failed institutions. More to the point, the monetary determinants of aggregate demand remained free from major shocks during the S&L crisis, and the one *possible* macroeconomic ripple was *debatably* the minor recession of 1990–1991.[13]

Yet the real proof of both the stark difference between Friedman and Bernanke and of the superiority of Friedman's approach comes from a close comparison of Greenspan's record as Fed Chairman and Bernanke's record. Many have forgotten that Greenspan actually faced three potential financial crises during his long tenure: the October 1987 stock market crash, the fear surrounding the year 2000 (Y2K), and the terrorist attack of September 11, 2001. His primary response to all three was not targeted bailouts but a flooding of the economy with liquidity in the short term.

Greenspan's Handling of Potential Crises

The crash of Black Monday, October 19, 1987 occurred almost exactly two months after Alan Greenspan had assumed his Fed post in August. He had initially tightened up on the growth of the monetary base and other monetary measures, whose growth rates had actually been quite high during the last

---

13. Bert Ely, "Savings and Loan Crisis," in *The Concise Encyclopedia of Economics*, ed. David Henderson, 2nd ed. (Indianapolis, IN: Liberty Fund, 2008), 459–63; Federal Deposit Insurance Corporation, *History of the Eighties—Lessons for the Future*, vol. 1, *An Examination of the Banking Crises of the 1980s and Early 1990s* (1997), http://www.fdic.gov/bank/historical/history/vol1.html; Marcia Stigum, *The Money Market*, 3rd ed. (Homewood, IL: Business One Irwin, 1990), 387–90. My figure for total failures covers *both* commercial banks and thrifts (some accounts report only one or the other) from 1980 to 1992 and comes from the FDIC website, "Historical Statistics on Banking," http://www2.fdic.gov/hsob/index.asp

four years of his predecessor, Paul Volcker. But when the Dow Jones Industrial Average plunged by 508 points, more than 20 percent, and before trading began the next morning, Greenspan issued a short, public statement, affirming the Fed's "readiness to serve as a source of liquidity to support the economic and financial system." He backed that up with high-profile, open market operations, frequently conducted an hour or more before normally scheduled market interventions by the New York Fed's trading desk. As a result, Fed holdings of Treasury securities jumped by more than $8 billion within two weeks, and its holdings of Federal-agency issues jumped by $4 billion. Most of these increases were repurchase agreements (RPs or repos), in which the Fed temporarily creates base money to buy securities that the dealer has agreed to buy back usually between one and fourteen days later (with interest added). The Fed also opened the discount window, although its loans to banks increased only temporarily by a little more than $2 billion.[14]

The most serious danger from the stock market crash was centered in the investment banks, coincidentally the same institutions that have played such a notorious role in the financial crisis of 2007–2008. In 1987, investment banks were not yet engaging in the massive proprietary trading that caused the recent difficulties, but their broker-dealer operations, specifically margin accounts, still depended heavily on loans to customers with money borrowed in turn from major New York and Chicago commercial banks. The lending banks became

---

14. Probably the best study of Greenspan's handling of the 1987 stock market crash is Mark Carlson, "A Brief History of the 1987 Stock Market Crash with a Discussion of the Federal Reserve Response" (Federal Reserve Board, 2006), but also worth consulting are Bob Woodward, *Maestro: Greenspan's Fed and the American Boom*, expanded paperback edition (New York: Simon & Schuster, 2001), 36–49; Justin Martin, *Greenspan: The Man Behind the Money* (Cambridge, MA: Perseus, 2000), 171–79; Steven K. Beckner, *Back from the Brink: The Greenspan Years* (New York: John Wiley & Sons, 1996), 34–62; Alan Greenspan, *The Age of Turbulence: Adventures in a New World* (New York: Penguin Books, 2008), 104–10; and "Statements and Comments of Alan Greenspan, Chairman of the Federal Reserve," *Black Monday: The Stock Market Crash of October 19, 1987*, Senate Committee on Banking, Housing, and Urban Affairs, Hearing, 100 Congress, 1 Session (Washington: Government Printing Office, 1987). For a wildly sensationalist account, see James B. Stewart and Daniel Hertzberg, "How the Stock Market Almost Disintegrated a Day after the Crash," *The Wall Street Journal*, November 20, 1987, 1. One can follow the change in the Fed's balance sheet during this period through its weekly H.4.1 releases, which are available online for download at http://fraser.stlouisfed.org/statreleases/h41/1987/

skittish, and if they had refused to roll over these call loans to the investment banks, the collapse of credit might have cascaded seriously. But Greenspan's prompt response ensured that securities loans at commercial banks actually increased during the crisis.[15]

At the same time, E. Gerald Corrigan, then president of the New York Fed, was making numerous calls to Wall Street players, leaning on the commercial banks to keep credit flowing. In addition to creating money, something else that the Fed has long done is to lend, for very short terms, securities from its own portfolio to primary dealers (either commercial or investment banks) who provide other securities as collateral. Except for the interest paid by the borrowing dealer, this deal is essentially a barter transaction in which securities briefly swap for other securities rather than for cash, leaving the impact on the monetary base neutral. After the crash, the Fed temporarily relaxed its restrictions on this type of security lending, by suspending limits per issue and per dealer as well as by suspending the requirement that the loans not facilitate a short sale.

So the Fed's actions during the 1987 crash were not a pure Friedmanite liquidity injection. Indeed, Greenspan considered the further step of loaning money directly to investment banks, something Bernanke would start doing in 2008, but this proved unnecessary because the crisis dissipated almost as quickly as it had emerged. The Fed's actions therefore left almost no noticeable imprint on any of the monetary measures, including the base and total reserves (in part because Treasury lending to the Fed in the form of Treasury deposits also went up temporarily at the same time). Some have even concluded that Greenspan's one-sentence announcement was alone sufficient to restore confidence, calming markets and averting panic. Yet the important point is that nothing the Fed did during the 1987 crisis involved or even hinted at a Bernankeite bailout of particular insolvent institutions.

Ironically the Y2K threat, arising from fear that computer programs were unequipped to handle the transition to the year 2000, made the biggest blip in the monetary measures, despite being the least remembered of the potential crises Greenspan faced. Y2K barely merits a few paragraphs in Greenspan's memoirs, and they relate only to the Fed's own computers and not to policy.

---

15. The most convincing, detailed discussion of how the 1987 crash might have spiraled into a full-fledged panic is in Beckner, *Back from the Brink*, 45–58.

Nonetheless, he was concerned "that people are going to draw too much out [of banks and other depositories], and walking around with a lot of hundred dollar bills is not the safest way to keep your money." Just a casual glance at Figure 6.1 shows Y2K's hefty impact on both the monetary base and total bank reserves (not seasonally adjusted), one that was far larger than the regular Christmas run-up of those two magnitudes. The base rose from $551 billion to $608 billion over three months before falling back to $577 billion in March 2001. Much of this spike was concentrated in reserves (properly measured), whose year-on-year growth rate started at 0 percent annually, peaked at 40 percent, and then fell down to negative 30 percent (as depicted in Figure 6.2). All of this was orchestrated through open market operations using repos. The Fed also established what it called a "Special Liquidity Facility" so banks could borrow through the discount window without the usual stigma that then attached to doing so, and it even sold banks options on the future discount rate at which they could borrow, but neither of these measures proved necessary when Y2K fizzled into a nonevent. [16]

---

16. Greenspan, *Age of Turbulence*, 203–04. Former Governor of the Fed, Laurence H. Meyer, gives Y2K more attention in *A Term at the Fed: An Insider's View* (New York: HarperCollins, 2004), 155–57. The Greenspan quotation comes from Jerome Tuccille (who served on Y2K task force for financial institutions), *Alan Shrugged: The Life and Times of Alan Greenspan, the World's Most Powerful Banker* (Hoboken, NJ: John Wiley & Sons, 2002), 245. The relevant Fed H.4.1 releases can all be found at http://www.federalreserve .gov/releases/h41/. The numbers that are the basis for Figure 6.1 come from the enormously convenient website of the St. Louis Federal Reserve, http://research.stlouisfed.org/fred2/. The monetary base is Board of Governors Monetary Base (monthly and not seasonally adjusted), Not Adjusted for Changes in Reserve Requirements: BOGUMBNS. Currency in circulation is the Currency Component of M1 (monthly and not seasonally adjusted): CURRNS. I have subtracted the latter from the former to get total reserves.

As David R. Henderson and I pointed out in "Greenspan's Monetary Policy in Retrospect: Discretion or Rules?" Cato Institute *Briefing Paper*, no. 109 (November 2008), all of the officially reported measures of bank reserves are deficient: "those compiled by the St. Louis Fed are adjusted for changes in reserve requirements, whereas those compiled by the board of governors exclude any excess reserves held in the form of vault cash, all required clearing balances, and Fed float. (You can find this critical detail only in the footnotes of the Fed's H.3 release.) For some idea of how massive the resulting distortion can be, consider December 2007. The Board of Governors reported total reserves (monthly, not seasonally, adjusted, and not adjusted for changes in reserve requirements) of $42.7 billion. If you add in vault cash not covering reserve requirements, that number jumps to $60.3 billion. And when you bring in required clearing balances and float, the number

Figures 6.1 and 6.2 display an equally dramatic although somewhat smaller increase in reserves following the terrorist attack of September 11, 2001, on the World Trade Center. The average monthly size of the base experienced a $20 billion temporary increase, mostly concentrated in reserves, whose year-on-year growth rate rose from 0 percent to 30 percent annually and then eventually, after the Christmas holidays, fell to negative 20 percent annually. This time the Fed relied more heavily on discount loans to banks, which soared from an average of $200 million to $45 billion on September 12. Greenspan recounts that this temporary credit extension was something "that the staff and the individual Federal Reserve banks were entirely capable of handling." The 9/11 attack also brought forth an innovation that would reappear under Bernanke—currency swap lines with foreign central banks—but the amounts ultimately involved were small and the swap lines expired after thirty days. Meanwhile, when the stock market reopened on Monday, September 17, trading was orderly.[17]

Of course, no one can know with certainty what might have happened to the financial system or the economy without Greenspan's three liquidity interventions. Perhaps none of them was necessary, in particular his preparations for Y2K. The recent unexpected fragility of the financial system, however, when faced with what seemed to be containable losses from subprime mortgages,

---

rises to $72.6 billion, 70 percent greater than the board's estimate. If the distortion were consistent across time, the board's reserve totals would still tell us something. But the distortion is not close to consistent across time, in part because banks increasingly used vault cash in their ATMs." Recently one of our graduate students, Justin Dean Rietz, has compared our estimates of total reserves as calculated above with estimates based on adding together bank deposits at the Fed, total vault cash, and service related balances from the weekly H.3 and H.4.1 releases. He found the two estimates comparable.

17. Greenspan, *Age of Turbulence*, 4–5; and Meyer, *A Term at the Fed*, 183–84. See also Greg Ip and Jim VandeHei, "Economic Front: How Policy Makers Regrouped to Defend The Financial System," *The Wall Street Journal*, September 18, 2001, A1. These central-bank currency swaps are covered in Dino Kos, "Treasury and Federal Reserve Foreign Exchange Operations," *Federal Reserve Bulletin* 87 (December 2001): 757–62. (From the 1960s through 1998, the Fed had earlier standing swap lines with several central banks, but their purpose was to facilitate foreign-exchange intervention rather than to provide liquidity. Most of these older swap lines were phased out by mutual agreement in 1998, although Canada and Mexico retained small swap lines under the auspices of the North American Free Trade Agreement.) Again, the relevant Fed H.4.1 releases can all be found at http://www.federalreserve.gov/releases/h41/

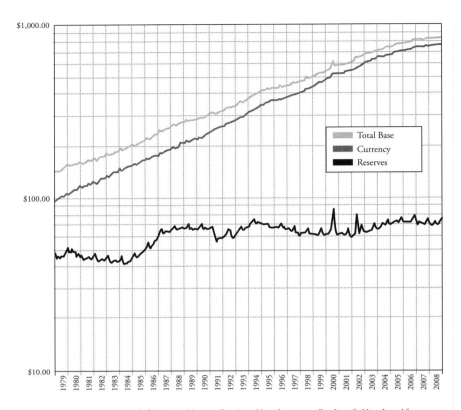

Note: The monetary base is Board of Governors Monetary Base (monthly and not seasonally adjusted), Not adjusted for Changes in Reserve Requirements: BOGUMBNS. Currency in circulation is the Currency Component of M1 (monthly and not seasonally adjusted): CURRNS. Total reserves are the latter subtracted from the former.

Figure 6.1. Monetary Base, 1979–2008 (Billions, Log Scale)

Source: Federal Reserve Bank of St. Louis 1979–2010

certainly raises the prospect that full-fledged financial panic may have ensued in one or more of these cases without the Fed action. Whether necessary or not, all three interventions constituted sudden, general injections of base money into the financial system that were just as quickly unwound. Even when flowing through the discount window, none of the liquidity was aimed *specifically* at any institution facing insolvency.

Greenspan's only significant deviation from the Friedman formula came before 9/11 and Y2K, when he permitted the head of the New York Fed—William

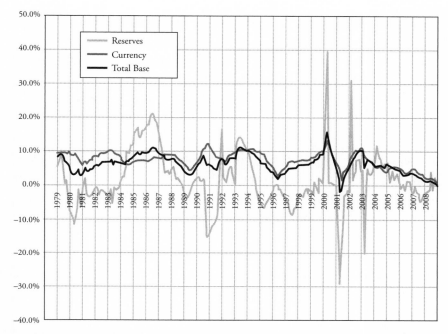

Figure 6.2. Year-on-Year Growth of Base, Currency, and Reserves, 1979–2008
Source: Author's calculations from the data for Figure 6.1

McDonough at that time—to "godfather," in Greenspan's word, a private bail-out of Long-Term Capital Management (LTCM) after the Russian sovereign default of August 1998. Although no Federal Reserve or taxpayer money was involved, this action represented a portentous signal to send to the financial community, encouraging moral hazard. For the first time, "too big to fail" was applied to a nondepository institution, uncovered by deposit insurance. LTCM was not a commercial bank, which the Fed normally oversees; nor was it an investment bank, which were still at this time outside the Fed's province; nor was it even a money-market fund, which despite also being beyond the Fed's purview at least affects the money stock. LTCM was a hedge fund, whose shares were legally confined to very wealthy individuals because of the risky investments the fund might undertake. If central bankers felt it necessary to step in to forestall the failure of a fund so seemingly unrelated to the Fed's traditional orbit, then creditors of other financial institutions surely might conclude that they could depend on being bailed out if their investments went sour in the future.[18]

Indeed, government assurances may have already been at work in a small way. David Mullins, Jr., previous vice chairman of the Fed, was a major LTCM partner. Warren Buffett of Berkshire Hathaway was offering, on his own initiative, $4 billion for the fund, but the partners rejected the unattractive offer. They were the ones who had alerted McDonough at the New York Fed to LTCM's difficulties and were now aware that he was backstopping Buffett's offer, calling together the parties to the rescue deal that ultimately went through. Greenspan privately did not fully agree with McDonough's assessment of the potential risk from an LTCM failure and believed that McDonough's brokering of the bailout was too aggressive, but publicly Greenspan made a show of solidarity with his subordinate. Perhaps just as bad as the signal that this Fed intervention sent to private creditors is the precedent it set for financial regulators such as Bernanke. A gross violation of the Friedman formula could now be credited with having averted a financial collapse, whether it actually had or not, thus reinforcing the perceived necessity of similar targeted bailouts in the future.[19]

Bernanke: Phase One

Ben S. Bernanke became chairman of the Federal Reserve Board on February 1, 2006. His subsequent response to the financial crises of 2007–2009 went through two phases. The first phase began in the fall of 2007, when it became apparent that rising mortgage defaults were having serious systemic effects. Until then, many if not most economists had concluded that potential subprime losses would be no larger and have no more macroeconomic down-

---

18. Greenspan, *Age of Turbulence*, 192; Meyer, *A Term at the Fed*, 112–18; Tyler Cowen, "Bailout of Long Term Capital: A Bad Precedent?" *New York Times*, December 28, 2008, BU5. Chapter 10 of Roger Lowenstein, *When Genius Failed: The Rise and Fall of Long-Term Capital Management* (New York: Random House, 2000) contains the standard account of the Fed involvement.

19. Woodward, *Maestro*, 197–209, suggests that the partners rejected Buffett's offer because they knew he would oust them. Lowenstein, *When Genius Failed*, 201–03, believes the rejection hinged on legal difficulties with the offer. Be that as it may, the fact that the partners knew the New York Fed was coming to the rescue made it easier to reject Buffett's offer, rather than try to negotiate improvements.

side than the losses from the S&L crisis of the 1980s. As late as May 17, 2007, Bernanke was predicting "that troubles in the subprime sector on the broader housing market will likely be limited, and we do not expect significant spillovers from the subprime market to the rest of the economy or to the financial system." The second phase of Bernanke's policies was initiated in September 2008, at the same time that he and secretary of the Treasury Henry Paulson decided to scare the hell out of the American people in order to gain passage of what became the Troubled Assets Relief Program (TARP). To fully understand these two phases, both their similarities and differences, we need to make a brief excursion into the events that culminated in the crisis.[20]

We now know from Gary Gorton's research that what generated the widespread systemic repercussions of the mortgage defaults was a panic that began in August of 2007, and its epicenter was investment banking.[21] The nature of investment banks had changed significantly during the new century. In the past they had served primarily as underwriters, brokers, and dealers—that is, as facilitators of the transfer of financial securities between two other parties. Insofar as they owned securities themselves, they did so predominately in conjunction with those functions. Back in 1994, the total financial assets of all investment banks, as reported in the Fed's flow of funds accounts, was less than $500 billion, compared with more than $4 trillion for commercial banks. But over the next decade investment banks began acquiring ever larger amounts of various securities on their own balance sheets, in what is called proprietary

20. Ben S. Bernanke, "The Subprime Mortgage Market" (speech at the Federal Reserve Bank of Chicago's 43rd Annual Conference on Bank Structure and Competition, May 17, 2007), http://www.federalreserve.gov/newsevents/speech/bernanke20070517a.htm
21. Gary B. Gorton, "The Panic of 2007" (prepared for the Federal Reserve Bank of Kansas City, Jackson Hole, Wyoming, Symposium, August 21–23, 2008), http://papers.ssrn.com/sol3/papers.cfm?abstract_id=1255362, reprinted in *Maintaining Stability in a Changing Financial System* (Kansas City: Federal Reserve Bank of Kansas City, 2009); Gorton, "The Subprime Panic," *European Financial Management* 15 (January 2009): 10–46; Gorton, "Slapped in the Face by the Invisible Hand: Banking and the Panic of 2007"(prepared for the Federal Reserve Bank of Atlanta's 2009 Financial Markets Conference, May 2009); Gorton and Andrew Metrick, "Securitized Banking and the Run on the Repo" (Yale ICF Working Paper No. 09-14, November 2009); and Gorton, *Slapped By the Invisible Hand: The Panic of 2007* (Oxford: Oxford University Press, 2010). For an accessible summary of this research, see Gorton, "Questions and Answers about the Financial Crisis" (prepared for the U.S. Financial Crisis Commission, February 2010).

trading, transforming these institutions into major financial intermediaries. By 2007 they held over $3 trillion in assets, a sixfold increase that made them collectively bigger institutions than such conventional intermediaries as thrifts, money market funds, or finance companies. And this total does not include any hedge funds managed by investment banks, whose assets are classified by the flow of funds accounts within the household sector. Over the same period the assets of commercial banks increased less than half as much, to $11 trillion.[22]

Investment banks still financed some of their expanded balance sheets with borrowing either from customer accounts or through bank loans. But more than $1 trillion worth of their funds came from repos. Although repos technically involve exchanging a security for cash, then reversing the transaction, they may also be thought of as a form of short-term borrowing, frequently overnight, with the underlying security pledged as collateral. In other words, like commercial banks and thrifts, investment banks were now borrowing short to lend long, in what has been designated the "shadow banking system." Nearly all of this borrowing was either from abroad or from large institutional investors within the financial sector, especially money market mutual funds. Moreover, although repos were once conducted predominately with Treasury securities, they now were collateralized with almost any marketable instrument, including complex securitized debt.

Commercial banks have also relied on repos as a source of funds, and in fact employed them extensively in the late 1970s and early 1980s, a period of

---

22. Quarterly *Flow of Funds Accounts of the United States*, from mid-1996 on forward, are available here: http://www.federalreserve.gov/releases/z1/default.htm. Most investment banks are listed as "Security Brokers and Dealers." For earlier reports, go to http://www.federalreserve.gov/releases/z1/Current/data.htm. The term "investment bank" is sometimes distinguished from security brokers and dealers, either to refer to firms that concentrate on underwriting (the brokering and dealing of securities when they are first issued) or to the financial holding companies that own broker-dealer subsidiaries. I am using the term in its broadest sense, to encompass the entire sector, including those investment banks or broker-dealers that are subsidiaries of banks or bank holding companies. This coincides with the flow of funds category of "Security Brokers and Dealers," except for nonbank financial holding companies, which are put into the "Funding Corporations" category. Adding the latter potentially increases the size of the investment-banking sector by another trillion dollars or more in 2007, but these holding companies do not themselves appear to employ repurchase agreements to raise funds, at least not on net.

high interest rates, to get around interest ceilings on bank deposits. A bank, for example, might convert a million-dollar checking account (on which, even after the deregulation of interest rates, it could not pay interest to corporate businesses) into an overnight loan secured by a Treasury bill (on which it could pay interest) and then the next day convert this repo back into an account with full check-writing privileges and the interest added in. As a result, the overnight repos *of commercial banks* were counted as money in M2, and their term repos in M3. Declining importance of this ploy with declining nominal interest rates was one factor that contributed to the Fed's moving overnight repos from M2 to M3 in 1997, and then the Fed discontinued reporting M3 in March of 2006.[23]

Investment bank repos were never counted in the monetary measures, and no one knows precisely how big this market became before August 2007. The flow of funds accounts put total repos for *all* institutions at nearly $2.4 trillion, but that amount is net of any repo loans between one commercial bank and another or between one investment bank and another. Thus, the net total fails to capture interbank lending through repos, which provided investment banks with their own analog to the federal funds market (the market where commercial banks and other depositories can loan each other reserves). Some financial institutions were even making what are called "matched book" repos, two transactions whereby they lend money on the asset side in exchange for a security and then use that security as collateral to borrow money on the liability side. As a result, the same underlying security can be used as collateral several times, in a process called "rehypothecation." Although Gorton has suggested that the gross size of the repo market may have reached $12 trillion, that estimate involves some double counting of both the asset and liability side of single transactions. An article by Peter Hördahl and Michael R. King puts the peak total closer to $6 trillion, with the amount arising from investment banks, both within the sector and with institutions outside the sector, accounting for

---

23. Marcia Stigum and Anthony Crescenzi, *Stigum's Money Market*, 4th ed. (New York: McGraw Hill, 2007), is the definitive reference on repurchase agreements. Older editions, by Stigum alone and entitled *The Money Market*, contain some details about practices that have since changed. A terminological anomaly: for banks or other private institutions, the repurchase agreement is the liability of the borrower and the reverse repurchase agreement is the asset of the lender; for Federal Reserve, this terminology is the opposite: a repurchase agreement is an asset, and a reverse repurchase agreement is a liability.

two-thirds of the total. This estimate for investment banks roughly agrees with estimates reported by the Securities Industries and Financial Markets Association and the U.S. Securities and Exchange Commission.[24]

Defaults on mortgages were already rising by mid-2006, and then in June 2007 Moody's began to downgrade its ratings on asset-backed securities containing subprime mortgages, while two Bear Stearns–managed hedge funds that had invested heavily in such securities were in danger of shutting down. These growing solvency problems turned into a liquidity run on investment banks, as the repo market began to contract in August (see Figure 6.3). Between the third and fourth quarter of 2007, the total amount of *net* repos fell by over $200 billion, most of which represented borrowing by investment banks. The run continued into 2008, as investment bank repos fell by another $550 billion. If we also count the additional repo transactions between two different investment banks, another trillion dollars worth had likewise disappeared. As a result, total financial assets of investment banks declined by almost as much. Some of this decline represents genuine losses from bad investments, of course, but much of it was induced by vanishing liquidity.[25]

The panic also affected another type of short-term borrowing by financial institutions: asset-backed commercial paper. Not only did stand-alone investment bank *holding companies* (that is, those unconnected with commercial banks) rely on borrowing through this source but so did another major part of the shadow banking system: the structured investment vehicles (SIVs). Set up by commercial banks, which had been encouraged by the Basel capital requirements to

---

24. Peter Hördahl and Michael R. King, "Developments in Repo Markets during the Financial Turmoil," *BIS Quarterly Review* (December 2008): 37–53; Securities Industries and Financial Markets Association, *Research Report* 4 (May 2009): 10; U.S. Securities and Exchange Commission, *Select SEC and Market Data Fiscal 2009*, 24, http://www.sec.gov/about.shtml. See also Tobias Adrian, Christopher R. Burke, and James J. McAndrews, The Federal Reserve's Primary Dealer Credit Facility," Federal Reserve Bank of New York, *Current Issues in Economics and Finance* 15 (December 2009), http://www.newyork fed.org/research/current_issues/ci15-4.html
25. For the Fed's *Flow of Funds Accounts*, I have calculated all changes in assets or liabilities from the level tables rather than the flow tables. The two do not always coincide, because the flow tables omit changes in market value.

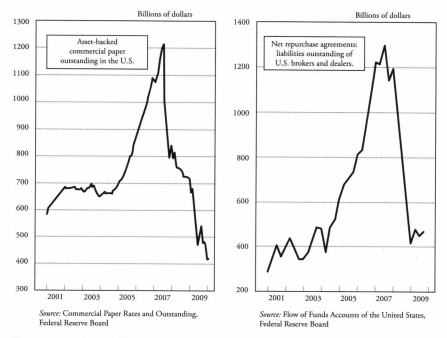

Figure 6.3. Selected Short-Term Collateralized Debt Instruments, 2001–2010

Source: From Matthew J. Eichner, Donald L. Kohn, and Michael G. Palumbo, "Financial Statistics for the United States and the Crisis: What Did They Get Right, What Did They Miss, and How Should They Change?" Finance and Economics Discussion Series, Division of Research & Statistics and Monetary Affairs, Federal Reserve Board (April 2010), p. 40.

securitize mortgages, SIVs were bank subsidiaries that issued their own debt of varied maturities to purchase assorted mortgage-backed securities and other financial products. Only about 20 percent of the SIVs' $4.5 trillion worth of assets was funded by commercial paper, but when added to the commercial paper issued by the investment-banking sector, the total outstanding had reached $1.2 trillion by mid-2007. As depicted in Figure 6.3, after the August panic hit, this market also collapsed. Evidence of the panic in these two markets was most visible in the rise of various interest-rate spreads that measure risk. The haircuts off the face value of the underlying securities for certain repo loans began to rise; the spread between the London Interbank Offered Rate and the overnight index swap rate (Libor–OIS) increased by a full percentage point; and the Treasury–Eurodollar (TED) spread jumped by nearly 2 percentage points.[26]

So what was the Fed's response in Phase One of Bernanke's policies? At first glance, it might appear to be a Friedmanite liquidity injection. Back in January 2003, the Fed had altered its policy with respect to discount loans to banks. Instead of setting the discount rate below the Fed's target for the federal funds rate and rationing its lending, the Fed began setting the discount rate slightly above the federal funds target and permitting unlimited short-term borrowing without any stigma. But the higher discount rate, relative to the rate at which banks could borrow reserves from each other, prevented this change from having any noticeable effect on total borrowing, which remained a trivial part of the Fed's balance sheet, ranging between $30 and $400 million, or always less than 1 percent of total assets. In reaction to the panic, the Fed announced on August 17, 2007, that it was reducing the spread between the two rates and allowing banks to borrow for as long as thirty days (later extended to ninety days). Finally in December of that year, Bernanke created the Term Auction Facility (TAF) to provide additional funds to banks for periods of up to eighty-four days. Unlike in the discount window, where the Fed sets the interest rates and the banks decide how much to borrow, under the Term Auction Facility, the Fed sets the amount to be lent and the banks determine the interest rate through auction. The Fed simultaneously reinstated currency swaps with foreign central banks.

By the summer of 2008, lending to banks through the Term Auction Facility had climbed to $150 billion, and discounts added another $18 billion. Other things being equal, this lending would have brought about a substantial

---

26. Matthew J. Eichner, Donald L. Kohn, and Michael G. Palumbo, "Financial Statistics for the United States and the Crisis: What Did They Get Right, What Did They Miss, and How Should They Change?" Finance and Economics Discussion Series, Divisions of Research & Statistics and Monetary Affairs, Federal Reserve Board (April 2010), which is also the source for Figure 6.3. The Fed's *Flow of Funds Accounts* tracks SIVs under the category "Issuers of Asset-Backed Securities," which excludes government agencies and government-sponsored enterprises. Asset-backed commercial paper is not reported directly, but it approximates the total of commercial paper reported as issued by ABS issuers and funding corporations. On the early unfolding of the crisis, see Paul Mizen, "The Credit Crunch of 2007–2008: A Discussion of the Background, Market Reactions, and Policy Responses," Federal Reserve Bank of St. Louis *Review* 90 (September/October 2008): 531–67.

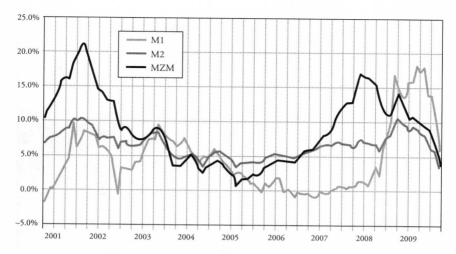

Note: M1 is from the Board of Governors, monthly and not seasonally adjusted: M1NS. M2 is from the Board of Governors, monthly and not seasonally adjusted: M2NS. MZM is from the St. Louis Fed, monthly and not seasonally adjusted: MZMNS. Annual year-on-year growth rates are author's calculations.

Figure 6.4. Monetary Growth (M1, M2, and MZM), 2001–2009
Source: Federal Reserve Bank of St. Louis 1979–2010

bulge in the monetary base. But other things were not equal. For *pari passu,* Bernanke was pulling money out of the economy by selling Treasury securities. As a consequence, during the year ending in August 2008, the monetary base had increased less than $20 billion, a mere 2.24 percent, which was well below its average annual growth of 7.54 percent during Greenspan's nineteen years in charge. Moreover, nearly all of the increase was in the form of currency in circulation. Total reserves during the first year of the crisis had risen from $72.4 to $73.0 billion, less than 1 percent. As for the broader measures of money, the annual growth rate of M1 rose somewhat, the growth rate of M2 fell a tad, and that of MZM was volatile around a roughly constant average (see Figure 6.4). Bernanke was not injecting liquidity, just redirecting it.

This complete sterilization of new Fed loans applied equally to the other initiatives it created before Bernanke's Phase Two kicked in, as depicted in Figure 6.5. Justified by the final failure of Bear Stearns, the Primary Dealer and Other Broker-Dealer Credit Facility (PDCF) and the Term Security Lending Facility (TSLF) were both set up in March 2008 (and both were terminated two years later). The former basically extended discount loans to investment

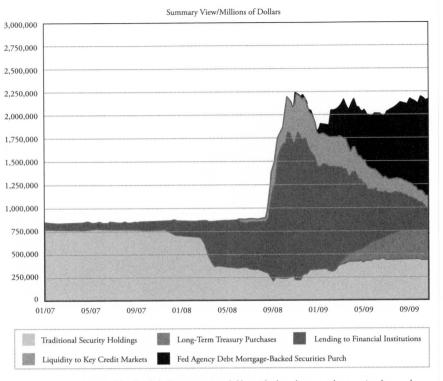

Summary View/Millions of Dollars

Note: "Traditional Security Holdings" includes Treasury securities held outright through open-market operations but not those acquired through repos (usually classified as open-market operations, but in this chart included with Lending to Financial Institutions). Beginning in 2009, long-term Treasury securities and federal-agency debt are separated out into other categories. "Lending to Financial Institutions" includes repos, discounts, Term Auction Facility, Central Bank Liquidity Swaps, Primary Dealer and Other Broker-Dealer Credit Facility, credit extended directly to AIG, and all miscellaneous Federal Reserve assets. "Liquidity to Key Credit Markets" includes Maiden Lane I, II, and III; Asset-Backed Commercial Paper Money Market Mutual Fund Liquidity Facility, Commercial Paper Funding Facility, and Term Asset-Backed Securities Loan Facility.

Figure 6.5. Federal Reserve Assets, 2007–2009

Source: Federal Reserve Bank of Cleveland 2007–2009

banks generally, while the latter lengthened the time that dealers could borrow securities from the Fed in exchange for other securities. Allowing dealers to swap their riskier assets temporarily for treasuries made it easier for them to borrow cash from other lenders in the repo market. Despite the fact that these two facilities greatly expanded the Fed's dealings with investment banks, they occupy the hazy boundary between Friedmanite and Bernankeite interventions. Even traditional open-market operations conducted with repos can admittedly be construed as short-term Fed loans to primary dealers. This ambiguity, however, does not apply to the direct bailout of Bear Stearns in the same month, channeled through a limited-liability company dubbed Maiden Lane and set up under the New York Fed.[27]

Monetary historian Michael Bordo questioned Bernanke's practices at the time. At the annual symposium of the Kansas City Fed in Jackson Hole, Wyoming, in late August of 2008, he pointed out: "The oddest part of the creation of these new discount window loans is that they are sterilized." Implicitly invoking the theoretical disparity between Friedman and Bernanke, Bordo further wondered "why this complicated method of providing liquidity has been introduced when the uncomplicated system of open market operations is available." The latter would leave "the distribution of liquidity to individual firms to the market," whereas the new facilities "exposed the Fed to the temptation to politicize its selection of recipients of its credit." Overall, we can say that Phase One represented an innovative, bold, and unproven attempt to stem onrushing financial panic, and it failed utterly.[28]

Given Bernanke's awareness of the growing crisis, why indeed did he preclude even a modest, short-term, reversible blip in the monetary base or reserves? Part of the answer probably involves his infatuation with inflation as the proper, long-run central-bank target. Through 2007 into 2008, people were quite concerned about rising commodity prices worldwide, particularly the price of oil.

---

27. Descriptions of all the additional facilities created by the Fed during both of Bernanke's phases can be found at both the Board of Governors website, http://www.federalreserve gov/monetarypolicy/default.htm, and the New York Fed website, http://www.newyork fed.org/markets/index.html. For good summaries of how these facilities affected the Fed's balance sheet, see William T. Gavin, "More Money: Understanding Recent Changes in the Monetary Base," Federal Reserve Bank of St. Louis *Review* 91 (March/April 2009): 49–59; and John Carlson, Joseph G. Haubrich, Kent Cherny, and Sarah Wakefield, "Credit Easing: A Policy for a Time of Financial Crisis," Federal Reserve Bank of Cleveland *Economic Trends* (November 11, 2009), http://www.clevelandfed.org/research/trends/2009/0209/02monpol.cfm
28. Michael Bordo, "Commentary: The Subprime Turmoil: What's Old, What's New and What's Next" (remarks for the Federal Reserve Bank of Kansas City, Jackson Hole, Wyoming, Symposium, August 21–23, 2008), reprinted in *Maintaining Stability in a Changing Financial System*, 118. See also Bordo, "The Crisis of 2007: The Same Old Story, Only the Players Have Changed" (remarks prepared for the Federal Reserve Bank of Chicago and International Monetary Fund Conference: Globalization and Systemic Risk, Chicago, September 28, 2007), http://sites.google.com/site/michaelbordo/home32

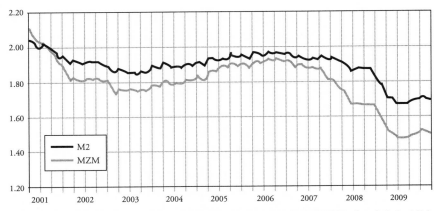

Note: M2 is from the Board of Governors, monthly and not seasonally adjusted: M2NS. MZM is from the St. Louis Fed, monthly and not seasonally adjusted: MZMNS. Nominal is the Bureau of Economic Analysis GDP, 1 decimal, quarterly, seasonally adjusted annual rate: GDP. Velocity divides GDP by the relevant monetary aggregate.

Figure 6.6. Velocity M2 and MZM, 2001–2009

Source: Federal Reserve Bank of St. Louis 1979–2010.

Driven to a large extent by increasing international demand, these hikes in certain relative prices represented a minor supply shock to the U.S. economy. Inflation targeting does not deal well with supply shocks, because to the extent that the central bank tightens to suppress rising prices, it will exacerbate any negative impact on output and unemployment. On top of that, a supply shock's positive impact on prices will partly disguise the negative impact from any velocity or monetary shock. Bernanke did not tighten as much as the European Central Bank did at the time, but his aversion to inflation left little room for a genuine liquidity injection.[29]

One might argue that because all of the broader monetary measures continued to grow at varying rates, pumping up base money was not the Fed's proper response. But because neither repos nor commercial paper were counted in any of the monetary measures, the contraction of those markets was not showing up as a fall in the money stock but as an increase in money demand. The panic therefore witnessed drastic declines in velocity, as Figure 6.6 illustrates. If Bernanke

29. Janet L. Yellen, "The U.S. Economic Situation and the Challenges for Monetary Policy," Federal Reserve Bank of San Francisco *Economic Letter* 2008-28-29 (September 19, 2008): 3. An Austrian advocate of free banking who agrees that prices should be permitted to rise with a supply shock is George Selgin. See his *Less Than Zero: The Case for a Falling Price Level in a Growing Economy* (London: Institute of Economic Affairs, 1997).

was going to prevent nominal GDP from also declining, with an attendant fall in output, he needed to offset the negative velocity shock with monetary expansion. It is no coincidence that this action is the exact policy that Scott Sumner, in his influential economics blog, *The Money Illusion*, has been stubbornly insisting should have been implemented to avoid the economic downturn. Surprisingly, it is also a policy that Bernanke should have implemented automatically if he really took seriously his supposition that the credit channel wreaks its havoc through velocity rather than through aggregate supply.[30]

Bernanke: Phase Two

All hell broke lose in September of 2008, a little more than a year after the panic had commenced. The investment bank Lehman Brothers went bankrupt; the government-sponsored mortgage agencies Fannie Mae and Freddie Mac were nationalized; a major money market fund, Primary Reserve Fund, "broke the buck" in industry parlance, meaning that it could no longer redeem its shares for a dollar each; and the enormous thrift holding company, American International Group (AIG), whose primary subsidiaries sold insurance, was unable to post the requisite collateral against its credit default swaps guaranteeing assorted securities. All these developments were manifestations of the ongoing collapse in the repo and commercial paper markets. The average haircut on repos for securitized debt spiked to 25 percent, the Libor–OIS spread reached 3.5 percentage points, and the TED spread approached 6 percentage points. Each of these spreads had been close to zero before August of the previous year. As a result, Bernanke hit the panic button on September 17 and inaugurated Phase Two of his crisis response.[31]

---

30. Velocity is calculated by dividing the relevant monetary measure into nominal GDP. These estimates, the basis for Figure 6.6, are somewhat crude, given that official GDP is reported only quarterly and seasonally adjusted, while the money stock figures used are monthly and not seasonally adjusted. Scott Sumner's blog, *The Money Illusion*, is at http://www.themoneyillusion.com/. See also Hetzel, "Monetary Policy in the 2008–2009 Recession."

31. For a detailed journalistic account of this period, see James B. Stewart, "Eight Days: The Battle to Save the American Financial System," *The New Yorker* 85 (September 21, 2009): 58–81.

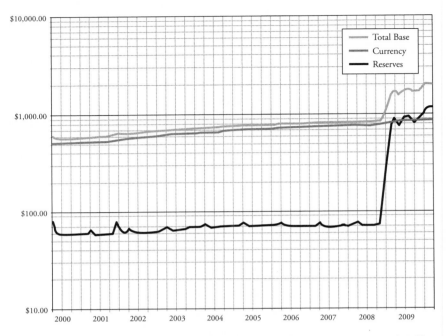

Note: The monetary base is Board of Governors Monetary Base (monthly and not seasonally adjusted). Not adjusted for Changes in Reserve Requirements: BOGUMBNS. Currency in circulation is the Currency Component of M1 (monthly and not seasonally adjusted): CURRNS. Total reserves are the latter subtracted from the former.

Figure 6.7. Monetary Base, 2007–2009 (Billions, Log Scale)
Source: Federal Reserve Bank of St. Louis 1979–2010

Along with the TARP, to which Congress appropriated $700 billion for targeted bailouts to be managed and funded by the Treasury Department, the most obvious feature of Phase Two was an unprecedented expansion of the monetary base, which doubled, in a mere four months, from $850 billion to $1.7 trillion (Figure 6.7). Nearly all of this increase was in bank reserves, whose year-on-year growth rate peaked at the astonishing rate of 1200 percent annually. The increase in the Fed's balance sheet was even greater, reaching $2.2 trillion, for reasons I explore later. By the time this expansion had tapered off, M1 was backed by more than 100 percent reserves. It would seem hard to deny that this response represented a massive liquidity injection. Yet all was not quite as it seemed.

The key to what Bernanke was doing was revealed earlier in 2008, when Fed officials began floating the idea of gaining authorization for the Fed to borrow money with its own securities. The Fed was running out of Treasury securities that it could sell to sterilize its targeted bailouts. Its holdings (not counting those acquired through repos) had dropped from $790.6 billion on July 12, 2007, constituting 90 percent of its balance sheet, to $479.8 billion on September 11, 2008, constituting 52 percent of its balance sheet. Moreover, $118 billion of the remainder was tied up in loans to dealers in exchange for other securities. If the Fed could market its own debt, it would be able to increase its total assets without affecting the monetary base. Its borrowings would simply pull money out of the economy on one end of its balance sheet, and then it would put that money back in on the other end through loans to favored firms and purchases of favored instruments. Notice how this is exactly the policy implied by Bernanke's analysis of the Great Depression. If the concern is that failing intermediaries will harm the economy mainly through the credit channel, then the goal is to subsidize them independently of what is happening to the money stock.[32]

The Fed in fact was already doing some borrowing indirectly. One insignificant way was through Maiden Lane, the Fed's very own SIV, set up to rescue Bear Stearns. As a subsidiary of the New York Fed, Maiden Lane had some liabilities that constituted funds not provided by the Fed. So Bernanke followed the same pattern after the explosion of the monetary base, creating four more limited-liability companies. Maiden Lane II and III, established in November and December 2008, were major parts of the AIG bailout. The Commercial Paper Funding Facility (CPFF), established in October 2008 and terminated in February 2010, purchased commercial paper. And the Money Market Investors

---

32. Greg Ip, "Fed Weighs Its Options in Easing Crunch," *Wall Street Journal*, April 9, 2008, 1, http://online.wsj.com/article/SB120768896446099091.html; Ip, "What Could the Fed Do?" *Wall Street Journal Blogs*, April 9, 2008, http://blogs.wsj.com/economics/2008/04/09/what-could-the-fed-do/?mod=WSJBlog; and Janet Yellin, "President's Speech," Federal Reserve Bank of San Francisco, March 29, 2009, http://www.frbsf.org/news/speeches/2009/0325.html. Friedman, in *A Program for Monetary Stability*, 34, 52–57, also once suggested that the Fed be granted "power to issue its own securities," but *not* for the purpose of buying other securities on the market but instead as a means of reducing the money stock in case the Fed ran out of government securities to sell. Concerned about the impact that the Treasury had on the money stock either through issuing its own base money (as with coins) or through issuing securities and then depositing the proceeds at the Fed, which Friedman recognized would contract base money, his ultimate *economic* solution was to merge the Treasury and Fed, eliminating Fed independence.

Funding Facility (MMIFL), established in October 2008, was never actually employed. The Fed, however, provided the bulk (when not all) of the money to these subsidiaries, whose other sources of funds never amounted to more than a few billion dollars.

Far more significant a beneficiary of indirect Fed borrowing was the currency swaps with foreign central banks, mentioned previously. By the beginning of 2009 swaps, which were coordinated with the U.S. Treasury's Exchange Stabilization Fund, had soared to more than half a trillion dollars. Yet much less than half of that total was financed by Fed money creation. The Treasury Department created a supplementary financing account that issued as much as $400 billion worth of securities *not* for the purpose of financing government expenditures; instead the money was deposited at the Fed. In essence, the Treasury was borrowing money from the general public and lending it to the Fed, which then relent it to foreign central banks. The Treasury through its deposits at the Fed withdrew money from circulation, while the Fed's purchase of foreign currencies put it back into circulation. The foreign currencies acquired as assets therefore showed up on the Fed's balance sheet but made no net contribution to the monetary base. These Treasury deposits explain why the increase of the balance sheet so greatly exceeded the increase of the base.[33]

Another source of divergence between the Fed's balance sheet and base money was some direct borrowing through more extensive *reverse* repos, in which the Fed uses its Treasury securities as collateral to secure short-term loans. In the past, this device was conducted almost exclusively with foreign central banks, and the amounts had run as high as $20 billion. But by late 2008, the Fed owed through reverse repos a total of $25 billion *domestically* to primary dealers, and as it repaid those loans, it went into debt for up to $90 billion from foreign central banks.[34]

---

33. Jeffrey Rogers Hummel, "Recent Fed Machinations," *Liberty & Power: Group Blog*, October 25, 2008, http://hnn.us/blogs/entries/56095.html; Hummel, "Is the Fed Reining Back," *Liberty & Power: Group Blog*, January 26, 2009, http://hnn.us/blogs/entries/60613 .html; Hummel, "Update on the Fed," *Liberty & Power: Group Blog*, February 2, 2009, http://hnn.us/blogs/entries/61061.html

34. Prior to December 2002, the Fed's H.4.1 Release treated its reverse repurchase agreements as "matched-sale purchase agreements," and so netted them out from the balance sheet, subtracting the amount from the asset side rather than adding it to liability side.

But the most important way that the Bernanke Fed began to borrow and continues to do so is indirect and largely unrecognized: by paying interest to banks on their reserves. The Fed was originally scheduled to gain this power in 2011, but on May 13, 2008, Bernanke sent a letter to House Speaker Nancy Pelosi asking for an immediate authorization. Permission was therefore included in the TARP act, and the Fed implemented this new power within days. To be fair, other central banks, including the European Central Bank, were already paying interest on reserves to help them hit their interest-rate targets, and even Friedman had once advocated this step, to facilitate the imposition of 100 percent reserves. Potential justifications for this policy are several.[35]

Nonetheless, many have come to recognize that interest-earning reserves have encouraged banks to raise their reserve ratios rather than expand their loans to the private sector. The rate that the Fed pays started out as high as 1.40 percent on required reserves and 1.00 percent on excess reserves but is now fairly low on both: 0.25 percent. Yet so are the alternatives available to the banks, especially after adjusting for risk. It is the gap between these rates that determines the incentive for individual banks to hang on to reserves. The interest on three-month Treasury bills remains lower, and both Treasury bills and reserves are assets that impose no legally mandated capital requirements on banks. Furthermore, an equally valid way to think about paying interest on reserves is that by doing so the Fed has made itself the preferred destination for a lot of bank lending. Bernanke in effect created money and then borrowed it back from the banks by paying them interest. The banks in turn partly financed their implicit loans to the Fed by reducing loans to the public by almost $500 billion as of the last

---

Thus, instead of increasing the balance sheet's size, the amounts involved were listed in a footnote.

35. Greg Ip, "Bernanke Asks Congress to Accelerate Authority to Pay Interest," *Wall Street Journal Blogs*, May 16, 2008, http://blogs.wsj.com/economics/2008/05/16/bernanke-asks -congress-to-accelerate-authority-to-pay-interest/; Jeffrey Rogers Hummel, "Interest on Bank Reserves and the Recent Crisis," *Liberty & Power: Group Blog*, October 13, 2008, http://hnn.us/blogs/entries/55621.html; Hummel, "Paradoxes of Paying Interest on Reserves," *Liberty & Power: Group Blog*, December 10, 2008, http://hnn.us/blogs/entries/ 58090.html; George Selgin, "Wholesale Payments: Questioning the Market-Failure Hypothesis," *International Review of Law and Economics* 24 (2004): 333–350; Friedman, *A Program for Monetary Stability*, 69–75.

quarter of 2009. Thus, the result is partly a net wash, with a shuffling of assets from the private sector to the Fed.[36]

Not all bank reserves earn interest—only those reserves held as deposits at the Fed. A bank's vault cash earns nothing, but vault cash currently amounts to only a little over $50 billion, less than total reserves before Bernanke launched Phase Two. What this means is that the payment of interest on reserves was tantamount to borrowing back from depositories the full $800 billion increase in reserves, and more. No wonder the impact of the base explosion on the broader monetary measures (except for M1) was so muted. Today in fact, the growth rates of M1, M2, and MZM are all declining. So Phase Two's seemingly massive injection of liquidity turns out to be not much of a liquidity injection at all.[37]

Who received the funds that the Fed was assiduously borrowing? In addition to the limited-liability subsidiaries and currency swaps already discussed, Bernanke created two other new facilities: the Asset-Backed Commercial Paper Money Market Mutual Fund Liquidity Facility (AMLF), in operation between October 2008 and February 2010, and the Term Asset-Backed Securities Loan Facility (TALF), initiated in November 2008 to work in conjunction with the Treasury's TARP subsidies and still in operation (as of January 2012). But the bulk of the money went to four other uses. First, lending to depositories through the Term Auction Facility doubled to half a trillion before falling back down to zero in mid-2010. Second, the Fed restored its holdings of Treasury securities to approximately the same dollar level it held before the panic began in August 2007, but with a much heavier proportion of long-term Treasury notes and bonds in its portfolio as compared with short-term Treasury bills.

---

36. The decline in bank lending, taken from the Fed's *Flow of Funds Accounts*, is for the commercial banking sector only and does not include savings institutions. It is based on totals for mortgages, consumer credit, security credit, and loans not elsewhere classified. It does not include bank holdings of securities, including securitized mortgages, which remained roughly constant anyway.

37. Figures on vault cash are available from the Fed's weekly H.3 Release: http://www .federalreserve.gov/releases/h3/. For a virtual admission that the Fed's goal was *not* a liquidity injection, see Todd Keister and James J. McAndrews, "Why Are Banks Holding So Many Excess Reserves?" Federal Reserve Bank of New York *Current Issues in Economics and Finance* 15 (December 2009), http://www.newyorkfed.org/research/current_issues/ ci15-8.html.

The third major asset in the Fed's new bloated balance sheet became securities issued by such federal agencies as Fannie and Freddie. Until the early 1980s, the Fed had frequently purchased small quantities of federal-agency securities when conducting open market operations, and it continued to use them in its repos afterward. By March 2010, however, its holdings of these securities had reached almost $170 billion. Finally, the fourth major and eventually largest asset on the Fed balance sheet was mortgage-backed securities, over a trillion dollars face value as of March 2010. Although the Fed had never purchased this particular type of security before January 2009, even this operation is not entirely without precedent. Up through 1984, the Fed had actually purchased a type of private securities known as bankers' acceptances, essentially bank-guaranteed private debt, which had figured prominently in open market operations during the 1920s and 1930s.

With this barrage of sometimes seemingly incremental steps when viewed individually, an amped-up Fed was bailing out such firms as Bear Stearns and AIG, assisting the Treasury with its TARP subventions, lending extensively to a new array of institutions including investment banks and money market funds, and purchasing large amounts of such new financial instruments as commercial paper and mortgage-backed securities. More than half of that activity was financed not by issuing true base money but by directly or indirectly borrowing from the private sector in one way or another. This is how Phase Two of Bernanke's policies transformed the Federal Reserve from a central bank confined primarily to managing the money supply into an institution that is also a giant government intermediary that borrows large sums in order to allocate credit. In that respect, it has become similar to Fannie or Freddie, with the important distinction that the Fed has greater discretion in subsidizing a wider variety of assets.

Bernanke's intention to continue down this path became apparent on April 30, 2010, when the Fed announced creation of the Term Deposit Facility (TDF). This is a mechanism through which banks can convert their reserve deposits at the Fed (which are just like Fed-provided, interest-earning checking accounts for banks) into deposits of fixed maturity at higher interest rates set by auction (which will be just like Fed-provided certificates of deposit for banks). Although the Fed so far has tested term deposits amounting to only a few billion dollars at maturities ranging from 14 to 84 days, term deposits make the Fed's borrowing more explicit. They also permit Bernanke to drop (at least for now) seeking permission for the Fed to issue its own securities. In his July 2010 testimony before Congress, he confided that "the Federal Reserve is putting in place the capacity to conduct large reverse repos with an expanded set of counterparties. Second, the Federal Reserve has tested a term deposit facility, under which instruments similar to the certificates of deposit that banks offer their customers will be auctioned to depository institutions." Both of these actions are ways for the Fed to maintain its hefty support of various financial markets without recourse to changes in the money stock.[38]

In sum, Phase One and Phase Two of Bernanke's policies turned out to be only slight variations on the same theme. Almost nothing that the Fed did during either phase can be accurately described as an effort to stimulate or even stabilize aggregate demand. Whatever the ostensible rationale, everything ended up being a supply-side intervention designed to prop up failing financial institutions. Helicopter Ben talks a good line about being ready to unleash quantitative easing, but this talk only imparts an aura of justification for the Fed's incredibly expanded role in allocating the country's scarce supply of savings. If anything, his policies were closer to a quantitative tightening. A better moniker would therefore be "Bailout Ben."

Central Banking as the New Central Planning

Three related arguments have been nested within the foregoing narrative. The first exposes the divergence between Milton Friedman and Ben Bernanke over the prescriptions they advocate during financial panics, a divergence arising from their contrasting emphasis on the money stock versus financial intermediation. The second credits Alan Greenspan with possibly averting panics using Friedmanite liquidity injections, whereas it blames the severity of the financial crises of 2007–2008 at least in part on Bernanke's consistent failure

---

38. The Fed press release announcing the Term Deposit Facility is at http://www.federalreserve.gov/newsevents/press/monetary/20100430a.htm; general details about the facility are at http://www.federalreserve.gov/monetarypolicy/tdf.htm. Bernanke's July 21, 2010 testimony before the Senate Committee on Banking, Housing, and Urban Affairs is at http://www.federalreserve.gov/newsevents/testimony/bernanke20100721a.htm

to do so. And the third alleges that Bernanke's targeted and sterilized bailouts have altered the fundamental nature of the Federal Reserve. The second argument, about the comparative efficacy of Friedman's and Bernanke's respective prescriptions, is undoubtedly the most controversial, and I have no illusions about having come to a full understanding of what caused the recent recession. But one does not have to accept this relative evaluation for the other two arguments still to be correct. Nor must one even agree about the critical theoretical differences between Friedman and Bernanke to recognize that the Fed that emerged from the crisis is no longer the same as the Fed before.

For the foreseeable future, Bernanke has added to the Fed's traditional function of simply manipulating the money supply and letting the market determine where the credit will flow, the function of centrally allocating credit, much of which it has borrowed. During his opening remarks at the August 2010 Fed symposium in Jackson Hole, Wyoming, he even revealed the terminology that goes along with this new approach. The Fed is now working through what Bernanke calls the "portfolio balance channel," in which policy is designed to change "the quantity and mix of financial assets held by the public." Based on the assumption "that different financial assets are not perfect substitutes in investors' portfolios," this goal is achieved by manipulating the "securities the central bank holds or is anticipated to hold at a point in time (the 'stock view'), rather than the current pace of new purchases (the 'flow view')."[39]

Most economists appear not to fully appreciate yet just how drastic are the changes that Bernanke has wrought. When the proposal of Congressman Ron Paul to audit the Fed was before Congress, hundreds of economists interpreted the proposal as a threat to the Fed's independence and rallied to the Fed's defense.[40] Granted, the independence of a central bank that is primarily confined

---

39. Ben S. Bernanke (speech at the Federal Reserve Bank of Kansas City Economic Symposium, Jackson Hole, Wyoming, August 27, 2010), http://www.federalreserve.gov/news events/speech/bernanke20100827a.htm; Caroline Baum, "Monetarists Follow Milton Friedman to the Grave," *Bloomberg*, August 29, 2010, http://www.bloomberg.com/news/ 2010-08-30/monetarists-follow-milton-friedman-to-grave-commentary-by-caroline -baum.htm

40. Catherine Rampell, "Petition for Fed Independence," *New York Times*, July 15, 2009, http://economix.blogs.nytimes.com/2009/07/15/petition-for-fed-independence/. Ultimately 386 economists, some quite prominent, signed the petition opposing an audit.

to monetary policy may provide an important safeguard against inflation and political business cycles. Another question altogether, however, is independence for a bloated central bank that has assumed on a grand scale the same task of those assorted government-owned and sponsored agencies that redirect credit flows into privileged markets and institutions, contrary to what would occur on the market.

Bernanke is undoubtedly honest and dedicated as well as very smart; favoritism and pull probably had little or no influence on who received the vast amounts that the Fed dispensed during the crisis. We can go further; Bernanke has even brought the Fed to new levels of transparency with respect to both proceedings of the Federal Open Market Committee and the Fed's releases and websites. Were this not so, I would have found it much more difficult to write this chapter. But can we depend in the future on always having someone of impeccable integrity at the Fed's helm, someone who will steadfastly insulate this enhanced intimacy with the U.S. economy from politics and corruption? An institution with such enlarged command over the financial system must not be free from close oversight. The excesses of Fannie and Freddie should have taught us that lesson.

And let us not deceive ourselves about Bernanke's promise to shed all the myriad new asset powers the Fed has acquired once the economy fully recovers. The problem is not simply dumping securities that are no longer marketable. Although many of the Fed's new facilities have been discontinued or are no longer functioning (at least for the time being), several Fed press releases left open the possibility that the Term Auction Facility, for instance, would be permanent.[41] Bernanke may be sincere about his intention, but when in the history of the Fed—or most other government agencies for that matter—has newly acquired authority and reach been easily, entirely, and voluntarily relinquished?

The unprecedented growth in the Fed's discretionary authority is actually in keeping with Bernanke's opinions about the proper role of government, another respect in which he differs from Friedman. Even before the financial crisis,

---

41. Board of Governors for the Federal Reserve System, Press Release (September 24, 2009), http://www.federalreserve.gov/newsevents/press/monetary/20090924a.htm; Press Release (December 12, 2007), http://www.federalreserve.gov/newsevents/press/monetary/20071212a.htm.

Bernanke expressed great admiration for President Franklin D. Roosevelt and his handling of the Great Depression. In a testament to what Bernanke termed "Rooseveltian Resolve," he wrote in 1999 that "Roosevelt's specific policy actions were, I think, less important than his willingness to be aggressive and to experiment—in short, to do whatever was necessary to get the country moving again. Many of his policies did not work as intended, but in the end FDR deserves great credit for having the courage to abandon failed paradigms and to do what needed to be done." Notice not just Bernanke's strong faith in government intervention, but also his embracing of the popular fetish of good intentions, where a policy is judged not according to systematic outcomes but according to hoped-for results. As long as the government *tries* something, what matter if its efforts do not work?[42]

My tedious rendition of the new lending facilities that Bernanke set up, each with its own acronym, reveals even an emulation of FDR's alphabet soup of New Deal agencies, however unconscious. In a speech on April 8, 2010, Bernanke reaffirmed his praise for Roosevelt's "bold experimentation," drawing explicit parallels with the Fed's recent actions under his own leadership. "[P]olicymakers must respond forcefully, creatively, and decisively to severe financial crises," he exclaimed. Or consider the following, which Bernanke included in his tribute to Friedman: "what we do know is that the central bank of the world's economically most important nation in 1929 was essentially leaderless and lacking in expertise. This situation led to decisions, or nondecisions, which might well not have occurred under either *better leadership or a more centralized institutional structure* [emphasis mine]." These are not the words of a sedate central banker reluctantly intervening in a crisis but rather of an activist regulator who views the economy as requiring expert, detailed management with constant, coordinated control. Still more recently at Princeton University, Bernanke explicitly called for improved "economic engineering" and "economic management" by the regulatory authorities.[43]

---

42. Bernanke, "Japanese Monetary Policy," 25; Ip, "Long Study of Great Depression Has Shaped Bernanke's Views"; John Cassidy, "Anatomy of a Meltdown: Ben Bernanke and the Financial Crisis," *The New Yorker*, December 1, 2008, 48–63.

43. Ben S. Bernanke, "Economic Policy: Lessons from History" (speech at the 43rd Annual Alexander Hamilton Awards Dinner, Center for the Study of the Presidency and

In the final analysis, central banking has become the new central planning. Under the old central planning—which performed so poorly in the Soviet Union, Communist China, and other command economies—the government attempted to manage production and the supply of goods and services. Under the new central planning, the Fed attempts to manage the financial system and the supply and allocation of credit. Contrast present-day attitudes with the Keynesian dark ages of the 1950s and 1960s, when almost no one paid much attention to the Fed, whose activities were fairly limited by today's standard. Even before Bernanke, the Fed's increasingly conspicuous targeting of interest rates had major economic players sitting on the edge of their chairs, waiting to hear the Open Market Committee's latest pronouncement, rationally oblivious to the fact that the Fed is basically a noise trader in the market for loanable funds and cannot ultimately control *real* interest rates.

This pretense of control led William A. Fleckenstein (a critic of Greenspan who is unduly harsh, in my opinion) to write aptly: "Central bankers are actually *central planners*. Like bureaucratic leaders of central-planned or command economies, they pick an interest rate to within two decimal places that they guess will be the correct one, and then they proceed to cram it down the throat of the banking system [emphasis his]." But now with Bernanke, the central-planning aspect of central banking has become far more encompassing. As George Selgin put it in an interview, "the Fed . . . has morphed into a central planning agency with a corporate welfare department." It requires a certain hubris to undertake such a daunting task, yet a hubris that Bernanke clearly does not lack. Unfortunately, as the prolonged and incomplete recovery from the recent recession suggests, the Fed's new central planning, just like the old central planning, will ultimately prove an unfortunate, and possibly disastrous, failure.[44]

Congress, Washington, D.C., April 8, 2010), http://www.federalreserve.gov/newsevents/speech/bernanke20100408a.htm; Bernanke, "remarks at the Conference to Honor Milton Friedman"; Bernanke, "Implications of the Financial Crisis for Economists" (speech at the Conference Co-sponsored by the Center for Economic Policy Studies and the Bendheim Center for Finance, Princeton University, September 24, 2010), http://www.federalreserve.gov/newsevents/speech/bernanke20100924a.htm
44. William A. Fleckenstein (with Frederick Sheehan), *Greenspan's Bubbles: The Age of Ignorance at the Federal Reserve* (New York: McGraw Hill, 2008), 3; Selgin interview in Thomas Oliver, "Fed Didn't Save the Economy," *Atlanta Journal-Constitution.* August 22, 2009, http://www.ajc.com/business/fed-didnt-save-the-121009.html

References

Adrian, Tobias, Christopher R. Burke, and James J. McAndrews. 2009. The Federal Reserve's Primary Dealer Credit Facility. *Federal Reserve Bank of New York, Current Issues in Economics and Finance* 15 (December). Available at: http://www .newyorkfed.org/research/current_issues/ci15-4.html

Ahiakpor, James C. W. 2003. *Classical Macroeconomics: Some Modern Variations and Distortions.* London: Routledge.

Baum, Caroline. 2010. Monetarists Follow Milton Friedman to the Grave. *Bloomberg,* August 30. Available at: http://www.bloomberg.com/news/2010-08-30/ monetarists-follow-milton-friedman-to-grave-commentary-by-caroline-baum .htm

Beckner, Steven K. 1996. *Back from the Brink: The Greenspan Years.* New York: Wiley.

Bernanke, Ben S. 1983. Nonmonetary Effects of the Financial Crisis in the Propagation of the Great Depression. *American Economic Review* 73, no. 3: 257–76.

———. 1988. Monetary Policy Transmission: Through Money or Credit? *Federal Reserve Bank of Philadelphia Business Review* (September–October): 3–11.

———. 2000a. *Essays on the Great Depression.* Princeton, N.J.: Princeton University Press.

———. 2000b. Japanese Monetary Policy: A Case of Self-Induced Paralysis. In *Japan's Financial Crisis and Its Parallels to U.S. Experience,* edited by Ryoichi Mikitani and Adam S. Posen, 149–66. Washington, D.C.: Institute for International Economics.

———. 2002a. Deflation: Making Sure "It" Doesn't Happen Here. Remarks before the National Economists Club, Washington, D.C., November 21. Available at: http://www.federalreserve.gov/boarddocs/speeches/2002/20021121/default.htm

———. 2002b. Remarks at the Conference to Honor Milton Friedman, University of Chicago, Chicago, November 8. Available at: http://www.federalreserve.gov/ boarddocs/speeches/2002/20021108/default.htm

———. 2007. The Subprime Mortgage Market. Speech at the Federal Reserve Bank of Chicago's 43rd Annual Conference on Bank Structure and Competition, May 17. Available at: http://www.federalreserve.gov/newsevents/speech/bernanke2007 0517a.htm

_____. 2010a. The Economic Outlook and Monetary Policy. Speech at the Federal Reserve Bank of Kansas City Economic Symposium, Jackson Hole, Wyo., August 27. Available at: http://www.federalreserve.gov/newsevents/speech/bernanke 20100827a.htm

_____. 2010b. Economic Policy: Lessons from History. Speech at the 43rd Annual Alexander Hamilton Awards Dinner, Center for the Study of the Presidency and Congress, Washington, D.C., April 8. Available at: http://www.federalreserve .gov/newsevents/speech/bernanke20100408a.htm

_____. 2010c. Implications of the Financial Crisis for Economists. Speech at a conference cosponsored by the Center for Economic Policy Studies and the Bendheim Center for Finance, Princeton University, Princeton, N.J., September 24. Available at: http://www.federalreserve.gov/newsevents/speech/bernanke20100924a .htm

_____. 2010d. Semiannual Monetary Policy Report to the Congress before the Committee on Banking, Housing, and Urban Affairs, U.S. Senate, Washington, D.C., July 21. Available at: http://www.federalreserve.gov/newsevents/testimony/ bernanke20100721a.htm

Bernanke, Ben S., and Mark Gertler. 1995. Inside the Black Box: The Credit Channel of Monetary Policy Transmission. *Journal of Economic Perspectives* 9, no. 4: 27–95.

Bordo, Michael D. 2007. The Crisis of 2007: The Same Old Story, Only the Players Have Changed. Remarks prepared for the Federal Reserve Bank of Chicago and International Monetary Fund Cconference "Globalization and Systemic Risk," Chicago, September 28. Available at: http://sites.google.com/site/michaelbordo/ home32

_____. 2008. Commentary: The Subprime Turmoil: What's Old, What's New, and What's Next. Remarks for the Federal Reserve Bank of Kansas City symposium, Jackson Hole, Wyo., Symposium, August 21–23. Available at: http://www.kc.frb .org/publicat/sympos/2008/Bordo.08.15.08.pdf. Reprinted in *Maintaining Stability in a Changing Financial System*, 111–20. Kansas City: Federal Reserve Bank of Kansas City, 2008.

Calomiris, Charles W. 2008. Banking Crises. In *The New Palgrave Dictionary of Economics*, 2d ed., edited by Steven Durlauf and Lawrence Blume, 1:348–52. New York: Palgrave Macmillan.

Carlson, John B., Joseph G. Haubrich, Kent Cherny, and Sarah Wakefield. 2009. Credit Easing: A Policy for a Time of Financial Crisis. *Federal Reserve Bank of Cleveland, Economic Trends* (November 11). Available at: http://www.cleveland fed.org/research/trends/2009/0209/02monpol.cfm

Carlson, Mark. 2006. *A Brief History of the 1987 Stock Market Crash with a Discussion of the Federal Reserve Response.* Washington, D.C.: Federal Reserve Board. Available at: http://www.federalreserve.gov/pubs/feds/2007/200713/200713abs.html

Cassidy, John. 2008. Anatomy of a Meltdown: Ben Bernanke and the Financial Crisis. *The New Yorker* 84 (December 1): 48–63.

Cowen, Tyler. 2008. Bailout of Long Term Capital: A Bad Precedent? *New York Times*, December 28: BU5.

Eichner, Matthew J., Donald L. Kohn, and Michael G. Palumbo. 2010. *Financial Statistics for the United States and the Crisis: What Did They Get Right, What Did They Miss, and How Should They Change?* Finance and Economics Discussion Series. Washington, D.C.: Divisions of Research and Statistics and Monetary Affairs, Federal Reserve Board, April.

Ely, Bert. 2008. Savings and Loan Crisis. In *The Concise Encyclopedia of Economics,* 2d ed., edited by David Henderson, 459–63. Indianapolis, Ind.: Liberty Fund.

Federal Reserve Bank of Cleveland. 2007–2009. Credit Easing Policy Tools. Available at: http://www.clevelandfed.org/research/data/credit_easing/index.cfm

Federal Reserve Bank of St. Louis. 1979–2010. Economic Research. Available at: http://research.stlouisfed.org/fred2/

Fleckenstein, William A., with Frederick Sheehan. 2008. *Greenspan's Bubbles: The Age of Ignorance at the Federal Reserve.* New York: McGraw Hill.

Friedman, Milton. 1960. *A Program for Monetary Stability.* New York: Fordham University.

———. 2003. The Fed's Thermostat. *Wall Street Journal,* August 19: A8.

Friedman, Milton, and Anna Jacobson Schwartz. 1963. *A Monetary History of the United States, 1867–1960.* Princeton, N.J.: Princeton University Press.

Gavin, William T. 2009. More Money: Understanding Recent Changes in the Monetary Base. *Federal Reserve Bank of St. Louis Review* 91, no. 2: 49–59.

Goodhart, Charles A. E. 1987. Why Do Banks Need a Central Bank? *Oxford Economic Papers* (new series) 39, no. 1: 84–89.

———. 1995a. *The Central Bank and the Financial System.* Cambridge, Mass.: MIT Press.

———. 1995b. Price Stability and Financial Fragility. In *Financial Stability in a Changing Environment,* ed. by Kuniho Sawamoto, Zenta Nakajima, and Hiroo Taguchi, 439–97. New York: St. Martin's Press.

———. 1998. *Money, Information, and Uncertainty.* 2d ed. Cambridge, Mass.: MIT Press.

Gorton, Gary B. 2008. The Panic of 2007. Paper prepared for the Federal Reserve Bank of Kansas City symposium, Jackson Hole, Wyo., symposium, August 21–23. Available at: http://papers.ssrn.com/sol3/papers.cfm?abstract_id=1255362. Reprinted in *Maintaining Stability in a Changing Financial System,* 131–262. Kansas City: Federal Reserve Bank of Kansas City, 2008.

———. 2009a. Slapped in the Face by the Invisible Hand: Banking and the Panic of 2007. Paper prepared for the Federal Reserve Bank of Atlanta's 2009 Financial Markets Conference, May. Available at: http://papers.ssrn.com/sol3/papers .cfm?abstract_id=1401882

———. 2009b. The Subprime Panic. *European Financial Management* 15, no. 1: 10–46.

———. 2010a. Questions and Answers about the Financial Crisis. Paper prepared for the U.S. Financial Crisis Commission, February. Available at: http://papers .ssrn.com/sol3/papers.cfm?abstract_id=1557279

———. 2010b. *Slapped by the Invisible Hand: The Panic of 2007.* Oxford, U.K.: Oxford University Press.

Gorton, Gary, and Andrew Metrick. 2009. *Securitized Banking and the Run on the Repo.* Yale ICF International Center for Finance Working Paper no. 09-14. New Haven, Conn.: Yale University, November.

Greenspan, Alan. 1988. Statements and comments for *"Black Monday": The Stock Market Crash of October 19, 1987: Hearing before the U.S. Senate Committee on Banking, Housing, and Urban Affairs,* Hearing, 100th Cong., 1st sess., February 2–5.

———. 2008. *The Age of Turbulence: Adventures in a New World.* New York: Penguin Books.

Hayek, Friedrich A. 1935. *Prices and Production.* 2d ed. London: Routledge.

Henderson, David R., and Jeffrey Rogers Hummel. 2008. *Greenspan's Monetary Policy in Retrospect: Discretion or Rules?* Cato Institute Briefing Paper no. 109. Washington, D.C.: Cato Institute, November.

Hetzel, Robert L. 2009. Monetary Policy in the 2008–2009 Recession. *Federal Reserve Bank of Richmond Economic Quarterly* 95 (Spring): 201–33.

Hördahl, Peter, and Michael R. King. 2008. Developments in Repo Markets during the Financial Turmoil. *BIS Quarterly Review* (December): 37–53.

Horwitz, Stephen. 2000. *Microfoundations and Macroeconomics: An Austrian Perspective.* London: Routledge.

Hummel, Jeffrey Rogers. 2008a. Interest on Bank Reserves and the Recent Crisis. *Liberty & Power: Group Blog,* October 13. Available at: http://hnn.us/blogs/entries/55621.html

———. 2008b. Paradoxes of Paying Interest on Reserves. *Liberty & Power: Group Blog,* December 10. Available at: http://hnn.us/blogs/entries/58090.html

———. 2008c. Recent Fed Machinations. *Liberty & Power: Group Blog,* October 25. Available at: http://hnn.us/blogs/entries/56095.html

———. 2009a. Is the Fed Reining Back? *Liberty & Power: Group Blog,* January 26. Available at: http://hnn.us/blogs/entries/60613.html

———. 2009b. Update on the Fed. *Liberty & Power: Group Blog,* February 2. Available at: http://hnn.us/blogs/entries/61061.html

Ip, Greg. 2005. Long Study of Great Depression Has Shaped Bernanke's Views. *Wall Street Journal,* December 7: A1.

———. 2008a. Bernanke Asks Congress to Accelerate Authority to Pay Interest. *Wall Street Journal Blogs,* May 16. Available at: http://blogs.wsj.com/economics/2008/05/16/bernanke-asks-congress-to-accelerate-authority-to-pay-interest/

———. 2008b. Fed Weighs Its Options in Easing Crunch. *Wall Street Journal,* April 9: A1. Available at: http://online.wsj.com/article/SB120768896446099091.html

———. 2008c. What Could the Fed Do? *Wall Street Journal Blogs,* April 9. Available at: http://blogs.wsj.com/economics/2008/04/09/what-could-the-fed-do/?mod=WSJBlog

Ip, Greg, and Jim VandeHei. 2001. Economic Front: How Policy Makers Regrouped to Defend the Financial System. *Wall Street Journal*, September 18.

Keister, Todd, and James J. McAndrews. 2009. Why Are Banks Holding So Many Excess Reserves? *Federal Reserve Bank of New York Current Issues in Economics and Finance* 15 (December). Available at: http://www.newyorkfed.org/research/current_issues/ci15-8.html

Kos, Dino. 2001. Treasury and Federal Reserve Foreign Exchange Operations. *Federal Reserve Bulletin* 87 (December): 757–62.

Lowenstein, Roger. 2000. *When Genius Failed: The Rise and Fall of Long-Term Capital Management.* New York: Random House.

Martin, Justin. 2000. *Greenspan: The Man behind the Money.* Cambridge, Mass.: Perseus.

Meyer, Laurence H. 2004. *A Term at the Fed: An Insider's View.* New York: Harper-Collins.

Mizen, Paul. 2008. The Credit Crunch of 2007–2008: A Discussion of the Background, Market Reactions, and Policy Responses. *Federal Reserve Bank of St. Louis Review* 90, no. 5: 531–67.

Oliver, Thomas. 2009. Fed Didn't Save the Economy. *Atlanta Journal-Constitution*, August 22. Available at: http://www.ajc.com/business/fed-didnt-save-the-121009.html

Rampell, Catherine. 2009. Petition for Fed Independence, *New York Times*, July 15. Available at http://economix.blogs.nytimes.com/2009/07/15/petition-for-fed-independence/

Schwartz, Anna J. 1986. Real and Pseudo-Financial Crises. In *Financial Crises and the World Banking System,* edited by Forrest Capie and Geoffrey E. Wood, 11–31. New York: St. Martin's Press.

Securities Industries and Financial Markets Association. 2009. *Research Report 4.* New York: Securities Industries and Financial Markets Association, May.

Selgin, George. 1988. *The Theory of Free Banking: Money Supply under Competitive Note Issue.* Totowa, N.J.: Rowman and Littlefield.

———. 1997. *Less Than Zero: The Case for a Falling Price Level in a Growing Economy.* London: Institute of Economic Affairs.

———. 1999. Japan: The Way Out. Unpublished essay, September.

———. 2004. Wholesale Payments: Questioning the Market-Failure Hypothesis. *International Review of Law and Economics* 24: 333–50.

———. 2010. Email to Jeffrey Rogers Hummel, September 9.

Stewart, James B. 2009. Eight Days: The Battle to Save the American Financial System. *The New Yorker* 85 (September 21): 58–81.

Stewart, James B., and Daniel Hertzberg. 1987. How the Stock Market Almost Disintegrated a Day after the Crash. *Wall Street Journal,* November 20: 1.

Stiglitz, Joseph E., and Bruce Greenwald. 2003. *Towards a New Paradigm in Monetary Economics.* Cambridge, U.K.: Cambridge University Press.

Stigum, Marcia. 1990. *The Money Market.* 3rd ed. Homewood, Ill.: Business One Irwin.

Stigum, Marcia, and Anthony Crescenzi. 2007. *Stigum's Money Market.* 4th ed. New York: McGraw Hill.

Sumner, Scott. 2009–2010. *The Money Illusion: A Slightly Off-Center Perspective on Monetary Problems.* Available at: http://www.themoneyillusion.com/

Tuccille, Jerome. 2002. *Alan Shrugged: The Life and Times of Alan Greenspan, the World's Most Powerful Banker.* Hoboken, N.J.: Wiley.

U.S. Federal Deposit Insurance Corporation. 1997. *History of the Eighties—Lessons for the Future.* Vol. 1, *An Examination of the Banking Crises of the 1980s and Early 1990s.* Washington, D.C.: U.S. Federal Deposit Insurance Corporation. Available at: http://www.fdic.gov/bank/historical/history/vol1.html

———. 2010. Historical Statistics on Banking. Available at: http://www2.fdic.gov/hsob/index.asp

U.S. Federal Reserve Board of Governors, U.S. Federal Reserve System. 1987. H.4.1 Weekly Releases: Factors Affecting Bank Reserves and Condition Statement of F.R. Banks. Available at: http://fraser.stlouisfed.org/statreleases/h41/

———. 1987–1995. *Flow of Funds Accounts of the United States.* Available at: http://www.federalreserve.gov/releases/z1/Current/data.htm

———. 1996–2010a. Quarterly *Flow of Funds Accounts of the United States* (quarterly). Available at http://www.federalreserve.gov/releases/z1/default.htm

_____. 1996–2010b. Weekly H.4.1 Releases: Factors Affecting Bank Reserves and Condition Statement of F.R. Banks. Available at: http://www.federalreserve.gov/releases/h41/

_____. 1998–2010. Weekly H.3 Releases: Aggregate Reserves of Depository Institutions and the Monetary Base. Available at: http://www.federalreserve.gov/releases/h3/

_____. 2007. Press release, December 12. Available at: http://www.federalreserve.gov/newsevents/press/monetary/20071212a.htm

_____. 2009. Press release, September 24. Available at: http://www.federalreserve.gov/newsevents/press/monetary/20090924a.htm

_____. 2010. Press release, April 30. Available at http://www.federalreserve.gov/newsevents/press/monetary/20100430a.htm

U.S. Securities and Exchange Commission. 2009. *Select SEC and Market Data Fiscal 2009*. Washington, D.C.: U.S. Securities and Exchange Commission. Available at: http://www.sec.gov/about.shtml

White, Lawrence H. 1999. *The Theory of Monetary Institutions*. Malden, Mass.: Blackwell.

Woodward, Bob. 2001. *Maestro: Greenspan's Fed and the American Boom*. Exp. paperback ed. New York: Simon & Schuster.

Yellen, Janet L. 2008. The U.S. Economic Situation and the Challenges for Monetary Policy. *Federal Reserve Bank of San Francisco Economic Letter*, no. 2008-28-29 (September 19): 1–5.

_____. 2009. President's Speech. *Federal Reserve Bank of San Francisco News* (March 29). Available at http://www.frbsf.org/news/speeches/2009/0325.html

7

The Great Recession and Monetary Disequilibrium

W. William Woolsey

Introduction

THE MILD RECESSION that began in December 2007 turned into the "Great Recession" during the fourth quarter of 2008. What had been a manageable reallocation of resources away from housing and towards more highly valued uses along with a modest slowdown in spending turned into a rapid drop of money expenditures on current output—a general glut of goods. While a modest recovery began soon after, money expenditures, output, and employment all remain depressed relative to their growth paths of the Great Moderation of 1984 to 2008. This collapse of money expenditures and its failure to return to trend is illustrated in Figure 7.1. Here, money expenditures is measured by Final Sales of Domestic Product.[1]

What happened? While there were many serious economic problems that manifested in the fall of 2008, the fundamental reason for the emergence of the Great Recession was monetary disequilibrium. In particular, there arose in late 2008 a pronounced excess demand for money—a desired amount of money that far exceeded the existing quantity of it.[2] This shortage caused the collapse in money expenditures that in turn triggered the Great Recession.

The fundamental proposition of monetary theory tells us we should not be surprised by this outcome. The fundamental proposition says that even though

---

1. "Final Sales of Domestic Product," U.S. Department of Commerce: Bureau of Economic Analysis, http://research.stlouisfed.org/fred2/series/FINSAL?cid=106
2. Leland B. Yeager, "Significance of Monetary Disequilibrium" in ed. George A. Selgin, *The Fluttering Veil: Essays on Monetary Disequilibrium* (Indianapolis: Liberty Fund, Inc., 1997), 218.

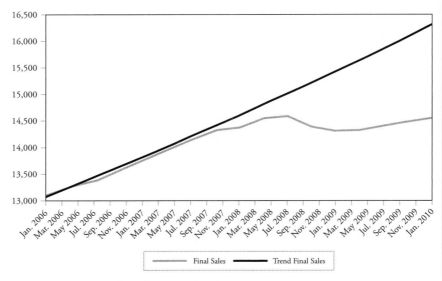

Figure 7.1. Final Sales of Domestic Product
Source: FRED Database

an individual can adjust actual money holdings to his or her desired holdings, the economy as a whole cannot, given a fixed amount of money. The individuals' efforts to adjust their desired money holdings to actual money holdings will therefore cause disruptive changes in interest rates, real production, employment, and income. Eventually, prices will adjust to restore monetary equilibrium. Until they do, though, an excess money demand shock like the one that occurred in late 2008 is bound to be contractionary, if not somehow offset, for example, by an adequate increase in the quantity of money.[3]

In this chapter, I further explore this monetary disequilibrium approach to money expenditures and recession. I begin in the second section entitled "The Direct Effects of Monetary Disequilibrium on Money Expenditures," by discussing the direct effects of monetary disequilibrium on money expenditures. Then, in the third section entitled "Indirect Effects of Monetary Disequilibrium on Monetary Expenditures," I explain the indirect effects of monetary disequilibrium on money expenditures, including how monetary disequilibrium affects the intertemporal coordinating role of interest rates and other assets. In the fourth section entitled "Keynesian Explanations of Depressed Money Expendi-

---

3. Yeager, "What are Banks?" in *The Fluttering Veil*, 127–28.

tures and Recession," I then critique the Keynesian approach to depressed money expenditure; and follow that up with an assessment of supply shocks from a monetary disequilibrium perspective in the fifth section entitled " Supply Shocks and Monetary Disequilibrium." I conclude in the section entitled "Monetary Policy and Monetary Disequilibrium" by discussing the policy implications for a monetary disequilibrium crisis like the Great Recession.

The Direct Effects of Monetary Disequilibrium on Money Expenditures

An imbalance between the quantity of money and the demand to hold it is likely to have a direct impact on money expenditures for final goods and services—particularly on the consumer goods and services and capital goods produced and sold in the private sector. While money is an asset, it serves as the medium of exchange. Incomes are generally earned as money payments, and, for the most part, that money is soon spent on various goods, services, and other assets. Money is not solely an asset that is held, but it is also something that flows through cash balances. If an individual is holding more or less money than desired, adjusting that outflow of monetary expenditures allows actual money holdings to adjust to desired money holdings.

With a shortage of money, an individual household can reduce the outflow of monetary expenditures on consumer goods and nonmonetary assets. Given the inflow of money receipts, this allows money holdings to increase to the desired level. Similarly, firms can adjust the expenditure of current cash flow on new and replacement capital goods.

However, the money expenditures of one individual are the monetary receipts of another. While any one household or firm can add to money balances by restricting the outflow of monetary expenditures, this simply shifts the shortage to those who would have received the matching payments. Those who are now short of money may also reduce their outflow of money expenditures.

To the degree that those initially short of money, or any of those whose reduced monetary receipts leave them short of money, respond by reducing expenditures on final goods and services, the result is a decrease in the demand for output. Nothing in this process suggests that anyone is less interested in selling resources or products to earn income, and so, the lower demand for products is matched by an unchanged desire to sell. This is what is traditionally described as a general glut of goods.

While firms that experience lower sales may lower prices, or at least reduce the rate of price increase, each firm is likely to respond by reducing production as well. To the degree firms reduce production, then the reduction in output and employment results in lower real income. Because the services provided by holding money are normal goods, the reduction in real income results in a decrease in the demand to hold money. The demand to hold money falls to match the existing quantity.[4]

This understanding, at the very least, suggests that the reason why money expenditures on final goods and services decreased in the fall of 2008 was that the quantity of money during that period was less than the demand to hold money. Households decreased expenditures on consumer goods, particularly durable consumer goods and also purchases of new homes. Firms, meanwhile, greatly reduced their expenditures on capital goods. While each household and firm may have intended to increase their money holdings by this process, their money balances were in fact limited by the change in the quantity of money over the period.

If the prices of goods and services, including wages, had dropped in proportion with money expenditures, the real volume of expenditures could have been maintained. Monetary disequilibrium could have been avoided and monetary equilibrium maintained without disrupting the volume of output and employment.

So did prices and wages drop in proportion to fall in money expenditures? On the contrary, both continued to increase despite the collapse in money expenditures. This development can be seen in Figures 7.2 and 7.3.[5]

These figures show that growth of wages and the price level did slow down, but nowhere near the level of decline in final sales. Consequently, most of the

---

4. Yeager, "Essential Properties of the Medium of Exchange," in *The Fluttering Veil*, 106–08.
5. Gross Domestic Product Chain Type Price Index, U.S. Department of Commerce: Bureau of Economic Analysis, http://research.stlouisfed.org/fred2/series/GDPCTPI?cid =21; Average Hourly Wages: Total Private Industry, U.S. Department of Labor: Bureau of Labor Statistics, http://research.stlouisfed.org/fred2/series/AHETPI?cid=11

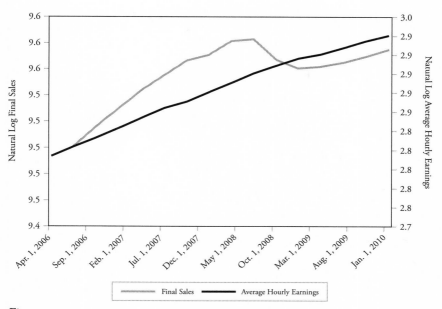

Figure 7.2
Source: FRED Database

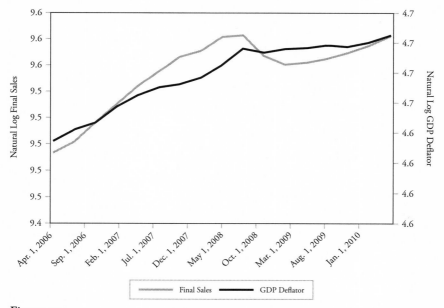

Figure 7.3
Source: FRED Database

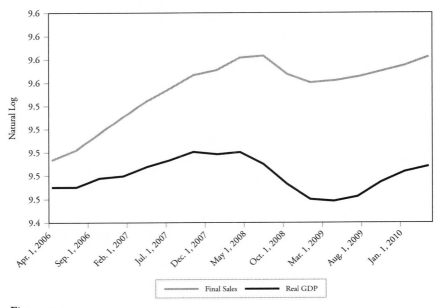

Figure 7.4
Source: FRED Database

adjustment to the excess money demand shock occurred via a drop in the real volume of output as seen in Figure 7.4.[6]

Indirect Effects of Monetary Disequilibrium on Monetary Expenditures

Households short on money do not necessarily reduce expenditures on consumer goods and services to accumulate desired money balances. They can instead change the form of their saving by refraining from purchasing nonmonetary assets such as bonds, stocks, or real estate out of current income. Similarly, by selling nonmonetary assets, it is possible to immediately adjust actual money holdings to desired money holdings rather than gradually letting them build up by restraining money expenditures out of current receipts.

6. Real Gross Domestic Product, 3 decimal, U.S. Department of Commerce: Bureau of Economic Analysis, http://research.stlouisfed.org/fred2/series/GDPC96?cid=106

Similarly, firms do not necessarily rebuild money holdings by refraining from purchasing new capital goods out of current cash flow. They can instead accumulate money rather than use current cash flow to purchase nonmonetary assets. And firms can sell off nonmonetary assets to accumulate money holdings.

Since those who fail to sell nonmonetary assets, or else purchase them, now have less money, the logic of monetary disequilibrium proceeds as before. Restrictions of expenditures, or else sales of nonmonetary assets, must continue until the demand to hold money adjusts to the existing quantity. To the degree that anyone who ends up with reduced money balances responds by spending less on output, then the reduced money expenditure depresses output and employment.

However, much of modern macroeconomics follows Keynes by emphasizing the impact of asset sales on the nominal yields on financial assets, especially bonds. The real yield on those assets, then, impacts consumer and investment expenditure.

Interest Rates and Long-Run Equilibrium

Before discussing how monetary disequilibrium can impact interest rates, it is useful to review the role of real interest rates as a price providing economic coordination. Real interest rates—the amount of purchasing power that borrowers pay lenders—depend on the supply of saving and demand for investment in the long run. Saving is that part of income not spent on consumer goods and services. By saving, a household uses income to accumulate assets or repay debts, resulting in an increase in net worth. Since the added net worth increases the ability to purchase consumer goods in the future, saving shifts consumption from the present to the future.

Investment is spending by a firm on capital goods—machines, buildings, and equipment. While the purchase and production of capital goods tends to increase the productive capacity of the economy, resources used to produce capital goods are not available to produce consumer goods and services now. Investment, then, is a shift in the production of consumer goods from the present to the future.

The price that coordinates spending on consumer goods and services with the ability of firms to produce consumer goods and services over time is the interest rate. The "natural interest rate" is the level of the interest rate that keeps saving and investment equal. That part of income that households don't spend on consumer goods and services today is matched by spending by firms on capital goods. The funds that households save results in an increase in net worth that matches the expansion in the amounts of capital goods—machines, buildings, and equipment. And the increase in net worth plus interest—the increase in the ability of households to buy consumer goods and services in the future— matches the expansion in the firms' ability to produce consumer goods and services in the future.

A supply of saving and demand for investment diagram can be used to illustrate the natural interest rate and saving and investment as illustrated in Figure 7.5. At interest rates above the natural interest rate, households receive the signal and are given an incentive to refrain from spending on consumer goods, and to instead accumulate assets to add to net worth and increase their ability to purchase consumer goods in the future. Firms receive the inconsistent signal to purchase few capital goods, freeing up resources to produce consumer goods now but adding less to their capacity to produce consumer goods in the future.

In this view, an increase in the desire by households to save, by accumulating assets (including money) or repaying debts, is represented by a shift of the supply of saving curve to the right. This is shown in Figure 7.6. The natural interest rate is lower, and both the amount saved and the amount invested increase. While lower interest rates dampen the decrease in expenditure on consumer goods, there is a shift in the composition of demand away from consumer goods and towards capital goods. Production follows the shift in demand, so that fewer consumer goods are produced now and instead capital goods are produced, adding to the ability to produce consumer goods in the future.

In a growing economy, spending on, and the production of, both consumer and capital goods are growing over time. The more likely scenario is that the added saving reflects a smaller increase in spending on consumer goods now, and a larger increase in spending on capital goods now. The result is a larger increase in the production of consumer goods in the future than would have occurred without the additional saving.

A less happy scenario would be a decrease in investment demand as shown in Figure 7.7. If firms become less optimistic about the future profitability of

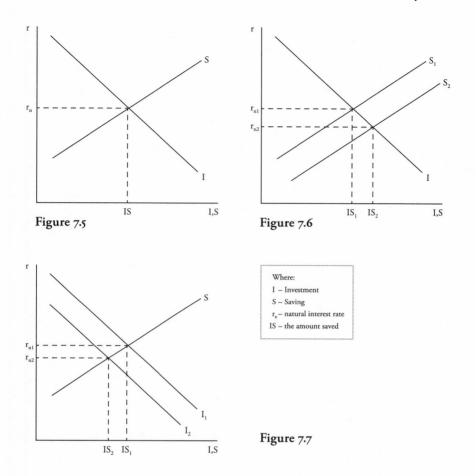

Figure 7.5

Figure 7.6

Figure 7.7

Where:
I – Investment
S – Saving
r_n – natural interest rate
IS – the amount saved

production, the result is a shift in the investment demand curve to the left. The natural interest rate falls, and both the amount invested and saved fall as well. While the lower interest rate dampens the decrease in investment demand, the result is a shift in the composition of expenditure away from the purchase of capital goods and towards the purchase of consumer goods. The composition of production shifts as well, with more consumer goods produced now. But because of reduced productive capacity, fewer consumer goods can be produced in the future.

In a growing economy, the most plausible scenario is that the decreased demand for investment reflects a more rapid increase in spending on consumer goods now and a smaller increase in the demand for capital goods. The production of consumer goods then would expand by less in the future than would have occurred if investment prospects were better.

Keynes rejected the traditional "classical" account of the interest rate (saving and investment), arguing that it assumed full employment of labor. He argued that changes in employment and income influence saving and so the level of the real interest rate at which saving equals investment.[7] While a bit simplistic, his argument is more or less correct. The natural interest rate is the level of the real interest rate consistent with saving equaling investment at a level of real output and income that matches the productive capacity of the economy.

The "IS curve" is a staple of Keynesian textbook macroeconomics. A variant can be used to illustrate the relationship between the natural interest rate and the productive capacity of the economy. The "IS curve" illustrates the negative relationship between the real interest rate and planned real expenditure. Lower real interest rates provide a signal and incentive for households to expand current consumption and firms to expand investment. Local government, especially, changes expenditures in response to changes in the real interest rate. Lower real interest rates can even depress the exchange rate and stimulate expanded exports while reducing imports.[8]

The natural interest rate is the level of the real interest rate where real expenditure matches the productive capacity of the economy. This is shown in Figure 7.8. Real interest rates below the natural interest rate create signals and incentives so that individual plans for real expenditure add up to a level beyond the productive capacity of the economy.

An increase in saving or a decrease in investment shift the IS curve to the left, and this reduces the natural interest rate. Figure 7.9 shows a decrease in the natural interest rate.[9]

---

7. John Maynard Keynes, *General Theory of Employment, Interest and Money* (New York: First Harbinger Edition, Harcourt, Brace & World, Inc., 1964): 175–85.
8. The "IS curve" is often constructed on a rather simplistic Keynesian basis by taking a given change in the real interest rate, and examining how the consequent increased investment expenditure stimulates output and real income. Part of the additional real income is saved, and real income supposedly rises enough so that the saved portion matches the initial increase in investment.
9. Unlike the more traditional supply of saving and demand for investment diagram, the shift in investment and implied shift in consumption is not shown. Only the level

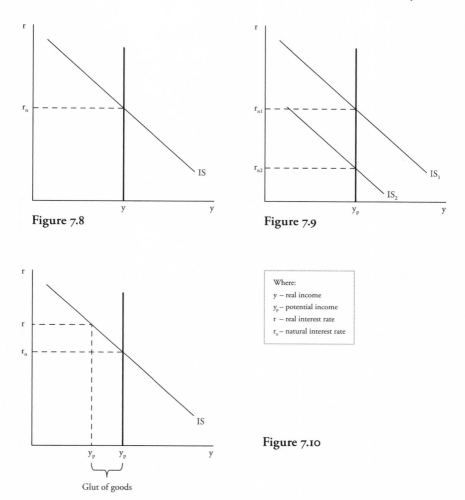

Figure 7.8

Figure 7.9

Where:
y – real income
y_p – potential income
r – real interest rate
r_n – natural interest rate

Figure 7.10

Glut of goods

Real interest rates above the natural interest rate, on the other hand, result in individual plans for real expenditure that add up to less than the productive capacity of the economy. In other words, real interest rates above the natural interest rate imply a "general glut of goods." Figure 7.10 shows a general glut of goods.

---

of the real interest rate, consistent with total real expenditures remaining equal to the productive capacity of the economy, is illustrated by the diagram, and not the composition of demand or the implied allocation of resources between capital and consumer goods.

The "Liquidity Effect" and Monetary Disequilibrium

Since individual households and firms facing a shortage of money are likely to respond, at least partly, by reducing purchases of financial assets out of current income or selling part of their current holdings, lower prices and higher yields on financial assets should be expected. If the nominal yield on money itself is assumed to be sticky, in the extreme, set at zero for conventional hand-to-hand currency, changes in the nominal yields on assets impact the opportunity cost of holding money.

For example, those short of money refrain from purchasing, or sell, non-monetary assets like bonds. The prices of the bonds fall, and the interest rate rises. If the yield on transactions accounts (or hand-to-hand currency) fails to rise in proportion, the opportunity cost of holding money rises. This will tend to reduce the amount of money people prefer to hold, closing off the shortage of money.

Unfortunately, this shortage of money has not reduced the supply of saving or increased the demand for investment. The "IS" curve has not shifted to the right. The "natural interest rate" that provides the signals and incentives to keep saving equal to investment and the real volume of expenditures equal to the productive capacity of the economy has not changed.

If a shortage of money is closed off by higher nominal interest rates on non-monetary assets, interest rates can no longer be expected to coordinate saving and investment. If the expected inflation rate were unchanged, then the higher nominal interest rates would raise real interest rates in proportion, pushing the real interest rate above the natural interest rate. Further, since the impact of a shortage of money on money expenditures is foreseeable, so is slower inflation, or even deflation. Real interest rates can be expected to rise through both higher nominal interest rates and lower expected inflation. Thus the indirect effect of a shortage of money acting on the prices and yields on financial assets tends to force the market real interest rate above the natural interest rate and reduce the real volume of expenditures to a point where there is a general glut of goods. A shortage of money could result in the situation shown by Figure 7.9.

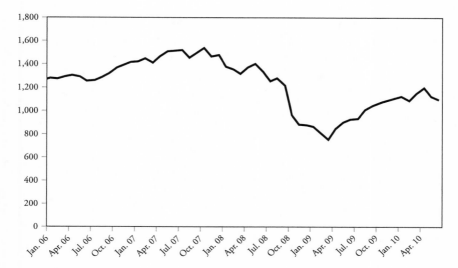

Figure 7.11
Source: FRED Database

Asset Prices and Interest Rates and the Great Recession

In this section, I will discuss the role that the sale of financial assets to accumulate money played in the Great Recession. Most obviously, people sold stock in order to hold "cash." One simple approach is to sell stock and leave the funds received in a transactions account. Of course, not everyone can do this simultaneously. The primary effect was a collapse of stock prices. Figure 7.11 shows that the S&P 500 index peaked at the beginning of the fourth quarter of 2007, then dropped at a 273.4 percent annual rate in October of 2010 and a 111-percent annual rate in November.[10]

Similarly, there was a sell-off of corporate bonds. An individual selling off bonds can leave the funds received in a transactions account, shifting from risky bonds to government-insured bank deposits. Not everyone can do this, and the result is that corporate bond prices fell and their yields rose.

There was even a spike in the yields of negotiable certificates of deposit and financial commercial paper. Generally, riskier and longer-term-to-maturity

---

10. S&P 500, Online Data Robert E. Shiller, http://www.econ.yale.edu/~shiller/data.htm

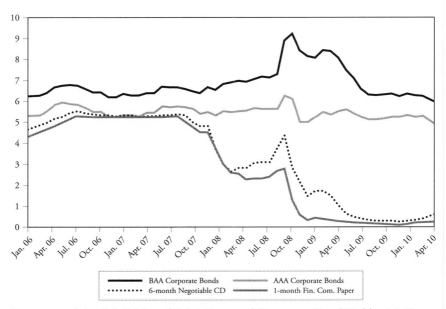

Figure 7.12. Moody's BAA and AAA-Seasoned Corporate Bond Yields, AA Financial Commercial Paper, and Six-Month CD Rate
on the Secondary Market

Source: FRED Database

financial assets had the larger decreases in prices and increases in yields. Figure
7.12 shows Moody's BAA and AAA-seasoned Corporate Bond yields, AA Financial Commercial Paper, and 6-month CD rate on the secondary market.[11]

While the spikes in the nominal interest rates on corporate bonds have
largely been reversed, the spike in the rates on certificates of deposit and financial
commercial paper were pauses in a continuing trend of lower rates. As shown
by Figure 7.12, by the middle of 2010, those rates were much lower than before
the initial spike.

11. Moody's Seasoned AAA Corporate Bond Yield, Board of Governors of the Federal Reserve System, http://research.stlouisfed.org/fred2/series/AAA?cid=119; 6-month Certificate
of Deposit-Secondary Market, Board of Governors of the Federal Reserve System, http://
research.stlouisfed.org/fred2/series/CD6M?cid=121; One Month AA Financial Commercial Paper Rate, Board of Governors of the Federal Reserve System, http://research
.stlouisfed.org/fred2/series/CPF1M?cid=120; Moody's Seasoned BAA Corporate Bond
Yield, Board of Governors of the Federal Reserve System, http://research.stlouisfed.org/
fred2/series/BAA?cid=119

The continued depressed state of the economy and the recent experience of slower inflation suggest that part of this decrease in nominal rates was not reflected in equally low real interest rates. But a much more important impact is on the natural interest rate. Expectations of depressed output and income in the future plausibly raise saving and reduce investment. As continued failure of the economy to recover leads households to reduce expectations of future income prospects, they cut back on consumption now. Similarly, firms' continued disappointment in seeing a rapid recovery in sales may lead them to reduce future expectations of sales and profits, and reduce investment. The effect of expectations of a depressed economy on the natural interest rate is shown in Figure 7.10.

While it is possible and likely that monetary disequilibrium will impact interest rates and disrupt their ability to provide proper signals and incentives to coordinate production over time, it is a mistake to assume that a return of interest rates to "normal" levels, or even lower-than-normal levels, means that monetary disequilibrium is not the reason for depressed money expenditures and real output.

Keynesian Explanations of Depressed Money Expenditures and Recession

That tight money could result in lower money expenditures is uncontroversial. However, the more important implication of the monetary disequilibrium approach is that depressed money expenditures on final goods and services is only possible if there is an excess demand for money. In particular, the Keynesian explanation of depressed money expenditure due to increased saving or reduced investment necessarily smuggles in monetary disequilibrium through the back door.

Monetary Disequilibrium and the Paradox of Thrift

The "Paradox of Thrift" is a staple of basic Keynesian economics. The argument is that while an individual may increase saving by reducing consumption, an increase in saving by the economy as a whole can result in reduced money expenditures, reduced output, and people becoming so poor that, on the whole, they no longer can afford to increase saving.

How does the process supposedly occur? Those seeking to save reduce their spending on consumer goods. The firms that would have sold the consumer goods produce less, so income and employment contract. The reduced income results in a further decrease in consumption expenditure, and so, further reductions in production, income and employment. This multiple contraction of money expenditures, income and employment only stops when growing poverty leads households to cease their efforts to save out of their depressed incomes.

How does the "Paradox of Thrift" relate to monetary disequilibrium? In an economy that only has money and current output, the relationship between expenditures on that output and monetary disequilibrium is simple. Planned sales of current output generate a matching income. That income can be spent either on currently produced output or else not spent at all. Any difference between income and expenditure must be matched by an accumulation of money—an increase in the demand to hold money.

If an increase in the demand for money—a planned accumulation of money over the period under consideration—is ruled out by assumption, then saving is only possible through the purchase of capital goods. Saving and investment are necessarily equal. However, if planned accumulation of money balances is considered and the quantity of money is given, then it becomes possible for saving to exceed investment by the amount of accumulated money balances. The planned excess of saving over investment is necessarily identical to the planned accumulation of money balances.

When there are a variety of assets that are neither output nor money, then it is possible to sell output, planning to earn income, and then use that income to accumulate nonmonetary assets. For example, it would be possible for people to plan to produce and sell output and purchase stock—existing equity claims on firms. Such a scenario appears to make possible a decrease in money expenditures on output without there being any increase in the demand for money. Can saving by the accumulation of nonmonetary assets lead to reduced money expenditures, depressed real output, and lower employment?

A key insight of monetary disequilibrium is that because money is the medium of exchange, those selling assets, such as existing stock, don't necessarily want to hold more money. And so, the question must always be asked: what do those who sell these nonmonetary assets do with the money they receive in payment? Too often, the implicit assumption is that they necessarily hold the money and so any shift in demand from output—say consumer goods—to financial assets becomes an increase in the demand for money.

Many financial assets trade on markets that come close to clearing continuously—prices and yields adjust almost immediately to keep quantity supplied and demanded equal. The notion that the difference between planned sales of output and the demand to purchase output could be matched by an unmet desire to accumulate financial assets like stocks or bonds is implausible. Leaving aside the possibility of a shortage of money, consider the implications of a surplus of output matched by a shortage of bonds or stocks. Brokers on the stock exchange or bond dealers respond to the shortage of the assets by raising their prices, which reduces their yields. With the markets for the financial markets clearing, there is no shortage on those markets to match the surplus of output.

The lower yields on assets is a lower interest rate, which creates an incentive for an expansion of consumer and investment expenditure. Further, higher prices of at least some assets can create a wealth effect that should result in increased spending on consumer goods and services. The monetary disequilibrium approach, however, is less focused on the particular pathway through which changing asset prices and interest rates might result in changes in the demand for (or supply of) currently produced output. The point is rather that surpluses of output must be matched by shortages of some other goods or services, and markets that continuously clear are not plausible candidates for shortages.[12]

There are some assets that trade on markets that do not clear continuously. Real estate is subject to protracted periods of buyers' and sellers' markets. Used consumer durables and used capital goods trade on markets that are sometimes little different from the markets for current output. However, many used goods are very close substitutes for output. While it is conceivable that there could be a surplus of new single homes matched by a shortage of existing homes or a surplus of new cars matched by a shortage of used cars, it seems very likely that some of those frustrated in purchasing used goods would instead purchase current output.

12. Yeager, "Essential Properties of the Medium of Exchange," in *The Fluttering Veil*, 103–04.

But what of assets that have no close substitutes: for example, beachfront land? Yeager describes this as the "old masters" problem. The artists have passed on and cannot contribute to current output. It is possible that the planned production of goods and services to earn incomes is matched partially by a demand for "old masters." There might be a surplus of output matched by a shortage of these old masters." If the market for "old masters" fails to clear, then there is a general glut of currently produced goods and services. Employment opportunities are curtailed because it is impossible to produce the particular goods and services demanded.

However, Yeager shows that if there is a shortage of "old masters," the result will not be a general glut of goods unless there is a shortage of money. If there is a shortage of "old masters," then some of those seeking to purchase them at current prices will be frustrated. They are earning income in the form of money, but are unable to spend that money on the goods they prefer. What do these frustrated buyers do? There are really just two possibilities: (1) These buyers might choose to purchase some other good or service that, by assumption, isn't a very close substitute for the desired "old masters"; or (2) the other alternative is for these buyers to simply hold onto their money. And if the "second-best" use of income is to accumulate money balances, then holding onto money is the source of the monetary disequilibrium consistent with the excess supply of goods.[13]

The monetary disequilibrium approach does not require that changes in the quantity of money or the demand to hold money arrive as a bolt from the blue—exogenous shocks to the quantity of money or the demand to hold money. As Yeager's arguments show, money disequilibrium can be a consequence of other economic changes. Leaving aside unusual situations where a seller's market in real estate could result in frustrated buyers holding money as a second best alternative, monetary disequilibrium could easily be a consequence of changes in asset prices. An increased demand for nonmonetary assets can raise their prices and lower their yields. Interest rates decrease. If the yield on money does not fall in proportion, this lowers the opportunity cost of holding money and so raises the amount of money people want to hold. If the quantity of money fails to increase, or by only a smaller amount, then the result is monetary disequilibrium—a general glut of goods matched by a shortage of money.

13. Yeager, "What are Banks?" in *The Fluttering Veil*, 126.

Money and Credit Confused

Monetary disequilibrium is an imbalance between the quantity of money and the demand to hold money. Unfortunately, it is common to describe the supply of loans as the "supply of money," and the demand to borrow money as the "demand for money." A shortage of money may be identified with a supply of loans that fails to keep up with the demand to borrow money, or worse, the increase in loan interest rates, which clears up what otherwise would be a shortage of loanable funds. While it is possible that a shortage of money could result in a decrease in the supply of credit and higher interest rates, this is a possible consequence of monetary disequilibrium and not monetary disequilibrium itself.

Perhaps more troubling is the assumed relationship between changes in the supply of credit and money expenditures. The argument seems reasonable. Households borrow money to purchase homes and consumer durables, if they are not running up credit card bills to pay for clothes or a night out on the town. Firms borrow money to fund purchases of capital goods. If the supply of credit falls, then fewer funds are available to purchase consumer goods and capital goods. An inadequate supply of credit results in lower money expenditures.

Even more troubling is the claim that deleveraging, paying down existing debts, results in less money expenditures and so reduced output. This argument also seems plausible enough, but it is nothing more than the paradox of thrift in a slightly different guise. If households reduce consumption out of current income to pay down debt, this is an increase in saving. If firms use revenue to pay down debt, this is an increase in business saving. Supposedly, saving results in reduced money expenditures, lower output, and reduced employment.

However, an inadequate supply of credit or deleveraging can only result in decreased money expenditures if an imbalance between the quantity of money and the demand to hold money somehow develops. Credit shifts funds between and among households and firms. For every borrower there is a lender. If fewer funds are lent to borrowers, the borrowers may reduce expenditures on output, but what do those who would have made the loans do with the funds? If they expand their money balances rather than make loans, then the increase in the demand for money results in a shortage of money.

Similarly, if borrowers use their income to pay down their debts rather than purchase consumer goods or capital goods, then those who had made the loans receive the repayments. If they expand their money holdings rather than relend the money or purchase some other good, service, or asset, then the increase in the demand for money results in a shortage of money.

It is possible that a central bank or commercial banking system might have created the money out of thin air and then lent it out. If less money is created and lent, then the quantity of money is lower. Again, the result is an excess demand for money—an imbalance between the demand to hold money and the quantity of money.

If there is no increase in the demand for money or decrease in the quantity of money, then reduced lending simply shifts expenditures away from borrowers to those who would have been lenders. Repayments of existing debts simply shift expenditures away from those "deleveraging" to the former creditors being repaid.[14]

The Keynesian "Multiplier" and the Yeager Effect

The "Paradox of Thrift" claims that a change in saving and consumption will result in a multiple change in money expenditures, income, and output. Changes in investment or government spending similarly have a multiplied impact.

How does the process occur? Those seeking to save reduce spending on consumer goods and services. The firms that would have sold the consumer goods produce less, so income and employment contract. The reduced income results in a further decrease in consumer expenditure, and further reductions in production, income, and employment. This multiple contraction of money expenditures, income, and employment only stops when growing poverty leads households to cease their efforts to save out of their depressed income.

This account of the multiplier has a more-than-passing resemblance to the fundamental proposition of monetary theory in the context of a shortage of money. Those short of money reduce their money expenditures. Those who would have received the money are now short on money. The process continues to contract monetary expenditures until falling real output and income leaves

14. Yeager and Robert L. Greenfield,"Money and Credit Confused?" in *The Fluttering Veil*, 179.

people so poor that their demand to hold money falls to match the given quantity. The Keynesian multiplier is monetary disequilibrium without the money.

More importantly, the "Yeager effect" shows that this process of cumulative rot is only possible in the context of monetary disequilibrium. Consider again the multiplier story. Increased saving and reduced consumption leads to reduced production, employment, and income. The reduced income supposedly leads to less consumption and to another round of reduced production and employment and consumption. But as income and employment decrease, the demand to hold money falls. If there had been no shortage of money before, the result is a surplus of money. Since what are now excess money balances are spent on output or other assets, the cumulative rot is arrested.[15]

Monetary Disequilibrium and the Liquidity Trap

The liquidity trap is an argument Keynes developed, suggesting that there may be situations in which monetary policy is ineffective.[16] During the fall of 2008 and on into the subsequent years of the Great Recession, the term "liquidity trap" came to be used to refer to problems associated with the "zero nominal bound." In this view, once the central bank has lowered its target interest rate to zero, then monetary policy can do nothing to expand money expenditures.

The monetary disequilibrium approach shows that any problem due to a lower bound on interest rates must be associated with an excess demand for money.[17] Suppose people plan to sell output and earn income in order to purchase short-term bonds. At current prices and interest rates, there is a surplus of output—a general glut of goods—matched by a shortage of bonds. If bond markets clear, the prices of the bonds rise and their yields fall enough to clear that market. Either the excess supply of output disappears, or else the shortage must shift to some other asset market. If those markets clear, then there is no shortage in those markets either. And if those markets don't clear and result in frustrated buyers, then those frustrated buyers are left with what are now excessive money balances. What do they do with them?

---

15. Yeager, "The Keynesian Diversion," in *The Fluttering Veil*, 200–03.
16. Keynes, *General Theory of Employment, Interest and Money*, 207.
17. Yeager, "A Cash-Balance Interpretation of Depression," in *The Fluttering Veil*, 13–14.

The point of these accounts is not to claim that there can never be a surplus of output, but to simply point out that the only plausible shortage to match a surplus of output is a shortage of money. If the initial shortage was for short-term bonds, and the yields on those bonds approach zero, then any further excess demand for those bonds will almost certainly be shifted to money.

The logic of the zero nominal bound on interest rates is that, rather than bear the cost of holding securities with negative yields, potential lenders can simply hold money. The assumption is that hand-to-hand currency has a zero nominal yield, and currency can be held in bank vaults or, if excess reserves are forbidden, in safety deposit boxes. The logic of the zero nominal bound is that if the interest rate becomes too low, people will instead hold money rather than lend. And that implies an increase in the demand to hold money.

Consider a market with a conventional price ceiling. The quantity demanded is greater than the quantity supplied. Because there is a shortage, some buyers are frustrated. They had money to buy the product, but they cannot. It is possible that some of those who are frustrated would simply hold the money as the next best alternative, but it is likely that purchasing some other good, service, or asset would be the choice of the typical frustrated buyer.

With the zero nominal bound on bonds, the "price ceiling" on Treasury bills is that the price cannot rise above the face value by more than the cost of storing currency. If there is a shortage at that "ceiling" price, some of the buyers will be frustrated. However, the very nature of this ceiling is that it exists because holding currency is better than holding securities with a negative nominal yield. It is likely that this shortage of bonds at the zero nominal bound will be shifted over to an excess demand for money.

Supply Shocks and Monetary Disequilibrium

Monetary disequilibrium focuses on the situation in which a decrease in money expenditures results in reduced production and employment. The key insight is that the source of the problem must be an imbalance between the quantity of money and the demand to hold money. This does not mean that aggregate output can only fall in response to reduced money expenditures. In particular, a decrease in potential output—the productive capacity of the economy— can lead to lower production without there being a shortage of money.

Typical examples of an adverse supply shock would be a poor harvest or a disruption in oil supplies. However, suppose that problems in credit markets prevent the efficient flow of funds from households to firms. Profitable production opportunities are not exploited because firms cannot obtain the needed credit. The production of goods and services is curtailed.

The lower levels of production result in depressed income and employment. A Keynesian "multiplier" process would suggest that these reduced levels of income and employment would then result in reduced consumption expenditure and further reductions in income and employment. The monetary disequilibrium approach, however, shows that, assuming money is a normal good, the reduced level of real income would lead to an excess supply of money. As those excess money balances are spent, the demands for goods rise. The resulting shortages of goods and services would result in higher prices. The higher prices then increase the demand for money enough so that people are again just satisfied to hold the existing quantity of money. Output contracts to reflect the reduced productive capacity of the economy, and the price level rises so that money expenditures remain unchanged.

Another scenario that would at least temporarily disrupt productive capacity would be a shift in the composition of monetary expenditures, such as decrease in the demand for new single family homes and an expansion in the demand for fixed capital goods by firms and consumer goods by households. In the short run, construction firms are set up to continue producing single-family homes. Some of the capital goods used in the construction field are specific to those endeavors. Similarly, many of the skills of carpenters and other skilled tradesmen may have limited usefulness in producing other goods and services.

Because the relevant productive capacity is for those things that are in demand, the result of a shift in demand is similar to a decrease in productive capacity. Those sectors facing falling demand contract production, while those sectors enjoying growing demand seek to expand production but run into bottlenecks due to inadequate capacity. Only gradually—as labor shifts, new skills are developed, and appropriate capital goods are produced—can total output recover. In the meanwhile, assuming money is a normal good, the depressed level of real output and income implies a lower demand to hold money. Given the quantity of money, the excess supply of money is cleared by a higher price level, causing the demand for money to rise to the given quantity of money.

Conclusion: Monetary Policy and Monetary Disequilibrium

The monetary disequilibrium approach to macroeconomics implies what appears to be a simple norm for monetary policy—avoid monetary disequilibrium and keep money expenditures growing with the productive capacity of the economy. If the quantity of money is equal to the demand to hold money, never cause a shortage or surplus of money by changing the quantity of money.

Unfortunately, since the demand for money can change, a better statement of the policy norm is to always adjust the quantity of money to the demand to hold money. One of the most important implications of the monetary disequilibrium approach is that if this norm is followed, then there will never be a general glut of goods.

What about a "liquidity trap" or the zero nominal bound? Suppose there is a shortage of Treasury bills resulting in a higher price and lower yield. The zero nominal bound is reached, but there remains a shortage of Treasure bills. Frustrated buyers hold money.

Further suppose the central bank responds to the shortage of money by appropriately expanding the quantity of money, however, it purchases the very same bonds for which the quantity demanded outstripped the quantity supplied at the zero nominal bound. To the degree the central bank purchases a larger quantity of those very same bonds, it will reduce the quantity of those bonds available for others to hold, leading to a larger shift by frustrated buyers to increased money holdings. While the quantity of money would increase with every purchase of bonds, the demand for money would increase as well, so this form of monetary policy is pointless.

If there is a shortage of money, and a central bank is expanding the quantity of money through open market operations, then it should purchase securities with nominal yields greater than zero. For example, if a central bank usually purchases T-bills, and the yields on four-week T-bills are driven to zero, then the central bank should begin purchasing three-month T-bills. If those yields are driven to zero, then it should move to six-month T-bills, and then, if needed, move on to notes and then bonds. If the entire national debt is purchased and still their remains a shortage of money, then private securities must be purchased, starting with short-term AA commercial paper and moving towards

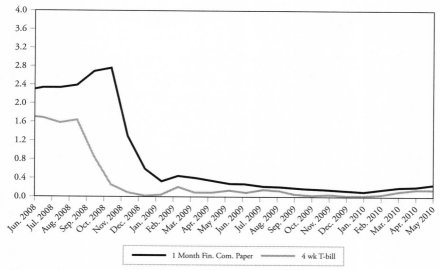

Figure 7.2
Source: FRED Database

longer maturities and higher risks. Only when the interest rate and credit risks become too great does monetary policy through open market operations become ineffective.

During the fourth quarter of 2008 and the first quarter of 2009, and on through the Great Recession, the yields on very short-term Treasury bills fell to very low levels.[18]

Perhaps most interesting is that during the spike in short-term interest rates in September of 2008, represented by one-month financial commercial paper in Figure 7.13, the interest rate on four-week T-bills moved in the opposite direction. Over the next few months, the interest rate on four-week T-bills continued to drop, reaching zero, and even less than zero on a few trading days, but averaging 0.1 percent.

Presumably, there was an excess supply of output and most financial assets, particularly risky and long term ones, but even one-month financial paper. While those reducing expenditures on output and financial assets, as well as

---

18. Four-Week Treasury Bill: Secondary Market Rate, Board of Governors of the Federal Reserve System, http://research.stlouisfed.org/fred2/series/TB4WK?cid=116

those selling financial assets, could simply accumulate money, at least some of them wanted to purchase T-bills. This pushed the yield on those T-bills down, coming close to the zero bound, which then caused frustrated buyers to shift to holding money. Perversely, the Fed began paying interest on reserve balances at this time, so that rather than the storage cost of currency becoming the lower bound on the nominal interest rates on those bonds, it became the 1.4 percent, and later the 0.2 percent, interest rate paid on reserve balances.[19]

While simple textbook explanations of monetary policy describe open market purchases with the Fed purchasing T-bills with newly created money, the Fed holds only $18 billion in Treasury bills versus $712 billion in Treasury notes and bonds.[20] Since the growing national debt includes an additional $4.5 trillion of Treasury notes and bonds, a substantial increase in base money still remains possible.[21]

The monetary disequilibrium approach to macroeconomics shows that the decrease in money expenditures in the fall of 2008 was due to a shortage of money, a quantity of money less than the demand to hold money. Because various measures of the quantity of money increased during that period, the demand to hold money must have increased tremendously. The increase in the demand for base money, and especially bank reserves, was truly astounding.

What should be done? The monetary disequilibrium approach appears consistent with a laissez-faire attitude, simply allowing the price level, including the level of wages, to fall enough to bring the real supply of money up to the demand. At some sufficiently low price level, the real supply of money will equal the demand to hold money. However, there is nothing in the monetary disequilibrium approach that suggests that such an adjustment would be smooth or painless. On the contrary, because money, the medium of exchange, does

---

19. Interest Rate Paid on Required Reserve Balances, Board of Governors of the Federal Reserve System, http://research.stlouisfed.org/fred2/series/INTREQ1?cid=118; Interest Rate Paid on Excess Reserve Balances, Board of Governors of the Federal Reserve System, http://research.stlouisfed.org/fred2/series/INTEXC1?cid=118
20. System Open Market Holdings, Federal Reserve Bank of New York, http://www.new yorkfed.org/markets/soma/sysopen_accholdings.html
21. Financial Management Service, U.S. Department of the Treasury, *Treasury Bulletin* (June 2010), http://www.fms.treas.gov/bulletin/index.html

not have a single price and lacks a particular market where it can be traded by specialists, the process of clearing up a shortage through changes in the prices of other goods on all other markets will necessarily be difficult and disruptive.[22]

The alternative solution is for the Fed to increase the quantity of money enough to meet the demand to hold money. Since the amount of nominal money people choose to hold depends on its purchasing power, the usual assumption has been that the quantity of money should equal the demand to hold money at a given price level, with real income equal to the productive capacity of the economy and real interest rates at levels consistent with coordinating saving and investment. An alternative approach is to target a constant growth path for money expenditures. For example, a 3-percent growth path of money expenditures should result in a stable price level on average. Returning to the 5.4-percent growth path of the Great Moderation implies choosing an inflationary growth path of prices—more or less equal to the 2.4-percent trend inflation rate from the Great Moderation.

However the fundamental nominal value of the economy is decided, how much base money should be created? Sadly, the monetary disequilibrium approach provides no simple quantitative rules of thumb. Instead, only the qualitative judgment is possible—the quantity of base money created by the Federal Reserve during the Great Recession may be high by historic standards, but it has been too little and too late.

References

Keynes, John Maynard. 1964. *General Theory of Employment, Interest and Money*, First Harbinger Edition.

Yeager, Leland B. 1997. "A Cash-Balance Interpretation of Depression," in *The Fluttering Veil: Essays on Monetary Disequilibrium*, George A. Selgin, editor. Indianapolis, IN: Liberty Press.

———. 1997. "Essential Properties of the Medium of Exchange," in *The Fluttering Veil: Essays on Monetary Disequilibrium*, George A. Selgin, editor. Indianapolis, IN: Liberty Press.

---

22. Yeager, "A Cash-Balance Interpretation of Depression," in *The Fluttering Veil*, 11–12.

_____. 1997. "The Keynesian Diversion" *The Fluttering Veil: Essays on Monetary Disequilibrium*, George A. Selgin, editor. Indianapolis, IN: Liberty Press.

_____. 1997. "What are Banks?" in *The Fluttering Veil: Essays on Monetary Disequilibrium*, George A. Selgin, editor. Indianapolis, IN: Liberty Press.

Yeager, Leland B. and Greenfield Robert L. 1997. "Money and Credit Confused?" *The Fluttering Veil: Essays on Monetary Disequilibrium*, George A. Selgin, editor. Indianapolis, IN: Liberty Press.

8

A Global Liquidity Crisis

Nicholas Rowe

Prelude to a Liquidity Crisis

IT WAS CLEAR to any macroeconomist who looked at international finances around 2007 that there was trouble ahead. We got that right. But we were wrong on what *sort of* trouble was ahead.

The United States government was running large fiscal deficits. If a government spends more than it gets in tax revenue, it has to borrow the difference. One place it can borrow is from its own citizens, but U.S. households were saving little—not enough to finance U.S. investment—so the U.S. private sector also needed to borrow. Government borrowing needs (G-T) plus private sector borrowing needs (I-S) together added up to net borrowing from abroad. The U.S. economy was buying more goods than it produced, so the difference was made up by net imports from abroad, and those net imports were financed by borrowing from abroad.

There's a flip side to this U.S. story. If one country is buying more than it produces—and borrowing—other countries must be buying less than they produce—and lending. You can't borrow and spend unless someone else saves and lends. The savers and lenders included China, Japan, and Germany.

There is nothing wrong with one country borrowing from another country, even if we call it a "global imbalance." It happens all the time, just as it happens all the time between individuals within a country. It would only be by sheer fluke that all individuals, and all countries, at all times, were exactly identical in their willingness to save or spend. And it's the job of financial markets, both within countries and internationally, to match savers with spenders, so the savers can lend to the spenders.

But it can't go on forever, of course. The lenders will eventually want to be paid back, and the borrowers will need to pay them back. So eventually the borrowers will need to stop spending and start saving; and the lenders will need to stop saving and start spending. But when that happens the U.S. must stop importing and start exporting, and China, Japan, and Germany must stop exporting and start importing. And to persuade individual households and firms to do that, the exchange rate would need to adjust. The U.S. dollar would need to depreciate against the yuan, yen, and euro, so that U.S.-produced goods would become more attractive to foreigners, and foreign-produced goods would become less attractive to Americans.

What can't go on forever must eventually stop. What we worried about was a sudden stop. If the lenders suddenly got scared of getting paid back, they would suddenly stop lending. That would have been very disruptive, because it's not easy to switch U.S. resources from producing for the home market to producing for the export market, and it's also not easy to do the reverse switch for other countries' resources.

That was what we were scared of. Sure, the U.S. housing market looked over-priced, but that seemed to be a detail of the bigger picture, caused by the low interest rates and easy loan conditions that were caused in turn by high foreign savings.

It didn't happen that way. U.S. house prices fell, as expected, but the U.S. dollar appreciated, which was not expected. And interest rates on U.S. government bonds fell even lower, even to 0 percent on short-term U.S. Treasuries. There was a global rush into, not out of, the U.S. dollar and any safe promise to pay U.S. dollars. The government bonds that people got scared of holding were the bonds of some Eurozone countries, like Greece, Spain, and Ireland, where interest rates rose.

Why did it happen differently? If you want my answer in one word, it's "liquidity."

Liquidity: the Basics

What does "liquidity" mean, and why does it matter? I'm going to answer this question in a roundabout way.

Think back to why we use monetary exchange, rather than barter. Suppose I'm trying to swap the apples I have produced for some bananas I want to eat. If I'm very lucky, I can find someone who wants to do the exact opposite trade—who wants to sell bananas for apples. But that requires a double coincidence of wants, and double coincidences are very rare. Usually I can only find a single coincidence—a banana producer who wants to eat carrots, or a carrot producer who wants to eat apples. So maybe I accept carrots for my apples, and later try to sell the carrots for bananas. If I do this, I am using carrots as a medium of exchange. A medium of exchange is a good you accept as payment, not because you want it, but because you plan to trade it for something you do want.

If all goods were equally easy to buy and sell, we wouldn't care what goods we accepted as a medium of exchange. So all goods would function as media of exchange. But they aren't all equally easy to buy and sell; they all have different transactions costs. People will tend to use those goods which have the lowest transactions costs as media of exchange. And it snowballs, because the more people use one good as a medium of exchange, the easier it is for other people to use that same good as a medium of exchange, since it's easier to find someone else who will accept it.

A monetary exchange economy is one where this snowball effect (a network externality of positive feedback) has reached its limit. Only one good is used as a medium of exchange, and we call that one good "money." If there are *n* goods, including money, then there are *n-1* markets. You can buy or sell every good for money, but you don't buy or sell any good except for money. Those markets in which non-money goods exchange directly for other non-money goods don't exist. They could exist; but they don't exist because nobody wants to use them. It's easier to use money.

Money is the most liquid of all assets. It's the one that is easiest to buy and sell. The liquidity of money is an emergent property. What starts out as a difference in degree, with one good being slightly easier to buy and sell than all other goods, becomes a difference in kind, when that good becomes the only medium of exchange. We then measure the liquidity of all other assets as the ease with which they can be bought and sold for money.

A financial crisis may start as a solvency crisis, but will generally turn into a liquidity crisis as well. And a liquidity crisis may lower the market values of some assets, and worsen a solvency crisis.

Here's how that works. Suppose U.S. house prices fall. Some homeowners now have negative equity—their house is worth less than the mortgage—and there's an increased probability they will default on the mortgage. The mortgage is now worth less. That's a solvency crisis for the homeowner; and it may also create a solvency crisis for the bank that owns the mortgage, which may now be unable to pay its own loans. The bank's liabilities, which will be the assets of someone else, are therefore also worth less.

But asset values don't just fall; they become more uncertain. If a bank tried to sell its assets, nobody knows what those assets are worth. They might be especially afraid that the bank might be selling off the bad mortgages and keeping the good ones. This is the classic "Market for Lemons" problem, in which there is asymmetric information because the seller knows more about the asset than the buyer. Used cars are a notoriously illiquid asset for this very reason. Lots of previously liquid financial assets became illiquid, just like used cars. And illiquidity creates a snowball effect just like money, only in reverse. Nobody wants to buy an illiquid asset, because they fear it would be hard to sell if they ever needed to sell it. So the volume of trade falls, and the asset becomes even less liquid.

Illiquid assets sell at lower prices and higher yields than liquid assets. Paper money, which is irredeemable and intrinsically worthless, is just the extreme example of this. People are willing to accept paper money, and hold it at least temporarily, even at high rates of inflation, when the real yield on money is very negative. They willingly accept it, and hold it temporarily, just because it is the most liquid of all assets, and accordingly has a very high liquidity premium. But all assets are liquid to a greater or lesser extent, and their price reflects their liquidity. So when the liquidity of assets fell, their prices fell too.

A financial crisis creates a reduction in the supply of liquid assets, as previously liquid assets become illiquid. It also creates an increased demand for liquid assets. In times of change and greater uncertainty, people, firms, and financial institutions expect they may need to sell assets quickly. The decrease in supply of liquidity, and increase in demand for liquidity, work together to raise the price of liquidity—the liquidity premium. Liquid assets increase in price, and illiquid assets fall in price. And previously liquid assets that have become illiquid are hit twice, and fall doubly in price.

International Liquidity: The U.S. Dollar

That simple story can explain what happened in the financial markets within an individual country, like the U.S. But it can also explain what happened in international finance.

The U.S. dollar is the world's reserve currency. What that means is that the U.S. dollar is money to all the other monies.

If I want to sell apples and buy bananas, I don't swap them directly; I first sell my apples for money, and then use the money to buy bananas. If I want to sell Canadian dollars and buy Australian dollars, I don't swap them directly. I first sell my Canadian dollars for U.S. dollars, and then use the U.S. dollars to buy Australian dollars. And so the world's banks and central banks hold reserves of U.S. dollars, just as people hold reserves of money. The U.S. dollar is the international medium of exchange between other media of exchange. It is the most liquid of all monies. It is the moniest of monies. It is meta-money. So the liquidity crisis increased the demand for U.S. dollars relative to other currencies in the same way that it increased the demand for all monies relative to other less liquid assets. And so when the crisis hit, the exchange rate of the U.S. dollar didn't depreciate as expected; it appreciated.

The financial crisis was a *global* financial crisis. The U.S. was not the only country with falling house prices and banks becoming insolvent. But it is too much of a coincidence that the crisis hit so many countries at about the same time.

Part of the reason for the global spread of the financial crisis is that financial markets are international. The assets in one country may be held by people and banks in many countries. And so when the assets in one country fall in value, that may affect the value and liquidity of assets in many countries.

But the central role of the U.S. dollar as the world's reserve currency gives it a special importance. The excess demand for liquid assets, and for money, was above all an excess demand for the U.S. dollar. That's why the U.S. dollar appreciated against other currencies. And that excess demand for the global currency probably played a large part in making the financial crisis a global financial crisis. And that also places a special responsibility upon the U.S. Federal Reserve, as central banker to the world.

244 | A Global Liquidity Crisis

Economists will probably spend the next few decades arguing whether the Fed could have acted more quickly and aggressively in the face of the increased demand for U.S. dollars. But since an appreciating U.S. dollar, falling prices of real assets, falling expectations of inflation, falling expectations of real growth, all point to an excess demand for the U.S. dollar, we can only say that whatever the Fed did, it wasn't enough.

Currency Wars: Back to the Prelude?

The prelude to the crisis was the U.S. fiscal and current account deficits. Those problems certainly didn't go away when the financial crisis hit, and the fiscal deficit became worse as tax revenues fell. One reason the U.S. and other countries are unwilling to reduce their fiscal deficits is the fear that doing so would reduce aggregate demand and worsen the recession. But monetary policy is normally an alternative to fiscal policy, and loosening monetary policy can compensate for any fiscal tightening.

One of the ways in which a looser monetary policy works is by causing a depreciation of the exchange rate, and so increasing net exports. And some economists believe that since monetary policy cannot lower interest rates when they are already at the zero lower bound, then exchange rate depreciation is the *only* way that monetary policy can work. And if those economists are right, then monetary policy just becomes a zero-sum game of "beggar my neighbor," which merely redistributes aggregate demand between countries, rather than increasing global aggregate demand. Direct intervention in foreign exchange markets, to increase foreign exchange reserves and reduce your exchange rate, is seen as the prime example of this strategy.

"Currency Wars" is a term used to describe the attempt by each country to depreciate its exchange rate and gain at others' expense. The flashpoint is U.S. annoyance with China for buying U.S. dollar reserves and preventing the yuan appreciating against the dollar.

In a real war, one country can only win if another country loses. They can't all win. "Currency Wars" is a metaphor that only makes sense if you accept the monetary policy is a zero-sum game of "beggar my neighbor." If, instead, you believe that a loosening of monetary policy by all countries could increase world aggregate demand, and help the whole world escape the recession, then you won't like the metaphor. You want a currency war to break out. What others call a "war" can be a good thing. You will admit that if one country loosens its monetary policy, some of the gains will come at the expense of other countries. But that just encourages other countries to retaliate. And you want them all to retaliate, because if they all loosen monetary policy, the world as a whole will see increased aggregate demand.

Even so, there are two ways to fight a currency war: a good way and a bad way. Direct intervention in foreign exchange markets is the bad way. If all central banks just swap domestic money and bonds for foreign money and bonds, the net effect on world monetary policy washes out.

This, I think, is where the U.S. does have a legitimate complaint against countries like China that intervene in foreign exchange markets to add to their U.S. dollar reserves.

A monetary economy is very different from a barter economy. In a barter economy, if I want to save some of my income, I must either invest those savings myself or persuade someone else to borrow my savings. I cannot force anyone to borrow from me. But in a monetary economy, I can save in the form of money. I don't need to persuade anyone to borrow from me; I just stop spending some of my monetary income, and hoard money. But if I hoard money, the central bank is forced to increase the money supply by an equal amount in order to prevent a recession. The central bank increases the money supply by buying bonds, which means it is lending the money to whoever sold it the bonds. And if, at some time in the future, I decide to spend my hoard of money, the central bank has to reverse course, and reduce the money supply by selling bonds to prevent inflation. So when I save by hoarding money, the central bank is forced to act as my loan placement officer and find someone who wants to borrow and spend the income I have saved.

When I hoard money, the central bank has to act as my loan placement officer; and it's a very difficult sort of loan to place. Because it's a loan I can call in any time I like, with no advance warning. Because I can change my mind any time I like, and spend the money I've hoarded, the central bank is forced to find someone willing to accept a demand loan, one that can be called in at any time. But most real investments are illiquid, and cannot be reversed instantly.

The U.S. dollar is the world's reserve currency. The Fed is the world's central bank. If China decides to hoard U.S. dollar reserves, the Fed is forced to act as loan placement officer for China, and find someone willing to borrow China's savings. It's especially hard to be a loan placement officer during a global recession, when the demand for loans, especially safe loans, is lower than normal. But if the Fed fails to do this, there is an excess demand for U.S. dollars, and the U.S. goes into recession. Most borrowers can say "no" to the offer of a loan. The U.S. Fed cannot say "no" to the offer of a loan from China's central bank. The Fed is borrower of last resort for all countries in the dollar bloc. By saving U.S. dollar reserves, China is forcing the U.S. to borrow from China.

Solutions?

The fact that the U.S. dollar is the world's reserve currency has both advantages and disadvantages for the U.S. It lets the U.S. borrow at low interest rates. Indeed, if the rest of the world holds U.S. currency that pays zero interest, it's like an indefinite zero interest loan to the U.S. That's good. But at the same time it's a loan the U.S. cannot refuse, and that can be called in at any time. That's bad. It's especially bad during a global recession, when nobody wants to borrow, and there are few safe borrowers.

It's easy to talk about establishing a new world reserve currency, perhaps as a basket of national currencies. But if the world's central banks want to increase their international reserves, who would be willing to replace the Fed as loan placement officer to the world?

International Liquidity: The Euro

Central banks do two things: they do normal monetary policy in normal times; and they act as lenders of last resort in abnormal times. The European Central Bank (ECB) is similar to other central banks in normal times. But in abnormal times, it faces a very different political challenge in acting as lender of last resort.

Monetary Policy in Normal Times

Most of macroeconomics is about normal monetary policy in normal times. Should central banks target 2-percent inflation? If so, how should they do it?

What should they look at in deciding when to tighten monetary policy to prevent inflation rising above 2 percent, or deciding to loosen monetary policy to prevent inflation falling below 2 percent?

All central banks face the "one-size-fits-all" problem. If Western Canada is in an inflationary boom, and Eastern Canada is in a disinflationary recession, the West needs tight money and the East needs loose money. But the Bank of Canada has only one monetary policy for the whole country, so it has to compromise. The ECB faces the same need to compromise, if different parts of the Eurozone are hit by different shocks and need a different monetary policy response.

But this problem may be worse for the Eurozone for two reasons: first, because the different languages and cultures may reduce labor mobility and make it harder for unemployed workers in a recessionary region to move to get jobs in a booming region; and second, because each country in the Eurozone has a separate fiscal budget, and there is no central fiscal authority to speak of. The Canadian federal government can spread the fiscal load between regions in boom and regions in recession, acting as a regional automatic stabilizer. Without a central fiscal authority, Eurozone governments in a recession see their tax revenues falling and expenditures rising, and they may be forced to increase taxes and cut spending to control the deficit, which may be a problem in its own right, and also worsen the regional recession. Other Eurozone governments in a boom see tax revenues rising and expenditures falling, and they may be tempted to cut taxes and increase spending, worsening the regional boom.

Given these two problems, it is less likely that the Eurozone will be an "optimal currency area" than any single country of a similar size, like the U.S. That means the costs of the "one-size-fits-all" problem may outweigh the benefits that a single currency creates by facilitating cross-border trade.

Monetary Policy in Abnormal Times

In abnormal times, like a financial crisis, central banks act as lender of last resort. Commercial banks hold short-term deposits as assets, and long-term loans as liabilities. Those long-term loans are typically illiquid because they are used to finance irreversible investments and because only the bank that made the loans has good knowledge about the quality of the loans. So the bank cannot call in the loans in a hurry and cannot sell them quickly for what the bank thinks they are worth. Potential buyers of those loans might think the bank is trying to sell them "lemons." All goes well, provided the bank can continue to roll over its short-term deposits. But if it is ever unable to roll over its short-term deposits, the bank is in trouble. The classic example is a bank run, in which each depositor runs to withdraw his money before all the other depositors withdraw theirs and the bank runs out of reserves. The prophecy of a bank run can be self-fulfilling. Fractional-reserve banking serves a need because lenders want to lend short and liquid, and borrowers want to borrow long and illiquid, but the situation is inherently unstable.

The job of a central bank is to act as lender of last resort to commercial banks that are unable to roll over their deposits—in other words, banks that face a run.

It's not just fractional reserve banks that face the danger of runs. Lenders want to lend short and liquid; borrowers want to borrow long and illiquid. Borrowers can also finance their long-term irreversible investments by issuing bonds. They can issue short-term bonds, hoping to be able to roll them over when they come due. Or they can issue long-term bonds, which lenders may buy because they believe those bonds can always be sold to other lenders if they need cash quickly. But this means that bond markets face exactly the same sort of danger that fractional reserve banks face.

Liquidity snowballs. Money is just the extreme example of this. The more people are willing to buy a good, the greater the incentive for others to buy it and hold it temporarily, because they know they can sell it again easily if they need to. But this snowball effect can also go in reverse. If a good becomes illiquid, fewer people are willing to buy it, because it is harder to sell, and so it becomes even less liquid. Illiquidity can become a self-fulfilling prophecy, just like a bank run.

In principle, central banks in a financial crisis should lend freely to illiquid but solvent borrowers. But they should lend at a penalty rate, to discourage borrowers from relying too much on the central bank. This is known as "Bagehot's Rule." But in practice it's not so easy to distinguish illiquidity from insolvency. A borrower facing a liquidity crisis, whether bank, business, or government, may have to borrow at abnormally high rates and sell its assets at abnormally low "fire-sale" prices precisely because it faces a liquidity crisis. At market prices and interest rates, the borrower may be unable to pay its debts, which means it is insolvent. But those market prices and interest rates may merely reflect temporary illiquidity. Or they may not. And the central bank has to act quickly, to prevent the crisis spreading, so good information on the solvency of borrowers is even harder to get. There is always the danger that a central bank acting as lender of last resort may lend to a fundamentally insolvent borrower, and so the central bank takes a loss.

The role of lender of last resort is therefore both monetary and fiscal. It's monetary because only the central bank can create unlimited quantities of irredeemable money. It's fiscal because if the loan goes bad, the central bank is ultimately spending taxpayers' money. It's taxpayers' money because all the profits from the central bank eventually go to the government. Central banks create money that pays zero interest and use it to buy assets that do pay interest, so they earn a stream of profits, which belong to the government that owns the central bank. If the bank makes a bad loan, the losses on that loan diminish the profits. If those losses were ever big enough, the government might even need to bail out the central bank, or else have the central bank resort to very high and inflationary rates of money creation to recoup those losses.

Now governments themselves are borrowers; they issue bonds. And sometimes governments issue short-term bonds, planning to roll them over to refinance the national debt when they come due, rather than paying them off by running a surplus of tax revenues over expenditures. And so governments themselves may need a lender of last resort. That makes monetary and fiscal policy even more closely intertwined when central banks act as lenders of last resort.

The coordination of monetary and fiscal policy isn't easy; but it's a lot easier when we are talking about one country with one government and one central bank, and the government owns the central bank. There's at least a chance that the government and central bank will share the same views about what is best for the country. The money all comes out of the same pot. And there are only two parties to agree. It's a lot harder in the Eurozone, where all the Eurozone governments, plus the European Central Bank, need to be consulted.

Printers Versus Non-printers

Some governments are "printers." That means they borrow in their own currency that they themselves can print. Other governments are "non-printers."

They borrow in a currency that they themselves cannot print. The central governments of the U.S., U.K., and Canada, for example, are printers. The national governments of the Eurozone countries, for example, are non-printers.

In normal times it makes a difference, but not a big difference, in being a printer. Being able to print money, virtually for free, is a good source of revenue for the government. But it's not unlimited. To give a very rough estimate, if the stock of currency is 10 percent of annual nominal GDP, and nominal GDP is growing at 5 percent per year (say 3 percent real growth, plus 2 percent inflation), then the revenue from printing money (called "seigniorage") is 10 percent × 5 percent = 0.5 percent of GDP. So the central bank will earn profits equal to 0.5 percent of GDP, which it gives to the government, and the government can use these profits to have higher spending or lower taxes than otherwise. But these seigniorage profits are limited. If the central bank prints at a faster rate, inflation will rise point-for-point. And inflation is a tax on holding currency, so higher inflation means people will hold a smaller amount of currency as a percentage of GDP. Governments that try to finance too much spending by printing money eventually end up with hyperinflation and total collapse of the currency, like Zimbabwe in 2009.

In abnormal times, during a financial crisis, and a deflationary recession, there are much bigger advantages to being a printer.

Recessions cause an increase in government budget deficits just through the normal operation of automatic stabilizers, as tax revenues fall and transfer payments increase. Add to that the costs of bailing out troubled banks. And add to that the fact that governments often want to use discretionary fiscal policy to help increase aggregate demand and fight the deflationary recession. All these things mean that government debt starts to climb. And the recession means a drop in real GDP, and deflation means a further drop in nominal GDP. So the ratio of nominal debt to nominal GDP increases for two reasons: the numerator rises, and the denominator falls. And since that ratio is a rough measure of a government's capacity to pay its debts, a rising debt/GDP ratio adds a risk premium on the interest rate that the government must pay to service its debt, which can cause a further rise in the debt.

A government that is a non-printer faces a risk of a debt-spiral, and default. It has very limited options. It can cut spending and increase taxes, but those will worsen the recession, and worsen the deflationary forces. It's even conceivable that tightening fiscal policy might make default more likely.

But governments that are printers can simply print their way out of their debts. It might be ugly, but it can be done. You owe a trillion dollars, coming due over the next ten years? Just print a trillion dollars, and pay your debts when they come due. Yes, it may indeed cause hyperinflation. And if it does so, your creditors won't be pleased to be repaid in worthless paper. And your credit rating will be shot, and you may be unable to borrow again for a long time. But it can be done. You don't have to default, unless you prefer default to the consequences of not defaulting.

But of course, it never need reach that extreme for printers. If you are in a deflationary recession, a little bit of inflationary pressure is just what you want to happen. So if the bond market vigilantes ever start to fear default, and require an increased risk premium to hold your bonds, the central bank can just buy the bonds with freshly printed money, forcing the interest rate down again. And that's just what the printers have been doing. And that's why interest rates in the U.S., U.K., and Japan—all printers—have stayed much lower than those in Greece, Spain, and Ireland, all non-printers.

The "Exit Strategy"

The printers face a very different problem than the non-printers. As long as inflation is not a problem, the printers can borrow and print as much as they like. But if their economy suddenly recovers, and the demand for safe nominal assets like government debt and money falls, they will need to reverse direction quickly to prevent inflation. The central bank will need to reduce the money supply again, which means selling back the bonds it had previously bought. And if bond prices have fallen in the meantime, as they will if interest rates return to normal, the central bank may not be able to buy back all the money it had previously issued. And the government will no longer be able to rely on printing money to cover its deficits, if it wants to avoid inflation, and it will need to cut spending and raise taxes to avoid default.

There's a paradox here. While the risks of recession and deflation continue, governments and central banks want people to fear future inflation, so people will try to sell their money and government bonds and buy real goods and invest in real assets instead. The fear of future inflation would end the deflationary recession. Yet governments and central banks themselves fear future inflation, and so want a credible "exit strategy" to prevent future inflation when the recession ends. But having a credible exit strategy prevents people fearing future inflation and so prolongs the deflationary recession. And needing to keep a credible exit strategy prevents governments borrowing enough and printing enough to end the recession.

It ought to be possible to find some middle ground, where expected future inflation is just high enough to promote a recovery—but no higher—and where governments and central banks will have just enough difficulty implementing an exit strategy to make it rational for people to expect enough future inflation to promote a recovery. But if people's expectations suddenly reach some sort of tipping point, where they suddenly switch from expecting future deflation to expecting high future inflation, there may be no middle ground. That's the problem the printers face.

Solutions

I don't have any magic solutions.

The best way to get out of a crisis is not to get into one in the first place. But that's easier said than done. Financial crises are not new. We haven't been very successful in avoiding financial crises over the last few hundred years, and I don't see any reason to expect we will be much more successful in the future.

The underlying problem is this. There are ultimate lenders, who want to spend less than they earn today, and ultimate borrowers, who want to spend more than they earn today. Lenders want to save in assets that are safe, liquid, and simple. But borrowers want to invest in assets that are risky, illiquid, and complicated. And "Finance"—the whole industry of financial intermediaries and financial markets—tries to satisfy both at the same time. And ultimately, it can't be done. The illusion works most of the time, and both sides get more or less what they want, which is really great. But if enough people lose faith in the illusion, for good reasons or bad, it all falls apart. And central banks, the ultimate providers of the ultimately liquid asset, are called on to clean up the mess.

For printers, I think the best policy would be for central banks to announce and stick to a clear target path for the price level, or perhaps nominal GDP. (This is a bit different from inflation targeting, because it means that if inflation comes in below target one year, the central bank will raise the target inflation rate temporarily, to get back onto the same long-run path for the price level.) A clear and credible target for the price level or nominal GDP would do much to prevent the destabilizing effects of expected deflation and recession.

And central banks need to be willing to do whatever it takes to get back onto that path, if it is to be credible and anchor people's expectations. That would include buying an index of stocks, like the S&P 500. Seeing stock prices rise as central banks bought stocks would have a direct effect on aggregate demand, and also inspire confidence that the central bank's actions were working and the economy were recovering. And since the central bank's exit strategy would be to sell those stocks at a higher price when the economy recovers and returns to the target path, it would be able to afford to buy back the extra money it had issued during the recession.

For non-printers? I don't know. Every non-printer needs to find a friendly printer, who will print whatever is necessary in a crisis. But that friendly printer will want to insist on some degree of regulatory control to try to reduce the probability of a crisis. Which means the non-printer will lose some degree of sovereignty.

PART III

Creating a Better Monetary System

9

Nominal Income Targeting and Monetary Stability

Joshua R. Hendrickson

Introduction

A SUCCESSFUL MONETARY policy should promote monetary stability by minimizing the economic fluctuations resulting from monetary disturbances. In recent years, there has been an increasing amount of research into the formulation of optimal monetary policy rules.[1] In fact, there now appears to be a growing consensus within the macroeconomic literature that monetary policy should be described by a rule.[2] A number of different proposals have arisen, with the two most prevalent rules being the Taylor Rule (1993)[3] and some form of an inflation-targeting rule.

An alternative to these rules is a nominal income-targeting rule in which the central bank adjusts monetary policy in response to deviations of nominal gross domestic product from some explicit target.[4] While this type of rule is

---

1. The rules are typically judged by the variability of the output gap and inflation evident in simulations. For a textbook treatment of the evaluation of alternative monetary policy rules, see Michael Woodford, *Interest and Prices* (Princeton: Princeton University Press: 2003) or Jordi Galí, *Monetary Policy, Inflation, and the Business Cycle* (Princeton: Princeton University Press, 2008). For a recent survey, see Michael Woodford, "Optimal Monetary Stabilization Policy" (NBER Working Paper No. 16095, 2010).

2. See, for example, the work collected in John B. Taylor, *Monetary Policy Rules* (Chicago: Chicago University Press, 1999) and Ben S. Bernanke and Michael Woodford, *The Inflation-Targeting Debate* (Chicago: Chicago University Press, 2005).

3. John B. Taylor, "Discretion Versus Policy Rules in Practice," *Carnegie-Rochester Series on Public Policy* 39 (1993): 195–214.

4. A nominal income target need not be defined in terms of nominal GDP. Robert J. Gordon, "The Conduct of Domestic Monetary Policy," in *Monetary Policy in Our Times,*

not as prevalent in the literature, it does have a number of desirable characteristics.[5] First and foremost, a nominal income-targeting rule is not dependent on structural assumptions about the economy and requires less stringent information requirements on monetary policymakers than alternative monetary policy rules. Second, a nominal income target implicitly creates a flexible price level, or inflation, target depending on the nature of the shock. Finally, there is reason to believe that such a rule would limit economic fluctuations caused by shocks to aggregate demand.

What follows is a detailed analysis of the theoretical underpinnings of a nominal income-targeting rule, its desirable properties, and a discussion of existing empirical evidence. It is shown that while a nominal income-targeting rule has a number of desirable properties in and of itself, it also exhibits advantages over both the Taylor Rule and inflation targeting. Finally, it is suggested that the Great Recession could potentially have been much less severe had the Federal Reserve had an explicit nominal income target.

Nominal Income Targeting: Explanation and Motivation

A Simple Framework for Analysis

In order to motivate a general analysis of the characteristics of a nominal income-targeting rule for monetary policy, this chapter employs the textbook aggregate demand–aggregate supply (AD-AS) framework. This framework, while somewhat simple, is useful in that it is able to capture many of the issues relevant for evaluating a number of important issues surrounding monetary policy.

The AD-AS model is depicted in Figure 9.1. As shown in the figure, the long-run aggregate supply curve, denoted LAS, is vertical in conjunction with the natural rate hypothesis or the concept of potential output. Thus, the long-

---

eds. Albert Ando et al. (Cambridge: MIT Press, 1985), for example, suggests that a measure of nominal final sales would be more appropriate.

5. Bennett T. McCallum and Edward Nelson, "Nominal Income Targeting in an Open Economy Optimizing Model," *Journal of Monetary Economics* 43 (1999): 553–78 and Joshua R. Hendrickson, "An Overhaul of Federal Reserve Doctrine: Nominal Income and the Great Moderation" (working paper, 2010) are recent examples.

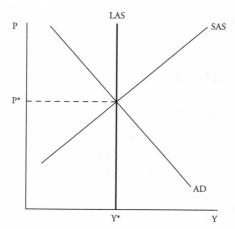

Figure 9.1 Aggregate Supply-Aggregate Demand Framework

run aggregate supply curve implies that the long-run level of output is independent of the price level; or, more broadly, that there does not exist a long-run trade-off between inflation and output (or correspondingly unemployment).

Aggregate demand, denoted AD, is downward-sloping thereby reflecting the inverse relationship between the price level and the level of output. This downward-sloping demand curve is motivated by the money demand function. The demand for real money balances is a function of a spectrum of interest rates as well as income. As the price level rises, this reduces real balances below the desired level causing the demand for nominal balances to increase. As a result, interest rates increase and output declines.

The short-run aggregate supply curve (SAS) is upward-sloping. The positive relationship between the price level and output is motivated by the idea that rising prices entail higher profits for firms. Thus, when prices increase, firms seek to expand production to capitalize on profit opportunities. A necessary condition for rising prices to cause higher profits is a slow adjustment of input prices. This condition can be motivated by nominal wages that are set by labor contracts or informal agreements. Alternatively, the slow adjustment of wages could be the result of the supply of labor being a function of not only the real wage, but also permanent income. Under such conditions, the wage would be slow to adjust as a result of individual revisions regarding permanent income.

In a stochastic environment, a number of factors might cause these curves to shift. First, consider shifts in aggregate supply. For example, aggregate supply might shift as a result of cost-push factors. In other words, workers expect higher prices and thus seek to negotiate higher wages. As wages rise, this increases the cost of production and reduces aggregate supply thereby shifting the SAS curve to the left. In addition, supply shocks due to droughts, natural disasters, or un-expectedly good (or bad) harvests can also shift SAS. What's more, technology and productivity can shift both the SAS curve and the LAS curve depending on the degree of persistence of the change. For example, if an increase in productiv-ity is temporary, the SAS curve will shift to the right. For a permanent increase in productivity, the LAS curve will shift to the right. Finally, shifts in SAS can result from deviations of output from potential. When output rises above po-tential, firms raise their prices. This change in prices, however, induces workers to negotiate higher nominal wages thereby shifting the SAS curve to the left.

The aggregate demand curve can shift for a number of reasons as well. First, a change in time preference would induce a change in the present demand for output. In addition, inflation expectations will also induce changes in the demand for present and future output. Also, fiscal policy, conditional on how monetary policy is determined, can also potentially shift the AD curve.

Most importantly for the remaining analysis, however, is that monetary pol-icy operates through changes in aggregate demand. The central bank, through its control of the monetary base, is able to adjust the money supply. This is typically done through open market operations in which the central bank buys financial assets, such as government debt. The increase in the money supply increases the prices of financial and later nonfinancial assets and results in a corresponding decline in the yields, both explicit and implicit, of these assets. The lower interest rate implies a higher present discounted value of the assets thereby raising net worth and stimulating the demand for goods and services and investment. Thus, expansionary monetary policy shifts the AD curve to the right and contraction-ary policy shifts aggregate demand to left.

Given this basic framework, it is now possible to consider the effectiveness of monetary policy in dealing with each type of shock. Before proceeding, however, it might be important to discuss the role of expectations is this environment. Over the last thirty years or so, macroeconomists have widely accepted the rational expectations hypothesis, at least as a first approximation. This hypothesis entails that individuals know the model and form expectations consistent with using the conditional mathematical expectation given all information available at the time.

As a result, changes in aggregate demand should cause simultaneous changes in the short-run aggregate supply. In other words, in the wake of a positive AD shock, workers who observe the shock immediately seek to increase their nominal wages. If wages and prices are perfectly flexible, a positive AD shock would lead to a simultaneous shift of SAS such that the level of output remains unchanged and the price level rises. In this instance, there is no role for monetary policy. However, if wages and prices are sticky, the SAS curve will not shift completely, thereby leading to a change in both the level of output and the price level. In other words, the *qualitative* change under such conditions is the same as implied above; the only difference is in the magnitude of the change. Given the existing evidence on the speed of wage and price adjustment (see, for example, the survey by Taylor).[6] This author views the simpler model without expectations outlined above as sufficient for analysis. The remainder of the discussion regarding AD-AS therefore proceeds by ignoring the role of expectations.[7]

Nominal Income Targeting in the AD-AS Framework

Given the outline of the general framework, it is now possible to consider the behavior of monetary policy under a nominal income target. As a matter of simplicity, the assumption of zero output growth is imposed to ensure the desirability of achieving the natural level of output. In addition, it is assumed that the central bank prefers zero inflation and seeks to correct previous deviations of inflation from the target rate of zero. In other words, the central bank not only prefers zero inflation, but also a constant price level. Under these assumptions, it follows that the central bank seeks to target a constant *level* of nominal income (P^*y^* in Figure 9.1).[8]

First, consider the effect of a positive aggregate demand shock shown in Figure 9.2. The positive shock shifts the AD curve to the right. The result is

---

6. John B. Taylor, "Staggered Price and Wage Setting in Macroeconomics," in *Handbook of Macroeconomics* I, part 2, eds. John B. Taylor and Michael Woodford (North-Holland: Elsevier, 1999).

7. Alternatively, one could simply assume that all shocks are completely unanticipated.

8. It is possible in practice for the central bank to target either the level of nominal income or the growth rate. Given the assumption of zero growth, this latter choice is irrelevant for the present analysis. Nonetheless, it is discussed further in the next section.

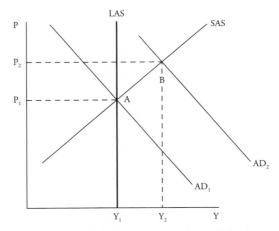

Figure 9.2. A Positive Aggregate Demand Shock

a short-run equilibrium with a higher price level and a higher level of output as shown by point B. The higher level of both prices and income imply that nominal income is greater that the target level. As a result, the central bank would engage in contractionary monetary policy (i.e. raise interest rates/contract the money supply) thereby reducing aggregate demand and returning the economy to the equilibrium at point A and maintaining constant nominal income. It is important to note that a zero inflation target, or a price-level target, would require the same policy response.

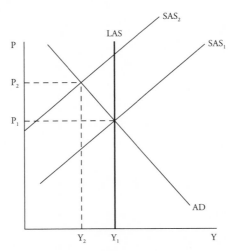

Figure 9.3. A Negative Aggregate Supply Shock

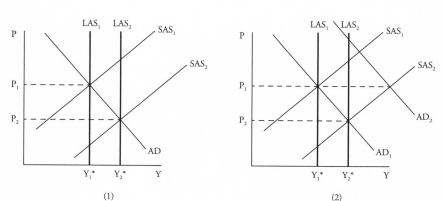

Figure 9.4. A Permanent Change in Aggregate Supply

Next, suppose that there is a temporary, negative shock to aggregate supply. As shown in Figure 9.3, the negative supply shock shifts the SAS curve to the left, raises the price level, and reduces output below potential. In this scenario, the rise in the price level offsets the decline in output. As a result, nominal income remains roughly constant. Under a nominal income-targeting rule, monetary policy does not respond. What's more, even under an inflation or price-level target, if the change is recognized as temporary, as is likely is the case of a natural disaster, the central bank is likely to abstain from a change in policy. Nonetheless, this conclusion does not hold for permanent changes in aggregate supply.

The final example to consider is the effect of a permanent shock to aggregate supply caused by an increase in technology. As shown in panel (1) of Figure 9.4, technological innovation shifts both the SAS and the LAS curve to the right. Again, this causes an opposite change in the price level and output. In this case, the price level declines and both actual and potential output increase. It follows that nominal income again remains roughly constant. Thus, under the nominal income-targeting rule, there is arguably no role for monetary policy. However, following an inflation or a price-level target, the central bank would shift to an expansionary policy to prevent the price level from falling. What's more, given that changes in technology and productivity are hard to identify in real time, it is unlikely that an inflation or price-level targeting regime would remain agnostic as in the case illustrated above. This type of policy is illustrated in panel (2) of Figure 9.4. As shown, this type of policy would temporarily increase output above its new potential level.

The central theme motivated by this analysis is that nominal income targeting requires that monetary policy respond solely to aggregate demand shocks. As shown in Bradley and Jansen,[9] so long as the nominal wage remains fixed, monetary policy can more formally be captured by a rectangular hyperbola where each point along the hyperbola represents a constant level of nominal income. As a result, monetary policy need not respond to aggregate supply shocks. The desirability of this type of policy is the subject of the subsequent section.

Desirable Properties of a Nominal Income Target

A nominal income target has a number of desirable properties both in and of itself and in reference to alternative policies. First, a nominal income target prevents monetary policy from responding to fluctuations in aggregate supply thereby preventing the accommodation of rising inflation to cost-push related shocks. Similarly, this prevents monetary policy from undertaking expansionary policies in response to rising productivity. Second, a nominal income target is more closely able to maintain monetary equilibrium, a desirable characteristic across a broad spectrum of monetary theories of the business cycle. Third, and finally, the use of a nominal income-targeting rule is desirable because it requires less restrictive informational assumptions for policymakers to be successful in formulating policy. Each of these properties is discussed in more detail below.

Supply-Driven Versus Demand-Driven Deflation

As discussed above, a nominal income target implies that the price level should be allowed to fall in response to an increase in productivity. Relaxing the assumption of zero growth, a nominal income target would effectively be formulated as the sum of the desired growth rate of real output (the potential growth rate) and the desired inflation rate. Even under this condition, an increase in productivity would imply that the inflation rate be less than the implicit target. If the desired rate of inflation is zero percent, this would similarly result in deflation.

---

9. Michael D. Bradley and Dennis W. Jansen, "Understanding Nominal Income Targeting," *St. Louis Federal Reserve Bank Review* (Nov./Dec., 1989): 31–40.

At first glance, a monetary policy that could potentially lead to deflation would seem like a drawback given the conventional wisdom on deflation. For example, DeLong (1999: 231) argues that deflation be "avoided at all costs."[10] Bernanke similarly expresses concern about the effects of deflation and expresses confidence that "the Fed would take whatever means necessary to prevent significant deflation in the United States."[11] Nonetheless, this is a very limited view of deflation. A more nuanced view suggests that not only would deflation not be harmful under certain circumstances, it would actually be desirable.

The conventional view on deflation finds its origin with Irving Fisher.[12] Specifically, Fisher emphasizes that a negative shock to aggregate demand will be captured by a modest decline in velocity, a corresponding decline in the price level, and liquidation of debt. This initial impact is followed by an increase in the cost of riskier loans, asset price declines, and an increase in real interest rates and the real value of debt. As a result, net worth and profits decline, thereby reducing output, increasing unemployment, and reducing the demand for deposit currency. Ultimately, this process can result in financial distress through bank runs, bank failures, and further debt liquidation.

Much of this sentiment is reflected in the current conventional wisdom. For example, Beckworth outlines three predominant mechanisms in the literature by which deflation results in adverse economic outcomes:[13]

1. With sticky, or rigid, input prices, a decline in the price level will result in higher real wages and therefore lower profits. Firms will then seek to reduce production and/or employment.
2. A decline in the price level will result in an unexpected rise in the real interest rate, further reducing the demand for interest-sensitive purchases.

10. J. Bradford DeLong. "Should We Fear Deflation?" *Brookings Papers on Economic Activity*, No. 1 (1999): 225–52.
11. Ben S. Bernanke, "Deflation: Making Sure 'It' Doesn't Happen Here" (speech to National Economists Club, 2002), http://www.federalreserve.gov/boarddocs/speeches/2002/20021121/default.htm.
12. Irving Fisher, *Booms and Depressions* (New York: Adelphi, 1932); Fisher, "The Debt-Deflation Theory of Great Depressions," *Econometrica* 1, no. 4 (1933): 337–57.
13. David Beckworth, "Aggregate Supply-Driven Deflation and Its Implications for Macroeconomic Stability," *Cato Journal* 29, no. 3 (2008): 365.

In addition, as deflation is realized, this will result in a lower nominal interest rate. If the central bank uses an interest rate as an intermediate target for monetary policy, the decline in nominal rates will leave less room for expansionary policy as the rate nears the zero lower bound.

3. Deflation results in lower assets prices and a higher real value of debt. As a result, net worth and collateral values decline leading to a rise in defaults and an amplification of the original shock.

Given the potential adverse effects from deflation, it is important to examine the conditions under which one could expect to observe these effects. For example, in the AD-AS framework above, a decline in the price level can occur for a negative aggregate demand shock and a positive aggregate supply shock. A careful reading of the literature suggests that the adverse effects of deflation are confined to the former. For example, footnote 1 to Bernanke's 2002 speech cited above states:[14]

> Conceivably, deflation could also be caused by a sudden, large expansion in aggregate supply arising, for example, from rapid gains in productivity and broadly declining costs. . . . Note that a supply-side deflation would be associated with an economic boom rather than a recession.

This quote adequately captures the role for nuance.

The fact that productivity-induced deflation results in a boom renders a number of the points raised above moot. To understand a distinct difference from the alternate forms of deflation, consider the effects on wages and profits from an increase in productivity. Following the increase in productivity, output prices fall. In addition, consistent with the assumption of sticky wages above, the real wage rises. However, contrary to the decline in aggregate demand, these changes do not result in adverse effects. As Selgin explains, rising productivity reduces the per unit cost of production thereby maintaining stable price markups per unit of production.[15] In addition, the increase in productivity results in a higher marginal product of labor. The increase in real wages therefore serves to compensate workers accordingly.

---

14. Ben S. Bernanke, "Deflation: Making Sure 'It' Doesn't Happen Here," footnote 1.

15. George Selgin, *Less Than Zero: The Case for a Falling Price Level in a Growing Economy* (London: Institute of Economic Affairs, 1997).

Debt deflation and financial concerns are also unwarranted following a productivity-induced decline in the price level. The rising value of debt in real terms is offset by an unexpected increase in real income. In addition, rising productivity implies that the value of collateral should also rise with the corresponding increases in expected earnings.[16]

Finally, concerns about the policy interest rate are similarly unwarranted. Rising productivity implies that the real rate of interest should increase. Thus, as Beckworth notes, "the higher real interest rate should counter downward pressure on nominal interest rates from the deflationary pressures and reduce the chance of hitting the lower interest rate bound."[17]

This nuanced view of deflation suggests that the existence of adverse effects from a falling price level is dependent upon the nature of the economic shock. As a result, there remains reason to believe that aggregate demand-induced deflation should be avoided. However, aggregate supply-induced deflation is desirable at best and harmless at worst. A growing amount of historical empirical research supports this distinction (Bordo and Redish for the U.S. and Cananda;[18] Bordo, Lane, and Redish for U.S., U.K., and Germany;[19] Beckworth for U.S.;[20] and the multi-country analysis by Atkeson and Kehoe).[21]

---

16. For a more formal analysis of a productivity shock in a model with endogenous asset prices, see Joshua Hendrickson, "Monetary Transmission in the New Keynesian Framework: Is the Interest Rate Enough?" (working paper, 2010); and Hendrickson, "A Re-Examination of Money and Business Cycles" (unpublished PhD. diss., 2010). The model incorporates agency costs into an otherwise standard New Keynesian sticky price model. As a result, entrepreneurial behavior is subject to a collateral constraint. Following a shock to productivity, asset prices increase thereby raising entrepreneurial net worth. Consistent with the AD-AS, both output and potential output rise and inflation declines below its steady state rate of zero.

17. David Beckworth, "Aggregate Supply-Driven Deflation and Its Implications for Macroeconomic Stability," *Cato Journal* 29, no. 3 (2008): 367–68.

18. Michael Bordo and Angela Redish, "Is Deflation Depressing? Evidence from the Classical Gold Standard," in eds. Richard C. K. Burdekin and Pierre L. Siklos, *Deflation: Current and Historical Perspectives* (Cambridge: Cambridge University Press, 2004).

19. John Bordo, Landon Lane, and Angela Redish, "Good Versus Bad Deflation: Lessons from the Gold Standard Era" (NBER Working Paper 10329, 2004).

20. David Beckworth, "The Postbellum Deflation and Its Lessons for Today," *North American Journal of Economics and Finance* 18, no. 2 (2007): 195–214.

21. Andrew Atkeson and Patrick J. Kehoe, "Deflation and Depression: Is There An Empirical Link?" *American Economic Review* 94, no. 2 (2008): 99–103.

Thus, based on a more complete view of deflation, nominal income targeting is a much more desirable policy objective than other alternatives such as inflation or price-level targeting, which would require the central bank to attempt to prevent deflation following an increase in productivity. Even with an understanding of the more nuanced view, policymakers would be required to distinguish between types of shocks in real time under a policy aimed at stabilizing the price level or inflation.[22] In contrast, nominal income targeting allows monetary policy to correct aggregate demand-induced deflation while preventing policy from responding to aggregate supply shocks as the nuanced view of deflation suggests is optimal. What's more, these responses (or lack thereof) are a direct byproduct of the nominal income target and therefore do not impose unrealistic informational requirements on policymakers who might otherwise want to satisfy these goals.

Monetary Equilibrium

The concept of monetary equilibrium broadly encapsulates the central theme of a number of business cycle theories including those advocated by monetarists Warburton, and Yeager,[23] coordination Keynesians (Leijonhufvud), and Austrians (Horwitz).[24] The central concept centers on the role of money as a medium of exchange. As a result, money has no market of its own; rather, money trades in all markets. Given this unique role, and consistent with Walras' Law, an excess demand or excess supply of money requires a corresponding excess supply

---

22. There is significant reason to believe that such a task would be arduous. See Beckworth (this volume).
23. Clark Warburton, "The Monetary Disequilibrium Hypothesis," *The American Journal of Economics and Sociology* 10, no. 1 (1950): 1–11; Leland Yeager, "The Significance of Monetary Disequilibrium," *Cato Journal* 6, no. 2, (1986): 369–99. This framework also fits with that of Milton Friedman and Anna J. Schwartz, "Money and Business Cycles"; Friedman and Schwartz, *A Monetary History of the United States* (Princeton: Princeton University Press, 1963); Friedman and Schwartz, *Monetary Trends in the United States and the United Kingdom* (Chicago: University of Chicago Press, 1982).
24. Axel Leijonhufvud, *Information and Coordination: Essays in Macroeconomic Theory* (New York: Oxford University Press, 1981); Steven Horwitz, *Microfoundations and Macroeconomics: An Austrian Perspective* (London: Routledge, 2001). See also the discussion of F.A. Hayek's views in Lawrence H. White, "Hayek's Monetary Theory and Policy: A Critical Reconstruction," *Journal of Money, Credit, and Banking* 31, no. 1 (1999): 109–20.

or excess demand for goods, respectively. It follows that in order for monetary policy to mitigate business cycle fluctuations, the goal of the central bank should be to seek to equate the money supply with the desired level of money demand. At first glance, this would seem to impose strict informational assumptions on policymakers. However, upon further inspection, this concept actually has straightforward policy implications.

Consider the equation of exchange:[25]

$$MV = Py$$

where M is the money supply, V is velocity, P is the price level, and y is the level of output. If M is broadly defined, this equation can be re-written as:

$$mBV = Py$$

where m is the money multiplier and B is the monetary base. This alternate form of the equation of exchange is particularly useful because the money multiplier, m, will capture changes in the demand for the monetary base; velocity, V, changes in the demand for the broader money aggregate, M. In addition, the monetary base, B, is directly controlled by the central bank.

The concept of monetary equilibrium suggests that the central bank should choose the monetary base that stabilizes money demand. In other words, the monetary base should adjust to changes in m and V. As stated above, this policy prescription seems to impose strict information restrictions on the monetary policymakers, as it is difficult to observe m and V in real time. In fact, this is not the case. As implied in the equation of exchange, for a given path of the monetary base, there exists a corresponding path for nominal income (Py),

---

25. It is important to note that the equation of exchange is an identity. Nonetheless, it is useful for analysis when one adds the auxiliary assumptions that the monetary base is exogenously determined by the central bank, and that output grows at its natural rate in the long run. Accordingly, it follows that changes in prices and therefore nominal income will be caused by changes in the left-hand-side variables. Beckworth and Hendrickson (see David Beckworth and Joshua R. Hendrickson, "Monetary Policy and the Great Spending Crashes" (working paper, 2010)) develop a micro-founded model that formalizes this prediction. Early empirical support for this broad framework is provided in Friedman and Schwartz (see Milton Friedman and Anna J. Schwartz, "Money and Business Cycles"; Friedman and Schwartz, *A Monetary History of the United States;* and Friedman and Schwartz, *Monetary Trends in the United States and the United Kingdom*).

ceteris paribus. If the monetary base is fixed to this given path, fluctuations in the demand for the components of the monetary base as well as the broader monetary aggregate cause deviations from the path of nominal income that would otherwise exist. Thus, in order to maintain monetary equilibrium and therefore mitigate the business cycle fluctuations that result from monetary disturbances, it follows that the central bank should adopt a nominal income target, as deviations from the target would necessarily provide guidance for the central bank as to the appropriate change in the monetary base necessary to achieve monetary equilibrium.

The concept of monetary equilibrium is a fairly broad theoretical construct that fits with a number of business cycle theories that emphasize monetary disturbances. The fact that nominal income targeting is a useful guide for monetary policy in this context is therefore important as it suggests that this type of policy is somewhat robust to more specific formulations of structural models. This is a key point emphasized by McCallum, who stresses the collective ignorance of the profession with regards to the true structural model.[26]

Nominal Income Targeting Alternatives

Presently, there are two predominate alternatives to nominal income targeting that exist in the literature. The first is the idea of inflation targeting under which the central bank adjusts its policy instrument to deviations in the rate of inflation from its target. The second and more popular alternative, at least in the United States, is the Taylor Rule under which monetary policy is adjusted according to both deviations of inflation from its target as well as the output gap. While each of these policies has desirable properties, they require more stringent assumptions about the information available to policymakers, thereby creating a greater potential for errors in policy.

One alternative to nominal income targeting emphasized in the literature and actually developed in practice is inflation targeting. Under an inflation target, the central bank sets a target for inflation and adjusts the stance of policy to

---

26. Bennett T. McCallum, "Robustness Properties of a Rule for Monetary Policy," *Carnegie-Rochester Conference Series on Public Policy* 29 (1988): 173–204.

deviations of inflation from its target. The benefit of this policy is that it targets a nominal variable that the central bank can directly affect through monetary policy. What's more, it gives the central bank a long-term goal for policy.

Nonetheless, there are reasons for reservations about inflation targeting. For example, critics as early as Hayek emphasized the importance of relative prices rather than the price level.[27] Specifically, Hayek emphasized the role of money creation in altering the structure of production and therefore relative prices. The behavior of the price level is therefore not of primary importance and might be misleading with regards to the effects of monetary policy.

More recently, Christiano, Motto, and Rostagno have recast this type of argument using a structural macroeconomic model.[28] These authors incorporate financial market frictions into an otherwise standard New Keynesian framework and consider the effects of inflation targeting. They find that a policy of inflation targeting can lead policymakers to unwittingly induce a boom-bust cycle that results from excess credit creation in the wake of productivity shocks. Specifically, the authors find that the monetary policy response to rising productivity under inflation targeting causes investment, consumption, output, and asset prices to exceed values that are socially efficient.

This view is broadly consistent with both the discussion of alternate forms of deflation and monetary equilibrium described above. As emphasized above, there is an important distinction between changes in inflation that are caused by shocks to aggregate supply and the changes that are caused by aggregate demand. As a result, monetary policy should respond only to shocks to aggregate demand. Unfortunately, this imposes strict informational assumptions on policymakers as it requires them to determine the underlying cause of changes in the price level, or the rate of inflation, in real time. While this distinction might not be arduous in the wake of easily observable, aggregate supply shocks that result from natural disasters, it is much more difficult to ascertain the effects of productivity on prices in real time.[29]

27. F.A. Hayek, *Prices and Production* (London: Routledge, 1931).
28. Lawrence J. Christiano, Roberto Motto, and Massimo Rostagno, "Two Reasons Why Money and Credit May be Useful in Monetary Policy" (working paper, 2007).
29. For more on productivity and monetary policy, see Beckworth (Chapter 2).

In theory, the Taylor Rule (1993)[30] corrects for the shortcoming in inflation targeting by incorporating a term for the output gap, or the deviation of output from its natural level. Formally, the Taylor Rule can be written as follows:

$$R_t = r + \pi_t + h(\pi_t - \pi^*) + g(y_t - y) \qquad (1)$$

where R_t is the short-term nominal interest rate targeted by monetary policy,[31] r is the long-run equilibrium real interest rate, π_t is inflation, π^* is the inflation target, $(y_t - y)$ is the percentage deviation of output from potential, and g and h are parameters.[32] The level of the nominal interest rate is therefore determined by the long-run equilibrium interest rate and deviations of inflation and output from their respective targets.

The inclusion of the output gap in the Taylor Rule is an improvement over an inflation target in that it explicitly requires the central bank to react differently to aggregate supply and aggregate demand shocks. Unfortunately, while the Taylor Rule lessens the informational requirements of central bankers about the nature of the economic shock, the rule creates a new informational requirement, as central bankers must know the true level of potential output.

There is sufficient reason to believe that this new informational assumption is problematic. For example, authors such as Taylor[33] and Clarida, Galí, and Gertler[34] estimate the parameters of the Taylor Rule for sub-periods in U.S. economic history. Most notably, they find that the Federal Reserve became much tougher on inflation following the appointment of Paul Volcker as chairman

---

30. Taylor, "Discretion Versus Policy Rules in Practice."

31. Here I have used the term "target" rather than "instrument" with reference to the monetary policy interest rate. The reason is that the instrument of the central bank, at least in the United States, is the monetary base. The policy interest rate, the federal funds rate, is effectively the intermediate target of monetary policy. This might seem to be a minor point to the reader, but it is important in terms of how monetary policy is conducted. For more, see Michael T. Belongia and Melvin J. Hinich, "The Evolving Role and Definition of the Federal Funds Rate In the Conduct of U.S. Monetary Policy" (working paper, 2009).

32. Taylor suggests, based on evidence from simulations, that the parameters should each equal 0.5.

33. Taylor, "Staggered Price and Wage Setting in Macroeconomics."

34. Richard Clarida, Jordi Galí, and Mark Gertler, "Monetary Policy Rules and Macroeconomic Stability: Evidence and Some Theory," *Quarterly Journal of Economics* 115 (2000): 147–80

as evident by the substantial increase in the estimated parameter on inflation.[35] The estimates of these authors, however, are based on the current data available. In reality, the members of the Federal Open Market Committee (FOMC) did not have access to this information. For example, initial government estimates of output are subject to subsequent and, at times, significant revisions. Thus, in order to properly assess the response of policymakers to certain variable targets, one must use estimates based on data available in real time.

In a series of papers, Orphanides estimates Taylor rules for the same sub-periods using the Federal Reserve's Greenbook forecasts of inflation and output. These estimates suggest that there was a strong response of monetary policy to forecasted inflation in each sub-period. In contrast to the earlier work, Orphanides does not find much of a change in policy between the sub-periods using the real-time data. The results presented by Orphanides suggest that the primary difference between policies during the Great Inflation and the post-Volcker era are not explained by the parameters of the Taylor Rule, but rather differences between the estimated output gap and the actual output gap.[36] In other words, policy mistakes were caused by inaccurate estimates of the output gap throughout the 1970s.

Similarly, Cukierman and Lippi develop a structural model of the U.S. economy in which the central bank cannot distinguish whether fluctuations in inflation and output are due to fluctuations in demand or the result of a shock to potential output.[37] This information problem causes monetary policy to become systematically too loose relative to the case of perfect information when potential output declines and is systematically too tight when potential output rises. What's more, the size of the policy mistakes vary proportionally to the size of the shock to potential output and are robust to instances in which the central bank forecasts optimally. The implication is that misperceptions about the output gap can be an important source of monetary policy mistakes

35. Taylor (see Taylor, "Staggered Price and Wage Setting in Macroeconomics") actually ignores the Volcker era in his analysis and chooses the sub-period that begins with Greenspan's tenure as chairman. Nonetheless, this remains the post-Volcker era.
36. See Figure 9.5 in Athanasios Orphanides, "Monetary Policy Rules, Macroeconomic Stability, and Inflation: A View from the Trenches," in *Journal of Money, Credit, and Banking* 36, no. 2 (2004): 151–75.
37. Alex Cukierman and Francesco Lippi, "Endogenous Monetary Policy with Unobserved Potential Output," *Journal of Economic Dynamics and Control* 29 (2005): 1951–83.

and therefore economic fluctuations when the central banks do not have perfect information.

What the above discussion highlights is the difficult nature of using inflation targeting or Taylor rules to conduct monetary policy. Each rule imposes strong informational assumptions on central bankers. Under an inflation target, those making monetary policy decisions are forced to consider the nature of the shock. The inflation target must therefore adjust relative to the perceived nature of economic shocks. The Taylor Rule, while eliminating this informational problem through the inclusion of the output gap, requires a new set of strong informational assumptions. Specifically, the Taylor Rule requires that central bankers know the equilibrium real rate of interest, the output gap, and the inflation rate in real time. There is sufficient reason for concern about these informational assumptions as the evidence described above suggests that the inability of the Federal Reserve to accurately estimate the output gap can explain the poor performance of monetary policy during the Great Inflation in the 1970s.

In contrast, a nominal income-targeting rule does not impose such stringent informational assumptions. As noted above, the nominal income target implies that monetary policy only responds to shocks to aggregate demand. As a result, and contrary to an inflation target, policymakers do not have to know the nature of the shock. What's more, a nominal income-targeting rule does not require any knowledge of the output gap. While a nominal income target requires an implicit target for inflation and real output growth, it is much more flexible to errors. For example, McCallum's proposal was to set the nominal income target equal to the long-run average rate of real output growth, or roughly 3 percent annually.[38] Thus, this rule implicitly implies that the central bank is targeting 3 percent real output growth and zero inflation. An error in this implicit target for output will naturally result in a corresponding error for the implicit inflation target, but this would likely be reasonably harmless for errors of small magnitude.[39] The nominal income-targeting rule

---

38. Bennett T. McCallum, "The Case for Rules in the Conduct of Monetary Policy: A Concrete Example," *Federal Reserve Bank of Richmond Economic Review* (Sept./Oct., 1987): 10–18.

39. If the implicit real output target is based on the past history of growth for a developed economy, it would certainly seem reasonable to assume that any error between the implicit target and the actual average rate of output growth would be small. McCallum

is therefore able to mitigate fluctuations in real output around its trend without an estimate of potential output. Meanwhile, the Taylor Rule requires that central bankers know inflation, real output, and potential output in real time. Errors in the output gap are not necessarily offset by a corresponding change in the inflation target.

Finally, a major benefit inherent in nominal income targeting is that it circumvents the imperfect knowledge of macroeconomists and policymakers with regard to the structure of the macroeconomy. While it is generally accepted that monetary policy directly impacts nominal variables, there does not exist a widely accepted dynamic theory of the relationships between real and nominal variables. Most notably, there is little agreement about the aggregate supply function, or Phillips curve–type relationship among macroeconomists. For example, the current monetary models often have a New Keynesian Phillips curve as part of the core of the model, which implies that the inflation rate is dependent on expectations of future inflation and the output gap. Empirical evidence, however, suggests that this relationship does not fit the data very well.[40] In fact, empirical evidence favors a backward-looking Phillips curve, at least in reduced form estimation, which is not consistent with the rational expectations framework that underlies modern macroeconomic models. As a result, it is important that any monetary policy framework developed should not be dependent upon any given structural framework that explains the division of nominal income between output and inflation. The nominal income target is the only policy considered above consistent with that proposition.

Evaluating Nominal Income Targeting

The previous section was concerned with the theoretical underpinnings and desirable features of a nominal income target. Given this outline, it is important to consider what a nominal income target might look like in practice and the corresponding implications for macroeconomic stability. As result, the next

---

(see Bennett T. McCallum, "The Case for Rules in the Conduct of Monetary Policy"), for example, suggests using the twenty-year average growth rate and updating this figure at infrequent intervals.

40. Jeremy Rudd, and Karl Whelan, "Modeling Inflation Dynamic: A Critical Review of Recent Research," *Journal of Money, Credit, and Banking* 39, no. 1 (2007); 155–70.

subsection discusses three alternative formulations of nominal income targeting. The remaining subsections examine evidence from empirical work and simulations as well as the behavior of nominal income during the Great Recession.

What Would a Nominal Income Targeting Rule Look Like?

Given the desirable features of a nominal income-targeting rule in theory, it is important to consider what such a rule would look like in practice. Broadly, there are three types of policies that have been outlined in the literature. Each is discussed in turn below.

The first proposal is that of McCallum,[41] who suggests that the growth rate of the monetary base should be set in response to deviations of nominal income growth from its target and long-term trends in base velocity. Specifically, this rule can be written as:

$$\Delta b_t = 0.00739 - (1/16)[x_{t-1} - x_{t-17} - b_{t-1} + b_{t-17}] + \mu(x^*_{t-1} - x_{t-1}) \qquad (2)$$

where b is the monetary base, x is nominal income, x^* is the nominal income target, and μ is a parameter that measures the responsiveness of base growth to deviations from the target.[42] All variables are expressed in logarithms and thus the constant implies a 3-percent annual growth rate. The term in brackets is the four-year average growth in base velocity.

An alternative to the aforementioned rule is that used by McCallum and Nelson[43] and Hendrickson.[44] This rule can be written as:

$$R_t = R + ß[E_{t-1}\Delta x_t - \Delta x^*] \qquad (3)$$

where R_t is the policy interest rate, R is the equilibrium interest rate, $E_{t-1}\Delta x_t$ is the nominal income growth forecast, Δx^* is the nominal income growth target, and ß is a parameter that measures the responsiveness of the policy interest rate

---

41. McCallum, "The Case for Rules in the Conduct of Monetary Policy"; McCallum, "Robustness Properties of a Rule for Monetary Policy."
42. McCallum (see McCallum, "The Case for Rules in the Conduct of Monetary Policy"; and McCallum, "Robustness Properties of a Rule for Monetary Policy," *Carnegie-Rochester Conference Series on Public Policy* 29 (1988): 173–204) suggests that $\mu=0.25$.
43. McCallum and Nelson, "Nominal Income Targeting in an Open Economy Optimizing Model."
44. Hendrickson, "An Overhaul of Federal Reserve Doctrine."

to expected deviations of nominal income from the target. This proposal differs from that of McCallum[45] in regards to how monetary policy is conducted. In the former case, the central bank is using its instrument to adjust to deviations of nominal income from the target whereas, in the latter case, monetary policy is conducted using an interest rate as an intermediate target.[46] It is also important to note that the rules differ in that the monetary base rule targets the level of nominal income whereas the interest rate rule targets the growth of nominal income. This distinction has important implications for monetary policy, but each rule is easily adapted to the alternative specification.

Finally, Sumner[47] suggests a market-oriented solution.[48] In this proposal, the central bank would offer to buy and sell unlimited quantities of a futures contract priced in terms of expectations for nominal income. Under this scenario, open market operations would effectively be conducted by the general public rather than by the central bank. For example, suppose that the Federal Reserve decided to announce a nominal income target of $16.6 trillion for the end of 2010, a target consistent with a 5-percent growth rate in nominal income from the start of the recession to the target date.[49] The Fed would then set the price of the contract to some fraction of the target. Those who believe that nominal

---

45. McCallum, "The Case for Rules in the Conduct of Monetary Policy"; McCallum, "Robustness Properties of a Rule for Monetary Policy."

46. There are other key differences between interest rate rules and monetary aggregate rules. Poole, for example, shows that the choice of policy instrument is dependent on the variance and covariance of the error terms in the IS and LM equations in a stochastic IS-LM model. In addition, the use of an interest rate rule is problematic for policymakers when the nominal interest rate approaches the zero lower bound, whether or not a liquidity trap exists. William Poole, "Optimal Choice of Monetary Policy Instruments in a Simple Stochastic Macro Model," *The Quarterly Journal of Economics*, Vol. 84, No. 2 (1970): 197–216.

47. Scott Sumner, "Let A Thousand Models Bloom: The Advantages of Making the FOMC a Truly 'Open Market'," *Contributions to Macroeconomics* 6, no. 1, art8 (2006).

48. The example in Sumner (see Sumner, "Let A Thousand Models Bloom") refers to a CPI futures market, although he notes that the same principle would apply to a nominal income target. Sumner has advocated nominal income futures elsewhere (see Sumner, "Using Futures Instrument Prices to Target Nominal Income," *Bulletin of Economic Research* 41 (1989): 157–62).

49. The 5-percent target is meant to be consistent with the average growth rate in nominal income over the last thirty years. This author would actually prefer a target closer to 3 percent, but the discussion and conclusions remain unchanged.

278 | Nominal Income Targeting and Monetary Stability

income will come in above the target will therefore take a long position on the contract, while those who believe nominal income will come in below target will take a short position.[50] If nominal income comes in above target, those who took a long position will earn a return while those who took a short position will have to pay the difference. The reverse would hold for the case in which nominal income comes in below target.

The implications for monetary policy under this type of framework are as follows. Those who take a long position on the contract are effectively forecasting that monetary policy is too loose. When an individual wants to take a long position, the central bank creates and sells the contract. Simultaneously, the central bank will undertake an open market sale. Conversely, when an individual wants to take a short position, the central bank will create and buy the futures contract while simultaneously conducting an open market purchase. Thus, under this framework, market participants who seek to earn a profit from their forecast of nominal income essentially conduct open market operations. As a result, the net change in the monetary base is dependent on the magnitude of purchases of the futures contract relative to sales.

Each of these rules has its relative merits, but ultimately they all provide the same general guide for monetary policy. Given the general outline of the rules above, it is important to consider how these rules would perform in practice. The subsequent subsection examines empirical evidence on nominal income targeting.

An Empirical Examination

Given the absence of monetary policy rules that explicitly target nominal income, empirical evidence on the particular rules described above relies on simulations. McCallum,[51] for example, conducts a simple simulation

---

50. Under this scenario the central bank would offer a futures contract at a par value of (1.0X)(Current nominal income) where X is the target rate for nominal income growth. Market participants would take a "long" position by purchasing the futures contract and a "short" position by selling the contract.
51. McCallum, "The Case for Rules in the Conduct of Monetary Policy."

by assuming that nominal income depends on its own lag and the lag of the monetary base. Combined with the monetary policy rule in equation (2) above, McCallum is able to simulate a time path for nominal income and compare it with the desired target of 3 percent per year. The simulations suggest that the deviation of nominal income from its target for actual monetary policy during the period from 1954–85 is over thirty times as large as that implied by the nominal income-targeting rule given by equation (2).[52]

One drawback of this simulation, however, is that it is generated using a model without a theoretical foundation. As a result, McCallum[53] conducts a number of simulations to examine the robustness of the earlier results using an atheoretical vector autoregressive model as well as alternative structural models.[54] The results suggest that the conclusions drawn in McCallum are robust to model specification.

Taylor[55] considers the implications of three alternative policies. Specifically, Taylor compares a nominal income growth target with actual monetary policy and a hybrid nominal income growth target in which the central bank adjusts the nominal income target by using the constant desired rate of growth plus the deviation of real output from its equilibrium level. The evidence suggests that the third rule produces the best performance. The first rule performs poorly as a result of the fact that the target is the growth of nominal income. Targeting the growth rate implies that the rule allows deviations from the target to accumulate. These results suggest that targeting the level of nominal income would be desirable relative to a growth target.

Similarly, Hall and Mankiw[56] compare the relative performance of alternative nominal income-targeting rules. The results suggest that a policy rule

---

52. The deviation from the targeted trend is measured by the root mean squared deviation.
53. McCallum, "Robustness Properties of a Rule for Monetary Policy."
54. A vector autoregressive model is an econometric model that consists of a vector of endogenous variables that are regressed on their own lags and the lags of the other variables. The model is used to estimate theory-free relationships between economic variables.
55. John B. Taylor, "What Would Nominal GNP Targeting Do to the Business Cycle?" *Carnegie-Rochester Series on Public Policy* 22 (1985): 61–84.
56. Robert E. Hall and N. Gregory Mankiw, "Nominal Income Targeting," in ed. N. Gregory Mankiw, *Monetary Policy* (Chicago: University of Chicago Press, 1994).

that targets the level of nominal income is preferable in terms of the volatility of the price level, inflation, and the output gap to both a nominal income growth target and actual monetary policy. A hybrid rule that targets the level of nominal income as well as deviations of output from the natural rate is slightly preferable to the nominal income level target. Nonetheless, this latter result assumes that the natural rate of output is known in real time by policymakers.

McCallum and Nelson[57] develop an open economy, rational expectations model and consider the variability of inflation and the output gap using a rule similar to that in equation (3), an inflation-targeting rule, and a Taylor rule.[58] Their results suggest the nominal income-targeting rule performs well in comparison to both rules. In fact, nominal income targeting performs as well or better than these rules except in the case of fairly activist policies.[59]

Finally, Hendrickson[60] argues that the significant change in monetary policy in the United States since 1979 is explained by an increased responsiveness to movements in nominal income. Specifically, the claim is that monetary policy moved from a cost-push view of inflation to a demand-pull view of inflation in the post-1979 period. As a result, changes in monetary policy should be reflected in the responsiveness to nominal income. Estimates for a reduced form equation similar to equation (3) verify that movements in the federal funds rates were larger in response to fluctuations in the Federal Reserve's Greenbook forecast of nominal income after 1979. What's more, comparing these models within both a semi-classical and New Keynesian model suggests that such a change in monetary policy can explain the reduction in the vari-

---

57. McCallum and Nelson, "Nominal Income Targeting in an Open Economy Optimizing Model."

58. The nominal income-targeting rule used by McCallum and Nelson differs only in the sense that they assume that the central bank seeks to smooth movements in the interest. This is done by assuming that movements in the policy interest rate are caused not only by changes in the goal variable(s), but also the lagged interest rate.

59. These "activist" policies refer to policies in which the coefficient(s) on the goal variable(s) are fairly high. Of course, it is also important to note that the policymakers do not face imperfect information in the model.

60. Hendrickson, Joshua R. "An Overhaul of Federal Reserve Doctrine: Nominal Income and the Great Moderation." *Journal of Macroeconomics*, forthcoming.

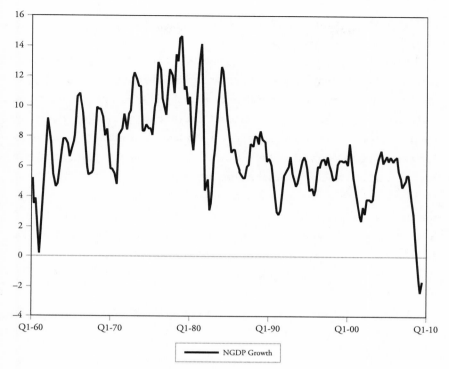

Figure 9.5. Nominal GDP Growth
Source: FRED Database

ability of inflation and the output gap observed during the Great Moderation rather well.

Nominal Income and the Great Recession

As noted above, it is a widely accepted proposition that monetary policy affects only nominal variables in the long run. Thus, in accordance with the natural rate hypothesis, the growth of real output should fluctuate around its natural rate. Accordingly, since monetary policy can affect only nominal income, a stable monetary policy should similarly imply that nominal income be stationary around some constant mean equal to the equilibrium rate of real output growth plus some equilibrium rate of inflation. Figure 9.5 plots nominal income growth, as measured by nominal gross domestic product, for the United States for the period from 1960–2009.

In examining Figure 9.5, there are a few points of particular interest. First, nominal income growth is not stationary for the entire sample.[61] In particular, the path of nominal income growth is upward-sloping beginning in the 1960s and extending through the 1970s. Second, the time series is stationary during the period commonly known as the Great Moderation beginning in the 1980s and extending through 2007. Finally, the Great Recession is characterized by a substantial collapse in nominal income growth. As noted in the reference to Hendrickson (forthcoming) above, the behavior of nominal income growth in the first two sub-periods can be explained by the behavior of monetary policy. It is therefore important to consider whether monetary policy can explain the sudden collapse of nominal income growth during the Great Recession and, if so, how a nominal income target could potentially have led to an alternative path for policy.

To motivate an analysis consider the simple monetary equilibrium framework outlined above. Recall that the equation of exchange can be written as:

$$mBV = Py$$

where m is the money multiplier, B is the monetary base, V is velocity, P is the price level, and y is real output. Here the product mB is defined as M2, which is similar to that used in the analysis of Friedman and Schwartz[62] and has been shown to have a statistically significant effect on aggregate demand by Hafer, Haslag, and Jones.[63]

---

61. This seems clear from casual observation, but it is also verified by augmented Dickey-Fuller tests. This is true of the subsample as well.

62. Friedman and Schwartz, *Monetary Trends in the United States and the United Kingdom.*

63. Aggregate demand is formulated as a backward-looking IS equation in Hafer, Haslag, and Jones (see R.W. Hafer, Joseph H. Haslag, and Garett Jones, "On Money and Output: Is Money Redundant?" *Journal of Monetary Economics* 54 (2007): 945–54). These authors also find it useful to include the money multiplier and the monetary base separately in the IS equation, which would seem to provide support for the analysis herein. A better measure of the money supply would be Divisia M2, which is consistent with economic, aggregation, and index number theory, whereas simple sum indexes are not. Unfortunately, this data is not available for the time period in question.

This framework is important because it reflects the potential effects of monetary disequilibrium. For example, following an economic shock, an increase in the demand for money will be reflected in m and V where changes in m reflect changes in the demand for the components of the monetary base and V reflects changes in the demand for the broader monetary aggregate (in this case M2). Consistent with monetary disequilibrium theory if there is an increase in the demand for money and that increase is not met by an increase in the money supply, this will result in a reduction in aggregate demand as individuals withhold purchases in order to hold the greater quantity of money. The existence of sticky prices implies that this will not only reflect a reduction in nominal income, but also in real income as well. This type of framework is thus in the spirit of Friedman and Schwartz,[64] who showed that the increase in the demand for base money resulted in a reduction in broader money aggregates and therefore both nominal and real income for a number of deep recessions in U.S. monetary history. What's more, the use of this framework can provide direct implications for monetary policy under a nominal income target.

Figure 9.6 plots the monetary base (in trillions of dollars), the M2 money multiplier, and M2 velocity. The monetary base is plotted on the right-hand axis whereas the other two variables are plotted on the left-hand axis. As shown, the money multiplier exhibits a sharp decline in the third quarter of 2008, which coincides with the failure of Lehman Brothers and the announcement of TARP. Meanwhile, velocity began experiencing a moderate decline starting at the beginning of the onset of the recession in late 2007. Finally, the monetary base sharply increased beginning in the third quarter of 2008 as well. In fact, between the second quarter of 2008 and the fourth quarter of 2009, the monetary base roughly doubled.

To put these changes into context regarding monetary policy, consider that through the fourth quarter of 2007, nominal income was $14.37 trillion. Taking the changes in velocity and the money multiplier as given, the monetary base would have to have increased by 140 percent for nominal income to remain constant through the fourth quarter of 2009. What's more, for nominal income

---

64. Friedman and Schwartz, "Money and Business Cycles"; Friedman and Schwartz, *A Monetary History of the United States.*

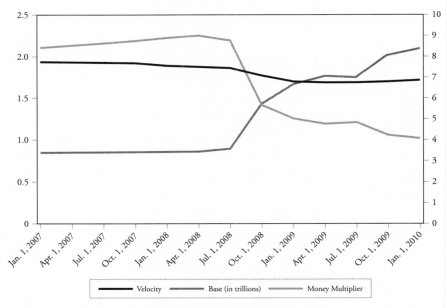

Figure 9.6. Monetary Equilibrium: the Money Multiplier,
Velocity, and the Monetary Base"

Source: FRED Database, Author Calculations

to average a 5-percent annual increase over this period, consistent with the average rate of growth throughout the Great Moderation, the monetary base would have had to increase by 165 percent. This would seem to suggest that monetary policy is an important source of the decline in nominal income.

This conclusion requires a couple remarks. First, this perspective on monetary policy has recently been called into question by Cochrane, who argues that the Great Recession does not fit with monetary disequilibrium theory because the "Federal Reserve flooded the country with money (reserves)." This would seem to cast doubt on the claim that the collapse in nominal income was the result, at least in part, of monetary policy.[65] While it is certainly true that the excess reserves increased from $6 billion to roughly $800 billion over this time

65. Cochrane (see John H. Cochrane, "Understanding Policy in the Great Recession: Some Unpleasant Fiscal Arithmetic" (NBER Working Paper No. 16087, 2010) argues that the reduction in aggregate demand was the result of a decrease in the discount rate on government debt.

period, Cochrane's analysis ignores an important distinction. As Friedman and Schwartz[66] explain, the negative impact from an increase in the demand for currency and/or bank reserves is the result of the fact that a greater proportion of the monetary base is needed to meet the demand for its components. Increases in the monetary base would offset the increase in demand and prevent the broader monetary aggregate from declining. However, the increase in bank reserves outlined above coincides with the Federal Reserve's decision in October 2008 to pay interest on excess reserves. Thus, the increase in the demand for base money was met by an increase in an interest-bearing asset.[67]

Second, the failure of monetary policy to prevent the collapse in nominal income, despite a substantial increase in the monetary base, speaks to the desirability of a nominal income-targeting rule. Without a stated goal, the Federal Reserve is conducting monetary policy in a difficult manner. The behavior of policymakers seems to reflect a view that a substantial monetary stimulus was necessary, but the decision to pay interest on excess reserves suggests that this expansion was to be done in a manner that prevented substantial inflationary pressures.

The use of a monetary policy rule would alleviate the difficulties with conducting policy described above. An explicit target for nominal income would provide a benchmark by which to judge the stance of policy. Under such a policy, the relation between nominal income and its target would reflect the stance of policy and therefore signal the proper response of policy to the central bank. The collapse of nominal income in this case would signal to the central bank that policy was too tight with the specific changes in the monetary base and interest rates of secondary importance.

Finally, as emphasized in Woodford,[68] an important component to monetary policy is how it affects expectations. Monetary policy works not only through the direct effect of open market operations, but also by influencing expectations about the future path of policy. Thus, a nominal income-targeting

---

66. Friedman and Schwartz, "Money and Business Cycles."
67. Reserves that earn interest from the Federal Reserve are effectively government debt. This debt is thus an asset on a bank's balance sheet in much the same manner as a U.S. Treasury bill would be. Curiously, Cochrane seems to agree on this point, but not on the distinction with regards to monetary equilibrium.
68. Woodford, *Interest and Prices.*

rule could have potentially stemmed, at least in part, the collapse in nominal income from the knowledge that the central bank would stand ready to facilitate any increase in the demand for base money.[69]

Conclusion

Nominal income targeting has a number of desirable characteristics. First, while there is widespread recognition that monetary policy affects nominal income, there is much less agreement about the division of those effects between output and the price level. As a result, a nominal income-targeting rule is desirable, as it does not require any assumptions about the structural character of the economy. Analogously, a nominal income target imposes less stringent information assumptions on monetary policymakers.

The second important characteristic of a nominal income target is the fact that it implicitly implies a flexible price level (or inflation) target in the wake of aggregate supply shocks. Specifically, a nominal income target implies that the price level (inflation rate) target should be allowed to rise following a supply shock and fall in the wake of an increase in productivity. What's more, this change in the price level (inflation) target is implicit in the nominal income targeting-rule and does not require any revision of the target on the part of monetary policymakers.

Finally, a central theme in monetary business cycle theories is the concept of monetary equilibrium defined as the condition in which the nominal supply of money is sufficient to satisfy the demand for real money balances. In these theories, cases of disequilibrium are the primary source of economic fluctuations. Nominal income targeting is desirable in that it implicitly maintains monetary equilibrium, thereby minimizing fluctuations that result from monetary disturbances.

A successful monetary policy should foster monetary stability by minimizing economic fluctuations that result from monetary disturbances. Along these lines, there has been a push in recent years to devise optimal monetary policy

---

69. In the context of the equation of exchange, the existence of an explicit monetary policy rule should stabilize both velocity and the money multiplier.

rules. These efforts have focused predominantly on inflation targeting and Taylor rules. Nonetheless, the theoretical and empirical evidence presented above speak to the desirability of nominal income targeting both in and of itself and in reference to popular alternatives.

References

Atkeson, Andrew and Patrick J. Kehoe. 2008. "Deflation and Depression: Is There An Empirical Link?" *American Economic Review*, Vol. 94, No. 2, p. 99–103.

Beckworth, David. 2007. "The Postbellum Deflation and Its Lessons for Today." *North American Journal of Economics and Finance*, Vol. 18, No. 2, p. 195–214.

———. 2008. "Aggregate Supply-Driven Deflation and Its Implications for Macro-economic Stability." *Cato Journal*, Vol. 28, No. 3, p. 363–84.

Beckworth, David and Joshua R. Hendrickson. 2010. "Monetary Policy and the Great Spending Crashes." Working paper.

Belongia, Michael T. and Melvin J. Hinich. 2009. "The Evolving Role and Definition of the Federal Funds Rate In the Conduct of U.S. Monetary Policy." Working paper.

Bernanke, Ben S. 2002. "Deflation: Making Sure "It" Doesn't Happen Here." Speech to National Economists Club. Available at: http://www.federalreserve.gov/board docs/speeches/2002/20021121/default.htm

Bernanke, Ben S. and Michael Woodford. 2005. *The Inflation-Targeting Debate.* Chicago: Chicago University Press.

Bordo, Michael and Angela Redish. 2004. "Is Deflation Depressing? Evidence from the Classical Gold Standard" in Burdekin and Siklos, eds. *Deflation: Current and Historical Perspectives.* Cambridge: Cambridge University Press.

Bordo, Michael, John Landon Lane, and Angela Redish. 2004. "Good Versus Bad Deflation: Lessons from the Gold Standard Era." NBER Working Paper 10329.

Bradley, Michael D. and Dennis W. Jansen. 1989. "Understanding Nominal Income Targeting." *St. Louis Federal Reserve Bank Review*, Nov./Dec., p. 31–40.

Christiano, Lawrence J., Roberto Motto, and Massimo Rostagno. 2007. "Two Reasons Why Money and Credit May be Useful in Monetary Policy." Working paper.

Clarida, Richard, Jordi Galí, and Mark Gertler. 2000. "Monetary Policy Rules and Macroeconomic Stability: Evidence and Some Theory." *Quarterly Journal of Economics*, Vol. 115, p. 147–80.

Cochrane, John H. 2010. "Understanding Policy in the Great Recession: Some Unpleasant Fiscal Arithmetic." NBER Working Paper No. 16087.

Cukierman, Alex and Francesco Lippi. 2005. "Endogenous Monetary Policy with Unobserved Potential Output." *Journal of Economic Dynamics and Control*, Vol. 29, p. 1951–83.

Fisher, Irving. 1932. *Booms and Depressions.* New York: Adelphi.

———. 1933. "The Debt-Deflation Theory of Great Depressions." *Econometrica*, Vol. 1, No. 4, p. 337–57.

Friedman, Milton and Anna J. Schwartz. 1963a. "Money and Business Cycles." *Review of Economics and Statistics*, Vol. 45, No. 1.

Friedman, Milton and Anna J. Schwartz. 1963b. *A Monetary History of the United States.* Princeton: Princeton University Press.

———. 1982. *Monetary Trends in the United States and the United Kingdom.* Chicago: University of Chicago Press.

Galí, Jordi. 2008. *Monetary Policy, Inflation, and the Business Cycle.* Princeton: Princeton University Press.

Gordon, Robert J. 1985. "The Conduct of Domestic Monetary Policy," in Ando, Eguchi, Farmer, and Suzuki (eds.), *Monetary Policy in Our Times*, Cambridge: MIT Press.

Hafer, R.W., Joseph H. Haslag, and Garett Jones. 2007. "On Money and Output: Is Money Redundant?" *Journal of Monetary Economics*, Vol. 54, p. 945–54.

Hall, Robert E. and N. Gregory Mankiw. 1994. "Nominal Income Targeting" in N. Gregory Mankiw (ed.) *Monetary Policy.* Chicago: University of Chicago Press.

Hayek, F.A. 1931. *Prices and Production.* London: Routledge.

Hendrickson, Joshua R. 2010a. "Monetary Transmission in the New Keynesian Framework: Is the Interest Rate Enough?" Working Paper.

———. 2010b. "A Re-Examination of Money and Business Cycles." Unpublished Ph.D. dissertation.

———. forthcoming. "An Overhaul of Federal Reserve Doctrine: Nominal Income and the Great Moderation." *Journal of Macroeconomics.*

Horwitz, Steven. 2001. *Microfoundations and Macroeconomics: An Austrian Perspective.* London: Routledge.

Leijonhufvud, Axel. 1981. *Information and Coordination: Essays in Macroeconomic Theory.* New York: Oxford University Press.

McCallum, Bennett T. 1987. "The Case for Rules in the Conduct of Monetary Policy: A Concrete Example." *Federal Reserve Bank of Richmond Economic Review.* September/October, p. 10–18.

———. 1988. "Robustness Properties of a Rule for Monetary Policy." *Carnegie-Rochester Conference Series on Public Policy,* Vol. 29, p. 173–204.

McCallum, Bennett T. and Edward Nelson. 1999. "Nominal Income Targeting in an Open Economy Optimizing Model." *Journal of Monetary Economics,* Vol. 43, p. 553–78.

Orphanides, Athanasios. 2001. "Monetary Policy Rules Based on Real-Time Data." *American Economic Review,* Vol. 91, No. 4, p. 964–85.

———. 2002. "Monetary Policy Rules and the Great Inflation." *American Economic Review,* Vol. 92, No. 2, p. 115–20.

———. 2004. "Monetary Policy Rules, Macroeconomic Stability, and Inflation: A View from the Trenches." *Journal of Money, Credit, and Banking,* Vol. 36, No. 2, p. 151–75.

Rudd, Jeremy and Karl Whelan. 2007. "Modeling Inflation Dynamic: A Critical Review of Recent Research." *Journal of Money, Credit, and Banking,* Vol. 39, No. 1, p. 155–70.

Selgin, George. 1997. *Less Than Zero: The Case for a Falling Price Level in a Growing Economy.* London: Institute of Economic Affairs.

Sumner, Scott. 1989. "Using Futures Instrument Prices to Target Nominal Income." *Bulletin of Economic Research,* Vol. 41, p. 157–62.

———. 2006. "Let A Thousand Models Bloom: The Advantages of Making the FOMC a Truly 'Open Market'." *Contributions to Macroeconomics,* Vol. 6, No. 1, Article 8.

Taylor, John B. 1985. "What Would Nominal GNP Targeting Do to the Business Cycle?" *Carnegie-Rochester Series on Public Policy*, Vol. 22, p. 61–84.

_____. 1993. "Discretion Versus Policy Rules in Practice." *Carnegie-Rochester Series on Public Policy*, Vol. 39, p. 195–214.

_____. 1999a. *Monetary Policy Rules.* Chicago: Chicago University Press.

_____. 1999b. "A Historical Analysis of Monetary Policy Rules," in John B. Taylor (ed.), *Monetary Policy Rules.* Chicago: Chicago University Press.

_____. 1999c. "Staggered Price and Wage Setting in Macroeconomics," in John Taylor and Michael Woodford (eds.) *Handbook of Macroeconomics*, North-Holland: Elsevier, Vol. 1, Part 2.

_____. 2009. *Getting Off Track: How Government Actions and Interventions Caused, Prolonged, and Worsened the Financial Crisis.* Stanford: Hoover Institution Press.

Warburton, Clark. 1950. "The Monetary Disequilibrium Hypothesis." *The American Journal of Economics and Sociology*, Vol. 10, No. 1, p. 1–11.

White, Lawrence H. 1999. "Hayek's Monetary Theory and Policy: A Critical Reconstruction." *Journal of Money, Credit, and Banking*, Vol. 31, No. 1, p. 109–120.

Woodford, Michael. 2003. *Interest and Prices.* Princeton: Princeton University Press.

_____. 2010. "Optimal Monetary Stabilization Policy." NBER Working Paper No. 16095.

Yeager, Leland. 1986. "The Significance of Monetary Disequilibrium." *Cato Journal*, Vol. 6, No. 2, p. 369–399.

10

Should Monetary Policy "Lean or Clean"?

William R. White

Introduction

SHOULD MONETARY POLICY *lean* against the wind of the ex-
pansion phase of credit upturns, in order to moderate boom conditions? Clearly,
no one would question the desirability of leaning enough to reduce associated
inflationary pressures. But should the reaction be stronger than that which
near-term inflation control might seem to warrant? In particular, should policy
be tighter than otherwise, given evidence of growing "imbalances" in the real
economy[1] or increasing systemic exposures in the financial system? Or should
an alternative strategy be relied upon to deal with such problems? In particular,
should monetary policy be content with trying to *clean* up afterwards, once the
boom has turned to bust? Indeed, should central banks go even further and
preemptively ease policy in order to short-circuit the bust altogether?

As a matter of logic, the answer to the *lean-or-clean* question must depend on
an evaluation of the relative merits of each approach, since alternatives cannot

---

This paper grew out of a presentation at a Monetary Roundtable at the Bank of England,
and has benefitted from comments made at conferences at Bank Negara Malaysia in Kuala
Lumpur, and at the Centre for Financial Studies in Frankfurt, Germany. The views in this
paper are entirely personal and do not necessarily reflect the views of the Organization for
Economic Co-operation and Development, the Bank for International Settlements, the
Federal Reserve Bank of Dallas or the Federal Reserve System.

1. Imbalances are defined here as significant and sustained deviations from longer-run
trends. Such deviations raise the possibility of mean reversion, perhaps with associated
macroeconomic costs. Evidently, such an outcome need not be inevitable, given that
underlying fundamentals might have changed enough to justify these unusual observations. Nevertheless, mean reversion seems a quite common historical phenomenon.

be evaluated in isolation. The dominant view until quite recently seems to have been in favor of cleaning up afterwards. However, the practical difficulties encountered in trying to do so, during the years following the crisis which began in mid 2007, have altered the balance of earlier arguments.

Indeed, the set of economic circumstances which then faced the official community were as difficult as any seen in the postwar period. Growth slowed sharply in both the advanced and emerging market economies. For a time, inflationary pressures were also rising, particularly in the emerging market economies, though they subsequently receded as recession took hold. In the major financial centers, many markets became dysfunctional, and some ceased to operate at all. Many financial institutions had to be closed down, nationalized, or supported in some way by governments.

The purpose of this paper is to suggest steps that might be taken to help avoid a repeat of such difficulties in the future. Evidently, this presupposes some understanding of what caused these dramatic events in the first place.

Liberalized financial systems seem to be inherently "procyclical."[2] That is, there are endogenous cycles in which some piece of good news leads to both an increased demand for and supply of credit. This positively affects both asset prices and spending, contributing to still more optimism and providing still more collateral for still more loans. Eventually, all these trends overshoot levels justified by the initial improvement in fundamentals and rational exuberance becomes irrational exuberance. In the end, the bubble bursts, and the process of speculation and leverage that powered it goes into reverse. Such processes have been seen repeatedly in history. The great recessions beginning in 1825, 1873, and 1929 all shared these characteristics[3], as did the more recent Nordic, Japanese, and Southeast Asia crises.[4] Moreover, in each instance, the crisis emerged

---

2. For a fuller description, see C. E. V. Borio and W. R. White, "Whither Monetary and Financial Stability? The Implications of Evolving Policy Regimes" (in "Monetary Policy and Uncertainty" Symposium sponsored by the Federal Reserve Bank of Kansas, August, 2003, 131–211).

3. On this, see J. Schumpeter, "Depressions: Can We Learn from Past Experience?" in *Economics of the Recovery Program*, 1934. Whittlesley House, McGraw Hill Book Co., New York and London.

4. See C.P. Kindleberger and R. Z. Aliber, *Manias, Panics and Crashes,* 5th ed. (New York: Palgrave Macmillan, 2005).

suddenly and unexpectedly, and without any significant degree of accelerating inflation beforehand.

There is a great deal of evidence to support the view that the crisis which began in 2007 had similar roots. The "New Era" and "Great Moderation" proclaimed in the latter part of the 1990s led to a variety of excesses, which suddenly collapsed around the turn of the century. This was met in turn by an unprecedented degree of monetary easing in the large industrial countries, and subsequently by very easy monetary policies in many emerging market countries (accompanied by massive foreign exchange intervention) as they tried to resist upward pressure on their exchange rates. The upshot was that global interest rates, both short and long, were held at unusually low levels for much of the first decade of this millennium. These lower rates contributed (a demand side effect) to a massive increase in monetary and credit aggregates. A further contribution to this credit growth (a supply side effect) was made by sharply declining lending standards. These easier lending terms were said at the time to be justified, both by an overall reduction in the risks to be managed and by improved risk management capacities. In both the advanced and emerging market countries, many borrowers obtained access to credit who would never have been able to do so in the past (subprime mortgages, for example) or did so on unusually easy terms (cov-lite corporate loans, for example). Speculation and leverage also expanded significantly, not least through the use of new structured products with high levels of leverage imbedded in them.

These developments contributed to record-high global growth rates in the years immediately preceding the crisis. Inflation, moreover, was quiescent for an unexpectedly long period under the influence of a variety of positive supply shocks, not least the process of globalization.[5] However, at the same time, these financial developments were also contributing to the gradual buildup of at least four major "imbalances" affecting both the financial and real sectors of the global economy.[6] As to the former, most asset prices (not least the price

---

5. For a fuller assessment of the relationship between globalization and domestic inflation, see W. R. White, "Globalisation and the Determinants of Domestic Inflation" (BIS Working paper no. 250, Basel, March 2008).

6. As noted above, imbalances are defined here as significant and sustained deviations from longer-run trends. Logically, individual deviations might be explained in a variety of

of housing) rose to unprecedented levels. The exposure of financial firms to risks of various sorts, as can now be clearly seen with hindsight, also increased sharply. As to the latter, household savings rates in many countries (especially the English speaking ones) fell to zero or even below. At the same time, the ratio of investment to GDP in China rose to over 40 percent,[7] a level never before seen in large countries in the postwar world. Finally, a number of countries with highly advanced financial systems, and associated low household savings rates, ran very large trade deficits. These were largely financed by capital inflows from surplus countries that had accumulated reserves in the process of resisting exchange rate appreciation.

With the onset of the crisis, the period of high global growth and essentially stable prices came to an end. Perhaps the first overt manifestation of the effects of the long period of rapid monetary and credit expansion was a sharp rise in commodity prices. With the influence of the earlier positive supply shocks having run their course, higher commodity prices quickly fed through to headline CPI in many countries. However, lower real wages subsequently weighed on spending and growth, and this deceleration was further aggravated as the imbalances noted above began to unwind. Indeed, the slowdown was so sharp, and the effects on commodity prices so appreciable, that the earlier worries about inflation were increasingly replaced by fears of near-term deflation.

The tipping point in this transition was arguably the "Minsky moment" in financial markets,[8] which occurred in August of 2007. The announcement that

---

idiosyncratic ways. However, when a wide variety of imbalances emerge simultaneously, this rather points in the direction of a joint underlying cause. This is pursued further below.

7. From a Wicksellian perspective, troubles arise whenever the financial rate (say, the long bond rate) differs from the natural rate (proxied by the prospective growth rate of the economy). Estimates of each for the global economy show that the financial rate fell below the natural rate in 1997, as the global growth rate of potential accelerated, and the gap continued to increase at least until the middle of 2008. See M. D. Knight, "General Manager's Speech" (remarks on the occasion of the BIS Annual General Meeting, Basel, June 30, 2008).

8. A "Minsky moment" refers to the analysis of financial crises initially put forward by Hyman Minsky. For a summary, see H. Minsky, "The Financial Stability Hypothesis," in P. Arestis et al., *Handbook of Radical Political Economy* (1992) Edward Elegar, Aldershot. He refers to various stages in the credit upswing, characterized by an ever-declining quality of loans, with the end result being a "Ponzi"-like financial structure. Interestingly,

BNP had suspended redemptions from three of their investment funds sparked a massive withdrawal of liquidity from the market for asset based securities, not least by money market mutual funds fearful of "breaking the buck." Subsequently, the process of financial deterioration continued relentlessly with a wide spectrum of asset prices falling sharply. Many financial institutions were merged, others went bankrupt, and still more feared that they were on the verge of bankruptcy.

Due in part to tighter credit conditions and the wealth destruction arising from lower asset prices, real growth in the advanced industrial economies slowed sharply. However, probably more important was the beginning of a process of mean reversion in spending patterns, in countries exhibiting such imbalances, and the spread of this effect to other countries through trade linkages in particular. The emerging market economies initially seemed somewhat immune to this slowdown, but after a time also became caught up in the global transition[9] to slower growth. This interactive process of deterioration between the real and financial sectors, as the various imbalances simultaneously unwound, had not fully run its course even by 2011. Fears also remained that the full impact on global currency markets, and on protectionist sentiment, of stubbornly large trade imbalances also remained to be seen.

Recognizing the potential economic costs of all these developments raises the important question of how such processes might be avoided, or at least the costs moderated, in the future. Given that the underlying problem is one of excessive credit creation, there should be a strong presumption that monetary policy will have a significant role to play in leaning against these excesses. In the same way that repairing a broken financial system might be a necessary

---

Irving Fisher painted a similar picture of this process. (*See* I. Fisher, "The Debt-Deflation Theory of Great Depressions," *Econometrica*, 1933.) The "Minsky moment" is that point in time when the market suddenly recognizes the scale of the accumulated potential losses and further lending ceases. According to this story, markets may look illiquid, but the underlying problem is one of fears about solvency. The word "arguably" is used in the text, because the panic in August 2007 had been preceded by well over a year of declining U.S. house prices and rising default and delinquency rates. The markets, however, initially chose to ignore these developments.

9. On the high likelihood of this happening, *see* W. R. White, "Emerging Market Finance in Good Times and Bad: Are EME Crises a Thing of the Past?" (speech at the IIF 25th Anniversary Membership Meeting, Washington, D.C., October 2007).

but not sufficient condition for restoring health to the real economy after a "bust," relying solely on regulatory mechanisms to moderate a "boom" might also prove insufficient.

The "Lean-Versus-Clean" Debate

Against this background, an attempt is made in this paper to evaluate what has been a dominant analytical paradigm guiding the conduct of monetary policy in recent years; namely, that it is impossible to *lean* against credit bubbles using tighter monetary policy, but that it is possible to *clean* up afterwards using easier monetary policy.[10] Should it be possible to throw doubt on either or both of these propositions, then support is provided for the arguments presented in the Conclusion of this paper entitled "The Need for a New Macrofinancial Stability Framework." It is suggested there that "preemptive tightening" should replace "preemptive easing."

While not alone, the Federal Reserve seems most evidently to have conducted its monetary policy in strict conformance with the dominant analytical paradigm. Over the last two decades, representatives of the Federal Reserve System repeatedly stressed that monetary policy had been tightened only in response to the prospective inflationary implications of asset price increases, not in response to accumulating credit related imbalances (as such) or increasing exposures within the financial system. Conversely, when financial disturbances threatened growth prospects, monetary policy was repeatedly eased significantly. This occurred in 1987 (the stock market crash), in 1990–91 (the property crash,

10. See, for example, B. S. Bernanke, "Deflation: Making Sure 'It' Doesn't Happen Here" (remarks before the National Economists Club, Washington, D.C., November 21, 2001); F. S. Mishkin, "Housing and the Monetary Transmission Mechanism" (paper presented at the Federal Reserve Bank of Kansas City Economic Symposium, Jackson Hole, WY, August 31, 2007); and D. Kohn, "Monetary Policy and Asset Prices Revisited" (speech presented at the Cato Institute's 26th Annual Monetary Policy Conference, Washington, D.C., November 19, 2008). For a more recent description (and also a qualified recantation), see J. Yellen, "A Minsky Meltdown: Lessons for Central Bankers" (presentation to the 18th Annual H. P. Minsky Conference on the State of the U.S. and World Economy, New York, April 16, 2009).

and the S&L crisis), in 1998 (LTCM), in 2001–04 (the end of the NASDAQ bubble), and, most recently, in 2007 in response to the financial difficulties that emerged at that time. In addition, in the context of the Asian crisis of 1997, monetary policy was not tightened, even though all of the traditional indicators said it should have been. This pattern of "preemptive easing" was referred to by (then) Chairman Greenspan as a risk-management paradigm. In sum, combining a refusal to lean with an eagerness to clean implies that the Fed's policy has been highly asymmetrical over the credit cycle.

Whether this approach is appropriate is already being implicitly questioned by some other central banks. The Bank of Japan, for example, has announced that its policy settings will be determined by two "perspectives." While the first perspective is very similar to the "gapology" methodology[11] favored by the Fed, the second perspective seems to be a promise to resist in the future the formation of the credit and associated debt excesses that plagued Japan in the 1980s. Given how long Japan was stuck in the "bust" period, with all its accumulated economic costs, that promise is not surprising. Similarly, the European Central Bank has a second "pillar" in addition to a conventional first one. While historically rooted in the belief of the Bundesbank that there is a low-frequency association between money growth and inflation, some people associated with the European System of Central Banks have grown more willing over time to suggest that the second pillar could also foretell other kinds of problems.[12] While this evolution is by no means complete, it seems clear that the grounds for a serious analytical debate have at least been laid.[13]

---

11. The gap referred to here is not the Wicksellian gap referred to in footnote 7. Rather, it is the gap between estimates of actual output and potential output, or the equivalent in terms of labor market variables. It is this gap that economists believe drives changes in the rate of inflation.

12. See A. Weber, "Financial Markets and Monetary Policy" (speech presented at the 12th Annual Conference of the CEPR/ESI, Basel, September 2008). Also, for one reference among many, see O. Issing, "The Monetary Pillar of the ECB" (paper prepared for the conference "The ECB and Its Watchers," Frankfurt, June 3, 2005).

13. For a discussion of some other significant differences between major central banks in how they conduct monetary policy, and why, see W. R. White, "Why Central Banks Differ" (paper presented at a monetary and banking seminar at the Reserve Bank of India, Mumbai, February 2009).

Nor is this a new issue. Indeed, it was at the heart of the famous debate between Hayek and Keynes in the early 1930s.[14] Keynes won this debate, in part because Hayek offered no hope that policy might be used to ameliorate the situation during the Great Depression. In the process, Hayek's message was lost; namely, that the size of the downswing is determined by the size of the imbalances (specifically "malinvestments") which had built up in the upswing of the credit cycle. This is one aspect of the debate that needs to be reopened. At the same time, the scope for policies to resist the downturn also needs to be reexamined in light of another Austrian insight. It is not self-evident that policies are desirable when they are effective only at the expense of creating even bigger problems in the future.[15] Whenever there is an intertemporal trade-off, at least some attention needs to be paid to the discounted net benefit offered by alternative policies.

The possibility that policies that are effective in the short run might have longer-term costs is also suggested by some of the insights from dynamic control theory, applied to economics in the 1950s by the engineer A. W. Philips.[16] Think of the economy as a system subject to shocks, and one in which the policy instrument has significant lagged effects on the real economy (say through encouraging procyclicality). In such a world, a problem of "instrument instability" can easily arise. In this situation, a successful effort to ensure that the actual level of output closely matches that desired by the policymaker comes at the cost of the stabilizing instrument having to move ever more sharply in

---

14. J. Hicks, *Critical Essays in Monetary Theory* (Oxford: Clarendon Press, 1967), noted how this debate "captured the imagination" of economists at the time, but had been almost forgotten by the late 1960s. For a fuller account, see J. P. Cochran and F. R. Glahe, *The Hayek-Keynes Debate: Lessons for Current Business Cycle Research*" (Lewiston NY: Edwin Miller Press, 1999).

15. Contrast Keynes' famous comment: "In the long run we are all dead," with von Mises: "No very deep knowledge of economics is usually needed to grasp the immediate effects of a measure; but the task of economics is to foretell the remoter effects, and so to allow us to avoid such acts as attempt to remedy a present ill by sowing the seeds of a much greater ill for the future." One is also reminded of Milton Friedman who, on being told that money growth only led to inflation in the long run, was said to have responded "I have seen the long run, and it is now."

16. A. W. Phillips, "Stabilisation Policy and the Time Form of Lagged Responses," *Economic Journal* 67 (1957): 265–77.

successive cycles. Evidently, such policies cannot be sustained forever.[17] The solution to this instrument instability problem was found by engineers to be a lightening of the control procedure, to allow deviations from equilibrium to be somewhat longer lasting. By analogy, this implies that policies of "preemptive easing" might in the end prove disruptive. Put otherwise, small recessions (temporary deviations from equilibrium) might sometimes serve to ward off bigger deviations later. Moreover, in the case of monetary policies, the dangers might be even greater than the analogy suggests. This is because the monetary control instrument (policy rates) must eventually be constrained by the zero lower bound, and asymmetric policies over successive cycles would make this a more and more likely outcome.

Can Monetary Policy Lean Effectively Against the Expansionary Phase of the Credit Cycle?

It is important to note that the arguments *opposing* this view have focused almost exclusively on the difficulties of using monetary policy to lean against asset price increases, rather than the underlying credit cycle itself.[18] Rising asset prices are, of course, only one imbalance of many that can be generated by easy credit conditions. However, this narrow focus does have the advantage of allowing a number of plausible arguments to be made against the straw man of "targeting" asset prices.

---

17. In making a similar point, Cooper (see G. Cooper, "The Origins of Financial Crises" (Harriman House Limited) makes delightful reference to early work on "governors" for steam-driven saws. If "over-governed," such that the steam pressure was quickly altered to keep the saw moving exactly at a predefined pace, the machine would literally shake itself to pieces after the wood had been put on the blade.

18. A. Weber is implicitly critical in this regard (see Weber, "Financial Markets and Monetary Policy"). He states: "The debate about monetary policy and financial markets is too often slanted to the question of how to deal with asset price bubbles. In my opinion, this view of monetary policy and asset prices is too narrow." He then goes on to suggest that the focus should be "redirected from financial bubbles to the issue of 'procyclicality,'" which is consistent with what is being suggested in this paper. See also C. E. V. Borio, "Towards a Macroprudential Framework for Financial Supervision and Regulation" (BIS Working paper no. 128, Basel, February 2003); and W. R. White, "Procyclicality in the Financial System: Do We Need a New Macrofinancial Stability Framework?" (Kiel economic papers 2, Kiel, September 2005).

The first argument is that there are a number of asset prices that might be targeted. Advocates of a policy of "leaning against the wind" are then invited to choose which asset price should be the focus of the authorities' attentions, and to explain why. Since there is no obvious right answer to such a question, the whole approach of leaning against the wind is made to seem questionable. A second criticism is that, absent any clear criteria for determining the level of the asset price consistent with "fundamental value," it is impossible to estimate deviations from such a price in order to lean against it. A third criticism is that, given expectations of further increases in any rising asset price, the interest rate increases required to "prick the bubble" would be so great as to cause material damage to other parts of the economy.[19]

A more general argument opposing leaning against the credit cycle is that it might result in an undershoot of the desired level of inflation, whether that level is expressed as an explicit target or not. Two sorts of concerns can be noted in this regard. The first is that the economy might inadvertently be pushed into deflation, with all of the problems said to be associated with such a development. The second is that, by undershooting the desired inflation levels, the credibility of the central bankers' fundamental commitment to price stability as a longer-term goal might be brought into question. If he/she can countenance undershoots, why not overshoots as well?[20]

Those *supporting* the use of monetary policy to lean against the expansionary phase of the cycle begin with a simple point. To favor leaning against the credit cycle[21] is not at all the same thing as advocating "targeting" asset prices. Rather, action is needed to restrain the whole nexus of imbalances arising from excessively easy credit conditions. The focus should be on the underlying cause rather than one symptom of accumulating problems. Thus, confronted with a

---

19. For a recent airing of such arguments, see A. Greenspan, "We Need a Better Cushion Against Risk," *Financial Times,* March 27, 2009.

20. A number of practical difficulties would also have to be faced should a central bank wish to lean against the wind of the credit cycle. These issues are addressed in the Conclusion of this paper entitled "The Need for a New Macrofinancial Stability Framework," supposing that the case for leaning has been accepted in principle.

21. A policy of leaning against the wind of procyclicality has been recommended in successive Annual Reports of the BIS and in many publications by BIS Staff. In particular, see the various papers on the BIS website.

combination of rapid increases in monetary and credit aggregates, increases in a wide range of asset prices, and deviations in spending patterns from traditional norms, the suggestion is that policy would have to be tighter than otherwise.

From this broader perspective, there is no need to choose which asset price to target. It is a combination of developments that should evoke concern. Nor is there a need to calculate with accuracy the fundamental value of individual assets. Rather, it suffices to be able to say that some developments seem significantly out of line with what the fundamentals might seem to suggest. Finally, there is no need to "prick" the bubble and to do harm to the economy in the process. Rather, the intention is simply to tighten policy in a way to restrain the credit cycle on the upside, with a view to mitigating the magnitude of the subsequent downturn. Note as well, that general inflation would normally also be tending upwards in such circumstances, so that what is at issue here is not likely to be the direction of policy, but rather only the degree of policy tightening.

As for the more general concerns about undershooting the inflation target, this could lead to outright deflation, but it need not. In any event, it needs to be stressed that the experience of deflation is not always and everywhere a dangerous development.[22] The experience of the United States in the 1930s was certainly horrible, but almost as surely unique.[23] There have been many other historical episodes of deflation, often associated with bursts of productivity increases, in which falling prices were in fact associated with continuing real growth and increases in living standards. As noted above, there can be little doubt that serious problems can arise from the interaction of falling prices and wages and high levels of nominal debt. But the essential point of leaning against the upswing of the credit cycle is to mitigate the buildup of such debt in order to moderate the severity of the subsequent downturn. The price undershoot, per se, would not

---

22. See C. E. V. Borio and A. Filardo, "Deflation in an Historical Perspective" (BIS Working paper no. 186, Basel, November 2005).

23. Atkeson and Kehoe (see A. Atkeson and P. J. Kehoe. "Deflation and Depression: Is There an Empirical Link?" *American Economic Review, Papers and Proceedings* 94, no. 2 (May 2004) note in their concluding remarks, based on a broad historical study of seventeen countries over 100 years, that "The data suggest that deflation is not closely related to depression." Elsewhere they state "Our main finding is that the only episode in which there is evidence of a link between deflation and depression is the Great Depression (1929–1934)."

seem to be a problem if the economy is still growing strongly under the influence of the credit cycle itself. As for an undershoot undermining the credibility of the price stability objective, this would seem far less likely than the effects of an overshoot and should be easily explainable to the general public.

There are also other arguments supporting the views of those wishing to lean against the upswing of the credit cycle. It is very possible that credible statements of official concern and determination to act would change private behavior in a more stabilizing direction. In particular, it might help moderate some of the excesses seen in banking and credit markets, with their subsequent effects on asset prices and spending propensities. This is not an outlandish suggestion.[24] Indeed, it is now widely believed that a similar change occurred in the way inflationary expectations were formed after central banks became more serious about controlling inflation. Finally, tightening policy more in the upswing would seem likely to mitigate the size of the downswing,[25] and it would also provide more room for policy easing in response. In particular, with interest rates higher at the peak of the cycle, there would less chance of running into the serious constraint of the zero lower bound for interest rates.

Can Monetary Policy Clean Up Effectively in the Contractionary Phase of the Credit Cycle?

The first argument used by those *supporting* this view (that monetary easing will effectively stimulate aggregate demand) is that it seems generally supported by the macroeconomic models now commonly used by central banks. These include large-scale structural models, not much changed since the 1970s, but increasingly the use of Dynamic Stochastic General Equilibrium Models

---

24. A. Greenspan (see Greenspan, "We Need a Better Cushion Against Risk") states: "I know of no instance where incremental monetary policy has defused a bubble." This may or may not be true, but the historical record might well have been different had there been a different countercyclical policy regime in place before the expansionary phase of the credit bubble began.

25. One reason for believing in such a relationship is that financial institutions might become less exposed to bad loans during the upturn. This, together with other policies designed to make them more resilient to downturns, would lessen the likelihood of a significant tightening of credit conditions during the downturn.

(DSGE)[26] as well. The second argument is that policy easing has consistently worked to stimulate demand in the past. As noted above, the Fed's typical response to financial turmoil since 1987 has been to ease monetary policy and, in every instance to date, the economy subsequently resumed growth. Indeed, prior to the downturn of 2008, recessions had been very mild and the variance of output growth had been very low.[27] Third, as for previous experiences of costly deflations, the United States in the 1930s and Japan in the 1990s, it is argued that these were primarily the byproduct of policy error. In particular, the authorities failed to ease monetary policy aggressively enough.[28]

A fourth argument, of increasing practical relevance as policy rates edge ever lower, is that monetary policy can still be effective even at (or very near) the zero lower bound for the policy rate. The argument rests upon the efficacy of three propositions.[29] First, it is suggested that long rates can be lowered by generating expectations that the policy rate will be kept very low for an extended period. Second, it is held that term and credit risk premia can be reduced through changes in the relative supply of securities, reflecting shifts in the composition of the central bank's balance sheet. Third, it is suggested that "quantitative easing," in which the central bank's balance sheet is allowed to expand beyond the size required to keep the policy rate at zero, can have expansionary effects through various channels.

Those *opposed* to the view that monetary policy can clean up effectively in the contractionary phase of the credit cycle rely, in part, on refuting the arguments

---

26. For an overview, see C. E. Tovar, "DSGE Models and Central Banks" (BIS Working paper no. 258, Basel, September 2008).

27. The low variance of output growth in the United States, together with inflation remaining both low and stable, led to the accolade "The Great Moderation" referred to above.

28. See A. Ahearn et al., "Preventing Deflation: Lessons from the Japanese Experience in the 1990s" (FRBG International Finance Discussion paper no. 792, Washington, D.C., June 2002).

29. See V. Reinhart, "Tools for Combating Deflation" (presentation to the National Association of Business Economists, Washington, D.C., March 1993); B. S. Bernanke and V. Reinhart, "Conducting Monetary Policy at Very Low Short Term Interest Rates" (paper presented at the International Centre for Monetary and Banking Studies, Geneva, January 2004); and B. S. Bernanke, "Stamp Lecture" (London School of Economics, London, January 2009).

above. The first argument rests on the reliability of models of the macroeconomy. Evidently, models must not be confused with reality, and, in fact, large structural models have had a very poor record in predicting the turning points of even standard cycles in the postwar period. To this must be added the reality of massive change in the real economy, the financial sector, and the policy regime in recent years. The assumption of parametric stability under such conditions is highly implausible, unless the parameters are so loosely estimated in the first place as to raise serious doubts about the model's reliability. Further, even the large structural models have very rudimentary financial sectors, and their predictions might therefore be particularly suspect at times of financial crisis. As for more modern DSGE models, even their supporters admit that they are "work in progress," and they possess even more rudimentary financial sectors than those seen in more structural models.[30]

As for the second argument, just because something has worked in the past need not logically imply that it is certain to work in the future.[31] Indeed, the degree of monetary easing required to kick-start the United States economy seems to have been rising through successive downturns as the "headwinds" of debt have become stronger.[32] Indeed, after the crisis began in the summer of 2007, it was disquieting that mortgage rates actually rose for an extended period even as the discount rate was being lowered at an unprecedented pace. A similar phenomenon was seen early in the previous cycle of easing. Then, lower short rates initially failed to feed through to standard channels of the transmission mechanism until asset prices started to rise strongly in the middle of 2003.[33] In

---

30. For a critique of some of the theoretical and empirical underpinnings of such models, see J. Rudd and K. Whelan, "Can Rational Expectations, Sticky Price Models Explain Inflation Dynamics?" (FRBG Finance and Economics Discussion Series no. 46, Washington, D.C., 2003).

31. On this theme, against a far wider historical and philosophical backdrop, see N. H. Talib, *The Black Swan* (New York: Random House Publishing Group, 2007).

32. Consider the path of the policy rate in the United States in the early 1990s, the first years of this decade, and most recently. Both the size of the policy rate reduction and its speed have increased through successive cycles. This is consistent with the instrument instability argument made above.

33. It is evident from casual inspection that almost all asset prices, most commodity prices, and implicit volatilities derived from option prices, had an inflection point around the middle of 2003. It is perhaps more than correlation that global nominal policy rates

the United States, in spite of unprecedented monetary and fiscal stimulus, the recovery after 2002 was the weakest in postwar history.

One way to explain this phenomenon might be in terms of the cumulative effects of previous policy actions. As noted above, the Fed has used "preemptive easing" on successive occasions since the stock market crash of 1987, and many other central banks more or less followed its leadership. In each case, it could be argued that the resulting demand stimulus came in the form of an unsustainable bubble, which was then subsequently replaced by yet another bubble. The series begins with the easing of monetary policy in the late 1980s which helped spur the subsequent property bubble in many countries. The subsequent period of very low rates in the early 1990s led to the decline in the value of the U.S. dollar (and the Asian currencies effectively linked to it) and contributed to the Asian bubble. The subsequent decision not to raise rates, in spite of tighter domestic conditions, contributed to the excesses of the LTCM period, and the subsequent easing of rates then induced the stock market speculation of the late 1990s. When this collapsed and rates were sharply reduced in response, the seeds of the housing market boom and bust were sown. Moreover, with many countries again resisting currency appreciation as the U.S. dollar fell through most of the first decade of this millennium, the imbalances referred to above became truly global.

Even four years after the crisis began, these imbalances (or "headwinds") remained an ongoing threat to the effectiveness of monetary stimulus. One particular source of concern was the state of household balance sheets in many countries. As a result of previous low household savings rates, debt levels remained very high and posed a continuing threat to consumption going forward. Moreover, it was thought possible that the real burden of this debt could rise even further, if prices and wages began to fall. Evidently, monetary policy in the major countries had very little room to lower nominal policy rates further. This implied that, even with inflationary expectations stable at some low level, real interest rates (ex ante) were positive. Moreover, the possibility remained at the time that declining prices might even be extrapolated into the future. This would imply

---

hit their low point at that time, with rates of zero, 1 percent and 2 percent in Japan, the United States, and the Euro zone respectively.

an even higher real rate of interest and would make the debt/deflation dynamic all the more resistant to the influence of monetary policy.[34]

As for the third argument, that the depressions in the U.S. and Japan were primarily the product of too timid monetary easing, it cannot be denied that still more aggressive easing might have made a material difference. However, this is a supposition rather than a statement of fact. What is a fact is that, in both cases, interest rates were eased very sharply at the beginning of each crisis, and in the latter case, significantly more than a Taylor rule would have implied.[35] A competing (or perhaps complementary) hypothesis would be that the difficulties seen in previous downturns were related to the excesses of the earlier upturns. In Japan, for example, it is a fact that investment levels collapsed after the crisis broke and that the corporate ratio of debt to value added fell continuously for over a decade.[36] Above, four major sets of global economic and financial imbalances were identified, of which only one had to do with the increased risk exposure (and inadequate capital) of financial institutions. The failure of the advanced market economies to subsequently grow robustly, in spite of the unprecedented degree of monetary easing seen after 2007, provides particularly clear evidence that underlying deflationary forces have their roots as much in the preceding "boom" period as in subsequent policy errors.

The fourth set of arguments, that monetary policy can still be effective even when policy rates are near zero, can be questioned (although not refuted) on various grounds. First, a credible commitment to keep policy rates low for an extended period to fight deflation assumes there are no other arguments for potentially having to raise policy rates. One such argument in the United States would be fear of a currency crisis arising from the long-standing increase in U.S. external indebtedness. The argument that changes in the composition of a central bank's balance sheet can effectively alter risk premia would seem to assume a high degree of non-substitutability between assets. This view has not

---

34. On this dynamic, the classic reference is I. Fisher, "The Debt-Deflation Theory of Great Depressions."

35. See Bank for International Settlements, chap. 4 (Annual Report, Basel, June 2001).

36. A still unsettled issue is whether Japan's poor performance throughout the 1990s was due to corporations not wishing to invest, because of earlier overinvestment, or because a weakened banking system was not prepared to lend them the money. Statements by Japanese officials seem more sympathetic to the former view than the latter.

been at all fashionable in academic circles in recent years, though it might now be being reassessed in light of the current degree of market dysfunction. Recall as well the failure of "Operation Twist" in the 1960s and various studies into the effectiveness (or rather the ineffectiveness) of foreign exchange rate intervention in large, liquid markets. Indeed, the fact that the Federal Reserve felt it necessary in the wake of the crisis to embark upon a policy of quantitative easing is itself testimony to the shortcomings of the policy initiatives taken previously. Whether this last recourse will work in stimulating real output growth remains to be seen, but the previous experience with quantitative easing in Japan cannot be considered wholly encouraging.[37]

This said, quantitative easing raises the possibility of two further channels through which monetary policy might regain its effectiveness. The first is a direct effect on inflationary expectations. The second is a direct effect on asset prices. Either could lead to a recovery of spending, as described below. However, the risks associated with each are also substantial. In effect, the cure might well prove as dangerous as the disease.

Skepticism about the efficacy of conventional monetary policy, when policy rates are already at zero, rests largely on a combination of two beliefs. First, a positive output gap is required to cause inflationary expectations to move in a positive direction. And, second, when policy rates are already zero, it is believed that monetary policy cannot produce such an outcome.[38] However, it is possible that quantitative easing could short-circuit this dynamic by having a direct effect on inflationary expectations. A number of academics have made such arguments.[39] Indeed, this view is also implicit in the credit given to central banks for having produced "The Great Moderation" over the two decades prior to 2007. Similarly, we have decades of observations from many Latin American

---

37. While there can be little doubt that massive increases in the nominal money stock will eventually result in increases in nominal quantities in the real economy, how this might be split between increases in real economic activity and prices (in anything short of the "long run") is not clear.

38. In the late 1990s, the Bank of Japan was advised by many to adopt an inflation-targeting framework to resist deflationary tendencies. The Bank refused to do so. They argued that they had no effective tools to influence aggregate demand, and therefore could not deliver on the promise of price stability.

39. For example, see L. Svensson, "Escaping from the Liquidity Trap and Deflation: the Foolproof Way and Others" *Journal of Economic Perspectives* 17, no. 4 (2003).

countries indicating the extent and speed with which inflationary expectations (and inflation) responded directly to perceived changes in the monetary regime.

These observations lead to the conclusion that quantitative easing could in theory moderate or even reverse a debt/deflation dynamic. However, the associated risk would be that the process could easily get out of hand. Expectations driven by forward-looking beliefs in the integrity of the monetary framework would seem more open to rapid revision than expectations based on recent historical experience.[40] The fact that the Federal Reserve took steps in 2009 to make its longer-term inflation objectives more concrete presumably indicates both an awareness of the potential problem and a willingness to confront it directly. An underlying problem, however, is the credibility of such commitments, given the usefulness of higher rates of inflation in eroding debt burdens that are difficult to reduce in any other way. This problem would be aggravated by any perception that central banks in various countries were increasingly acting like agents of their respective Ministries of Finance.

One possible route to inflation rising more than desired might be a process of self-fulfilling expectations, either in financial markets or in the market for labor. Suppose that foreign holders of U.S. debt, almost wholly denominated in dollars, began to fear an inflationary outcome. They would then presumably try to protect themselves by selling their dollar-denominated assets, putting downward pressure on the prices of both those assets and the dollar itself.[41] In short, the risk premia on dollar-denominated assets would rise. This could conceivably raise aggregate demand (if the effect on domestic demand of higher domestic rates was less than the net effect of the currency depreciation) and would also directly raise U.S. inflation through higher import costs. Perhaps worse, the

---

40. Schumpeter (Schumpeter "Depressions: Can We Learn from Past Experience?," 4) refers to an even more sinister possibility. He notes that in 1896 in the U.S. there was a significant possibility that bimetallism might replace the gold standard. The implication of this inflationary threat was not higher inflation, as might have been expected. "On the contrary, although underlying conditions were by no means unfavorable for an upswing, business went to pieces."

41. A related problem is the state of health of the U.S. financial system. G. Kaminsky and C. Reinhart document the ease with which banking crises can turn into exchange rate crises with significant macroeconomic costs. (*See* Kaminsky and Reinhart, "The Twin Crises: The Causes of Banking and Balance of Payments Problems," *American Economic Review* 89 (1999): 473–500).

combination of falling asset prices and a weaker dollar might well culminate in stagflation. Similarly, domestic wages might also react more sharply than desired if wage earners began to fear an inflationary policy directed to reducing the real burden of debt at their expense.

The second channel through which quantitative easing might work would be a direct effect on asset prices, with higher wealth then leading to higher spending. As to a direct, significant, and lasting effect on asset prices, this would have to be judged unlikely, unless inflationary expectations were also moving upwards with all the risks just described. Against the background of initial asset price declines from the "unsustainable" levels of 2007, there seemed little likelihood of previous peaks being repeated. Indeed, were this to happen, it would constitute a repeat of the previous bubble with presumably even greater costs at some later date. As for the effect of higher asset prices on spending, this is also unclear. There has been growing agreement that, aside from asset price movements based on expectations of higher future productivity, higher asset prices do not in fact constitute an increase in wealth.[42] They do, however, provide more collateral to support more borrowing, which might in turn lead to more spending. However, the difficulty with this mechanism is that, in the wake of a financial crisis, banks generally do not want to lend and potential borrowers do not wish to borrow.

Finally, another risk must be confronted. Should any or all of the extraordinary monetary measures taken to stimulate aggregate demand prove effective, then these measures will have to be reversed in a timely way. This leaves open the possibility of policy mistakes. While presumably no policymaker would be expected to desire anything other than a modest increase in inflation, history teaches us that control over this process is by no means perfect. For example, there are a number of reasons why policymakers might have an exaggerated view of the level of potential following a financial crisis (and therefore the size

---

42. In particular, consider the case of rising house prices. An increase in wealth, by definition, allows an increase in living standards. In contrast, living standards do not rise with house prices since the rising asset value is offset by the higher implicit rent required to live in the house. For a more formal analysis of this matter, see W. R. White, "Measured Wealth, Real Wealth, and the Illusion of Saving," *IFC Bulletin* 26, Basel, July 2007, and J. Muelbauer, "Housing, Credit and Consumer Expenditures" (paper presented at the Federal Reserve Bank of Kansas City Symposium, Jackson Hole, WY, August 31, 2007).

310 | Should Monetary Policy "Lean or Clean"?

of the output gap).[43] First, after a bubble period, misallocated resources must be shifted to more productive uses. More concretely, after 2007 it became evident that the automobile, financial services, and construction industries in many advanced market economies had all become too large, as had the potential of Asia to export consumer goods. During such a process of adjustment, the level of global potential shifts down and the structural rate of unemployment shifts up.[44] Second, hysteretic effects, as unemployed workers lose contact with the labor market, could aggravate such developments, particularly in countries with badly functioning labor markets. Third, were there to be some rethinking (say, given the threat of protectionism) of the integrated global supply network that has built up over many years, potential would also be affected. Since there were grounds for believing that globalization had made a material contribution to lower inflation in the years preceding the crisis, a reversal of such trends might be expected to have the opposite effect.[45] Fourth, economic downturns commonly result in reductions in capital formation and in total factor productivity. Fifth, and finally, new legislation together with reregulation and nationalizations since the crisis have all had the effect of reducing potential. These supply side uncertainties must be added to those that, even in the past, led to potential "gaps" being very difficult to estimate in real time.

Another concern, given the extent to which central banks had massively increased the size of their balance sheets, was whether they would have the technical skills to reverse the expansion as quickly as they might like. Recall that all of this is effectively unchartered territory. In particular, the price at

---

43. Many central banks estimate potential using statistical "filters" based on past output levels. Evidently, if those previous output levels were not sustainable, such estimates of potential would be biased upwards.

44. This point was made more broadly and much earlier by Schumpeter, among others. He states (*see* J. Schumpeter, "Depressions: Can We Learn from Past Experience?", 16): "The chief difficulty lies in the fact that depressions are not simply evils, which we might try to suppress, but perhaps undesirable forms of something which has to be done, namely, adjustment to previous economic change. Most of what would be effective in remedying a depression would be equally effective in preventing this adjustment. This is especially true of inflation (i.e., monetary stimulus)."

45. See W. R. White, "Measured Wealth, Real Wealth, and the Illusion of Saving," *IFC Bulletin* 26, Basel, July 2007.

which central banks might be able to sell the kinds of assets they have purchased remains to be determined. This implies that withdrawing bank reserves
could have disruptive effects in some financial markets at least. Thus, a delicate
balancing act is required. As the real economy improves, tightening must be
"measured" enough not to destabilize still fragile confidence and financial
markets, but also fast enough not to allow inflationary expectations to rise too
much. This will be particularly difficult if the source of demand expansion was
itself a rise in inflationary expectations associated with quantitative easing.
And to all this must be added the risk of political pressure being applied by
governments worried about the cost of debt service on rapidly rising debts. The
experience of the United States and Japan in recent years indicates that the exit
problem is not inconsequential.[46]

By way of summary, Keynes worried that the use of monetary policy to
reverse downturns would eventually be like "pushing on a string." For this
reason, he advocated the use of fiscal stimulus in severely depressed economic
conditions.[47] Hayek was similarly skeptical about the role of monetary policy.
His argument, essentially, was that, if excessive money and credit was the source
of the economic problem, it was not self-evident that still more money and credit
was part of the solution.[48] Indeed, pre-War business cycle theorists worried that

---

46. Consider the process of "measured" tightening, which took place in the United States
from 2005 to 2007. A principal motivation for the Fed giving advance warning of its intentions was to allow those exposed to such tightening to cover their positions. In contrast, it
could be contended that this policy might have had the opposite effect of that intended.
The highly predictable nature of forthcoming policy moves reduced significantly the risks
of position-taking, and this could have encouraged the further buildup of leverage. Indeed, if the size of the "carry" was constantly declining, an increase in leverage would
have been essential to keep up the rate of return on capital. In sum, a shorter-term problem might have been avoided, but again at the expense of aggravating a longer term one.
Consider also the case of Japan, where high levels of short-term Government debt have
been said to have led to political pressure to keep policy rates down to ease debt servicing
requirements.
47. Of course, recommending the use of fiscal stimulus in such extreme conditions does
not necessarily imply a similar recommendation in the face of minor downturns, much
less "preemptive" policies.
48. In his later years, however, Hayek admitted that he had been wrong in the 1930s in
resisting the use of monetary and fiscal stimulus to offset the effects of a "secondary

the end game of this monetary and credit expansion might be hyperinflation, as occurred in central Europe in the early 1920s. While most central banks today seem firmly committed to the pursuit of price stability, the technical questions just referred to could still raise doubts as to its attainability. Both prospective inflation and deflation remain serious risks. All these considerations strengthen the arguments for not getting into such a dangerous situation in the first place. Further support for this proposition is provided by recognizing other longer-term problems associated with the maintenance of very expansionary monetary policies in such a situation.[49] These problems were emphasized by many pre-war theorists,[50] but can also be illustrated using more recent examples.[51]

Can Other Policies Be Used to "Clean Up" Regardless?

Considering the possibility that stimulative monetary policy might either not work effectively in the downturn, or might expose the economy to other risks over a longer horizon, raises the issue of other remedies. Should these also be deemed unreliable in restoring growth, or also have undesirable longer-term side effects, then the dangers associated with not leaning against the upswing of the credit cycle become still more evident.

Fiscal stimulus is the obvious way to increase demand. However, the level of government debt in many jurisdictions was already so high when the crisis began as to invoke concerns about "Ricardian Equivalence." That is, seeing

---

depression." By this, Hayek seemed to have meant a downward deflationary spiral sparked by, but independent of, the imbalances he saw as being at the heart of the initial downturn. See G. Haberler, "Reflections on Hayek's Business Cycle Theory" (*Cato Journal* 6, no. 2 (1986).

49. See W. R. White, "Is Price Stability Enough?" (BIS Working paper no. 205, Basel, April 2006), for a fuller description of all these problems.

50. The classic reference providing an overview of such theories is G. Haberler, *Prosperity and Depression* (Geneva: League of Nations, 1939).

51. First, as was seen in Japan, low rates can actually encourage forbearance and impede the balance sheet restructuring and/or bankruptcies necessary to reduce excess capacity. Second, this environment can encourage mergers and acquisitions having little long-term merit. Third, as seen in Japan in the early 1990s, and in many countries more recently, very low rates sustained for long periods can impede the functioning of the interbank market leaving the central bank as the market maker of last resort.

through the "veil" of government, taxpayers might tighten their belts as governments loosened theirs. In this regard, the muted response of the U.S. economy to the fiscal package of 2007 was particularly disappointing. Moreover, in some cases, further fiscal stimulus might even lead risk premia and interest rates to rise, which would further mute the overall stimulus provided to spending.[52] If such fears were also to interact with concerns about monetary financing, exchange rate depreciation, and eventual inflation, as discussed above in the case of the United States, the negative feedback would presumably be even greater. In Europe, the fact that sovereign spreads began in 2010 to move up in countries with high debt levels became a matter of increasing concern. So too was the associated increase in CDS spreads for sovereign debts issued by a number of countries, and the growing threat of rating downgrades. In sum, even fiscal stimulus might have its limitations and longer-term dangers.

Of course, the ultimate remedy for a problem of over-indebtedness is to recognize the facts and to write off in an orderly way those debts that cannot be serviced. However, here too there have been grounds for concern in recent years. Unlike previous sovereign debt crises, when all the principals involved could be assembled in one room, there were literally millions of households whose debts were not likely to be serviced under the initially agreed conditions. Moreover, many of these debts were encumbered by second mortgages,[53] or were parts of structured products implying that property and foreclosure rights

---

52. At the time of the Swedish banking crisis and associated deep (if short) recession, the authorities felt it would be imprudent to use discretionary fiscal stimulus to offset the downturn. This was particularly so since the Swedish krona had been under much pressure and the current account deficit was still large. See L. Heikenstein, "The Crisis in Asia—Experiences from Sweden" (presentation at the OECD, Paris, March 1998). In the downturn which began in 2008, the Irish government has also chosen to use tighter discretionary fiscal policy to offset a massive deterioration in the fiscal position arising from automatic stabilizers and a sharply weakening economy. Many other countries have stated the view that high initial debt levels imply they can do nothing more than let the automatic stabilizers work.

53. Ashcroft and Schuerman (see A. B. Ashcraft and T. Schuermann, "Understanding the Securitization of Subprime Mortgage Credit" (Federal Reserve Bank of New York Staff Report no. 318, 2008) estimate that by 2006, around 40 percent of AltA and 25 percent of subprime mortgages were encumbered by a "silent second" mortgage. The "silent" refers to their contention that, in most cases, this fact was hidden from the bank that subsequently bought the mortgages to incorporate them into structured products.

were less clear.[54] These complications threatened to impede any process of nego-
tiating debt reduction, implying that the ultimate losses could be much larger
than otherwise.[55] The new reality of credit transfer instruments constituted a
a further complication, since it implies that the interests of creditors were no
longer aligned. Some creditors would as a result profit more from a default than
a negotiated settlement.

Compared to these problems, the difficulties facing policymakers in restoring the normal functioning of the financial system after a crisis might actually
seem less daunting. Yet, it is obvious from recent developments, especially but
not exclusively in the United States, that even this task can be highly complicated. Alternative approaches (price support, recapitalization, "bad" banks and
temporary nationalization) all have both advantages and disadvantages that
must be assessed and weighed. The complications posed by large, internationally active and complex international banks are also substantial. Moreover,
however it is done, support for the financial system will have costs for taxpayers
(or at least potential exposures), which could also spark the fiscal concerns just
noted above.

Finally, and for the sake of completeness, two other sets of policies have
been suggested as potentially useful in the face of major economic downturns.
On closer examination, both have serious drawbacks. The first is, in principle,
extremely sensible as a medium-term proposition. Policies that encourage declining industries to adjust quickly should be pursued (including debt write-
downs and bankruptcies) since they serve to ensure that factors of production
are available to support emerging industries.[56] Unfortunately, in practice, the

---

54. Indeed, many structured products contain clauses expressly ruling out changes in
the original debt instruments.

55. A further very practical complication is that renegotiating contracts to mutual advantage takes time. The current institutional infrastructure in the United States, and perhaps
elsewhere, is simply inadequate to the task. Consider that there were 3 million foreclosure
filings in the United States in 2008 alone.

56. Schumpeter (*see* J. Schumpeter "Depressions: Can We Learn from Past Experience?")
and others in the Austrian school emphasized the crucial importance of such adjustments.
A number of private sector commentators have made similar points with respect to the
current cycle, noting that expansionary policies are likely to impede necessary longer-term
adjustments in the auto, real estate and financial services industries. In all these sectors,

William R. White | 315

short-term effects of such policies would be to make the downturn more severe and, thus, they have never had much (if any) political support. Indeed, after 2007, great efforts were made by the official sector in many countries to prevent the inevitable downsizing of the automobile from happening. The second set of policies has to do with wages. It was suggested by the Hoover administration, in the United States in the early 1930s, that industrial wage levels be maintained since wage income would contribute to consumption and aggregate demand. Unfortunately, the implication was lower profits and a lower demand for labor. While this left the overall effect on the wage bill and consumption indeterminate, the lower profits did imply lower investment.[57] In sum, there are no magic bullets in these policy suggestions either.

Conclusion:
The Need for a New Macrofinancial Stability Framework

The global economic and financial crisis which began in 2007 was the most disruptive since the 1930s. Moreover, even four years later, a variety of risks still threatened: financial disruptions, currency crises, and uncertain price developments among them. This raises the question of steps that might be taken to reduce the likelihood of similar risks arising in the future; i.e., crisis prevention. Such steps would seem desirable in themselves. Moreover, they would seem all the more desirable given the need to take unprecedented measures to manage the current crisis. Many of these measures will clearly have undesirable side effects over the medium term, consistent with the analysis above.[58] A credible

---

significant global overcapacity emerged during the crisis. See G. Tett, "Curse of the Zombies Rises in Europe Amid an Eerie Calm," *Financial Times*, April 3, 2009, 24, for a set of broader concerns about how needed corporate restructuring is currently being impeded.

57. For a fuller discussion of this wage issue, see G. Haberler, *Prosperity and Depression,* chap 11.

58. For example, consider all the longer-term problems noted above that are associated with monetary stimulus. With respect to fiscal easing, major increases in the ratio of government debt to GDP reduce the policy room for maneuver going forward. Private sector debt reduction invites moral hazard over a longer horizon, and further consolidation in the banking sector has the unwanted implication that still more banks become "too big to fail" or even "too big to save."

commitment to an institutional framework to ensure that similar problems would not arise in the future might then go some way to offset these undesirable side effects.

Not surprisingly in the circumstances, the possibility that liberalized financial systems might be inherently "procyclical" is already receiving increasing attention. Similarly, the possibility that accumulated imbalances might significantly reduce the effectiveness of stimulative monetary policy is being increasingly accepted. In particular, it cannot be denied that the period of financial market turmoil, which began almost four years ago, has been met with an extraordinary and creative response on the part of central banks. Nevertheless, the financial turmoil has continued unabated and the real side of the global economy still looks highly vulnerable.

Moreover, looking forward, there are grounds for belief that the problem of procyclicality could well get worse. Three major structural shifts within the financial sector have encouraged procyclicality: securitization, globalization, and consolidation. After some pause associated with the current crisis, these secular trends seem likely to resume since they have been driven in large part by improving technology, which will not be easy to roll back by government decree. In addition, there are grounds for belief that fair value accounting, in spite of the unwanted contribution it makes to the procyclicality of the system, will be increasingly adopted. Whatever its faults, it seems better than the available alternative accounting benchmarks. Finally, the great advantage of Basel II and Basel III is that they allow relative risk weights to change to reflect changes in underlying fundamentals. But, at the same time, they also allow the absolute weights to change over time. Evidently, in and of itself, this too could exacerbate procyclicality. In sum, there are numerous grounds for belief that the problem of procyclicality, already severe, will worsen going forward.

The fundamental conclusion to be drawn from balancing all the arguments above is that we need a new macrofinancial framework to resist procyclicality.[59]

---

59. This suggestion is presented in more detail in W. R. White, "Procyclicality in the Financial System: Do We Need a New Macrofinancial Stability Framework?"; and in various BIS Annual Reports. See also C. E. V. Borio, "Towards a Macroprudential Framework for Financial Supervision and Regulation" (BIS Working paper no. 128, Basel, February 2003); and C. E. V. Borio and I. Shim, "What Can (Macro-) Prudential Policy Do to Help Support Monetary Policy?" (BIS Working paper no. 242, Basel, January 2008).

This can be done in a market-friendly way. The intention must be to preserve the efficiencies generated by new financial developments, while at the same time mitigating inherent threats to safety and stability. Focusing on the development of a new framework to reduce procyclicality, the fundamental problem, could also mitigate the tendency for politicians to rely on heavy handed and punitive regulation designed primarily to stop the recurrence of yesterday's problems. While some such changes are surely needed,[60] care must be taken to address underlying causes of problems as well as their symptoms.

The central characteristics of such a system would be three in number. The first one would be an increased emphasis on *systemic* exposures. In particular, attention would be focused on the dangers associated with many different economic agents (households, corporations and financial institutions) having similar exposures to possible common shocks, and also the possibility of common responses. It is the shared exposures that contribute the most to systemic problems within the financial sector and to the joint vulnerability of the real and financial sectors.

Given that this is essentially a macroeconomic problem, rather than one confined to the financial system, it might also be suggested that central banks (with their "top down" view of things) should be given ultimate responsibility for resisting procyclicality and systemic distress.[61] Such a mandate for the central bank would in fact be consistent with the generally accepted view that price stability should be its principal objective. This consistency becomes obvious if one accepts the fact that price stability can be as easily threatened by deflation as inflation, if a boom-bust cycle is allowed to become sufficiently severe. Indeed, a deflationary spiral might in the end prove significantly more dangerous than an inflationary one since, as suggested above, monetary instruments can lose their potency in the face of high debt levels and the zero interest rate bound.

If central banks are to be given responsibility for "macroprudential" or systemic issues, what should be the role of traditional regulators? Evidently, there would still be need for a "microprudential" form of regulation that would focus

---

60. See the report of the Financial Stability Forum (2008) on "Enhancing Market and Institutional Resilience" to the G-8 for a long list of useful suggestions.
61. This is consistent with the thrust of the proposals made recently by the de Larosière group and by Lord Turner, for the Euro area and the United Kingdom, respectively.

on the safety and soundness of individual instituitions, particularly those that are large and complex. While this function could also reside in the central bank, it might be better to leave this in a separate institution also charged with ensuring appropriate market conduct and consumer protection. This "Twin Peaks" model (now in place in Australia and being suggested elsewhere) has the particular advantage of clarity about institutional objectives, a characteristic which also helps to ensure accountability of the agencies responsible.

A second characteristic of such a framework is that it would be much more *symmetric*. That is, the instruments used to resist procyclicality would attempt to lean against the upturn of the credit cycle rather than relying on cleaning up after the bubble had burst. In effect, "preemptive tightening" would replace "preemptive easing," for all of the reasons suggested above. This argument having been accepted at the level of principle, it must also be accepted that the practical implementation of such a policy would not be without difficulties.

As suggested above, conventional models (especially those based on recent data) are not likely to be very helpful in identifying problems that accumulate slowly during upturns and then suddenly materialize. That is the principal reason why most forecasters missed the current downturn. In contrast, indicators of growing "imbalances" in the economy do seem to have useful predictive powers.[62] Unusually rapid credit and monetary growth rates, unusually low interest rates, unusually high asset prices, unusual spending patterns (say very low household saving or unusually high investment levels) all ought to attract the attention of those charged with resisting procyclicality. Unusually high external trade positions (whether deficits or surpluses) are another indicator that unsustainable exposures are being built up.[63]

---

62. *See* C. E. V. Borio and P. Lowe, "Asset Prices, Financial and Monetary Stability: Exploring the Nexus" (BIS Working paper 114, Basel, July 2002); and C. E. V. Borio and M. Drehmann "Towards an Operational Framework for Financial Stability: 'Fuzzy' Measurement and Its Consequences" (BIS Working Paper 284, Basel, June 2009).

63. These might be defined as "macrosystemic indicators" of potential systemic stress. In addition, there might well be other "microsystemic indicators" (for example, measures of leverage or concentration in financial markets) that might also provide useful warning signals of accumulating stress. See Borio and Shim, "What Can (Macro-) Prudential Policy Do to Help Support Monetary Policy?" (BIS Working Paper 242, Basel, December 2007).

How might these indicators influence the setting of policy instruments? Here, much more work remains to be done, particularly with the calibration of monetary instruments. Nevertheless, all the arguments presented above suggest that interest rates in the expansion phase of the credit cycle would have to be tighter than inflation control alone would warrant. Absent higher interest rates, the underlying problem of excessive credit expansion will be extremely difficult to address. This will be particularly the case if current trends to disintermediated finance continue, implying that currently regulated institutions account for a steadily shrinking proportion of total credit growth. Evidently, this policy would then have to be explained to the public, currently conditioned to believe that meeting price stability objectives is sufficient to achieve good macroeconomic performance.

Regulatory policies would have a similar bias, with measures being taken to ensure that risk spreads (for expected losses), provisioning (for changes in expected losses) and capital (for unexpected losses) were built up in good times and run down in the bad.[64] Similarly, these regulatory actions would also have to be explained, particularly to the accounting profession and the fiscal authorities. Both groups, for understandable microeconomic reasons, have in many cases strongly opposed such policies in the past. Note as well that the use of such regulatory actions would likely be insufficient to deal with the underlying problem of credit growth and the wide range of imbalances to which it might lead. As indicated by developments in Spain in recent years, contracyclical measures such as "dynamic provisioning" allowed Spanish banks to be better prepared for the downturn (thus moderating the need to tighten credit conditions more recently). However, they did not prove very helpful in moderating the preceding upturn. Again, one is led to the conclusion that both regulatory and monetary instruments will have to be mobilized to deal effectively with the procyclicality problem.

Regulatory instruments do have one natural attribute. In the face of the many impediments to the discretionary use of both regulatory and monetary

---

64. This suggestion is consistent with the thrust of the argument in M. Brunnermeir et al. (July 2009) "The Fundamental Principles of Financial Regulation" (Geneva Report on the World Economy 11).

instruments,[65] it is not difficult to envisage the introduction of regulatory rules that would avoid many of these problems. Dynamic provisioning as introduced by the Bank of Spain, is one possibility. Another possibility would be to continue to calculate capital requirements as currently proposed under Pillar 1 of Basel II and Basel III. This relates capital requirements to the perceived risk of the portfolio of individual institutions. This figure might then be grossed up (using the existing authority of Pillar 2) to reflect system wide imbalances indicating the growing risk of systemic disturbances. Such an approach would act to offset the procyclicality inherent in variable risk weights, while building on the strengths of these arrangements at the same time.

The issue of how to deal with currently unregulated institutions also needs further reflection, since there can be no doubt that tighter requirements on regulated players will encourage migration elsewhere. The creation of SIV's and conduits to escape the capital requirements of Basel I attest to this. Presumably, the scope of regulation will have to be extended, at least to systemically important players, though in a globalized world this too has pitfalls. For this reason too, automatic (rule based) regulatory measures might still prove insufficient to deal with the underlying problem of procyclicality. In this case, both regulatory and monetary policies might also have to be tightened in a discretionary way at a second stage.

A third characteristic of such a macrofinancial stability framework is that the authorities involved would have to be much more mutually *supportive* than they appear to be at the moment. This implies more cooperation, both nationally and internationally. With respect to national authorities, silo mentalities currently prevail in many countries. With respect to international cooperation, national authorities remain almost wholly driven by questions of national interest. Hopefully, this might be changed.

At the *national level*, assuming adoption of the Two Peaks model, which allocates ultimate responsibility for different objectives to different agencies, central bankers and regulators should work much more closely together. This would involve ongoing discussion about both the indicators of growing imbalances and exposures and the appropriate policy responses. Central bankers

---

65. White, "Procyclicality in the Financial System."

(mostly economists) and regulators (often from a legal or accounting background) need to recognize that they have a great deal to learn from each other. Their respective "top down" and "bottom up" approaches also complement each other. Treasuries should actively encourage such cooperation since, should an unresisted boom turn to bust, it is the taxpayers who ultimately have to pay for any resulting bailouts.

As for mutual support at the *international level*, countries wishing to counter procyclical tendencies at home must pay more attention to the international dimension. Three points seem particularly important.

First, the oversight of internationally active financial institutions must have an international dimension. In many cases, foreign banks are so important that their failure could threaten macroeconomic stability in the host country (think of Central and Eastern Europe). At the same time, the international exposure of some banks is so large that losses elsewhere could threaten the health of the home country (think of Iceland). Indeed, it is not inconceivable that the home country would not have the fiscal means to save a bank that might be thought in principle "too big to fail." Everyone would then pay a price for the disorderly failure of a bank that proved "too big to save."

Second, more recognition must be given to the fact that international economic and financial linkages have been steadily growing. One implication of this greater integration is that domestic indicators of procyclical behavior will underestimate the threat posed to stability (and to inflation as well) to the extent that other countries are subject to similar pressures. A second implication, now all too evident, is that a "bust" in an important debtor country (say the U.S.) can have significant effects on output in creditor countries (say Germany, Japan, and China) that do not in fact seem to share the domestic imbalances generated by procyclical tendencies. From a policy perspective, this greater integration implies that everyone has a legitimate interest in encouraging debtor countries to moderate domestic excesses. But, by the same reasoning, creditor countries also have a responsibility to change their own policies to the extent that they are encouraging excesses elsewhere by providing the financing to sustain them.

Third, and closely related, much more attention needs to be paid to the role of exchange rates in fostering procyclical behavior. The efforts of many countries in emerging market countries to prevent their currencies from rising against the U.S. dollar, both through easy monetary policies and explicit intervention, effectively imported U.S. "imbalances" into their own countries. Since the U.S. dollar had been trending down for over a decade, this policy served to increase their domestic inflationary pressures as well. Moreover, these policies not only had undesirable domestic effects but undesirable international implications as well. First, by preventing the U.S. dollar from falling and by lowering U.S. long-term rates in the process of reserve accumulation, both the elasticity and absorption channels of trade adjustment were impeded. As a result, global trade imbalances became ever bigger and more dangerous. Second, with many currencies prevented from moving against the U.S. dollar, an unwarranted degree of upward pressure was diverted to freely floating currencies like the euro.[66] For all of these reasons, it is now in the interests of all countries to rethink urgently what currently passes for an international monetary system.[67]

---

66. Against this backdrop of very easy global liquidity conditions, another problem also emerged. Smaller countries that wished to tighten their domestic monetary policy found such efforts undermined by international capital flows, which pushed down long rates and pushed up asset prices. In principle, this should not happen if the theory of Uncovered Interest Rate Parity (UIP) prevails. In practice, UIP seems to prevail only over long horizons implying that unhelpful capital flows can continue for long periods. This was clearly a problem for New Zealand and for the United Kingdom as their central banks sought to tighten policy in the years preceding the crisis of August 2007. Indeed, as the U.S. dollar continued to weaken, even as domestic policy rates rose from 2005 onwards, capital inflows provided a significant degree of offset to the general thrust of U.S. policy. This raises the broader issue of whether even the United States must now be treated as a Small Open Economy.

67. This gives some urgency for calls to reform the Fund itself (the question of "chairs and shares"). If large, emerging market countries shared a sense of "ownership," the Fund might find it easier to produce a more universal floating exchange rate system, at least among the bigger currency blocks. Moreover, a more effective Fund might also find it easier to convince the large creditor nations (China, Germany, and Japan, in particular) that in a closed global economy everyone must contribute to measures to reduce global trade imbalances. Indeed, the need for creditors to adjust takes on added importance when the overall environment is deflationary rather than inflationary. Against this background of external imbalances, the fact that the United States introduced by far the largest set of domestic stimulus measures at the beginning of the crisis looks positively anomalous.

References

Ahearn, A., J. E. Gagnon, J. Haltmaeir and S. B. Kamin. 2002. "Preventing deflation: Lessons from the Japanese Experience in the 1990's." FRBG International Finance Discussion Paper No. 792, June, Washington, D.C.

Ashcraft, A. B. and T. Schuermann. 2008. "Understanding the securitization of subprime mortgage credit," Federal Reserve Bank of New York Staff Report no. 318.

Atkeson, A. and P. J. Kehoe. 2004. "Deflation and Depression: Is There an Empirical Link?" *American Economic Review*, Papers and Proceedings, Vol. 94, No. 2, May.

Bank for International Settlements. 2001. Annual Report, Basel, June.

Bernanke, B. 2002. "Deflation: Making Sure 'It' Doesn't Happen Here." Remarks before the National Economists Club, Washington, D.C., 21 November.

———. 2009. "Stamp Lecture" London School of Economics, January, London.

Bernanke, B. and V. Reinhart. 2004. "Conducting Monetary Policy at Very Low Short Term Interest Rates." Paper presented at the International Centre for Monetary and Banking Studies, January, Geneva.

Bernanke, B. S., V. R. Reinhart and B. P. Sack. 2004. "Monetary Policy Alternatives at the Zero Bound: An Empirical Assessment." FRBG Finance and Economics Discussion Series, No. 48, Washington, D.C.

Borio, C. E. V. 2003. "Towards a Macroprudential Framework for Financial Supervision and Regulation" BIS Working Paper No 128, February, Basel.

Borio, C. E. V. and M. Drehmann. Forthcoming. Towards an Operational Framework for Financial Ftability: "Fuzzy" Feasurement and its Fonsequences." Paper presented at the 12th Annual Conference of the Central Bank of Chile, November, Santiago.

Borio, C. E. V. and A. Filardo. 2005. "Deflation in an historical perspective." BIS Working Paper No 186, November, Basel.

Borio, C. E. V. and P. Lowe. 2002. "Asset Prices, Financial and Monetary Stability: Exploring the Nexus." BIS Working Paper 114, July, Basel.

Borio, C. E. V. and I. Shim. 2008. "What Can Macro-Prudential Policy Do To Help Support Monetary Policy?" BIS Working Paper No. 242, January, Basel.

Borio, C. E. V. and W. R. White. 2004. "Whither Monetary and Financial Stability? The Implications of Evolving Policy Regimes." BIS Working Paper No. 147, February, Basel.

Brunnermeir, M., A. Crocket, C; Goodhart, A. Persaud, and H. Shin. Forthcoming. "The Fundamental Principles of Financial Regulation." Geneva Report on the World Economy 11.

Cochran, J.P. and F. R. Glahe 1999. *The Hayek-Keynes Debate: Lessons for Current Business Cycle Research*. Lewiston NY: Edwin Miller Press.

Cooper, George. 2008. *The Origins of Financial Crises*. Hampshire: Harriman House Limited.

Financial Stability Forum. 2008. "Report of the FSF in Enhancing Market and Institutional Resilience" 7 April, Basel.

Fisher, I. 1936. "The Debt-Deflation Theory of Great Depressions." *Econometrica*.

Greenspan, A. 2005. "Economic Flexibility." Remarks to the National Association of Business Economists Annual Meeting, 27 September, Chicago.

———. 2009. "We Need a Better Cushion Against Risk." *Financial Times*, March 27, p. 9.

Haberler, G. 1939. "Prosperity and Depression." League of Nations, Geneva.

———. 1986. "Reflections on Hayek's Business Cycle Theory." *Cato Journal* Vol. 6, Number 2.

Heikensten, L. 1998. "The Crisis in Asia—Experiences from Sweden." Presentation at the OECD, March, Paris.

Hicks, J. 1967. *Critical Essays in Monetary Theory*. Clarendon Press, Oxford.

Issing, O. 2005. "The Monetary Pillar of the ECB." Paper prepared for the conference: The ECB and its watchers, 3 June, Frankfurt.

Kaminsky, G. and C. Reinhart. 1999. "The Twin Crises: The Causes of Banking and Balance of Payments Problems." *American Economic Review*, Vol. 89, p. 473–500.

Kindleberger, C.P. and R. Z. Aliber. 2005. *Manias, Panics and Crashes*. Fifth edition. New York: Palgrave Macmillan.

Knight, M. D. 2008. "General Manager's Speech," on the occasion of the BIS Annual General Meeting, 30 June, Basel.

Kohn D. 2008. "Monetary Policy and Asset Prices Revisited," speech presented at the Cato Institute's 26th Annual Monetary Policy Conference, 19 November, Washington, D.C.

Minsky, H. 1992. "The Financial Stability Hypothesis." WP74 in *Handbook of Radical Political Economy* by E. Arestis and M. Sawyer. Aldershot: Edward Elgar.

Mishkin, F. S. 2007. "Housing, and the Monetary Transmission Mechanism." Paper presented at the Federal Reserve Bank of Kansas City Economic Symposium, 31 August, Jackson Hole, Wyoming.

Muelbauer, J. 2007. "Housing, Credit and Consumer Expenditures." Paper presented at the Federal Reserve Bank of Kansas City Symposium, 31 August, Jackson Hole, Wyoming.

Phillips, A. W. 1957. "Stabilisation Policy and the Time Form of Lagged Responses." *Economic Journal* 67, 265–77.

Reinhart, V. 2003."Tools for Combating Deflation." Presentation to the National Association of Business Economists, March, Washington, D.C.

Rudd, J. and K. Whelan. 2003. "Can Rational Expectations, Sticky Price Models Explain Inflation Dynamics?" FRBG, Finance and Economics Discussion Series No. 46, Washington, D.C.

Schumpeter, J. 1934. "Depressions. Can We Learn from Past Experience?" in *Economics of the Recovery Program.*

Svennson, L. 2003. "Escaping from the Liquidity Trap and Deflation: The Foolproof Way and Others." *Journal of Economic Perspectives* Vol. 17, No. 4.

Talib, N. H. 2007. *The Black Swan.* New York: Random House Publishing Group.

Tett, G. 2009. "Curse of the Zombies Rises in Europe Amid an Eerie Calm." *Financial Times*, 3 April, p. 24.

Tovar, C. E. 2008. "DSGE Models and Central Banks." BIS Working Paper No. 258, September, Basel.

Weber, A. 2008. "Financial Markets and Monetary Policy." Speech presented at the 12th Annual Conference of the CEPR/ESI, September, Basel.

White, W. R. 2005. "Procyclicality in the Financial System: Do We Need a New Macrofinancial Stability Framework?" *Kiel Economic Papers* 2, September, Kiel.

_____. 2006. "Is Price Stability Enough?" BIS Working Paper No. 205, April, Basel.

_____. 2007a. "Measured Wealth, Real Wealth, and the Illusion of Saving." *IFC Bulletin* 26, July, Basel.

_____. 2007b. "Emerging Market Finance in Good Times and Bad: Are EME Crises a Thing of the Past?" Speech at the IIF 25th Anniversary Membership Meeting, October, Washington, D.C.

_____. 2008a. "Globalisation and the Determinants of Domestic Inflation." BIS Working Paper No. 250, March, Basel.

_____. 2008b. "The US, Europe and China: Different Tools, Different Realities." Paper presented at a monetary and banking seminar at the Central Bank of Argentina, September, Buenos Aires.

Yellen, J. 2009. "A Minsky Meltdown: Lessons for Central Bankers." Presentation to the 18th Annual H. P. Minsky Conference on the State of the U.S. and World Economy, 16 April, New York.

11

Limited-Purpose Banking

Laurence J. Kotlikoff

T'WAS THE YEAR the country stood still. Not a car, truck, or bus rode the roads. No one drove to work, no one drove to shop, no one drove to visit. No one drove anywhere. The reason was simple. No one could buy gas. Gas stations had gone broke. Their owners had tired of netting pennies on the gallon. They wanted to surge their earnings. The big money, they learned from a Harvard MBA, was in securitizing their services. So they started selling GODs—gas options for drivers. Each GOD gave the driver the option to fill her tank for $3 per gallon. Drivers bought GODs religiously. And with gas selling for $2 a gallon, station owners didn't worry.

Then the unthinkable happened. Gas prices skyrocketed to $6 a gallon, and drivers began invoking their GODs. Each GOD could save $3 per gallon per tank, and if you didn't need gas, you held up a sign—"Gods for Cash!" Station owners began cursing the GODs. They now had to buy gas at $6 a gallon and sell it for $3. In short order, the owners went bust. They closed their stations and started looking for jobs in financial services. GODs became worthless, and the economy ground to a halt. The economic moral is simple. If you want markets to function, don't let critical market makers—those who connect suppliers and demanders (e.g., refineries and motorists) of essential products—gamble with their businesses. Apply the moral to banks and the regulatory prescription is clear. Don't let banks take risky positions. Make banks stick to their two critical functions—mediating the payments system and connecting lenders to borrowers.

Trust, Not Liquidity

The fundamental problem facing our financial system is not insufficient liquidity, a shortage of credit, or capital inadequacy. The fundamental problem is a well-deserved lack of trust between borrowers and lenders at nearly all levels. To be blunt, the financial sector played the big con and lost big time. No one is going to trust insider raters, banks that borrow to gamble, hedge funds that fake returns, and insurers that concentrate rather than spread risk. No one is going to trust assets that can't be disclosed, are self-custodied, are valued by models calibrated with limited data that ignore systemic risk—and that are parked in secrecy jurisdictions like Antigua. Above all, no one in his or her right mind is going to trust bankers with me-first business plans—people who have seemingly lost the capacity to distinguish between conscience and greed.

The fact that most financial players have been honest and that most financial plays over the past decade were sound now means nothing. Everyone has been tarred by the scale and implications of dishonest and selfish behavior among a not-so-small minority. Uncle Sam could buy every toxic asset on earth and stuff a "bad bank" to its gills, and we'd still have a banking crisis. When people buy things, they want to know what they're getting. They won't buy Tylenol if they don't trust that Tylenol is in fact in the bottle, and they won't buy bank paper at a decent rate or bank equity at a decent price if they can't trust what the bank is doing.

Recapitalizing the banks is therefore not the answer. Left to their own wiles, bank managers will take that new capital and invest it in their latest Sure Thing, largely in order to convince us to do the same. They'll do this because it's not their capital. Their livelihood flows from their commissions and bonuses, which are based on sales of the Sure Thing, not the return on it. And they'll collect their loot long before the Sure Thing slithers away down the proverbial rat-hole.

Raising capital requirements for banks is equally futile as a solution to the present crisis. Banks in trouble know that their liabilities are limited by their terms of incorporation, and that the only chance of surviving is doubling down on risky bets—which is exactly the behavior we have seen as several financial giants lumbered recently toward the precipice. How many Long-Term Capital Managements, Bear Stearns, Lehman Brothers, AIGs, Merrill Lynches, and

Madoffs do we need before we realize that we're not dealing here with moral hazard? We're dealing with immoral certainty.

Since the core problem is trust, it's not going to be solved by resurrecting a failed financial system. Nor can it be resolved by nationalizing the financial sector, which will throw out the baby with the bathwater and introduce all manner of political agendas into financial decision-making. Instead, the solution is to fundamentally redefine what a bank can and cannot do, so that we never again face financial collapse.

Limited-Purpose Banking

Strange as it may seem to so many who have grown used to the American financial subculture of the past few decades, the core purpose of banks and other financial corporations isn't to gamble with other people's money. That core purpose is instead to connect—that is, to intermediate between—suppliers and demanders of financing. In this respect, banks are no different from gas stations. Gas stations intermediate between suppliers of gas (refineries) and demanders of gas (drivers); they don't gamble on the price of gas and leave the country exposed to a huge common bet, the loss of which will lead nearly all of them to close down.

To re-establish trust and resurrect our financial system we need to limit banks and all other financial corporations to their original purpose: financial intermediation. Here's how limited-purpose banking would work.

Every incorporated enterprise engaged in financial intermediation would operate strictly as a mutual fund company and live under a common set of rules. Whether they would call themselves commercial banks, investment banks, trust companies, hedge funds, savings and loans, mortgage brokers, or something else would be immaterial. They would all be free to do the same thing—namely, intermediate, and to make a profit by charging for that service, but take no risks with their company's money.

Banks (shorthand for financial corporations) would sell two main types of mutual funds: a cash mutual fund that would provide checking account services and other mutual funds that would provide investment opportunities in bonds, mortgages, stocks, private equity, real estate, and other financial securities.

Cash Mutual Funds

Consider first the checking account operations. In the current system, banks take in customer deposits and are required to keep only 10 percent in reserve against the possibility that customers will demand their deposits back right away. The other 90 percent is, in effect, the banks' gambling stakes. It is money banks can lend out on risky projects, spend on risky stocks, or invest in risky private equity and real estate. If these investments work out, everyone's happy. If not, well, the bank gets to flip the problem to the FDIC (i.e., to taxpayers), which insures the deposits. If everyone suddenly comes to believe, whether correctly or not, that the banks have lost their money, everyone will run to the teller windows and demand it back. It won't be there, as it wasn't there in 1873 or in 1930.

So we have a depository system that's very fragile because it is exposed to bank runs. Today, the FDIC is insuring close to $4 trillion dollars in deposits, and it's frankly very scary that it has less than $36 billion (just around 1 percent) in reserve to cover this massive liability. Were all Americans to panic and demand back their deposits, Uncle Sam would have to print up nearly $4 trillion on the spot—a formula for hyperinflation if ever there were one. Sound extreme? It is. But these are extreme times, and the public is getting close to full panic mode.

Under limited-purpose banking, bank runs could never arise. Every dollar deposited in a checking account would be held via a cash mutual fund in cash or U.S. Treasuries, meaning banks would hold not 10-percent reserves, but 100-percent reserves against these liabilities. Banks would always have all of our money on hand, either in cold cash or short-term T-bills.

Cash mutual fund assets would be held by third party custodies (to be supervised by a new government agency—the Federal Financial Authority or FFA), so if Sophie buys, say, $1,237 of shares in a cash mutual fund, she will know there are literally 1,237 dollar bills (or the electronic equivalent) sitting in an account, under the control of the third-party custodian, with Sophie's name on it.

All mutual funds under limited-purpose banking would be marked to market. Cash mutual funds would obviously be valued at $1 per share and could, therefore, never break or exceed the buck. Owners of cash mutual funds would be free to write checks against their holdings, use debit cards to access their cash from ATM machines, and use debit cards to pay for purchases online or in stores. These cash mutual funds would, thus, represent the demand deposits (checking accounts) under limited-purpose banking.

This is not a new idea. One-hundred-percent reserve requirements on checking and other accounts subject to immediate demand was, by the way, advocated under the heading Narrow Banking by Irving Fisher, Henry Simons, and Frank Knight in the 1930s and endorsed by Nobel Laureate Milton Friedman, Robert Litan, and other economists in the postwar era.[1] Simons and seven of his colleagues at the University of Chicago developed a specific narrow banking plan, called the Chicago Plan, which they presented to Congress for its consideration. Yale's Irving Fisher was sufficiently intent on narrow banking that he wrote a book on the subject entitled *100% Money.*[2]

Narrow banking, however, is a small feature of limited-purpose banking and would hardly suffice to deal with today's multifaceted financial problems. The problem is not that banks are borrowing just from those with FDIC-insured deposits and then gambling, at our potential expense, with simply those borrowed funds. The problem is that banks are also borrowing from many other lenders (including sovereign nations) whose loans are implicitly guaranteed by the government because the banks individually, or as a group, are too big to fail.

The "too big to fail" problem references another elegant strand in economic theory and modeling, namely, the economics of moral hazard and the optimal design of private and social insurance contracts.[3] I view limited-purpose banking from these headlights. It's not a proposal to restrain free financial trade with all the excess burden such a policy would entail. It's the opposite. It's a proposal to resolve market failure, and moral hazard is a form of market failure arising from incomplete information.

---

1. http://www.atimes.com/atimes/Global_Economy/JI17Dj03.html; http://papers.ssrn.com/sol3/Delivery.cfm/99041603.pdf?abstractid=160989&mirid=1; http://en.wikipedia.org/wiki/Narrow_banking; http://www.imes.boj.or.jp/english/publication/mes/2000/me18-1-4.pdf

2. Irving Fisher. *100% Money and the Public Debt.* London: Pickering & Chatto Ltd., 1996. http://www.answers.com/topic/irving-fisher#Biography

3. See Harvard economist and law professor Steven Shavell's seminal article, "On Moral Hazard And Insurance," *Quarterly Journal of Economics* (Nov. 1979) 541–62. http://www.law.harvard.edu/faculty/shavell/pdf/92_Quart_J_Econ_541.pdf.

Implications of Cash Mutual Funds for Monetary Policy

A byproduct of 100-percent-reserved checking accounts is that the government would gain full control of the M1 money supply. M1 is the sum of currency held by the public (money tucked in our pant pockets or, these days, hidden under our pillows) and our checking account balances. Under limited-purpose banking, M1 would equal the sum of currency plus our cash mutual fund balances.

Since the Federal Reserve creates every dollar of currency in the economy, and since each of those dollars would either reside, at any point in time, in our own physical possession or in a third-party custodian's physical possession (as custodied securities of the cash mutual funds), the sum of the currency printed would equal the sum of our own physical holdings plus the value of our cash mutual fund shares, which exactly equal the custodians' holdings.

Under limited-purpose banking, since M1 is currency plus the value of the holdings of the never-break-or-exceed-a-buck cash mutual funds, M1 corresponds to precisely what the government has printed. Thus, under this system, the Federal Reserve has direct control of M1 through its conduct of open market operations.

This is far from true under the current system. Currently, the Federal Reserve has only indirect control of the money supply because the extent to which checking account balances are created depends, in large part, on the *money multiplier*, which is ultimately determined by the banking system. When the banking system contracts its lending, the amount of checking account balances in the financial system declines as borrowers deposit less money into their checking accounts for the simple reason that they've chosen to borrow less or have been able to borrow less and just don't have as much to deposit.

So when the banks stop lending, M1 shrinks, as does the ratio of M1 to the amount of money originally printed by Uncle Sam, which is what we call the money multiplier. During our current financial crisis, the M1 multiplier declined from 1.6 to .8, although it now appears to be slowly heading back up.

Milton Friedman and Anna Schwartz argued strongly that the cause of the Great Depression was the collapse of M1, as opposed to, for example, the economy's flipping from a good to a bad equilibrium.[4] In their view, there is

---

4. Milton Friedman and Anna J. Schwartz. *A Monetary History of the United States*. Princeton: Princeton University Press, 1963.

a tight connection between M1 and the price level, and the contraction of M1 put downward pressure on prices, which caused the substantial deflation that arose in the early years of the Great Depression. Wages fell as well, but not as fast as prices, so the real cost of hiring labor—the real wage—rose, leading firms to lay off workers.[5]

One can question the Friedman-Schwartz view of the Great Depression, but my goal here is not to debate the origins of the Great Depression. My point is that, under limited-purpose banking, M1 would be fully determined by the central bank, so that the Friedman-Schwartz concern about the Federal Reserve losing control of the money supply and, thus, the economy's price level and performance, *to the extent that it's valid*, would not arise.

Today, just as in the 1930s, we have seen a huge decline in the money multiplier. This has forced Federal Reserve Chairman Ben Bernanke to expand the monetary base—to print massive amounts of money, in layman's terms—to stabilize M1. Printing all this money (Bernanke has more than doubled base money since late 2008) holds its own risks, of course: If the multiplier shoots back up, we could see the money supply and prices explode.

To summarize, we've got a depository system that's subject to moral hazard, bank runs, and wild swings in the money multiplier. In normal times these risks are theoretical; in times of crisis, they tend to ensure that we suffer maximum feasible calamity. It's not worth the risk, and limited-purpose banking would eliminate all three problems.

We now progress to the banks' second job under limited-purpose banking: selling bond, equity, and real estate mutual funds. Let's start with bond funds.

Other Mutual Fund Services

Under our system, banks would initiate, but not hold, loans. Banks would send their initiated loans, whether to individuals (e.g., a mortgage) or businesses (e.g., a credit line), to the Federal Financial Authority (FFA)—which would rate the loans after using tax records to verify the income reported and

---

5. The increase in real wages in the early 1930s was modest and may reflect a change in the composition of the employed workforce with the most productive workers being retained (earning higher real wages), and the least productive workers being laid off.

spot-checking the appraised value of collateral. Once processed by the FFA, the banks would package the fully disclosed, government-rated loans within mutual funds for purchase by the public. Once purchased, the loan would be activated. The public, not the banks, would own the mutual funds and hold the loans.

Banks could borrow money on their own account to buy office furniture, bank buildings, and make other investments in their operations—but not to gamble. Banks would never be leveraged because their purpose is intermediation, not gambling. Bank owners, on the other hand—including the owners of holding companies that include banks and other kinds of businesses—would still be completely free to gamble on high-risk investments, but only with their own personal money, not with the bank's assets.

There is, of course, a clear precedent for government loan rating; namely, Fannie Mae and Freddie Mac's conforming loan standard. And the idea of securitizing loans within mutual funds isn't new either. What's new here is the scope of the rating system, the degree of disclosure and the absolute prohibition against banks taking risks.

Next, consider bank issuance of mutual funds that hold stocks, private equity, and real estate. Banks would sell shares of the mutual funds and use the proceeds to purchase these securities. The banks themselves, however, would not own any of the securities held within their mutual funds. They'd simply connect savers to investors and collect a fee for the service.

What's the role of insurance companies under limited-purpose banking? This is a good question because the difference between financial securities and insurance policies is simply a matter of words. Today we can purchase financial securities that insure us against the stock market crashing, the dollar falling, the price of oil rising, and company X's bond defaulting (via the CDSs mentioned above).

Given that today's insurance companies are fundamentally engaging in the same business as today's banks, insurance companies would be considered banks under limited-purpose banking. And like all banks under limited-purpose banking, they would be free to market mutual funds of their choosing. But the mutual funds that insurers would issue would be somewhat different from conventional mutual funds. The first reason is that their purchasers would collect payment contingent on personal outcomes and decisions as well as economy-wide conditions. The second reason is the insurance mutual funds would be closed-end mutual funds, with no new issues (claims to the fund) to be sold once the fund had launched.

Take, for example, a three-month closed-end life insurance mutual fund marketed by a financial company called Die With Us First Bank to males age 50 to 55. Let's assume the fund closes on January 1, 2012, meaning males in this age bracket can buy shares up to that date. Like all other limited-purpose banking mutual funds, FBH would be required to custody its securities. In this case, FBH would simply hold every dollar contributed to the fund (spent on shares) in three-month Treasury bills.

At the end of three months, the pot (the principal, plus interest on the Treasuries, less the fee paid to fund managers) would be paid out to all those who died in proportion to the number of shares they purchased. Shareholders who don't die collect nothing. Now clearly, the dead can't literally receive payments, but their heirs can, so when I say the decedents collect, I really mean their estates.

There are two important points to convey right off the bat. If Arthur and Edward both die, but Arthur bought twice the number of shares as Edward, Arthur collects twice as much as Edward. So the way to buy more insurance under limited-purpose banking is simply to buy more insurance mutual funds shares.

Second, once the fund closes, the size of the pot is given, so, other things being equal, the more shareholders who kick the bucket, the less any decedent will collect. Thus, insurance mutual funds have a natural firewall, given by the size of the pot, when it comes to what they have to pay out. The firewall is the pot. What's in the pot is everything that's available to distribute, and not a penny more. All investors in the mutual fund will realize that no one is going to add to the pot after the fact, particularly not taxpayers.

Federal Financial Authority

The Federal Financial Authority (FFA) would audit the books of all publicly traded companies (to insure against any more Enrons), require full disclosure of the private equity and real estate being packaged within mutual funds, and establish a custodial system to ensure that title to all assets owned by mutual funds is secure and verified. Never again would a Bernie Madoff be free to custody his own accounts; i.e., to lie about the actual investments being made with investor money.

The FFA would replace the roughly 115 federal and state financial regulatory bodies and be the single financial regulator overseeing the financial system. The FFA can be thought of as an FDA (Food and Drug Administration) for financial products. The FFA would verify, supervise custody, fully disclose, and oversee the rating and trades of all securities purchased, held, and sold by the limited-purpose banking mutual funds.

Here's an example of how the FFA would operate. Consider Robby, who seeks to borrow money to buy Frank's house in Cleveland "using" a bank, call it WLMB (which stands for the We Love Money Bank). WLM would initiate the mortgage, by which I mean it would help Robby fill out a mortgage application. Next, WLMB would send the paperwork to the FFA for processing. The FFA would verify Robby's income statement using federal income tax records; it would certify his credit rating; it would verify, using independent local appraisers, the value of the home he intends to purchase; it would verify the property taxes and insurance costs on the home, and it would specify all other pertinent information that would help a mutual fund understand the value of buying Robby's mortgage.

Most important, the FFA would hire private rating companies to provide independent ratings of the risk of Robby's mortgage. The rating companies would be free of any financial conflicts of interest; i.e., they would not be permitted to work for companies or individuals whose securities they are rating.

The FFA would disclose everything it has learned about Robby's mortgage on a public website, without disclosing Robby's identity or the precise location of the house in question. And once the FFA has done its work, it would return the now fully disclosed mortgage to WLMB, which would put the mortgage up for public auction and purchase either by its own mutual fund that invests in home mortgages or by the mutual funds of other banks investing in home mortgages.

Robby's mortgage would fund when purchased, and not a second before, with the acquiring mutual fund wiring the funds to Frank's account. Hence, WLMB would never hold the mortgage and never be exposed to the risk of Robby's defaulting. It would simply intermediate the transaction, for which it would charge Robby a fee.

Conclusion

Limited-purpose banking may sound radical, but it's not. Fidelity Investments, TIAA-CREF, and other mutual fund companies have been operating as limited-purpose banks for decades and, no surprise, they aren't going under. While banks take on zero risk under limited-purpose banking, this new system wouldn't limit the public's investment opportunities. Today's mutual funds companies offer some 10,000 different products to choose from. Any of us can invest in junk-bond funds, blue-chip stock funds, real estate investment trusts, emerging-market equity funds—you name it. And we can invest directly, as well, not just by buying into a mutual fund. We can still gamble and lose our shirts if we want to; limited-liability banking does not try to spite human nature, close the casino, end the American penchant for rolling the dice, or subvert any other facet of our liberty to spend our money how we choose. It just eliminates the ability of banks and other financial institutions to act irresponsibly with other people's money.

Since all financial institutions "selling" securities would be mutual funds capable of issuing checking accounts, with 100-percent reserves, we'd have one set of regulations that apply to all financial corporations. Hence, this plan envisions no return to the old Glass-Steagall provision that limited the types of assets in which banks can invest, introduced in the 1930s but abandoned in the 1990s. To repeat, under limited-purpose banking, banks don't invest; they intermediate and nothing else.

Apart from running the FFA, limited-purpose banking costs nothing. It doesn't waste huge sums, relieving banks of their past mistakes. It restores trust via the only possible source available right now—the government—and it gets credit flowing through financial intermediaries because lenders (purchasers of mutual funds of loans) will know what they are buying. It is a cheaper solution than all the others being contemplated, and it is vastly cheaper than failing to solve the problem, which is precisely what these other "solutions" will accomplish.

Trust is a precious and ultimately fragile commodity, particularly the impersonal social trust bound up in institutions. Wall Street's masters of the universe squandered our trust unconscionably, and Jimmy Stewart is not coming back from Bedford Falls to save the day. We need a new system that takes the con out of financial services once and for all. We need limited-purpose banking.

References

Fisher, Irving. *100% Money and the Public Debt*. 1996. (Pickering Masters Editions). London: Pickering & Chatto Ltd.

Friedman, Milton and Anna J. Schwartz. 1963. *A Monetary History of the United States*. Princeton: Princeton University Press.

Shavell, Steven. 1979. "On Moral Hazard And Insurance," *Quarterly Journal of Economics* (Nov.) 541–62. http://www.law.harvard.edu/faculty/shavell/pdf/92_Quart _J_Econ_541.pdf

12

Central Banks as Sources of Financial Instability

George Selgin

THE RECENT FINANCIAL CRISIS set in bold relief the Jekyll-and-Hyde nature of contemporary central banks generally, and of the Federal Reserve System in particular. It has made apparent both our utter dependence upon central banks as instruments for assuring the continuous flow of credit in the aftermath of a financial bust, and the capacity of the same institutions to fuel the financial booms that make severe busts possible in the first place. To succeed, any reform aimed at forestalling future boom-bust cycles must somehow act to restrain the latter capacity.

Yet theoretical treatments of central banking place almost exclusive emphasis on its stabilizing potential, that is, on central banks' positive role in managing the growth of national monetary aggregates and in supplying last-resort loans to troubled financial (and sometimes non-financial) firms in times of distress. This one-sided treatment of central banking reflects both the normative nature of much theoretical work on the subject—that is, its tendency to focus on ideal rather than actual central bank conduct—and the (usually tacit) assumption that, however much central banks may depart in practice from ideal, financially stabilizing policies, they nevertheless serve to reduce the amplitude of booms and busts compared to what would ensue in the absence of centralized monetary control.

The present essay seeks to redress, if only to a small extent, the imbalance that characterizes most theoretical work on central banking, and to thereby supply more solid underpinnings for needed reform, by arguing that, contrary to conventional wisdom, central banks are *inherently destabilizing*, that is, that financial systems are rendered more unstable by central banks than they might be without them. To make this argument I must delve into the history of central banking, both to explain why governments encouraged the establishment of destabilizing institutions, and to account for the tendency of modern writers to look upon central banks as a stabilizing presence.

The Origins of Central Banking

An objective understanding of the macroeconomic and financial consequences of central banking requires, first of all, a value-free definition of the term "central bank," that is, a definition that doesn't presuppose any particular sort of conduct, whether beneficial or malign. Common textbook definitions of central banks as institutions devoted to combating inflation, dampening business cycles, or serving as lenders of last resort, won't do, because such definitions involve a tacit counterfactual the validity of which is open to doubt, and because they are in flagrant disagreement with the conduct of many real-world central banks.

So what, really, is a central bank? It is, fundamentally, a bank possessing a national monopoly, or something approaching a national monopoly, of the right to issue circulating paper currency. Although outright monopolies are most common today, in a few instances (e.g., the United Kingdom, Ireland, and China), other (commercial) banks also enjoy highly circumscribed currency-issuing privileges.

The privilege of issuing paper currency was not always so limited, however. On the contrary, it was once enjoyed by practically all banks, which depended on it as a source of credit at a time when the custom of transferring deposits by means of checks was as yet undeveloped. Although the earliest central banks began as "public" banks that typically enjoyed a monopoly of the banking business of their sponsoring governments only, while sharing at least to some limited extent the right to issue currency with other banks, they gradually acquired currency monopolies as well. Indeed, the transition to central banking in its modern guise tended to follow public banks' consolidation of currency-issuing privileges, for reasons to be made clear in due course.

Nevertheless, the first steps toward modern currency monopolies long predated modern notions of central banking, with their emphasis on central banks' stabilizing role. Instead, the public banks that later became full-fledged central banks were established solely for the purpose of catering to their sponsoring governments' fiscal needs—by managing their deposits, by administering their debt, and especially by accommodating their short-run credit needs. Despite their close relationships with national governments that helped to establish them these proto-central banks were profit-maximizing firms, and as such were managed solely in their owners' interest, rather than in the interest of the broader financial community. The notion that public banks' privileges obliged them to promote general economic stability came only in the aftermath of numerous financial crises—crises which, I intend to show, the public banks themselves helped bring about.

Although the Bank of England was not the first major public bank, the Swedish Riksbank having preceded it by a quarter century, the Bank of England was to become the prototype "modern" central bank, having been the earliest to acknowledge, at first tacitly (and grudgingly), and at length officially, its duty to rescue other financial firms by serving as a lender of last resort during periods of financial distress. The fiscal origins of the Bank of England, and its founders' corresponding unconcern for any broad macroeconomic consequences its creation might entail, are evident in the 1694 "Tonnage" Act (5 and 6 Will. & Mar. c 20) granting the Bank of England its original charter, an act "for securing certain Recompences and Advantages . . . to such persons as shall voluntarily advance the sum of Fifteen hundred thousand Pounds towards carrying on the War against France." Other early central banks had similar beginnings. The Bank of France, for example, was established by Napoleon for the express purpose of buying up French government securities, for which there was no other market at the time, while Germany's Reichsbank, predecessor of the present Bundesbank, itself grew out of the former Royal Bank of Berlin, founded by Frederick the Great for the purpose of managing the funds of the Prussian State. Yet the fiscal origins of early-modern central banks are often overlooked, and especially so by their proponents, including central bankers themselves.[1]

The fact that the first central banks evolved from public banks established for purely fiscal reasons suggests that any stabilizing potential they harbored was

---

1. The Bank of France's website, for instance, says that Napoleon established the bank "to foster renewed economic growth in the wake of the deep recession of the Revolutionary Period"! For a review of the origins of central banking in Western Europe and the United States, see Vera Smith, *The Rationale of Central Banking* (London: P.S. King & Son, 1936).

unanticipated by their founders. That could mean simply that, by a sheer stroke of good luck, institutions originally designed to serve governments' narrow fiscal ends just happened to be ideally suited, allowing for appropriate constitutional modifications, for scientific crisis management. I shall, however, argue that the public banks themselves were sources of instability, and that their vaunted stabilizing potential was at bottom little more than a potential for self-discipline, and a rather limited one at that.

The "Principle of Adverse Clearings"

To explore the possibility that central banks' unique privileges may themselves have contributed to financial instability, we must consider precisely how those privileges alter the scope for credit expansion. Doing so in turn requires that we consider the limits to such expansion in a competitive or "free" banking system, meaning one in which numerous banks enjoy equal rights to issue their own distinct brands of circulating notes.[2] In keeping with circumstances surrounding the early development of central banking, I shall assume that banks, whether enjoying exclusive privileges or not, are obliged to redeem their notes on demand in specie, that is, in gold or silver coin.

In a free banking system, banks treat rival banks' notes much as they treat checks drawn on rival banks today, that is, they routinely return them to their sources for redemption. Indeed, the modern practice of daily "clearing" of checks, with net dues settled by transfer of base money, usually on the books of some central bank, grew out of the pre-central banking practice of regular note exchange, with banks returning rivals' notes directly to them or to central clearinghouses, and settling accounts in specie.

This routine note-exchange and settlement process imposes very strict limits on credit expansion by individual note issuing banks and, hence, by the banking system as a whole, creating a tight connection between those limits and the available supply of specie reserves. Domestic monetary equilibrium in such a system can be understood as a state in which individual bank lending policies are

---

2. Strictly speaking, a "free" banking system, to use the expression in its European sense, is one in which banks are generally free from restrictive regulations, and not simply free to issue their own notes. But it is the implications of free and competitive note issue that particularly concern us.

consistent with zero long-run or expected net reserve drains, and bank reserve ratios just suffice to guarantee an optimally low probability of default owing to random variations of net reserve drains around their zero mean. Starting from such an equilibrium, and assuming an unchanging demand for money balances, any bank that further expands its balance sheet independently of its rivals will face a corresponding absolute and relative increase in the return flow of its notes (or checks) through the clearing system, and a corresponding net loss of reserves, which will leave it with an inadequate reserve cover, if it doesn't default outright. Banks in a free banking system may thus be likened to prisoners in a chain gang: escape is impossible for any single prisoner acting alone, and hardly less so for the group as a whole, because of the difficulty its members will encounter in trying to coordinate their steps. The greater the size of the gang, the more difficult escape becomes.

Elsewhere[3] I've referred to this competitive check against over-issuance of bank money as the "principle of adverse clearings." Thanks to it, the total volume of money and credit in a free banking system cannot easily expand beyond limits consistent with a stable overall volume of payments. Once banks have expanded to the point where their reserve cushions have fallen to some minimal, prudent level, they can expand further only if the demand to hold their notes or deposits increases, that is, if the value of the flow of their outstanding liabilities through the clearing system, whether notes or checks drawn against deposits, declines.

Thus, for the system as a whole, and assuming that all payments are conducted with bank money rather than with specie itself, the demand for (precautionary) reserves can be understood as increasing, though perhaps less than proportionately, with the volume of payments, MV, where M is the stock of bank liabilities, including outstanding notes and demand deposits, and V is the velocity of circulation of that stock, or its rate of turnover. It follows that, for any given domestic stock (supply) of specie reserves and real rate of interest (the last of which influences the demand for precautionary reserves), there will be a unique volume of payments at which reserve demand and supply are equal. Should a change in the public's demand for real money balances, as manifested

3. George Selgin, *The Theory of Free Banking: Money Supply Under Competitive Note Issue* (Totowa, NJ: Rowman and Littlefield, 1988).

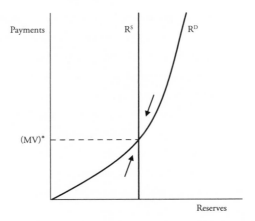

Figure 12.1. Reserve and Spending Equilibrium Under Free Banking

in a change in V, result in a level of spending no longer consistent with such an equilibrium, the banks will respond by expanding or contracting credit until equilibrium is restored. Specifically, an increase in V, for example, will result in an excess demand for reserves, prompting banks to reduce their lending and thereby reduce their outstanding liabilities, while a decline in V will have the opposite effect. These implications of the principle of adverse clearings are summarized in Figure 12.1.[4]

The tendency of a free-banking system to stabilize total spending has the obvious macroeconomic advantages of helping to maintain "natural" values of employment, interest rates, and real output. It also serves to prevent changes in the general price level except in connection with shifts in an economy's long-run supply schedule.

International Monetary Equilibrium

This "tight" nature of domestic monetary equilibrium under free banking also has implications for the preservation of international monetary equilib-

---

4. For details, see George Selgin, *The Theory of Free Banking*, 37–85; Selgin, "Free Banking and Monetary Control," *The Economic Journal* 104, no. 427 (1994): 1449–59; Selgin, "In-Concert Overexpansion and the Precautionary Demand for Bank Reserves," *Journal of Money, Credit, and Banking* 33, no. 2 (2001): 294–300, the last of which addresses the particular possibility of a coordinated overexpansion.

rium. In the context of an international specie—let us say gold—standard, the condition for such an equilibrium, that of "purchasing power parity," implies that a given sum of gold bullion should purchase approximately the same bundle of tradable goods in all gold standard countries: "approximately" because prices can persistently differ by amounts reflecting the costs of importing goods from abroad, including transport costs and duties. Should the bundle's price in any one country vary from its price elsewhere beyond upper and lower boundaries, known as "gold points," consistent with the aforementioned costs, the difference will cause more goods to be imported into, and fewer to be exported from, the country where prices are higher, with gold flows serving to finance the increased trade deficit. This Humean "price-specie-flow" mechanism will eventually restore purchasing power parity by promoting monetary contraction in the country where goods are more expensive and monetary expansion where they have been less expensive.

A virtue of free banking is that it limits occasions in which the Humean mechanism must operate, by checking a domestic overexpansion of money and credit *before* it has a chance to drive domestic prices above their values consistent with international purchasing power equilibrium. That the virtue is considerable will become apparent when we examine the workings of a central banking system, where the preservation of international monetary equilibrium is far more likely to depend on long-run corrections based on international specie movements. International gold flows would of course still occur even in a world consisting solely of national free banking systems: national shares of the world supply of gold reserves would alter for reasons analogous to those that can alter individual banks' market shares within a particular country. But such flows would not be evidence of a prior, substantial disturbance to international equilibrium brought about by the arbitrary overexpansion of credit in any one nation.

Central Banks: Pied Pipers of Credit

What happens if, instead of allowing all or at least many banks to issue circulating notes, that privilege is granted to a single bank only? For domestic exchanges, paper notes are generally more convenient than gold and silver coins, and so will typically be preferred. Consequently, banks that are denied the right to issue their own notes will stock and reissue notes from the privileged bank.

These less-privileged banks will, in other words, tend to treat those notes as a superior substitute for specie reserves. Two important consequences follow from this: first, the less-privileged (henceforth "commercial") banks will tend to send their specie to the privileged (henceforth, "central") bank, which will consequently become the sole custodian of the nation's specie reserves. Second, the central bank will be exempt from the principle of adverse clearings. The central bank is therefore able to operate on a very slim cushion of specie reserves, with a correspondingly greater "leveraging" of central bank capital. It will also be able to expand credit, and thereby increase the effective supply of commercial bank reserves, without having to fear any immediate internal drain of precious metal from its own coffers.

These last observations account for the perceived fiscal advantages of central banking, and thus for government's ability to secure generous fiscal support from central banks in return for the monopoly rights granted to them. But these fiscal advantages come at the cost of greater potential macroeconomic and financial instability, because the privileges they are based upon also make it far more likely that domestic credit expansion will proceed beyond sustainable limits, with equilibrium being restored in the long run by means of an external drain of specie. In other words, central banking set the stage for the "classical" nineteenth-century business cycle.

To see this, imagine a "typical" central bank of the early nineteenth century, pressed by its sponsoring government to supply it with additional credits. Because the central bank is exempt from adverse clearings, it has no certain way of ascertaining, in the short run, when it has expanded too far. It might even be tempted to lend its entire specie reserve, were it not often faced with unexpected (if modest) changes in the balance of payments. Nor can it easily determine whether domestic prices are approaching levels that must trigger an external drain of specie, because available price statistics, both domestic and international, are limited and crude, and because a general discrepancy may not be apparent in price indexes constructed for any particular goods "bundle."

Although commercial banks themselves remain constrained like so many members of a chain gang, the central bank's own exemption from adverse clearings allows it to lead them all, Pied-Piper fashion, in a general overexpansion, by adding to the aggregate, effective supply of commercial bank reserves. Referring again to Figure 12.1 above, as the central bank expands, the reserve-supply schedule shifts to the right, and the equilibrium volume of aggregate spending (MV) increases accordingly. Assuming given aggregate (goods) supply schedules, prices will be bid up, eventually triggering an external drain of specie from the central bank. The central bank consequently finds itself in danger of imminent default, and so proceeds to save itself by aggressively contracting credit. The contraction reduces commercial banks' reserves, forcing them to contract as well, and so triggers a general credit crunch.

From Villains to Heroes:
The Origins of the Classical Lender of Last Resort

If central banks are in fact sources of financial instability, how is it that they've come to be regarded as just the opposite? The explanation resides partly in modern economists' limited understanding of the workings of competitive currency arrangements, which causes them to assume that such arrangements must necessarily be less stable (because less subject to central "control") than monopolistic ones, and partly on a failure to appreciate the origins of the idea that monetary systems require a "lender of last resort."

The Bank of England was the first central bank to assume the role of last-resort lender. During the crises of 1857 and 1866 it did so informally and reluctantly; but at length it came to acknowledge, under public pressure, a duty to rescue other banks threatened by cash shortages, though otherwise solvent.

The chief architect of this newfound understanding was Walter Bagehot, best known today as the second and most illustrious editor of *The Economist*. It was Bagehot who, in *Lombard Street* (1873)[5], outlined what is now known as the "classical" lender-of-last-resort doctrine, according to which central banks, during times of financial distress, ought to continue to lend freely, though at high rates aimed at attracting capital from abroad and also at discouraging borrowing by insolvent (as opposed to merely illiquid) banks.

While many economists are aware of Bagehot's role in developing the modern lender-of-last-resort doctrine, few appreciate his position as one of the foremost *critics* of central banking. Indeed, some even imagine that Bagehot, in

---

5. Walter Bagehot, *Lombard Street: A Description of the Money Market* (London: Henry S. King, 1873).

recommending that the Bank of England be held responsible for last-resort lending, actually meant to endorse its monopoly privileges, and to (at least implicitly) recommend that all nations create similar institutions. In fact, as even a casual perusal of *Lombard Street* will attest, nothing could be further from the truth. On the contrary: Bagehot believed that central banks were financially destabilizing and hence undesirable institutions, and that it would have been far better had England never created one. He offered his lender-of-last-resort formula, not as an ideal, but as sort of first-aid repair to what was, in his view, a fundamentally unhealthy arrangement, the healthy alternative to which was free banking, with numerous banks issuing their own notes and maintaining their own reserves, as in the pre-1845 Scottish banking system.[6] England needed a lender of last resort, not to rescue it from crises inherent to competitive banking, but to limit the severity of crises that were inevitable consequences of the monopolization of currency. Here is Bagehot's own apology, from the closing pages of *Lombard Street*:[7]

> I know it will be said that in this work I have pointed out a deep malady, and only suggested a superficial remedy. I have tediously insisted that the natural system of banking is that of many banks keeping their own cash [i.e., specie] reserve, with the penalty of failure before them if they neglect it. I have shown that our system is that of a single bank keeping the whole reserve under no effectual penalty of failure. And yet I propose to retain that system, and only attempt to mend and palliate it.
>
> I can only reply that I propose to retain this system because I am quite sure that it is of no manner of use proposing to alter it. . . . You might as well, or better, try to alter the English monarchy and substitute a republic. . . .

Today, indeed, it appears that a proposal to do away with the English monarchy would meet with far less opposition than one to do away with the Bank of England's monopoly of paper currency!

---

6. The thoughtless extension of Peel's Act to Scotland in 1845 began a process of currency centralization there that is as of this date (2011) still incomplete. On the Scottish system in its free-banking heyday, see Lawrence H. White, *Free Banking in Britain: Theory, Experience and Debate 1800–1845*, 2nd ed. (London: Institute of Economic Affairs, 2009).
7. Bagehot, *Lombard Street*, 329.

Despite Bagehot's explicit disavowal of the Bank of England, posterity has managed to treat him, not as an opponent of central banking, but rather as one of its high priests—a fate that must surely have him spinning furiously in his grave. And so generations of monetary economists have been taught, quite wrongly in my opinion, that central banks are absolutely indispensable tools for financial stabilization. Yet central bankers themselves, having thus come to be lionized, do little justice to the man who was their (admittedly inadvertent) champion, honoring his "last-resort" lending rules mainly in the breach.

The U.S. Case

According to my "stylized" history of central banking, the concentration of currency-issuing privileges in favored public banks was an important cause of financial crises, which crises in turn supplied a rationale for reinforcing and enhancing public banks' monopoly privileges while forcing the public banks to acknowledge a public duty to serve as last-resort lenders.

Readers may observe, however, that financial crises have not been limited to those nations in which currency-issuing privileges were concentrated in a single bank. The United States, in particular, endured a series of severe crises—in 1873, 1884, 1893, and 1907—prior to its decision to embrace central banking in the shape of the Federal Reserve System, which was created in 1914. The U.S. case therefore appears to contradict my claim that central banks are properly regarded as destabilizing rather than as stabilizing institutions.

But the contradiction is more apparent than real. First of all, by almost any measure, the major financial crises of the Federal Reserve era—those of 1920–21, 1929–33, 1937–38, 1980–82 and, most recently, 2007–2009—have been more, rather than less, severe than those experienced between the Civil War and the World War I, even overlooking outbreaks of relatively severe inflation during 1917–1920 and 1973–1980. More importantly, the pre-Fed crises can themselves be shown to have been exacerbated, if not caused by, regulations originally aimed at easing the Union government's fiscal burden. The U.S. case therefore represents a special instance of the general pattern according to which central banking emerged as an unintended byproduct of fiscally-motivated government interference with the free development of national financial institutions.

The interference in the U.S. case consisted in part of Civil War legislation that limited commercial banks' ability to issue their own banknotes.[8] National banks were allowed to issue their own notes only if every dollar of such notes was backed by $1.10 in federal government bonds, while state chartered banks were forced to withdraw altogether from the currency business by a prohibitive tax assessed against their outstanding circulation beginning in August 1866. The result of these combined regulations was an aggregate stock of paper currency geared to the available supply of government securities. From the late 1870s onwards, as the government took advantage of regular budget surpluses to reduce its outstanding debt, the supply of eligible backing for National bank notes dwindled, and the total stock of such notes dwindled as well until, by 1891, the latter stock was only half as great, in value terms, as it had been a decade before. Regulations also prevented the stock of currency from adjusting along with seasonal increases in currency demand. Yet the U.S. economy was growing, and the seasonal demand for currency tended to rise sharply during the harvest season, that is, between August and November of each year. Under the circumstances it is hardly surprising that the U.S. endured frequent crises, and that these crises all involved more-or-less severe shortages of paper currency.

Canada's experience, on the other hand, gives the lie to the claim that the U.S. could put an end to crises only by means of more complete centralization of its currency system. Canadian banks, unlike their U.S. counterparts, were free to issue notes on the same general assets that supported their deposit liabilities. Consequently, they were perfectly capable of accommodating both secular and seasonal changes in the demand for currency. Figure 12.2 displays the course of Canada's well-behaved banknote currency, regulated solely by unfettered market forces, alongside that of regulation-bound National bank notes in the U.S., for the years 1880 to 1900. To anyone familiar with normal patterns of currency

---

8. Of other forms of interference, the most notorious consisted of barriers to branch banking erected by state governments which, by generally preventing branching both within and across state lines, gave rise to an exceedingly decentralized, undercapitalized, and underdiversified banking industry while forcing "country" banks to rely on correspondents for access to the New York money market. This arrangement caused specie reserves to become concentrated in New York, much as they tended to be concentrated in privileged banks of issue elsewhere, with a similar tendency toward the excessive "pyramiding" of credit on available specie reserves during booms, and to corresponding disruptive contraction during busts.

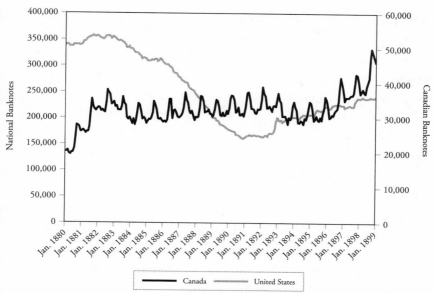

Figure 12.2. National (left scale) and Canadian (right scale)
Banknotes Outstanding, Thousands of Dollars, 1880–1900.

demand, the superiority of the less-regulated arrangement ought to be obvious. Considered in light of Canada's highly successful arrangement, which avoided all of the antebellum crises to which the U.S. economy had been subject, and also in light of the Fed's own performance, to characterize the U.S. turn to central banking in 1914 as a "second-best" solution is perhaps being over-generous.[9]

The Path to Fiat Money

Understood as a means for preventing crises and preserving the international gold standard, Bagehot's lender-of-last-resort solution was a failure. Crises

---

9. For details, see Roelift M. Breckenridge, *The Banking System of Canada 1817–1890* (New York: Macmillan, 1895). Although numerous legislative attempts were made, mainly between 1893 and 1907, to reform the U.S. currency system along Canadian ("Asset Currency") lines, all of them failed owing, in large part, to reformers' (well-founded) belief that asset currency would have to be combined with branch banking if it was to be sufficiently "elastic." Their proposals were for this reason aggressively, and successfully, opposed by established unit bankers. It was only following these failed efforts to deregulate the U.S. currency system that reformers began to champion a "central reserve bank" alternative.

continued, and even worsened, in part because the rules for last-resort lending were often disobeyed, but also because such lending alone could limit but could not eliminate violent changes in credit conditions, and associated disruptions of gold payments, stemming from prior central bank misconduct. Eventually it became evident that the international gold standard and central banking were incompatible arrangements, one of which had to go (Redish 1993).

The dismantlement of the international gold standard, temporarily at the outbreak of the first World War, and permanently in the course of the Great Depression, marked the end of "classical" financial crises: no longer was there a Humean price-specie-flow mechanism to snap back to equilibrium those national monetary systems that had temporarily escaped beyond its confines. Fiat money instead allowed central banks to expand without any clear constraints, permanently and with impunity, though at the cost of persistent inflation. Yet these new circumstances did not bring an end to financial crises, or even reduce their severity. They merely altered the nature of crises. The former Humean *denouement*, in which central banks were forced to retrench by an external drain of reserves, was replaced by a more subtle turning-point mechanism, consisting of the tendency of factor prices, caught behind other prices during booms, to catch up, raising interest rates, eliminating inflation-based profits, and exposing and bursting related asset-price bubbles. Such "post-classical" crises are today no less frequent than their classical counterparts had been during the nineteenth century. And they are equally attributable to central banks' mismanagement of money.

But while the advent of fiat money, far from rendering central banks less capable of generating booms and busts, has actually enhanced their capacity to do harm, it has also considerably complicated the possibility of fundamental reform. For unlike a gold or silver standard a fiat standard *must* be monopolistically administered if it is to retain any value. A reform allowing commercial banks the right to issue their own redeemable notes, even supposing that it could gain a sympathetic hearing, would by itself no longer serve, as it might have done in the days of metallic money, to deprive established central banks of their base-money creating powers and the crisis-making capacity that goes hand-in-hand with such powers.

But even allowing that paper currency must continue to be administered by government monopolies, it is nonetheless crucial that would-be reformers recognize the true nature of such monopolies, by discarding the essentially romantic depiction of central banks contained in most academic writings, and viewing them instead the way Walter Bagehot viewed the Bank of England, that is, as fundamentally dangerous institutions, in greater need than ever of strict confinement.

References

Bagehot, Walter. 1873. *Lombard Street: A Description of the Money Market.* London: Henry S. King.

Breckenridge, Roelift M. 1895. *The Banking System of Canada 1817–1890.* New York: Macmillan.

Redish, Angela. 1993. "Anchors Aweigh: The Transition from Commodity Money to Fiat Money in Western Economies." *Canadian Journal of Economics* 26 (4): 777–95.

Selgin, George. 1988. *The Theory of Free Banking: Money Supply under Competitive Note Issue.* Totowa, NJ: Rowman and Littlefield.

———. 1994. "Free Banking and Monetary Control." *The Economic Journal* 104 (427): 1449–59.

———. 2001. "In-Concert Overexpansion and the Precautionary Demand for Bank Reserves." *Journal of Money, Credit, and Banking* 33 (2): 294–300.

Smith, Vera. 1936. *The Rationale of Central Banking.* London: P.S. King & Son.

White, Lawrence H. 2009. *Free Banking in Britain: Theory, Experience and Debate 1800–1845,* 2nd ed. London: Institute of Economic Affairs.

Index

About the Contributors

Editor

DAVID BECKWORTH is Research Fellow at The Independent Institute, Assistant Professor of Economics at Western Kentucky University, and former international economist at the U.S. Department of the Treasury. He has done research on the measurement of monetary policy, the transmission mechanisms through which it works, and its impact on the global, national, and regional economies. He has published in journals such as *Economic Inquiry, Applied Economics Letters, Journal of Macroeconomics, Journal for the Scientific Study of Religion, Cato Journal*, and the *North American Journal of Economics and Finance*. Beckworth's blogging at *Macro and Other Market Musings* has been cited by the *Washington Post, New York Times, Financial Times, The Economist, CNN/Fortune, Bloomberg/Businessweek, Newsweek, Christianity Today*, and other prominent blogs, and his popular articles have appeared in *The New Republic, National Review Online, Investor's Business Daily*, Barron's, and *Focus*.

Contributors

CHRISTOPHER CROWE is an Economist at the International Monetary Fund, currently on leave and working in the private sector in London. He has a Ph.D. and M.Sc. in economics from the London School of Economics and a B.A. in economics from the University of Cambridge, and has also worked at the Caribbean Development Bank in Barbados. His research is mainly on monetary economics and monetary policy, macro-financial linkages and the housing market, and it has been published in the *Journal of Monetary Economics* and the *Journal of Economic Perspectives*, among other journals. He was born in Scotland, and is married with two children.

DIEGO ESPINOSA is a hedge fund manager and private investor. He successfully predicted the 2006–2009 housing crash and financial crisis. During that period, his portfolios carried concentrated short and/or put positions in subprime mortgage originators, homebuilders, bond insurers, GSEs, banks, and investment banks. Mr. Espinosa was previously Director of European Research at the equities research boutique Sanford C. Bernstein & Co. He was also a Portfolio Manager at Scudder Investments, where he co-lead managed the $10 billion Global Equity product. At Scudder, he also served as a Latin America equities analyst and ran the NYSE-listed Argentina Fund. Before joining Scudder, Mr. Espinosa was a #1-ranked (by *Institutional Investor*) Latin America equity research analyst at Morgan Stanley & Co. His non-investment experience includes working as a strategy consultant for the Boston Consulting Group in Boston, and as a commercial banker for Citibank, N.A. in Latin America. Mr. Espinosa has an M.B.A. in Finance from The Wharton School and an M.A. in International Relations from the Johns Hopkins University School of Advanced International Studies.

JOSHUA R. HENDRICKSON is an Assistant Professor of economics at the University of Mississippi. His primary areas of interest are monetary theory and policy. In particular, he is interested in the mechanisms through which monetary policy affects economic activity and the role of the supply and demand of monetary assets in explaining economic fluctuations.

JEFFREY ROGERS HUMMEL is Associate Professor at San Jose State University, where he teaches both economics and history. He is the author of *Emancipating Slaves, Enslaving Free Men: A History of the American Civil War* and has published articles in the *Journal of Economic History*, *Texas Law Review*, *International Philosophical Quarterly*, *The Independent Review*, and *Econ Journal Watch*, among others. Prior to joining San Jose State University in 2002, Professor Hummel taught at Golden Gate University and Santa Clara University. He also served in the U.S. Army as a tank platoon leader during the early seventies, was Publications Director for The Independent Institute in Oakland, CA, in the late eighties, and was a National Fellow at the Hoover Institution, Stanford University, for the 2001–2002 academic year. He received his Ph.D. in history from the University of Texas at Austin.

LAURENCE J. KOTLIKOFF is a William Fairfield Warren Professor at Boston University, a Professor of Economics at Boston University, a Fellow of the American Academy of Arts and Sciences, a Fellow of the Econometric Society, a Research Associate of the National Bureau of Economic Research, President of Economic Security Planning, Inc., a company specializing in financial planning software, a columnist for *Bloomberg*, a columnist for *Forbes*, and a blogger for the *Economist*. Professor Kotlikoff received his B.A. in Economics from the University of Pennsylvania in 1973 and his Ph.D. in Economics from Harvard University in 1977.

From 1977 through 1983 he served on the faculties of economics of the University of California, Los Angeles, and Yale University. In 1981–82 Professor Kotlikoff was a Senior Economist with the President's Council of Economic Advisers.

Professor Kotlikoff is author or co-author of 14 books and hundreds of professional journal articles. His most recent books are *Jimmy Stewart Is Dead*; *Spend 'Til the End*, co-authored with Scott Burns; *The Healthcare Fix*; and *The Coming Generational Storm*, co-authored with Scott Burns.

He publishes extensively in newspapers, and magazines on issues of financial reform, personal finance, taxes, Social Security, healthcare, deficits, generational accounting, pensions, saving, and insurance.

Professor Kotlikoff has served as a consultant to the International Monetary Fund, the World Bank, the Harvard Institute for International Development, the Organization for Economic Cooperation and Development, and many other institutions, and he has provided expert testimony on numerous occasions to committees of Congress including the Senate Finance Committee, the House Ways and Means Committee, and the Joint Economic Committee.

NICHOLAS ROWE is an Associate Professor in the Department of Economics, Carleton University, Ottawa, Canada. Originally from England, Rowe graduated with a B.A. in Philosophy from Stirling University, Scotland, and M.A. and Ph.D. in Economics from the University of Western Ontario, Canada. His main areas of interest are macroeconomics and monetary policy.

He is a member of the C.D. Howe Institute's Monetary Policy Council, which brings together Canadian academic and private-sector economists to act as a "shadow" to the Bank of Canada in providing recommendations for monetary policy. The recent financial crisis and recession triggered his 2008 decision to become active as an economics blogger, to increase communication between academic economists, policymakers, and the public. Rowe is one of five bloggers at the Canadian economics blog *Worthwhile Canadian Initiative*, http://worthwhile.typepad.com/worthwhile_canadian_initi/

GEORGE SELGIN is Professor of Economics at the University of Georgia, a Senior Fellow at the Cato Institute, and an Associate Editor at *Econ Journal Watch*. His areas of expertise are monetary economics, macroeconomics, and economic history. He is the author of *The Theory of Free Banking, Less than Zero: The Case for a Falling Price Level in a Growing Economy*, and *Good Money: Birmingham Button-Makers, the Royal Mint, and the Beginnings of Modern Coinage*, as well as numerous scholarly articles for the *Journal of Economic History*, the *Economic Journal*, the *Journal of Money, Credit, and Banking*, and the *Journal of Economic Literature*.

SCOTT SUMNER is Professor of Economics at Bentley University. His areas of interest are macroeconomics, monetary theory and policy, and history of economic thought. He has published articles in the *Journal of Political Economy*, the *Journal of Money, Credit and Banking*, and the *Bulletin of Economic Research*. He also writes a blog on public policy issues for *TheMoneyIllusion.com*.

LAWRENCE H. WHITE is Professor of Economics at George Mason University. He specializes in the theory and history of banking and money, and is best known for his work on free banking. He received his B. A. from Harvard and his M.A. and Ph.D. from the University of California, Los Angeles. He previously taught at New York University, the University of Georgia, and the University of Missouri, St. Louis.

White is the author of *The Clash of Economic Ideas*, *The Theory of Monetary Institutions*, *Free Banking in Britain*, and *Competition and Currency*. He is the editor of *F. A. Hayek, The Pure Theory of Capital*; *The History of Gold and Silver*; *Free Banking (3 vols., Edward Elgar, 1993)*; *The Crisis in American Banking*, and other volumes. His articles on monetary theory and banking history have appeared in the *American Economic Review*, the *Journal of Economic Literature*, the *Journal of Money, Credit, and Banking*, and other leading professional journals.

WILLIAM R. WHITE is a Canadian, born in Kenora, Ontario, who is now based in Basel, Switzerland. He is currently the Chairman of the Economic Development and Review Committee, which makes policy recommendations to members and aspiring member countries of the OECD. A member of the Issing Committee, which advises Chancellor Merkel of Germany on matters pertaining to international financial stability, he has also been a featured speaker at numerous events organized by the G-20.

White held the position of Economic Adviser at the Bank for International Settlements (BIS) in Basel between 1995 and 2008, heading one of the world's most highly regarded teams of macroeconomists. He and his colleagues repeatedly warned of the many "imbalances" building up under the smooth surface of the Great Moderation. Well before the subprime crisis began, he noted that accelerating credit growth in many countries and an associated deterioration in credit standards would have global implications that could last for years.

Prior to joining the BIS, White spent 25 years in central banking, leaving the Bank of Canada in 1994 as Deputy Governor (International). He received his Ph.D. in 1969 from the University of Manchester, where he was supported by a Commonwealth Scholarship.

W. WILLIAM WOOLSEY received a B.A. in Economics and Philosophy from Virginia Tech in 1979, and completed a Ph.D. in Economics from George Mason University in 1987. He taught economics at Talladega College for four years, and has served on the Faculty of The Citadel since 1986. He teaches Principles of Macroeconomics and Money and Banking to undergraduates in the Corps of Cadets and Foundations of Economics in the M.B.A. program. He has published papers on monetary economics in the *Journal of Money, Credit, and Banking*, *Contemporary Economic Policy*, the *Atlantic Economic Journal*, the *Southern Economic Journal*, and the *Cato Journal*.

Woolsey served as Chairman of the Faculty Council at The Citadel for three terms, and he has also been involved in James Island politics where he was elected for two terms on the town council in 2002 and 2004, and mayor in 2010. The Town of James Island lost its court battle last summer and Woolsey now chairs Free James Island, which seeks to reform the Town of James Island. Woolsey also has a blog, *Monetary Freedom*, that focuses on monetary issues.

Independent Studies in Political Economy